D0934230

Twenty-First Century World Order and the Asia Pacific

Twenty-First Century World Order and the Asia Pacific

Value Change, Exigencies, and Power Realignment

Edited by James C. Hsiung

Withdrawn

palgrave

TWENTY-FIRST WORLD ORDER AND THE ASIA PACIFIC
Copyright © James C. Hsiung, 2001

First published 2001 by PALGRAVE™
175 Fifth Avenue, New York, N.Y. 10010 and
Houndmills, Basingstoke, Hampshire RG21 6XS.
Companies and representatives throughout the world

PALGRAVE is the new global publishing imprint of St. Martin's Press LLC Scholarly and Reference Division and Palgrave Publishers Ltd. (formerly Macmillan Press Ltd).

ISBN 0–312–23879–7 hardback

Library of Congress Cataloging-in-Publication Data
Twenty-first century world order and the Asia Pacific / edited by James C. Hsiung.
        p.   cm.
    Includes bibliographical references and index.
    ISBN 0–312–23879–7
    1. Asia—Politics and government—21st century.   2. World politics—21st century.   3. National security—Asia.   4. Security, International.   5. Globalization.   I. Title: 21st century World order and the Asia Pacific.   II. Hsiung, James Chieh, 1935-
DS35.2. T86   2001
327'.095—dc21

                                                                  2001032761

A catalogue record for this book is available from the British Library.

Design by Letra Libre, Inc.

First edition: August 2001
10   9   8   7   6   5   4   3   2   1

Printed in the United States of America.

To my former colleagues at Lignan University, Hong Kong

CONTENTS

Acronyms

ABAC	APEC Business Council
AEI	Enterprise for Americas Initiative
ANZCER	Australia-New Zealand Closer Economic Relations
APEC	Asia Pacific Economic Cooperation forum
ARF	ASEAN Regional Forum
ASEAN	Association of Southeast Asian Nations
ASEAN-PMC	ASEAN Post-Ministerial Conference
ASEM	Asian-European Meeting
CACOM	Caribbean Common Market
CAP	collective action plan
CFSP	common foreign and security policy
CSCE	Conference on Security and Cooperation in Europe; now OSCE
DPP	Democratic Progressive Party
EC	European Community, which was preceded by the European Economic Community (EEC) and succeeded by the European Union (EU)
EMU	Economic and Monetary Union
EPG	Eminent Persons Group
EU	European Union; *see* EC
EVSL	early voluntary sectoral liberalization
FTA	free trade area
FEER	*Far Eastern Economic Review*
FTAA	Free Trade Area of the Americas
GATT	General Agreement on Tariffs and Trade, replaced in 1995 by WTO
GDP	gross domestic product
G-8	group of the seven most industrialized nations plus Russia
GMS	Greater Mekong [River] Subregion
GNP	gross national product
IAP	individual action plan
ICBMs	Inter-Continental Ballistic Missiles

IDB   Inter-American Development Bank
IES   International Economic Structure
ISI   import substitution industrialization
IMF   International Monetary Fund
IPR   Intellectual Property Rights
IR   International Relations, as a field of study
ISIS   Institute of Strategic and International Studies
KMT   Kuomintang (Nationalist Party)
MAP   Manila Action Plan
MERCOSUR   Southern Common Market
NAFTA   North American Free Trade Agreement
NATO   North Atlantic Treaty Organization
NGO   snon-governmental organizations
NMD   National Missile Defense system
OAS   Organization of American States
OSCE   Organization of Security and Cooperation in Europe,
                successor to CSCE
PECC   Pacific Economic Cooperation Council
PFTAD   Pacific Trade and Development Conference
PKO   peace keeping operation
PLA   People's Liberation Armed Forces
PRC   People's Republic of China
RTA   regional trade arrangements
SAR   Special Administrative Region, as in Hong Kong
                SAR, or Macao SAR
SDF   Self-Defense Forces (Japan's armed forces)
SLORC   State Law and Order Restoration Committee (the
                current military junta in Mymmar, former Burma)
SRTA   sub-regional trade arrangement
TGPF   Joint Fact-Finding Team (Indonesia)
TILF   Trade and Investment Liberalization and Facilitation
TMD   Theater Missile Defense system
TPF   Trade Policy Forum
UK   United Kingdom
UN   United Nations
UNECLAC   UN Economic Commission for Latin America and
                the Caribbean
WEU   Western European Union
WMD   weapons of mass destruction
WTO   World Trade Organization

FOREWORD

LEGACY OF THE PAST CENTURY: PARADOXES

The century we left behind was full of paradoxes never seen before at any time since Westphalia. For instance, its many epochal advances in technology brought unheard-of amenities like automobiles, aircraft, radio and television, computers and the Internet, and antibiotics and bioengineering, to name just a few. But it also introduced awesome destructive power into modern weaponry, such as long-range artillery, aerial bombers, submarines, the atom bomb, ballistic missiles, nuclear and other weapons of mass destruction, etc. The century was full of triumphs and tragedies. The latter included the two most destructive wars in history and the Cold War, which could have led to a nuclear holocaust and the end of civilization. The triumph was that nuclear deterrence did work, and the Cold War proved to be a period of "long peace" (cf. Perry 2000, 1; Hoffman 1998, 1–12).

Despite the twentieth century's notoriety as the "century of total war," empirical studies have, however, shown a sustained decline, since the Korean War (1950 - 1953), in international armed conflicts involving at least one major power.[1] In the words of one scholar (Mueller 1989), major-power armed conflicts have since retreated to the point of obsolescence. But the sad story is that civil wars have been on the increase. In the years since the end of the Cold War, for instance, the world's armed conflicts have been mainly civil wars, as found in Africa, the Balkans, Russia, and the Asia Pacific (notably in Indonesia). Another sad development is the recurrence of terrorist acts in different parts of the world. The October 12, 2000 tragic attack on the U.S. destroyer *Cole,* during a refueling stop in Aden, is but the latest reminder of rampant terrorism in the world.

Another paradox was in the collapse of the great European monarchies and of the sprawling Western colonial empires, in some cases built over several centuries. In its wake came the proliferation of over 80 new sovereignties (i.e., postcolonial states), but many, ironically, have since remained mired in poverty and instability. This irony is matched only by the unmistakable erosion of state sovereignty, as witnessed in the rise of the individual and the growing prominence of nonsovereign actors including international organizations.

The twentieth century was the first century to see the rise of universal peace organizations such as the League of Nations and its successor, the United Nations. Inspired by these examples as the institutional embodiment of a new avenue to peace building, thousands of other international governmental organizations (IGOs) and non-government organizations (NGOs) have mushroomed into being like never before. These have become, and joined the ranks of, a growing number of nonsovereign actors, again in ways unforeseen in previous centuries. To the array of nonsovereign actors came two new additions at the end of the century, both in the Asian region. After exiting in close succession (1997 and 1999) from British and Portuguese colonial rule, respectively, Hong Kong and Macao reverted to motherland China under an unprecedented "one country, two systems" formula.[2] The arrangement endows both postcolonial autonomous entities with the capacity to act internationally—more so than before—without sovereignty of their own, while under China's sovereign umbrella. The rise and proliferation of these and other nonsovereign actors undeniably poses the question as to whether our Westphalian system can still be understood purely from the state-centric perspective that has been held to be true for all previous centuries.

Furthermore, the triumph of democracy, as a form of government, spreading from Europe and North America to other lands (including the Asian region) during the century, was accompanied by the disconcerting emergence of the totalitarian state, not to mention autocracies of various stripes. Likewise, the uninhibited proliferation of free ideas and liberal values, following the rise of the modern mass media, only imperfectly aided in the dissemination of the liberal democratic ideal and tradition. The same process also engendered recurrent ideological divisions endemic to much of the century, such as between fascist and antifascist forces, between socialist and antisocialist camps, and increasingly between Western and non-Western ethos. At century's end, the division was only transmuted into what Samuel P. Huntington (1996) calls the "clash of civilizations," which he sees likely to continue into the new century.

The twentieth century, again paradoxically, gave us the Great Depression early on but also brought unprecedented prosperity by virtue of the global free market system after the end of World War II. Yet, for all the flaunted expansion in world wealth, the gaps separating the poor and the rich nations were becoming wider, rather than narrower. The successive revolutions in communications have brought us face to face in a shrinking global village; but as the recent Asian financial crisis (1997 - 1998) has amply demonstrated, the world has yet to learn how to reconcile internal peace of a nation with the at times ravaging forces of globalized capital.

A New World Order Emerging

At the dawn of a new millennium, an overriding, almost irrepressible, question is: What is in store for the global community in the time ahead? While we cannot divine the future, we can at least ascertain the general directions that the emergent world order is going to take in the new century now upon us. If somehow a contour of the emergent world order can be inferred from the known and knowable variables on hand, we may be on to a preview of what is likely to happen in the relations of nations in our Westphalian system in transition.

In a thought-provoking essay on "reconceiving change in the Westphalian system," Kurt Burch (2000, 201) raised a rhetorical question as to whether we "build" a world order or whether a world order will be "constituted" without our direct effort. In chapter 1, below, it will be shown how the new world order that this book addresses will "emerge"— not exactly out of nowhere nor entirely by willful "building" on our part.

As will be shown, in addition to the bequests of time, the new world order is going to reflect the collective aspirations of nations as well as their responses to new challenges, plus the unfulfilled agendas from the past century. For instance, the rising concern of "comprehensive security" (beyond the traditional national defense)—which in part is a reaction of nations to the threats posed by the environmental deterioration due to the spread of modern technology—is a human response for the survival of our ecosystem, calling for international collective action. Likewise, in the domain of collective human (or systemic) values, the new century is most likely to see the rise of social justice (including distributive justice) as a guide for world affairs, challenging the international social Darwinism that underscored the lore of the "Whiteman's Burden" of yore. This is a crucial development as the world collectively confronts its battles with widespread poverty and its attendant plagues, such as the AIDS epidemic, affecting almost all continents. As such, if materialized, it will be the living out of a latent unfulfilled dream for large segments of humankind that virtually had no voice until now.

Our Approach and Premises

This book is premised upon one cardinal assumption, viz.: that although the fundamental structural dimensions of our Westphalian system, such as sovereignty, territoriality, public authority, and nationality, will remain basically unaltered (Caporaso 2000, 8), they will come under increasing pressures (such as the rising voices of the impoverished and their supporters, and the erosion of state sovereignty) that will affect how the system operates within changing parameters. One other crucial element in the Westphalian order, the unilateral self-help reflex of states, may come under increasing constraint due to the imperative of collective action, as called for by deepening complex interdependence and globalization. This is so because collective action requires greater reliance on multilateral institutions and regimes of international governance, which mitigate the effects of systemic anarchy (lack of a supranational authority over and above states) that have justified unilateral self-help thus far.[3]

Another cardinal premise of the book is really a skepticism as to whether matter alone is what moves history. Without recreating the Marxian-Hegelian debate over matter/spirit as the motive force of history, let me make a hint of how we define world order (as laid out in chapter 1 below): While in agreement with neorealism that power distribution across the "agents" (states) in the Westphalian system is extremely important, we believe, nevertheless, that it is not the only "determinant" of the world order emerging on the horizon for the new century.

What we ought to be looking for is a combination of three factors: (1) the emergent body of first principles (systemic values) that will provide a new guiding light for world affairs and a "grammar" of international relations; (2) the exigencies—such as the forces of technological advance, rise of geoeconomics, and globalization—that will set the agendas of nations in their domestic and foreign policy; and (3) the changing power configuration across the international system that, in conjunction with the first two factors, will foreshadow the behavior and policies of nations at home and abroad. Thus, the subtitle of our book, "Value Change, Exigencies, and Power Realignment," is meant exactly to capture the synergistic essence of these three factors bearing on the emergent world order.

Under its conjoined title, this book in fact attempts to address three, not two, complex but interrelated topics: first, the new century's world order on a global scale; second, the state of the Asia Pacific at the regional level; and third, Asia Pacific's role (at both the receiving and giving ends) in the total context of the emergent global order. This book does not aim at dispensing policy recommendations to decision makers per se.[4] Rather, its purpose is to offer what we hope will be a coherent conceptual composite for thoughtful reflection to those whose job it is to make such recommendations (hence, advice to advisors) and, in addition, to students of international relations in general, especially those who share a curiosity—nay, anxiety—about what to expect of the emergent world order of the new century.

While we eschew the word "holism,"[5] our approach to world order is broader than Hedley Bull's (1977, 21) in his classic study of "order in world politics," although we share his main thrust that world order is "more fundamental . . . and morally prior to" what he calls by contrast "international order." We are aware that "world order" is a catch-all term (a conceptual distillation) for what constitutes, and yet transcends, the sum total of diverse dimensions that range from the ecological/economic, to the cultural/ideological, to the political/military. Even a contour of world order, as we hope to be able to etch out, must take account of these various elements, which are always in the background of our discourses even if they are not each articulated in full as one would wish.

Concededly, globalization is fast becoming a worldwide phenomenon as well as a force from whose reach no region can escape (Kris Olds et al. 1999). We have ample opportunity to address the question of globalization from both global and regional perspectives (especially in chapters 2, 3, 4, and 11). Nevertheless, despite its broad sweep, globalization is not the exclusive ingredient in the new world order; in the sense as we use the term here, that phrase will define the game of international relations over a broad spectrum of issue areas, including globalization itself.

Nevertheless, the Asia Pacific region, which has just shaken off a whopping financial crisis in the late 1990s, brought on by globalized capital, deserves to be examined in a number of ways, with undoubtedly relevant implications for all other regions equally faced with the onslaught of globalization. Within the context of the emergent world order, the book provides a scrutiny into: (1) the Asia Pacific's internal strengths/weaknesses that became obvious under the impact of the forces of globalization (chapters 2, 3, 4, and 11); (2) the region's approach to problems of "comprehensive security," a concern that commands mounting attention of many countries and regions in the world (chapters 3, 8, 9, and 10); (3) the success or failure in Asia Pacific's region-wide institution building, as compared with other regions (chapters 5, 6, and 7); and (4) the region's post-crisis sensitivity to its economic security and political stability (chapters 7 and 11).

INSIGHTS FROM THE GLOBALIST LITERATURE

In its conceptual frame of reference, the book is inspired by the rich scholarship available in the literature on "globalism"—a point that needs a brief explanation in its own right. As Andre Gunder Frank (1998, 340) demonstrates, globalism (a historically longer-existing and larger phenomenon than globalization) was a fact of life since at least 1500 (after Columbus' discovery of America in 1492) for the whole world. In fact, a few observers—such as McNeill (1963; and 1990), Hodgson (1993), Wilkinson (1987, 1993), Frank and Gills (1993), and Chase-Dunn and Hall (1997)—argue that at least an Afro-Eurasian "eucumene" or "central world system" was already functioning as a single unit long before 1500.

From the perspective of globalism, Frank (1998, 52–130) sees the rise of the West from 1500 onward in conjunction with the decline of the East after 1800. Europeans, he reminds us, used the silver extracted from the American colonies to buy entry into an expanding Asian market, which already flourished in the global economy by means of the very productive commercial and institutional mechanisms that were supposedly unique to Europe. In the introductory chapter below, we have occasion to refer to the level of achievement in China's economy from the 1400s through 1800, when its decline began. In terms of its over 33 percent share of the world's manufacturing product even in 1800, China rivaled the United States in its share of the global GDP at the peak of U.S. power (at 38 percent in 1950) and far surpassed the United States post-1980 share of less than 22 percent In fact, Asian output in 1700 accounted for 62 percent of world production, and as late as 1820, China's output alone exceeded all of Europe's.[6] It would be of interest to know if Asia, despite the slowing effects of the recent crisis on its growth, will live out its potentials of surpassing the economies of Europe and North America, as the eminent economist Staffan Linder (1986) had forecast over a decade before the crisis hit the region.

Returning to Frank in his globalist comparisons, let us note his argument that as the East entered into a declining phase of the cyclical world economy after 1800, the nations of the West resorted to import substitution and export promotion in the world market to become newly industrialized economies. That, Frank poignantly adds, is precisely what East Asia is doing today to recover its earlier dominance in the world economy, the "center" of which is once again moving to the "Middle Kingdom" of China. So concludes Frank (1998, 127), agreeing in essence with the conclusions independently arrived at by Huntington (1996), Khalilzad et al. (1999), and the Organskiite group (Tammen et al. 2000),[7] among others.

I must add that Frank, like Wallerstein (1974), Chaudhuri (1990), and Abu-Lughod (1989), belongs to the school of scholars that subscribe to the long-cycle view of history after the Kondratieff tradition, which requires the mastery of a macrohistory of world development. From this macrohistorical perspective, they variously came to the same position that the rise of the East preceded that of the West in human history. True to their belief in the Kondratieff cycles, they, with the support of massive statistics, are unanimously agreed that, as is most eloquently articulated by Frank (1998), the East (namely Pacific Asia) is to rise again.

In briefly reviewing this literature on globalism, I do not mean to suggest that the present book merely echoes the above Frankian thesis. The globalist perspective such as Frank represents, nevertheless, offers a healthy corrective for the habitual unquestioned tilt toward the Western experience in international relations (IR) theory,[8] to the neglect of the non-Western "periphery," and even to the exclusion of Asia (except for the Middle East). Indeed, Asia in academic political science is banished to "area studies," which in itself is often a derogatory term, implying it has no methodological focus nor inferential value to offer. In this book, we place the Asia Pacific in the course of a research aimed at prospecting the future global order of the new century. We hope that we will thus be able to reach a more balanced conclusion than if we adopted the usual Atlantic-centric approach, no matter whether the once- projected "Pacific Century" materializes or not. To say the very least, we hope the addition of an Asian dimension will help us unravel the puzzles that Western-derived theories are not equipped to deal with. A case in point is that, as will be shown in the book, many of the theories associated with Western neoliberal economics, for example, failed to explain the origin of the financial crisis hitting the Asian region, much less the peculiar responses that led to unexpectedly prompt recovery.

After acknowledging the macroperspective that Frank and company brought to bear in the study of human economic development, I must reiterate that our focus in the present volume is not exclusively economic. It is much broader. The point about Pacific Asia's place in the totality of the new world order, which as stated above is the third concern of this book, boils down to an intriguing question, namely: What role, if any, does the Asian region have to play in the emergence of the new global order? This question goes beyond what Bryce Harland, in the *International Herald Tribune,* 3 May 1996, said in a column titled "America Must Learn to Respect Asia's Way of Doing Things," to the effect:

> Westerners have been accustomed to telling Asians what to do. That period is coming to an end.... Westerners need to accept the equality of Asians, and their right to do things their own way ... and [assert] the validity of "Asian" values.

Echoing the same view in a follow-up column titled "At Issue Is the Nature of the International System," Jim Hoagland, of the same paper, 3–4 May 1996, added:

The conflict over China is a conflict about the nature of the international system, and its political, financial, and trade agencies. By design or otherwise, China is aggressively pushing to shape an alternative international system friendlier to Beijing's aims evident in the Chinese struggle to remake WTO rules for admission.

Like Frank's, these two views were written before the Asian financial crisis of 1997–1998 and, in Hoagland's case, before the negotiations were complete for China's entry to the WTO. The writers may not even in their wildest dreams have anticipated the Asian region's demonstrated resilience to the scourge of the "casino effects" of the global hot money flows. Much less could they have anticipated the upshot of the crisis to confirm China as the exemplary model for the region. As demonstrated by China's ability to ride out the storm like no other economy—for example, it did not devalue the renminbi, as many analysts had repeatedly predicted, during the competitive round of currency devaluations across the region—the safest way to sustained development for a nation, in the face of the ravaging forces of globalization, is to exercise measured control in the process of its liberalization, as the Chinese do.[9] As such, in the eyes of many, China has replaced Japan not only as the locomotive of Asia's economic growth but also as its model for safeguarded liberalization in the globalization age.

This is not another China-centered book, but it is nevertheless drawn to an angle explored neither in the world-system literature nor in the China-watching literature concerning China's role. The point bears on the extent to which China possibly wields the potential of contributing to the reshaping of the world's systemic values, such as in the promotion of greater social justice internationally. We raise this question with a contingency in mind: What if it should come to pass that China, true to the prediction of the power transition theory adherents (Tammen et al. 2000) and others (e.g., Khalilzad et al. 1999), should indeed "overtake" the United States by mid-century (2050) to become the next superpower?

FOUR INTERRELATED FOCI OF THE BOOK

In its endeavor to address the emergent global order and the Asia Pacific regional order within it, the book revolves around a number of interrelated foci, viz.: (1) the systemic values guiding world affairs, and the exigencies of concern to states, in the changing reality of the new century; (2) comprehensive security, both approached in light of the global trends as it bears on the Asian region, and viewed from three selected country perspectives (United States, China, and Japan); (3) globalization and its

manifestation in, and impact on, the Asian region; and (4) regional institution building, in comparison with other regions.

In sum, the conjoined title of the book, *Twenty-First Century World Order
and the Asia Pacific,* recalls to mind the proverbial horse-buggy relationship,
which has three, not two, dimensions, to wit: the horse, the buggy, and the
horse-buggy-ness. The analogy, however, is not a perfect one. Despite its
conjoined title, this book is not strictly about the relationship *between*
world order and the Asian region. Indeed, its prior concern is the emergent world order of the new century engulfing all regions. The Asian region is placed in its totality and, as such, is discussed as an illustration of
its manifestations, while the region also offers a test of the universality
(or lack of it) of the emergent world order. The horse-buggy analogy
merely suggests, implicitly, that global order cannot exist independently
of the society of nations in all regions, just as no region (Asia Pacific included) can stay outside the reach of the overarching global order. Put
differently, just as the global order may redirect, as well as reflect, the orientation of nations in the region, thus redefining the "game" of their external relations both within the region and with other regions, so too the
aspirations and behavior of the Asian nations may likewise provide in-
puts into the larger whole of world politics and the global economy, in effect contributing to the shaping or reshaping of the global order that
governs our Westphalian system. This will be especially true in the event
that the "Pacific Century" projected by many analysts should materialize.
In this sense, the relationship between the two parts in the book's conjoined title is a dialectical one.

The initial germ of this book goes back to the convening of a symposium in April 2000, under the same topic as the book's title, at Lingnan
University, Hong Kong. The planning for the symposium began when I
was a visiting Chair Professor and Head, Department of Politics-Sociology, at Lingnan, during 1997–1999. The topic of the symposium was a
spin-off from a process I presided over in the department's updating and
revamping of its instructional curriculum in order to adequately prepare
students for the coming century with its manifold challenges. During this
endeavor, somehow I was bitten by the "twenty-first century bug," as it
were. The idea of an international symposium to examine, at the theoretical level, the complex question of what lies ahead in the twenty-first
century for the world at large and for the Asian region in particular was
thus hatched. The mandate of the conference was to examine "what the
new millennium is going to bring to Planet Earth and how it is to affect,
among other regions, the Asia Pacific as a whole," as the conference
prospectus stated. A team of 22 scholars were invited to attend and share
their expertise from different angles, hailing as they did from different

localities including the United States, Japan, Singapore, Taiwan, Macao, Europe, and mainland China as well as Hong Kong. In addition to the 15 papers read and the comments given by their discussants, the symposium had extensive fruitful discussions among its participants on issues of relevance to the symposium's general theme.

The book project, whose conception came after the meeting, is an extension of these enlightening discussions. Eight chapters of the book are revised papers selected from the symposium. One additional chosen paper had already been committed for publication elsewhere, but its author, Professor Loksang Ho, Chairman of the Economics Department, Lingnan University, wrote a fresh chapter (chapter 11) for the volume, bringing theoretical insights to bear on a proper understanding of the Asian financial crisis, for which I am truly grateful. Interestingly enough, his finding that the Asian crisis was not associated with internal structural flaws confirms the conclusion independently arrived at in other chapters. Furthermore, he finds a close relationship between exchange rates and currency crises, but discovers that neither individual economies nor the market can have a solution to the problem. It would take a global effort to bring about the right exchange rates that are compatible with stability of the financial markets and the economy. This task, though a challenge not just for the Asian region, is based on lessons learned from the Asian financial crisis. This is one more indication of the kind of circular global-regional linkage that this book tries to demonstrate.

My introductory chapter (chapter 1), which offers an overarching theoretical framework for the entire volume, is an expanded and totally revised version of my keynote speech given at the symposium. Chapter 3 was written afterwards. In it, my attempt is to present an up-to-date overview of the Asia Pacific region in light of the discussions of the emergent global order. Among other things, it tries to draw cogent lessons from the region's recent bout with the ravaging force of globalized capital. The fate of the so-called "Asian values" and the peculiar Asian model of development, which came under cynical external criticisms during the crisis, were singled out for particular scrutiny. The concluding chapter (chapter 12), taking off from the key points and findings presented in the preceding chapters, attempts to integrate everything together in a final commentary, rounding out the topic addressed by the book while keeping a gaze on the future.

We hope that because of the global-regional linkage in its design, the book will be useful to both those interested in a contour of the emergent global order, such as is sketched out here, and others who are interested in how the new global order manifests itself at a regional level. For the latter group, our discussions concerning the Asian region, especially the inherent mode of analysis they offer, may be transferable to other regions of their choice.

ACKNOWLEDGEMENTS

Before concluding this already long foreword, I wish to thank many quarters and individuals who have helped make the symposium a success and this book possible. My first thanks go to Lingnan University for my two-year visiting stint at a critical juncture of history. It allowed me to witness more than the reversion of Hong Kong to Chinese sovereignty in 1997. I was able, coincidentally, to experience first hand the onslaught of the worst economic attack ever to hit the entire Asian region under the dark clouds of a financial crisis, which drove home to me the complex implications of the impact of globalization. I am equally thankful for the opportunity to have participated in the curricular updating exercise at Lingnan, as noted above. For it gave me a chance to reflect schematically on the implications of the dawn of a new millennium and its complex challenges to tertiary education, to IR research, and, more important, to the survival and future of humankind in our present habitat. To Professor Brian Bridges, at Lingnan, who served as my co-convenor of the symposium, I owe a special debt for having taken over, after my departure and return to New York University, my home institution, all the tedium of having to follow up on corresponding with the invitees to the symposium and securing the participation of an excellent team of experts for the project. For the funding support of the symposium, I wish to acknowledge my thanks in part to Lingnan's Center for Asian Pacific Studies (CAPS), directed by Professor Y. Y. Kueh, and in part to its Department of Politics-Sociology, now chaired by my successor, Professor David Phillips. Equally, I wish to acknowledge the logistical support lent by the able staff at CAPS, more especially David Ji, who discharged the local-arrangements function will skill and dedication. On the intellectual side, Dr. Xiangdong Wei, of the Economics Department at Lingnan, provided me many insights into the complexity of the nebulous role played by the international financial manipulators in connection with the Asian crisis.

To all contributors, I owe a heavy debt for their conscientiousness in delivering their revised essays (and in Lokang Ho's case, a brand new chapter) on time and, in three cases, way before the deadline. I have also benefited from comments from some contributors on my own chapter 3, which are duly acknowledged at appropriate places in the endnotes. In addition, among the outside readers of parts of the manuscript who have offered comments, space will allow me only to acknowledge my colleague, David Denoon, at New York University, Peter Yu, at the East Asian Institute, National University of Singapore, and Xiangdong Wei and Y. Y. Kueh at Lingnan. It goes without saying that the ultimate responsibility for any possible faults or omissions in the final product rests with me as the architect of the volume.

James C. Hsiung
New York University

NOTES

1. Based on findings of the Correlates of War (COW) project by David Singer and Melvin Small, as reproduced in Table 3, Small and Singer 1979, 66.
2. On the origin of the "one country, two systems" model and how it works in Hong Kong after reversion, see Hsiung 2000.
3. Cf. Hsiung 1997.
4. Some examples of such policy-oriented studies with recommendations are: Council on Environmental Quality 1980; Zoellick and Zelikow 2000; and Economy and Oksenberg 1999.
5. Environmentalists, going beyond the holistic orientation of the neorealists, whose concern is exclusively with the total power configuration across the whole system, urge that we direct our attention to the *wholeness* of the ecosystem we live in (see Pirages 1978). Ernst B. Haas (1990, 66) even proposed an "eco-wholist" (sometimes spelled "ecoholist") paradigm to highlight that our global system is so interdependent that it is "nondecomposable."
6. For figures like these and relevant discussions, see Kristof and WuDunn 2000.
7. This group is made up of former students or associates of the great master, A. F. K. Organski, founder of the power transition theory. The Tammen (2000) book grew out of a project looking into the twenty-first century world politics from the perspective of the theory.
8. For an illuminating exposition of this Western tilt in IR theory, see Bobrow 1999, 3–5.
9. On China's macroeconomic control and its ability to ride out the storm, see Li Xioaoming, "China's Macroeconomic Stabilization Policies," *Asian Survey,* 15, no. 6 (November-December 2000): 938ff.

REFERENCES

Abu-Lughod, Janet. 1989. *Before European Hegemony: The World System,* A.D. 1250–1350. New York: Oxford University Press.

Bobrow, Davis. 1999. Prospecting the Future. In *Prospects for International Relations: Conjectures about the Next Millennium,* special issue of *International Studies Review,* 1, no.2 (summer):1–10. Published by Blackwell Publishers (Malden, MA) for the International Studies Association.

Bull, Hedley. 1977. *The Anarchical Society: A Study of Order in World Politics.* Second edition, reissued in 1995, with a foreword by Stanley Hoffmann, by Columbia University Press, New York.

Burch, Kurt. 2000. "Changing the Rules: Reconceiving Change in the Westphalian System." *International Studies Review.* 2, no.2 (Summer): 181–201.

Burke, Edmund III, ed. 1993. *Rethinking World History.* Cambridge: Cambridge University Press.

Caporaso, James A., ed. 2000. "Changes in the Westphalian Order: Territory, Public Authority, and Sovereignty." In *Continuity and Change in the Westphalian Order,* Special issue of *International Studies Review.* 2, no.2 (summer): 1–28. Published by Blackwell Publishers (Malden, MA) for the International Studies Association.

Chase-Dunn, Christopher and Thomas Hall. 1997. *Rise and Demise: Comparing World Systems.* Boulder, CO: Westview Press.

Chaudhuri, K. N. 1990. *Asia Before Europe.* Cambridge: Cambridge University Press.

Council on Environmental Quality. 1980. *The Global 2000 Report to the President.* Prepared in conjunction with the U.S. Department of State. Washington, D.C.: Government Printing Office.

Economy, Elizabeth, and Michel Oksenberg, eds. 1999. *China Joins the World: Progress and Prospects.* New York: Council on Foreign Relations Press.

Frank, Andre Gunder. 1998. *ReOrient: Global Economy in the Asian Age.* Berkeley, CA: University of California Press.

Frank, Andre Gunder and B. K. Gills, eds. 1993. *The World System: Five Hundred Years or Five Thousand?* New York and London: Routledge.

Haas, Ernst B. 1990. *When Knowledge Is Power.* Berkeley, CA: University of California Press.

Hodgson, Marshall G. 1993. In Edmund Burke III 1993.

Hoffman, Stanley. 1998. *World Disorders: Troubled Peace in the Post–Cold War Era.* Lamham, MD: Roman & Littlefield.

Hsiung, James C. 1997. *Anarchy and Order: The Interplay of Politics and Law in International Relations.* Boulder, CO: Lynne Rienner.

———, ed. 2000. *Hong Kong the Super Paradox.* New York: St. Martin's Press.

Huntington, Samuel P. 1996. *The Clash of Civilizations: Remarking of World Order.* New York: Simon & Schuster.

Khalilzad, Z. et al. 1999. *The United States and a Rising China.* Santa Monica, CA: RAND.

Kristof, Nicholas, and Shirley WuDunn. 2000. *Thunder from the East: Portrait of A Rising Asia.* New York: Alfred Knopf.

Linder, Staffan Burenstam. 1986. *The Pacific Century: Economic and Political Consequences of Asian-Pacific Dynamism.* Stanford, CA: Stanford University Press.

McNeill, William. 1963. *The Rise of the West: A History of the Human Community.* Chicago: University of Chicago Press.

McNeill, William. 1990. "The Rise of the West after Twenty-Five Years." *Journal of World History.* 1, no.1: 1–22.

Mueller, John. 1989. *Retreat from Doomsday: The Obsolescence of Major War.* New York: Basic Books.

Olds, Kris, Peter Dicken, Philip F. Kelly, Lily Kong, and Henry Yeung, eds. 1999. *Globalisation and the Asia Pacific.* London and New York: Routledge.

Perry, William. 2000. Security and stability in Asia Pacific. *PacNet Newsletter,* No.18 (5 May 2000). Pacific Forum, CSIS; available on the Internet at: http://www.csis.org/pacfor/pac0018.html.

Pirages, Dennis. 1978. *Global Ecopolitics.* North Scituate, MA: Duxbury Press.

Small, Melvin and David Singer 1979. "Conflict in the International System." In *Explaining War: Selected Papers from the COW Project,* edited by J. David Singer and Associates. Beverly Hills, CA: SAGE Publications.

Tammen, Ronald, et al. 2000. *Power Transitions: Strategies for the 21st Century.* New York: Seven Bridges Press (Chatham House Publishers).

Wallerstein, Immanuel. 1974. *The Modern World System.* Vol. 1. New York: Academic Press. Vols. 2 and 3 were published in 1980 and 1989, respectively.

Wilkinson, David. 1987. Central civilization. *Comparative Civilizations Review* (fall), 31–59.

———. 1993. "Civilizations, Cores, World Economies, and Oilumenes." In Frank and Gills, eds., *The World System.*

Zoellick, Robert B., and Philip D. Zelikow, eds. 2000. *America and the East Asian Crisis.* New York: W. W. Norton.

PART I

THE GLOBAL PERSPECTIVE

CHAPTER 1

WORLD ORDER OF THE NEW CENTURY: PROSPECTS AND PERILS

JAMES C. HSIUNG

Conventional wisdom has it that with the advent of the twenty-first century, a new world order will replace the old in our Westphalian system, just as happened before, when each new century followed the preceding one. I hasten to add, however, that what we are witnessing is no ordinary transition from one century to the next, for a number of reasons. First, the end of the twentieth century followed on the heels of the Cold War, the magnitude and idiosyncrasy of which were unmatched in history. For one thing, its nuclear confrontation was not found in any previous period of bipolarity the world has seen since the dawn of the Westphalian system in 1648. Second, the turn of the new century also coincided with the onset of what can be called the age of "communications revolution,"[1] which both accentuated and accelerated the process of globalization. And, third, as a result of globalization, all parts of the world came under the sway of a universal spread of ideas, economic innovations, and cultural and political adjustments that accompany such diffusion, like never before. I shall not belabor the obvious but vacuous, namely, that the new century also ushers in a new millennium, to boot.

Like interdependence even at the most complex stage, globalization will most likely manifest itself differently in different regions. But it remains true that in the age of globalization, more than ever before, the ultimate global order that is to emerge from the initial fluidity beyond the collapse of the Cold War bipolar system, invariably, will bear on the order of all regions. For students of international relations, it means that while no region can be properly understood without a prior grasp of the global order at large, conversely, no understanding of the latter will be complete without looking at how it manifests itself and holds sway in a given region, preferably in comparison with other regions in comparable issue areas.

This book is designed precisely to respond to this dual challenge. To begin with, it (1) inquires into the pathway by which the new world order will emerge from its initial uncertainty and fluidity, and (2) attempts to speculate on the final shape the new world order will likely take. This dual task is the function primarily of chapters 1 and 2, paving the way for the follow-up inquiry into the question of how the world order at large will impact on, and interface with, the Asia Pacific region. The follow-up task will be undertaken in chapters 3 through 11, in which various aspects of the Asian region will be singled out for scrutiny within the context of the emergent world order. Where appropriate, relevant comparisons will be made with other regions, for example, Europe (EU) and North America (NAFTA). The concluding chapter (chapter 12) will tie everything together in a final look at both the global and regional order.

In methodological terms, Asia Pacific serves as both an illumination and a test of the emergent global order of the new century: An *illumination,* because its manifestation in the region will reveal how the new world order will set the parameters within which international relations will play out. A *test,* because discernible variations will testify to how well the new world order, as can be so deduced, will hold true despite the regional deviations from the global mean.

In Search of a Contour of the New World Order

Admittedly, given our present level of collective wisdom, no honest analyst can claim to know for sure what is likely to emerge from the initial period of fluidity as that which will replace the world order of the defunct bipolarity of the Cold War vintage.[2] Our effort here, nonetheless, is to identify and etch out a contour of what is likely to cohere as the new world order that will be the grammar of international relations through the rest of the twenty-first century. At a minimum, we hope to be able to find, or point to, a way whereby a meaningful quest can proceed.

The best way to begin is to scrutinize a number of interrelated subquestions. In raising them, I will explain why they demand careful scrutiny in our quest for an ultimate answer regarding the emergent world order. Three such subquestions stand out:

1. What will be the "systemic value(s),"[3] if any, that are to serve as the guiding light for world affairs and as a "grammar" of international relations in the new century?
2. What will be the burning issues, or agenda, engaging the attention of nations to the extent that they will reshape their domestic and foreign policy formulations and influence their international behavior in response to the changing reality?
3. What is likely to be the power distribution across the international system, say, by 2050, halfway through the new century? And, how is this new power balance likely to reshape major-power alignments, requiring substantive foreign-policy adjustments in the realm of international relations?.

The three subquestions are raised in the given order above because of our conception of what constitutes world order and the hierarchy of its components. In contrast to the neorealist view that power distribution across the system is the sole determinant of the behavior of nations (Waltz 1979), our view of world order is much broader. We believe that while power and its distribution across the system is important, the balance of power exercise does not take place in a vacuum. Instead, it is played out in accordance with the nature of the "game" of international relations in a given system, which has to be redefined in response to changes in a number of factors, only one of which is the system's power distribution. Other factors include a consensus regarding certain systemic values defining the "game" nations play,[4] the strategic concerns of nations, the international institutional constraints, the structure of expectations of principal decision makers, etc., that obtain at a given period of time.

Together, these factors constitute what we in this book call "world order."[5] Hence, our three subquestions follow the sequence that best reflects this inherent definition we subscribe to.[6] It reflects our belief that non-power factors (such as systemic values) actually set the parameters in which power is given meaning and, more important, which determine how power is to be employed and for what purpose. For instance, power may be used in competitive pursuit of colonial empires abroad (as in the nineteenth century), in a mission to counteract the ubiquitous threats of a totalitarian power (as during the Cold War), or in collective action to contain noninternational strife in the name of humanitarianism (such as in Bosnia, in the post–Cold War era).

Hedley Bull (1995, 21), in a classical work first published in 1977, distinguishes "world order" from "international order" in that he considers the former to be the "[o]rder of mankind as a whole . . . something more fundamental and primordial than [international order]; and also . . . something morally prior to it." To him, order and justice are compatible in the international society in which we live (83f). In fact, he argues, "justice, in any of its forms, is realizable only in a context of order. . . ." As will become increasing clear, our conception of world order agrees largely with Bull's, in the sense that it is larger than and prior to international order, if the latter means the maintenance of peace by the balance of power or other forms of statecraft. I wish to emphasize in particular Bull's point that world order is more fundamental and morally prior to international order, for a similar reason. Bull arrives at the same point by looking at the "value of world order and its place in the hierarchy of human values." For us, one crucial component of world order (i.e., "systemic values"), to reiterate, actually sets the parameters of the "game" nations play in a given age, thereby establishing the priority of their concerns and interests, and anticipating the means they resort to, including the balance of power technique among other forms of diplomacy, in defense of their national interests. The rules or norms pertaining to the strategy and behavior of states in pursuit of their goals, in a game thus circumscribed by the systemic values, constitute what Bull calls "international order," at the next echelon.

Now a few words of elaboration are in order about the three subquestions we posed above. Systemic values will be addressed first, followed by the other two elements in the sections below.

SYSTEMIC VALUES OF THE NEW CENTURY

The first subquestion we raised, concerning "systemic values," is far more pregnant than meets the eye. Since the birth of the Westphalian system, each century was guided by a distinct, clearly identifiable, systemic value (or set of values) that defined the "game" of nations and propelled nations onto the pursuit they undertook. Before we proceed any further, let me note that war and peace were always high on the agenda of the concerns of states in a given system; that being the case, the rational choice of a dominant strategy to maintain peace and, when necessary, to aggrandize one's national power in conditions of "anarchy" (i.e., in the absence of a world government) was a fixed feature in statecraft that preoccupied the attention of decision-makers of all times. So too, generations of diplomatic historians and other students of international relations were almost exclusively concerned with how states acted in defense of their national interests (Hinsley 1967; Lauren 1979).

For our purpose, however, the choice of a strategy as such is secondary to a precondition, namely, the determination of what kind of a system nations find themselves in and what kind of a game they find themselves playing vis-à-vis one another. Both the "system" and the "game" are defined by the combination of factors mentioned above, the first of which is the set of systemic values prevailing in a given epoch.[7]

We need not rehash at length the rise of sovereignty as a systemic value legitimizing the birth of separate entities—now called states—in the seventeenth century, marking off the Westphalian system from the erstwhile feudal and ecclesiastic order and imperial pretensions that had prevailed before 1648.[8] Nor the eighteenth century preoccupation with dynastic legitimacy based on the "divine right to rule" that, under the lingering influence of "Christendom," was reinforced by bonds between the ruling houses through intermarriages (Liska 1963). Under this new systemic value, the question of who should sit on the Spanish throne, for instance, was something that did not just precipitate a war of succession but riveted the attention of all powers at the time, until, that is, the rise of popular nationalism brought in a new order of things following the French Revolution.[9]

Let us turn our attention to the nineteenth century. While much has been said about the "concert" system that helped Europe maintain order following the Napoleonic wars, a woefully neglected development was the subsequent rise of a systemic value in support of (colonial) empire building overseas, with the potential of deflecting international conflicts to other continents (Albrecht-Carrie 1958, 214ff; Hinsley 1967, 264ff). Throughout the rest of the nineteenth century, European powers, starting with Britain, France, and the Netherlands, scrambled to establish their colonial empires stretching out from Africa to Asia and the Oceania. But, after self-determination became the new ultimate guiding star (systemic value) in the second half of the twentieth century, the table turned on the European colonial countries.

The powerful reach of this new systemic value fueled the unstoppable momentum of decolonization. A rapid succession of over 60 colonies and dependencies were swept into independence[10] less than 30 years after self-determination became codified as a universal human right in 1960, through the medium of the United Nations. Not even the colonial powers themselves (like Britain, France, etc.) voted against its adoption as GA Res.15114 (XV) (Hsiung 1997, 129–138). This universally flaunted systemic value, spearheading the drive of total decolonization, brought to a swift end the Western colonial empires that had been built over at least a century and a half. Not only that, it also fired the centrifugal (secessionist) drives that brought down the Soviet empire and spawned the turmoil in the former Yugoslavia at the end of the process.

If such outcomes speak eloquently for the power of systemic values whose time had come in history, the question is: What will be the overriding systemic value(s) of the twenty-first century? I see two inklings thus far. One is the rise of geoeocnomics, as will be discussed under a separate heading below. (In the age dominated by geoeconomic desiderata, in short, a country's economic security rivals, even outweighs, its military security in importance.) The other is found in the flip side of the "global village" syndrome. Undeniably, globalization of the economy has worked for the benefit of the corporate world at the expense of the working class, not to mention the environment. The outbursts and massive demonstrations staged by the odd coalition of labor movements, environmental groups, and social-rights advocates that disrupted the Seattle meeting of the World Trade Organization in November 1999 offered a brutal reminder of the extent of their disgruntlement with the prevailing international economic order installed since the end of World War II. Their collective demands for building labor rights, environmental protection, and social standards into trade accords and the protocols of international financial institutions were a wake-up call for all (Mazur 2000).

In view of this development, it will not be too far-fetched to suggest that the call for greater socioeconomic equality and, by extension, for the leveling (or narrowing) of the hierarchy between rich and poor nations and between the capital-owning class and the laboring masses will most probably be the new guiding light for the world. For lack of a better term, let us call it the "social justice" value at the systemic level for the new century.[11] Not coincidentally, this dovetails with the world's growing concerns for human security, as will be seen below as part of the so-called "comprehensive security" high on the agenda of nations' concerns in the new century.

Not long ago, the World Bank launched a study entitled "Voice of the Poor," which found that the deepening crisis of poverty presented what James C. Wolfensohn (2000, 6), president of the World Bank Group, calls a "challenge of inclusion," covering the widening numbers of the world's poor. "Poverty," according to this study, "is much more than a matter of income alone. The poor seek a sense of well-being which is peace of mind; it is good health, community, and safety" (quoted in Wolfensohn 2000, 7). As Wolfensohn put it, "the voices of the poor will be louder; but will they be heard?" (8).

Hence, while "social justice" may seem appealing, therein also lie potential perils. For it may become a dragnet for two overlapping genres of conflict: (1) between the less developed countries (the South), on the one hand, and the rich and more industrialized nations (the North), on the other; and (2) between certain non-Western countries (e.g., Asian) and the West, often cutting across the levels of economic development.

As a forerunner of conflicts of the first genre, let me cite the battle drawn in the United Nations General Assembly in which the Southern states, since the 1980s, have launched a "right to development" crusade. At the strategic level, the South identifies its past "economic subjugation" by the predatory West, as well as the "unjust" distribution of wealth in the postcolonial stage, as the sources of the South's misery (UN Doc.: C/CN.4/Sub.2/1987/23, 44). Tactically, the South insists that all human rights are "indivisible" and defines development as an "inalienable human right" of nations (GA Res.41/128: Arts. 6[2], 9[1], and 1[1]). By this linkage, the Southern nations deftly placed their claims to the right of (national) development on a par with the West's concerns about individual rights, such as the right to liberty and security of person. This particular view of the South is called an "alternative" approach to human rights (GA Res.39/145), thus potentially upstaging the traditional Western concerns for individuals' rights to be asserted against their own governments (Hsiung 1993a, 137).

The South's "alternative" approach, in effect, redirects the limelight of the world's human rights fight to the poor nations' claim that the West has a responsibility to help them realize their right to development. Through a number of UN General Assembly resolutions, it was made into a "primary responsibility" of states to create international, as well as domestic, conditions "favorable to the realization of the right to development" (e.g., GA Res.41/128: Arts. 3(1) and 4). It is apparent to which group of states this "primary responsibility" was attributed. There is every reason to assume that the drive will continue well into the new century, possibly flowering into a crusade for "human development" (UNDP 1993), equating "empowerment of the poor" with democratization (UNDP 1998). This crusade can be expected to consume the energies of the less developed countries, most of them postcolonial states, with the same fervor as did the drive of decolonization during 1960 through 1990.[12]

While the South's drive, as such, was limited to the economically underdeveloped nations, mostly in Africa (though some in Latin America and elsewhere), the more affluent Asian bloc of nations has also stood up in a different challenge to the West (more particularly the United States), in what clearly falls under the second genre of conflict alluded to above. A typical example was the convocation of a meeting in Bangkok in 1993, when 49 Asian countries, including the most economically successful, gathered to air their collective grievances against the West (read: the United States) for imposing its own standards of human rights on the non-Western countries and, moreover, for its "double standards" approach to human rights at home and abroad (see Hsiung 1997, 113). The

Bangkok Declaration issued at the end of the 49-nation conference, while reaffirming the importance of human rights, stressed "the universality, objectivity, and *non-selectivity* of all human rights" (Art. 7, emphasis added). This recalls the "alternative" approach of the Southern nations, although in the latter's concern, their self-proclaimed economic deprivation by the West outweighs the human-rights issue per se. Nonetheless, a crucial connection between the two protests, the African and the Asian, was in the "right to development," which the countries made into a universal human right not to be abridged by anyone, not in the least the Western powers.

Comparing the two instances, we find a few noteworthy lessons relevant to the future. First, both typify a deep-seated resentment of the West, though to varying degrees, that is apparently built on nationalism (cf. Mortimer and Fine 1999). While the first instance represents a genre of clashes between the poor South and the rich North, both terms (i.e., "South" and "North") are vestiges of the Cold War period. Following the end of the Cold War and the collapse of the Soviet bloc, what used to be known as "North," including, in the loosest sense of the word, the more industrially advanced Communist bloc countries in Europe, boiled down to just the industrial West. Therefore, the term "South-North conflicts" should be renamed "South-West conflicts," to conform to the changed reality. On the other hand, the second example above represented a different genre of conflicts, stemming from resentments against the West by another non-Western (i.e., Asian) group that included the most affluent nations in the non-Western world.

The second lesson is that the non-Western revolt today is increasingly directed at the United States, not only because it is the sole surviving superpower but also because the other, once "detestable" Western powers (such as England, France, etc.) have ceased to be colonial powers and, besides, have shown greater understanding than has the United States of the views, needs, and interests of non-Western states.[13] Besides, many in the South can even find theoretical support, as have Latin American nations, in *dependencia* theory. The elaborate explanation offered by the theory confirms their intuition that, as the theory claims, the source of their underdevelopment lies in the built-in bias in the post-1947 international economic structure founded on U.S. hegemony (Frank 1970; Dos Santos 1970; Emmanuel 1972; Wallerstein 1979).

While for the Asian group the human-rights disputes are the real reason behind its anti-U.S. sentiments, one new development is worth watching: the group's purposeful drift toward Europe, begun with Asem−1 in 1996.[14] If the trend continues, as is likely, the United States has to be prepared to live with a geoeconomic alignment between Asia (including some of the most prosperous countries, like Singapore and Malaysia) and members of the European Union (EU) in the time ahead.

The third and ultimate lesson is that both the "right to development" crusade and the human-rights dispute can equally fuel the structural conflicts between non-Western countries and the West, more particularly the United States. In this light, the emergent systemic value of international social justice paradoxically spells grave perils for the twenty-first century, despite the hopes it may inspire.

So much for the first of the three subquestions raised above. Next, I will comment on the two other subquestions briefly, just enough to provide an overview of the interrelationship of the three subquestions we raised. The necessary details will come in separate sections below. This way, I hope, the flow of ideas presented here will be easier to follow.

In a nutshell, our answer to the second subquestion, regarding the agenda of nations in the international relations of the new century, is that nations will be concerned with what can be lumped together under "comprehensive security." This umbrella rubric subsumes economic security, environmental security, the traditional military security, and human security. The last mentioned refers to the security of individuals from debilitating inequities of society (such as grotesque income gaps) or even the atrocities committed by their own government (such as in Rwanda, and in Bosnia and Kosovo in the disintegrating Yugoslavia, etc.). I might add that if human security involves, among other things, distributive justice at home, then it is consistent with and complementary to the call of international social justice, which, as seen above, is likely to become a foremost systemic value in the new emergent world order.

Likewise, the third subquestion, concerning the new power distribution across the international system and the challenge this factor presents, can be answered in a nutshell here first, leaving the elaboration to a separate section below. On this point, there can be as many answers as there are analysts. But the most tantalizing one, for our purpose, is the projection made by analysts who subscribe to A. F. K. Organski's "power transition theory." Without stealing the thunder from our discussion below, let me mention briefly their prognostication: Just as there has been a geological shift in the locus of international conflict from the once Eurocentric world to Asia, the foremost challenge that will arise, in this view, is the coming ascendancy of China as a superpower, possibly even overtaking the United States by 2050 (Tammen et al. 2000, 153ff). I will just note that, for our overview purpose here, this eventuality, if it materializes, will tie everything in this book together in its study of the new century's world order and the place of Asia Pacific in it.

Strategic Concerns of
Nations in the New Century:
Comprehensive Security

In our conception of world order, as briefly stated above, the next most important determinant of the behavior of nations is the strategic concerns and interests of nations in the new realty. These are at the center of the second of the three subquestions we raised in search of an answer to the new century's world order. These national concerns are in turn anticipated by a number of factors including the nature of the "game" nations play as circumscribed by the overriding systemic values already discussed. Another factor is the structure of the system as defined by its power configuration or, in neorealist parlance, power distribution across the system, which will be discussed in the next section.

In our discussion above, we have noted the rise of the social-justice dictate, along with the rising importance of the environment, while the rise of geoeconomics was mentioned in passing. I wish to point out that there is an inherent interrelationship among the three elements. The links between social justice and the environment were noted in reference to the moral we can derive from the cacophony of protests at the 1999 WTO meeting in Seattle. Our focus now is on the third element. As a prefatory remark, I would note that in combination, the three elements—geoeconomics, environment, and social justice—account for the rise of economic security, environmental security, and human security on the agenda of nations in their strategic concerns, under the rubric of "comprehensive security."

Economic Security (geoeconomics)

In contrast to all previous eras, geoeconomics has risen to rival, even outweigh, geopolitics as a desideratum determining a country's national interest and its foreign-policy behavior. This has come about not only because of the end of the Cold War but, more important, because of the globalization of the world economy beyond the stage of complex interdependence that Keohane and Nye (1977) wrote about. Despite its by now relatively wide usage, the term "geoeconomics" is nowhere defined,[15] except in my 1997 work (Hsiung 1997, 203).

Let me summarize that formulation for the sake of our discussion here. On the macro level, in the geoeconomic age, matters pertaining to manufacturing, marketing, financing, and research and design (R & D) are transnationalized, ultimately globalized. On the micro level, besides, national power is no longer measured exclusively, or even mainly, by a state's military might. And economic security has eclipsed, though not displaced, military security on the scale of strategic importance to a country's national interest. National power in this context is the aggregate of a number of components, such as human and technological resources, exportable capital, efficient production of modern goods, influence over global economic decision-making, and the will to mobilize economic capability for national ends (cf. Hunter 1992, 9).[16]

This formulation, which combines both a change in macrolevel economic power management and the new era's microlevel implications for individual states caught in the shifting global power game, captures, I think, the essence of the age of geoeconomics. In addition to redefining what power is and what the new system's power configuration implies, it also points up the paramountcy of geoeconomic calculations in the concerns of nations in their foreign-policy calculus and behavior.

I hope, by now, it is apparent why this discussion, as well as that of systemic values above, must precede our examination of the structure of the system (as redefined by the power distribution across its members), which is the last of our three subquestions. For an example of how geoeconomic desiderata may command a country's foreign policy priorities, we only need to recall Japan's response to the Persian Gulf crisis of 1990–1991, precipitated as it was by Iraq's invasion and annexation of Kuwait. That event taught the Japanese a lesson about economic security, because it drove home the vulnerability of their economy arising from its total dependency on extraregional supplies of vital resources. As the event woefully showed, access to these supplies could be disrupted at any flare-up of a crisis in a far-off place. Even more than before, Japan learned to appreciate the value of closer-to-home sourcing of strategic resources. Thus, while the world's industrial nations were carrying on their post-Tiananmen sanctions, Japan began in the fall of 1990—during the height of the Gulf crisis—to switch gears and to be the first industrial country to return to China in a deliberate effort to uplift its ties with the Chinese, thus breaking ranks with the rest of the G-7 (Hsiung 1993b, 10). It not only resumed bilateral trade but even extended to China U.S.$54 billion in credits.[17] In fact, during the next five years, 1991–1995, Japan's trade with China witnessed a double-digit increase over the already high pre-1989 level (Chen 2000, 104).

Another instance demonstrating how the geoeconomic reflex held sway was the decision of the Hong Kong SAR government to intervene in the market, in August 1998, during the course of the financial crisis hitting the Asian Pacific region. While well-intentioned critics condemned the move as a betrayal of Hong Kong's long tradition of laissez-faire, the fact is, considering the dictate of economic security in the age of geoeconomics, the SAR government reacted in the same fashion as would all traditional governments when their national security was breached by external military inroads.

I do not want to leave the impression that geoeconomics has thus replaced geopolitics. It has not. The implication is simply that in what we have called the "geoeconomic age," for instance, Switzerland or Turkey, in deciding some business question about which Germany and France disagree, will not necessarily decide in favor of Germany simply because it has a bigger GNP than France. But the fact that both Germany and France are in a strong enough economic position to help or hurt other countries is a crucial factor that, more than ever before, neither Switzerland nor Turkey, nor any other country, can afford to ignore or subsume under any consideration based on other factors (Singer and Wildavsky 1993, 29).

For a keener appreciation of the shift in the concerns of nations brought on by the age of geoeconomics, a brief comparison with geopolitics may be helpful. If we can extrapolate from the rich literature on geopolitics, it seems that the two most important ingredients—other than power itself—guiding the balance-of-power reflex of nations, in an essentially geopolitical game, are geography and ideology (Spykman 1944; Strausz-Hupe 1972; Gray 1977; Smith 1986; Ward 1992; Ross 1999). In a purely geopolitical context, two assumptions underpin the priority attached to ideology.[18] The first is the assumption that ideological homogeneity conduces to international stability. The other assumption is that ideological homogeneity unifies the principles of legitimacy (Kyung-won Kim 1970, esp. xvi-xix).

In a geoeconomic game, in contrast, a lot is determined by a player's strategic autonomy, which can be defined by reference to a number of conditions, including: (1) self-sufficiency in basic natural resources, such as energy; (2) relative freedom from long-term dependency on overseas market; and (3) access to inexhaustible, inexpensive, and relatively reliable labor force (Ross 1999, 93).

We have seen a geoeconomic redefinition of power above. Here, let me suggest that the redefinition is made necessary by a geoeconomic shift to considerations of a player's strategic autonomy, as distinguished from geography and ideology. Such being the case, it is plain that, in the geoeconomic age, not even the United States, the sole superpower today, has absolutely sufficient economic capacity and tools for influencing global economic decision-making, for affecting the behavior of other nations, or for shaping the global political-economic environment (Hunter 1992, 9). This means that "shared decision-making" will become increasingly the rule, rather than the exception, in the age of geoeconomics. To the uninitiated, let me note that "shared decision-making" is a concept first developed by Jeffrey Hart (1976) to account for the imperative of states engaging in collective action, when each of them only has partial control over certain events that are consequential to all, such as in bailing the world economy out of a recession. Industrial nations, Hart notes, only have *partial control* over the recovery of the world economy in a global recession; yet such recessions are consequential for all. Hence, joint control, as such, calls for joint decision-making and collective action. For our purpose here, joint decision-making and collective action is potentially the trademark of a geoeconomic age, just as "self-help," or unilateralism, has been a distinct characteristic of the age essentially dominated by the geopolitical reflex.

In the geoeconomic age that is upon us, when geopolitics still has a lingering influence on international relations, a foreign adversary in the geopolitical sense may very well be a great economic partner, such as in the case of China. Conversely, an ideologically defined ally like Japan may prove to be a potential economic threat, despite its protracted economic doldrums of the past decade.[19] The place of ideology as a strategic desideratum is now at best uncertain.

Environmental Security (Ecopolitics)

Strictly speaking, ecopolitics has a much broader connotation than the combination of the three terms—economics, ecology, and politics—of which it is a contraction. In its original formulation, proposed by Dennis Pirages (1978), global ecopolitics involves "the use of environment issues, control over natural resources, scarcity arguments, and related concerns of social justice to overturn the international political hierarchy, and related system of rules established during the period of industrial expansion" (5). Placing it in the context of total human history, Pirages speaks of an ecopolitical revolution, on a par with the two preceding human revolutions: the Agricultural Revolution (c. 8000 B.C.) and the Industrial Revolution, which began to gather momentum during the fifteenth and sixteenth centuries and culminated in the rapid advance of technology characteristic of the twentieth century (4). As such, the ecopolitical revolution encompasses a number of developments affecting all nations, subsumed under what he calls a "new scarcity" resulting from the "exponential growth of population." It includes resource depletion, energy shortage, water shortage, and scarcity of food and nonfuel minerals. In addition, the problem is compounded by a related issue of natural waste disposal (8–9). More important, global ecopolitics entails a paradigmatic shift on our part in approaching the reality surrounding us. It requires different solutions to problems of human development, which Pirages spells out in various chapters of his book.

In our concerns here, however, our main focus is the environment, although not for its own sake so much as for the challenge it presents to nations in their mutual relations.[20] Hence, in our usage, "ecopolitics" refers to the ecological and political dimensions of the concept only, because the "economic" component was singled out for discussion above, in the context of geoeconomics, a term which was unknown at the time when Pirages' study appeared. Besides, despite Pirages's urging that the trilogy of "ecopolitics" be taken seriously as "the new context of international relations," the appeal seems not to have made a proper impact in the two decades since. Scholarly attention, as can be ascertained from a cursory survey of subsequent publications, indicates that the "ecology" part of his trilogy has not been properly heeded to relative to the other two components, economy and politics. The latter two have by themselves received increasing attention in the meantime, so much so that a flowering subfield of international political economy (IPE) has helped transform the IR field and how it is taught in American academe. This unexpected slant, in the face of the world's continuing environmental deterioration, has caused Lester Brown (2000, 8–10) to plead for "replacing economics by ecology."

While Brown's argument was that the continuing deterioration in our ecosystem has led to global economic declines (9), our concern here is different, as is self-apparent in the following two points, both bearing on the future direction of international relations: First, there is a dual linkage between international conflict and the environment. Disputes over control of shared resources (such as shared waters of international rivers) may lead to conflict, while renewal of resources (for example, fish stocks) may be depleted as a result of conflict. Second, environmental degradation, which is oftentimes the result of impersonal social and economic forces, requires cooperative solutions among nations.

Arnold Wolfers (1962) long ago called attention to the distinction between "possession goals" and "milieu goals" pursued by states in the conduct of international relations. While nations clash over the former (e.g., disputed territories), they cooperate in pursuit of the latter, such as improvement of the environment, which equally affects their interests and well-being. Writing nearly four decades ago, he was almost prophetic. To the extent that environmental deterioration gives occasion to international cooperation, reversing the Hobbesian image of international politics as a state of war that all realists and neorealists have embraced, it offers a ray of hope for the future, though it also has its perils. Control and containment of AIDS and other epidemics, of ozone depletion, of deforestation, of human-induced soil degradation, of mass migration and inundation of illegal immigrants, of drug traffic across national boundaries, etc.—all this unquestionably requires, and does spawn, cooperation of nations. The reason is that the harm resulting from the loss of control over these common evils will affect all nations, which makes a triviality of the "relative gains" question that realists consider an insurmountable hurdle to international cooperation (Grieco 1990, 40–49).

Like clean water and air, the "milieu goals" are collective goods, which entail joint production by joint efforts, though with the ancillary problem of "free riders." The proliferation, over recent decades, of global environmental conventions covering a widening range of areas, from wildlife and habitat, oceans, atmosphere, to hazardous waste, is one indication of this growing awareness, on the part of nations, of the need for international collective action. One account gives a total of 230 environmental treaties to date,[21] three-fourths of them concluded since the first UN conference on the environment in 1972 (French 2000, 200f). Likewise, the mushrooming of cooperative institutions like the "international agricultural research centers" in the last three decades, seated in various parts of the world, from the Philippines to Kenya, from Peru to Syria, and from India to Nigeria, is another such indication (Hughes 1997, 452, table 18.5).

However, there is also evidence of a widespread temptation by certain countries to shift the burden of their problems to others. For instance, Greenpeace uncovered 500 efforts to export more than 200 million tons of waste from OECD countries between 1989 and 1994. After forty African countries protested in 1991 and called for an outright ban on waste exports to Africa, Greenpeace discovered that some waste exporters then targeted Central and Latin America. Those countries in turn had to tighten their controls on imports (Hughes, 470f).

Thus, we see perils in the face of environmental deterioration, which is expected to continue well into the new century. The kind of burden-shifting involving waste disposal is an example that illustrates both the perils of globalization and the dire need for greater international control of the flow of imports as well as domestic regulation over such hazards as the discharge of industrial wastes and release of carbon dioxide into the atmosphere. Here lies a giant dilemma. If vigilant control as such is widely enforced on the international flow of imports, what will guarantee that it will not turn into restraint of trade? On the other hand, in the absence of such a safeguard, where is the guarantee of environmental protection and the environmental security of nations? More or less the same can be said of the financial vigilance that Asia Pacific has learned to live with in the wake of the financial attack of 1997–1998 that racked the region as a price of globalization, a topic to which we will return in chapter 3.

HUMAN SECURITY (HUMAN DEVELOPMENT)

Human security and human development fall into a continuum concerning human well-being. As discussed above, in reference to the South's crusade, self-claimed right to human development is an ideal to be achieved through no less than a redistribution of the wealth of nations. Human security, in the narrower sense, deals with the psychological end state of development instead of the more mechanical aspects of development (UNDP 1993). At a minimum, it is based on an individual and collective sense of protection from perceived present and potential threats to physical and psychological well-being from all manner of agents and forces affecting lives, values, and property (Weiss et al. 1997, 260).

In this discussion, our sight is trained on human security, which is often subject to structural conflict, or what we have earlier called "inequities of society" (such as gross inequality in income distribution), and brute atrocities committed by the victims' own government, as has happened with increasing frequency in the last 15 years. Since 1985, most conflicts in the world occurred within states, rather than between states, and most of the casualties have been civilian (such as in Rwanda). The Kosovo crisis, in particular, dramatized the modern vulnerability of individuals to state aggression (Axworthy 1999). Large-scale atrocities, crime, and terrorism committed by governments against their own people, such as in the "ethnic cleansing" conducted by the self-designated central government in a disintegrating Yugoslavia, were shocking to human conscience. But they also helped call into question how the world community would deal with state terrorism.

Incidentally, conventional wisdom may assume that state terrorism is a problem endemic only to the "rogue states." But, Alexander George (1991) points out that in transmuted forms, it is at times committed by Western states like Britain (in Northern Ireland) and the United States, which, according to this view, engaged in state terrorism in Vietnam and Nicaragua. During the Reagan presidency, Washington even colluded with South Africa in waging a "secret war" (including terrorism) in southern Africa. But I wish to note that such instances of state terrorism as were attributed to Western states in the volume edited by George were acts committed mostly abroad, in foreign countries (except Northern Ireland). By contrast, the kind of state aggression noted above was perpetrated at home, by the home government against its own people, the civilian population of whom it was supposed to be the guardian and protector.

While state terrorism is the most sensational and outrageous assault on the sanctity of human security, there are other less dramatic, although no less disconcerting, sources of human insecurity (Renner 1996, 81), such as:

· Income inequality
· Shortage of clean water
· Illiteracy
· Food shortage
· Housing shortage
· Infectious diseases.

The last mentioned is, for example, a devastating scourge to Africa. A reported 23 million people in sub-Sahara Africa are beginning the twenty-first century with a death sentence imposed by HIV, the virus that leads to AIDS. For the first time in the modern era, life expectancy for a whole region is declining, threatening the economic future of 800 million people in sub-Sahara Africa. And it is declining by 20 years or more (Brown 2000, xviii; 4).

Yet, the epidemic is not limited to Africa. Two countries in the Caribbean—Haiti and the Bahamas—are, outside the African continent, the worst hit, according to a United Nations report. In Haiti, more than five percent of adults are infected, and in the Bahamas the rate is more than four percent. AIDS has made inroads in Asia, although so far it is unclear whether infection rates will explode to rival those in Africa and, if that happens, when it might occur. In India, while only 7 adults in 1,000 are infected, 3.7 million people were living with HIV at the beginning of the year 2000. According to the New York Times, 28 June 2000, the total number in India is second largest in the world, behind South Africa. Closer to home, reports showed a small but sharp rise in new HIV infections in San Francisco, over three years ending with the close of 1999. This finding was considered "deeply troubling" by health officials because San Francisco was one of the principal centers, along with New York and Los Angeles, of the AIDS epidemic, which was first detected in 1981. Despite aggressive prevention campaigns mounted in 1982, the New York Times, in a report on July 1, 2000, estimated that the number of new infections in San Francisco nearly doubled since 1996. The discovery gave no comfort to those who had hoped that the epidemic would be brought under control by the turn of the century. If the trend continues, it is sure to pose a growing threat to human security in many parts of the world.

In addition to infectious diseases, poverty may be one more threat to human security. In the New York Times, 11 July 2000, President Thabo

Mbeki of South Africa was quoted as saying, while an international conference on AIDS was being held in his country, that "extreme poverty," rather than AIDS, was the "biggest killer."

In sum, comprehensive security is going to gain importance in the new century. The three separate kinds of security just noted will compete with the traditional military security (otherwise known as "national defense") for the attention of national decision-makers. These three securities are the utmost concerns of nations and will be the nexus of their mutual relations. They will dominate the international agenda and demand collective action across national boundaries, at grave perils to noncooperative players. As such, they deserve our attention in our search for a definitive answer to the question of what will be the new world order in the twenty-first century.

STRUCTURE OF THE NEW SYSTEM: THE POWER CONFIGURATION

In this section, we will deal with the power distribution across our Westphalian system and its effects on how states will act and interact. As we have indicated above in our view of world order, power configuration is only one of the "determinants" of the identity and behavior of states. Again, what constitutes power (e.g., power in a geoeconomic context as contradistinguished from that in a geopolitical milieu), the purposes for which power is to be employed, and how the balance of power is to be played out cannot be determined in a vacuum. Hence, this discussion about power configuration comes only after the other two ingredients have been addressed.

John Herz (1962, 7) makes a distinction between "structure" and "system." To him, the concept of structure refers to "the basic features which characterize the given units [states] of international politics at or within a particular period." System, on the other hand, connotes "the ways in which these units [states] organize their relationships (formally, or informally) on the basis of such structure." In the way Herz uses the term "structure" there is a faint echo of what we conceptualize as world order. Clearly, Herz's "basic features" in his structure could include elements other than the distribution of power across the community of states although he did not specify beyond references to "rights" and "duties" of states and to a presumptive collective will of the community as manifested in collective security (39–42). It is as though he was saying that history was not moved by matter (power) alone.

In the neorealist (or structural realist) literature since Herz, however, structure and system are almost identical. "Any international *system*," writes K. J. Holsti, for example, "has a definable *structure,* a characteristic configuration of power and influence or persisting forms of dominant and subordinate relationships" (1995, 24, emphasis added). This formulation follows closely that laid out in the most fundamental neorealist treatise (i.e., Waltz 1979), in which everything is factored out of an international system except the power distribution across its agents (states).

In our usage here, "structure" refers to a given state of power configuration across the world of states in a particular period. But, unless otherwise implied, "system" means more than the power-defined structure, encompassing elements such as systemic values and strategic national concerns, as discussed above. Largely agreeing with the neorealists, nevertheless, we believe that the structure of power configuration, or how power is distributed across a system, has a way of influencing the behavior of states and, hence, their mutual relationships. In the neorealist paradigm, each state is positional, not atomistic, in a given system, in which power distribution determines the hierarchy of states in their relations with one another. It follows, in this view, that behavior of states is system-induced (Kaplan 1957; Waltz 1979). In our conception of world order, the behavior of states is also system-induced, except it has a different connotation. Such behavior, in short, is induced or anticipated by what we call world order, with its multiple components including, but not limited to, the power configuration factor.

Nevertheless, we accept the notion that a crucial way of classifying international systems is by the number of major powers, or poles, found in a system, which is an indication of the system's power configuration. A "major power" is one that acts with significant independence from other major actors; it is its own master in its choice of initiatives or responses in foreign relations (Russett, Starr, and Kinsella 2000, 78). Scholars are divided, however, on whether a major actor, or pole, is either one nation-state or a coalition of states (Sabrosky 1985). In our usage, we tend to adopt a more flexible view. A pole could either be a single actor, like the United States or China, or a coalition of states, such as the European Union (EU). We also accept Mearsheimer's (1990, 7, n.5) formulation that to qualify as a pole in a global or regional system, an actor "must have a reasonable prospect of defending itself against the leading state in the system by its own efforts.[22] But scholars are agreed on one thing, namely, that systems vary and acquire their distinctive names in accordance with their specific patterns of power distribution, such as "unipolar," "bipolar," and "multipolar," depending on how many major powers are dominant actors.

The importance of polarity is that it is a convenient device for telescoping (1) the hierarchy of the international system, (2) the stratification of its units (states), and (3) the balance-of-power structure (e.g., the alliance and counter-alliance networks), all of which provide an overview of the system itself and a reasonable expectation of what is likely to happen among the units given the set of stimuli and demands arising from the system in a given period.

Hence, since the end of the Cold War, scholars, especially neorealists, concerned with the forthcoming new world order have been watching what type of a new polarity will emerge to replace the bipolar system dominated by the United States and the Soviet Union that ended in 1990. But a decade into the post–Cold War era and despite the fanfare with which the alleged "dawn" of a new world order (NWO) was ushered in by Washington after Desert Storm (1991), we do not as yet know the exact nature of the new international system (as defined by its power configuration) that is upon us, much less the new order enwrapping it.[23] We know that NWO does not stand for the defunct NorthWest Orient airline. Other than that, we only know that it is a complex system *in evolution.* But, evolution toward what? President George H. Bush, who first trumpeted the NWO with exuberant enthusiasm, thought it was going to remain a unipolar system, dominated by the United States as the sole surviving superpower. The Pentagon's initial defense planning guide for the fiscal years 1994–1999, as leaked to the *New York Times,* 8 March 1992, was geared toward discouraging other large industrial nations from "challenging [U.S.] leadership" and maintaining "the mechanisms for deterring potential competitors from even aspiring to a larger regional or global role." Although this controversial draft was later revised, the Bush administration's strategic reflex of endeavoring to maintain the United States-led unipolarity was transparent. But such a notion was immediately challenged by Christopher Layne (1993), who argued that unipolarity was an "illusion," because other competing new great powers would inevitably arise. Others shared the view that unipolarity would be untenable and multipolarity would replace the Cold War bipolarity (Mearsheimer 1990; Hsiung 1991; Jervis 1991/92; Waltz 1993). With gains in hindsight, however, analysts are beginning to question whether either epithet, unipolar or multipolar, may not be premature.

As Hans Binnendijk (1999) suggests, we may seek guidance from history for an answer. After identifying and defining the five previous international systems—stretching from 1713 (the Treaty of Utrecht) through the bi-superpower Cold War system[24]—he found that each of the previous five systems had a life cycle, to wit: There was a tendency for fluidity and initial multipolarity (presumably following a brief, uncertain period in which one state aspired to becoming the unipolar power) to turn into rigidity and bipolarity. In turn, bipolarity would result in large-scale conflict (of a "cold war" genre) and the demise of the existing system. In other words, each of the preceding five international systems was initially multipolar (following a very brief period of unipolarity). As usual, under conditions of multipolarity, movement in the system was relatively fluid and followed complex paths. But each system ended as bipolar, and in at least four of the five systems, Binnendijk found bipolarity had ideological underpinnings.

In view of this tendency of multipolarity moving eventually toward bipolarity, as was found in all previous systems, Binnendijk concluded that the next, or sixth, system will also tend toward bipolarity. Although he cites Russian Prime Minister Primakov as once conceiving of a loose Russian-Chinese-Indian alliance directed against Western dominance, Binnendijk really thought that a Russian-Chinese alliance against the West was a more likely possibility. We do not have to take Binnendijk's word as final. We need be skeptical as to whether the next system, conceivably heavily tinged by the geoeconomic factor, will find ideological underpinnings as important as previous systems did. But, Binnendijk's projection that the post–Cold War multipolar system, the one prevailing at the turn of the twenty-first century, will eventually develop toward bipolarity is tantalizing. My main skepticism is that even assuming we agree that bipolarity is likely to emerge in the new century, how can we be sure which two opposing great powers will lead the way in the resultant bipolar system? And when will the system develop?

If Binnendijk's projection from history as such is bold, the assessment of the "state of the world" ahead by a group of adherents to A. F. K. Organski's power-transition theory is even bolder. In a joint study (Tammen et al. 2000), they applied the theory developed by the Michigan University professor, their mentor, to the next century, after first testing it against developments in the nineteenth and twentieth centuries. After scanning massive data on population, productivity (GDP growth rates), and political capacity, the Organskiite group concluded: "China has the demographic, economic, and political potential to catch and overtake the United States, first in the size of its economy and then in power" (154). Thus, it not only saw the intensification of the U.S.-China rivalry (bipolarity?) but the eventual rise of China as a challenger, possibly "overtaking" the United States to become the next superpower, most possibly after a "hegemonic war."[25]

I might add that "overtaking" is a crucial concept in the power-transition theory, which sees the root cause of "hegemonic wars" not in the loss of equilibrium (or power parity between contending states), as generations of balance-of-power advocates believe (cf. Morgenthau 1985, 222). Rather, the root cause lies in a "rear-end collision," when the second most powerful state, a "dissatisfied" power at that, catches up from behind with the incumbent dominant power (Organski 1968, 286). The data and analyses cited by the Organskiite group indicate that China has the potential of overtaking the U. S. economy in terms of GDP during the first quarter of the twenty-first century (154) and later, in terms of power, probably by mid-century (190). Thus, according to this study, a hegemonic war in the "rear-end collision" fashion is likely by 2050, unless, of course, the United States as the reigning superpower can maintain its current preponderance[26] or, alternatively, succeeds in converting China, in time, from a dissatisfied power into one very much attuned to, and with high stakes in, the prevailing system. Other scattered sources, both private and public (e.g., Linder 1986; World Bank 1997; Morrison 1998) have provided the same statistical analysis about China's economic potential. But the study by the Organskiite group is the first of its kind to put that analysis in a much larger context and, in so doing, to prognosticate on how and when the forthcoming dominant power is to challenge and replace the incumbent one.

True to the legacy of the progenitor of the power transition theory (Professor Kenneth Organski, who believed that the ultimate purpose of research was to make its findings relevant to policy), the study, released shortly after the master's death, likewise recommended three scenarios for the United States on how best to respond to the challenge ahead. We will have occasion to return to this particular point in chapter 3. What concerns us here is "what if" China remains a dissatisfied power by the time it "successfully bests" the reigning superpower in the coming hegemonic war? The answer is twofold: (1) Asia eventually will emerge as the "center of the international system with an Asian state [China] as the global dominant power"; and (2) that under the influence of China as the new dominant power, a very different type of world order will appear (Tammem et al. 2000, 193). Of course, as its name suggests, the power-transition theory never takes any state of power configuration as terminal, for every status is transitory. The concluding part of the Organskiite study looks beyond 2050 to the next question: What will be China's "eventual challenger" after then? The answer need not sidetrack us from raising a question of our own that is relevant to this inquiry, to wit: If all the Organskiite assessment is true, what is likely to be the world order under Chinese influence?

Two points come to mind. First, the kind of bipolarity that Binnendijk presages will evolve from the initial post–Cold War fluidity will come to an end when China overtakes the United States by mid-century, starting another cycle of evolution. Following Binnendijk's logic, the initial period after China's mid-century triumph will probably see, initially, a unipolar system in place, one that will be in evolution, moving from multipolarity to bipolarity in another cycle. Second, and more important to our interest here, as long as China is in a position to provide a decisive input into the future world order after mid-century, it will most likely speak for today's dissatisfied nations. The bulk of this group will comprise the states in the postcolonial South and other countries with their own ax to grind against the United States, including the most prosperous in the Asian group, which we noted above in reference to the crusade for "social justice" in the post–Cold War world. This, in other words, will be the coalition of those countries that equate "empowerment of the poor" with democratization and other states that oppose the alleged U.S. practice of "double standards" on human rights and favor alternative paths to democratization. The alignments will be redrawn accordingly.

I will now turn to the reasons why I see a link between the systemic value of "social justice" that we have postulated above and the likely support it is to receive from the Chinese, if indeed China becomes the next dominant power. The best way to begin is to hark back to the making of Article 2(3) of the United Nations Charter, which now reads: "All Members shall settle their international disputes by peaceful means in such a manner that international peace and security, and *justice,* are not endangered" (emphasis added). A careful reader will notice that the words "and justice" are separated by two commas on either side and that they come after "peace and security," in what appears to be an afterthought. The answer is that it was an insertion into the original draft, made at the insistence of the Chinese government, through Ambassador Wellington Koo at the Dumbarton Oaks talks. It was here that the representatives of the Allied powers—United States, Britain, the Soviet Union, and China (France was in exile)—met in 1944, to discuss the Dumbarton Oaks Proposals,[27] which later became the draft of the United Nations Charter as adopted in 1945. The original draft of the proposals, prepared by the United States in consultation with Britain, spoke only of "peace and security" (note the "and" joining the two words in a closed phrase). In the Chinese view, however, peace, even if achieved, would not necessarily be "just," for it could simply be an imposition of the arbitrary will of the more powerful. And no peace without justice could be stable or secure. Hence, the final, seemingly odd wording in Art. 2(3), "that peace and security, and justice, are not endangered," resulted from this insertion (China Institute 1956, ch. 1). Otherwise, why shouldn't it just read "peace, security, and justice"?

Two questions might be raised here by skeptics. First, where on earth did this idea, "justice," come from? Second, why would the Chinese government be so uptight about getting "justice" into the original U.S.-drafted wording of "peace and security"? To the first question, the notion that justice must be the cornerstone of all human relations (by logic, this could extend to international relations as well) can be traced back to Confucius (Peerenboom 1990; Chen 1997). The answer to the second question, as explained by Ambassador Koo at the Dumbarton Oaks talks, has to do with China's painful experience with over a century of brute power-politics inroads imposed by the West. During the long 100 plus years since the 1830s, China was at the mercy of Western powers, beginning with Britain, which forced the sale of opium down its throat. When China resisted, the British, relying on their superior might, waged a war in 1839, euphemistically dubbed in Parliament as the "war to open trade with China." When it was all over, peace and security were restored all right; but, China, defeated and humiliated, had to sign the unequal 1842 Treaty of Nanking. Worse still, this signing set the precedent for all unequal treaties to follow in China's relations with European powers (including Russia) and Japan, until 1942 (Tung 1970).[28] Hence, insisted Ambassador Koo, "peace and security" in the absence of justice would be futile and could conceivably contain seeds of more conflict and destruction in the time ahead (China Institute 1956, ch. 1).

Realist cynics, paraphrasing a line once attributed to Hitler's question regarding the value of a pound of public opinion, might raise a question of their own, to wit: How much is a pound of "international justice" worth? This, admittedly, is a troublesome question. One cannot find an answer anywhere. A search through the most authoritative work on the subject of justice (Rawls 1971), for example, has turned up no discussion, not even mention, of international justice. Anything that comes close is the Rawlsian notion that social and economic inequities should be rectified by society (60). This recalls the postcolonial South's crusade for righting the wrongs in the world that were considered to be the structural sources of its underdevelopment.

While we cannot exactly put our finger on what is international justice, at least we know what it is *not,* or, to be more exact, which international systems are not just systems. A brief look at how discriminately the international economic structure (IES) installed after the end of World War II has worked for the two separate groups of states, the industrial and the nonindustrial, may be instructive. The post-1947 IES, founded on the twin pillars of the Bretton Woods System (encompassing the World Bank and the IMF) and the GATT/WTO,[29] has worked well for the industrial states, but at the expense of the others. For instance, from the 1970s through the 1990s, the industrial group, with 25 percent of world population, commanded from 79 percent to 86 percent of the world's GNP, and claimed 75 percent to 82 percent of the world's export earnings.[30] A UNDP report in 1992 showed that 45 years after the postwar IES was put in place, the top 20 percent of the world's nations had an average per capita GNP 65 times that of the bottom 20 percent of nations, and, worse, that the gap was widening.[31] By 2000, one report had it that 1.3 billion population in the world lived under the poverty line, squeaking by with less than U.S.$1 a day.[32] While the GATT helped the industrial countries in boosting their trade volume by as much as 500 percent during the period of 1950 to 1975 alone, against an increase in global output of 220 percent, the nonindustrial countries had no share of any of these benefits, as reported by *The Economist* on 22 September 1990. With its provisions against state-subsidized economies, the GATT was forbidden to most of the less developed countries.

In sum, the above data spoke eloquently for what is not international justice, or at least what structural biases must be rectified before our system can be a more just one. No wonder the less developed countries have, since 1974, pushed for a "new international economic order," a dream that has been kept alive into the post–Cold War era. In challenging the senior President George Bush's version of the new world order, for example, China, in 1991, launched a campaign to promote a counterversion of what the post–Cold War world order should be. One of its three tenets was that the new world order should contain a "new economic world order" as well, in which the developed nations have an obligation to help the developing nations in their path to development (Sutter 1991, 4; Hsiung 1993b, 72).

Domestic developments in China in recent years may or may not have advanced the cause of human rights or democratization to the liking of Freedom House or Amnesty International.[33] On the other hand, however imperceptibly, they seem to complement China's international posture in support of social justice. In 1995, for instance, the Chinese Communist Party (CCP) for the first time officially celebrated the birthday of Confucius. The Haidian District in Beijing, home to two of China's best universities, Beida and Qinghua, has become known as the center for the re-blossoming of Confucian culture, with its emphasis on justice, as already noted. In addition, Jiang Zemin, the Chinese president and head of the CCP, has called on his fellow countrymen to uphold *zhengqi* (justice and upright behavior), among other things, in his much touted "three exhortations." There is enough to lead one to speculate that if China indeed should be the next dominant actor, as the Organskiite group says it will, the forthcoming world order beyond mid-century is most likely to be one that seeks to reverse the social Darwinian notion of "might makes right" that has prevailed through the nineteenth and the twentieth centuries.[34] As such, the new world order will most likely accentuate social justice in the community of nations where, as a Chinese ideal (enshrined in their five principles of Peaceful Coexistence) goes, all nations, big and small, should be equal in more than juridical sense.

Realist skeptics might ask: Wouldn't the Chinese be corrupted by power by then? That is a question we should leave to history. However, if history is any guide, China's past may shed some light on the future. Let us briefly examine the record in "near-modern" (post-1368 A.D.) Chinese history. During the mid-fourteenth through the mid-seventeenth centuries (the Ming Dynasty), China's GNP was 28–30 percent of the world's total output. By 1800 A.D. China did even better, accounting for 33 percent of world manufacturing output (Segal 1999, 25). But even the lower figure during the Ming Dynasty (i.e., 28–30 percent) already exceeded by far the U.S. share of the global GNP today, at the turn of the twenty-first century. During Emperor Yong Lo's reign (1403–1424), China, in a departure from its agrarian continent-bound tradition, began to dispatch seafaring expeditions, which by 1433 totaled seven in all. The first expedition, in 1405 A.D.,[35] preceded Christopher Columbus' discovery of the New World by 87 years. In the largest expedition, Zheng He (Cheng Ho), who led all seven ventures, had 30,000 sailors and 400 ships under his command. The group sailed out from southern China, through Southeast Asia, to reach as far as the Persian Gulf and east Africa. But contrary to expectations, and in stark contrast to Western maritime expansion, Zheng He and his men did not establish a single colony overseas nor lay claims to any piece of the territories they visited, claiming "discovery."[36]

What does this tell us about Chinese behavior when the country wielded superior power vis-à-vis other peoples and lands? A comparison with Western powers in comparable stages in history (e.g., during the nineteenth century) would be revealing as well as fascinating. While that ambitious endeavor is beyond the ken of this study, let me make a passing remark that the above brief recount of history may reveal a very different, hidden Chinese attitude toward power. It finds support in the Confucian motto that, in paraphrase, can be translated as: "Resorting to brute power (as opposed to suasion and exemplification) is a terrible way to gain acceptance." A vulgar but more expressive way of putting it would be: "You don't have to use your power on others just because you know you have it."

Benjamin I. Schwartz (1968, 279f), seems to have captured the essence of this inherent Chinese view when he observes a parallelism in Chinese Buddhism: Throughout history, Chinese Buddhism, even during the height of its power (when emperors were sometimes obliged to "bolster imperial authority by claiming bodhisattvaship," or appropriating

Buddhist regalia symbols), "never carried out the sustained and aggressive assault on the claims of the Chinese world order on its own ground that papal Christianity carried out against the claims of the Holy Roman Empire." While the Chinese in the past regarded their culture as "superior," Schwartz also notes, it was not in any way different from other ancient peoples (such as in Mesopotamia and central Asia) that had similar "sedentary agrarian cultures" (282). Although modern times have added nationalism and communism to the equation, as Schwartz is quick to point out (284–287), the fact is that modern China, even during the Maoist era, seemed to have learned to "live within the confines of an ongoing multi-state world" (288).

William Perry (2000, Part 2, 3), former secretary of defense during the first Clinton administration, made a similar claim about the U.S. attitude on power, when he said: "At least we know how *not* to use our power" in furtherance of imperialism (emphasis added). This may or may not be true in fact. But, even assuming it is true, I wish to note two significant differences: First, the Chinese view on avoidance in the use of brute power is premised on the desirability of the power of suasion and exemplification, which is absent in Perry's view. Secondly, there is a vast difference in people's perceptions of the United States as opposed to China on the point of the use of power. Perry's view, which can count on the support of a reasonable number of Americans in the post-Vietnam era, was endorsed by Israeli Prime Minister Yitzhak Rabin (3), among leaders in the Judeo-Christian world. But very few people in the West would agree with Benjamin Schwartz. On the contrary, it was once a favorite pastime in much of the West to depict post-1949 China as the proverbial fire-spitting dragon, always posing as a threat. No matter how anachronistic, sentiments in the Republican-controlled Congress after 1994, especially in the Senate Foreign Relations Committee, did not seem to have changed much. Outside of Congress, the reported rise of the so-called "Blue Team" and other peddlers of a new McCarthyism (Bill Gertz, to name just one) have added their voice to the China-bashing camp. They not only painted China as preparing for war with the United States but indulged in "character assassination" against any analysts they rated as not sufficiently anti-Beijing (including U.S. Ambassador Joseph Prueher), calling them "panda huggers."[37]

One crucial guide for us to help maintain our balance, let me hasten to add, is that, unlike its sister Communist country, the Soviet Union (under Stalin through Brezhnev), China, even under Mao, was never caught with material evidence of exporting wholesale communist revolution or of building a Communist empire in its own image abroad (after the fashion of Soviet control of Central and Eastern Europe), alarmist

U.S. charges to the contrary notwithstanding.[38] And this is all the more revealing when viewed against the occasional vitriolic Chinese criticisms of the United States in the latter's alleged efforts to "export democracy" (read: to destabilize other regimes) abroad, such as in respect of Sandinista Nicaragua and Castroite Cuba.[39] Peter Van Ness (2000, 270), reacting to the U.S.-perceived "China threat," offers an illuminating comment on why the Chinese have behaved quite differently from U.S. perception. "[T]he Chinese," he explains, "have argued that a peaceful and stable international environment is absolutely indispensable for their efforts to modernize their country. On balance, they have practiced what they preached."

If anything, modern Chinese nationalism and post-Mao communism will most likely coalesce to fuel China's zeal for promoting the acceptability of distributive justice, as well as communitarianism, in the new world order.[40] This will probably be all the more true should it come to pass, as predicted by the Organskiite group, that China, a dissatisfied power, replaces the United States by mid-century as the next dominant power. If that should ever happen, let me add, it will be China, not the United Sates, that is going to worry about, among other things, the world's proliferation of weapons of mass destruction, and how to deal with the so-called "rogue states" (or "states of concern," in more up-to-date language) that will then exist. However, there will be a difference in China's approach. To the extent our speculation about the Chinese commitment to "social justice" is empirically borne out, China will probably be concerned not only with the preservation of "peace and security" in the post–mid-century world but equally with "justice," in such a manner that the expectations of the framers of Article 2(3) of the UN Charter will be fulfilled. A caveat, though, is that everything said thus far will be way off in the unlikely event that China abandons its traditional position on the relationship of social justice to power.

CONCLUSION

We have seen in the above discussions the likelihood of a number of developments bearing on the evolution of a new world order for the twenty-first century. First, the world is likely to see the rise of a set of new systemic values marking off the new century as distinct from previous centuries. For lack of a better term, we have subsumed them under the rubric of "social justice." This norm will serve as the grammar of world affairs and redefine the "game" that nations play in the conduct of their mutual relations. While it holds hope for the future, the new dictate, as we have noted, may also spell perils in relations between the underdeveloped and the industrialized nations and between parts of the affluent non-Western world (e.g., the Asia Pacific group) and the West, barring unforeseen changes.

Second, we have seen that a wide range of strategic concerns will dominate the policy and behavior of nations. Under the general rubric of "comprehensive security," these concerns will comprise economic security, environmental security, and human security, in addition to the traditional military security. We have also argued that in the pursuit of "comprehensive security" goals, countries will have to collaborate and learn to live with collective decision-making and action. A positive development is that the habit of community collaboration, such as in combating environmental deterioration, may erode the erstwhile reflex of unilateral self-help. Creating a global society that will meet the challenge of the twenty-first century will require more than the reform of economic institutions such as the IMF or the WTO, although their reform is also needed in response to the rise of the systemic value of social justice (French 2000, 200). It will also require strengthening international environmental institutions and, no less important, the inauguration of institutions and regimes capable of safeguarding human security and human development. In the end, all these endeavors are interrelated in that they answer the crying need for global governance in amelioration of anarchy (i.e., lack of a world government) in the age of globalization.

And, third, we have reviewed two alternatives to the once prevailing views that saw either the continuance of a U.S.-dominant unipolarity or the emergence of a multipolar system, in which the United States would share leadership with a number of other powers. The first alternative view, as espoused by Hans Binnendijk, extrapolating a common pattern from all previous systems since 1713, foresees that the post–Cold War system, out of its current fluidity and evolving multipolarity, will eventually return to a bipolarity of a different sort. The other alternative view, in fact a forecast based on an imaginative application of A. F. K. Organski's power transition theory to a wealth of empirical data available thus far, foresees that China will overtake the United States, first in economic output during the first quarter of the new century and then in total power by mid-century. Both Binnendijk and the Organiskiite group agree on the rising prominence of a changing China. The crucial difference is that while one sees China sharing the burden of hegemonic leadership with the United States in a new bipolarity the other forecasts that China will even replace the United States as the next "dominant power" by mid-century. The United States, as the reigning superpower, may or may not be able to convert China into a game player fully integrated, and having high stakes, in the world system before mid-century. But, according to the latter view, the United States will not be able to stop China from catching up from behind and overtaking U.S. power.

As a follow-up to this inquiry, we have come upon the possible consequence of this last mentioned outcome. Agreeing with the Organskiite group, we have speculated that barring the probability that China will have been converted into a satisfied power, the new world order under Chinese influence will most likely be totally different. If China assumes the role of the next dominant actor as a dissatisfied power, it is most likely to play the champion of the world's "underdogs." As such, it will support and sustain their crusade for a "right to human development" and entitlement to assistance from the wealthy countries, all under the aegis of the social-justice dictum. Should Binnendijk's bipolar scenario come true, however, whereby China will share the burden of world leadership with the United States, Chinese influence will have to contend with any possible crosscurrents from the U.S. co-superpower. Nevertheless, it will most probably still make a difference in world events.

At the dawn of a new millennium, some analysts, conscious of the limitations of our ecosystem, already bursting at the seams, may look to humankind's next stop, the Moon and other celestial bodies. The National Aeronautics and Space Administration (NASA) announced in 1998 that in eight to ten years, humans will be technologically able to set up colonies, bases, and international space stations on the Moon. The time frame would place it in the first decade of the new century. The question is: Would this extension to the Moon make international relations any different? My gut feeling is that it will blissfully usher in an age of inter-celestial relations, speculations on which we might as well leave to celestial beings somewhere out there who presumably have superior intelligence beyond the reach of us Homo sapiens.

To sum up the above, in retrospect, it is as though the cycle were complete, from our postulated arrival of a systemic value that prizes international distributive justice, to the foreseeable rise of collective action by the community of nations, to the potential ascendancy of China either as the next dominant actor or, alternatively, as a co-hegemon (with the United States)—a development that holds positive potentials for the fulfillment of the systemic value of international social justice. As we have seen, the Chinese disposition to be the spokesman and defender of those disillusioned with the system can be traced to its cultural bent, its own deep-seated disgruntlement with Western inroads and insolence over a century and a half, and its communist commitment to the ideal of doing away with social inequities. But this "cycle" is not contrived. Rather, it has emerged logically from the three subquestions we have raised in our search for an overall answer to the new century's world order. Inherent in this incidental coherent loop is a contour of the new world order that can be derived from the wide array of facts and views we have examined. This contour stands to be borne out or falsified by future events unfolding before us. But until this derived contour is proven wrong by unfolding events, our analyses in this book will be guided accordingly.

NOTES

1. Different analysts have used different terms for the development. For example, Joseph Nye (1999) calls it the "information age," while Henry and Peartree (1998) use the "information revolution." Robert Kurdrle (1999) refers to it as the "communication globalization." But they all describe the changes brought by it in no less than revolutionary terms. Hughes (1997, 432) does lump a lot about future technological developments under the term "communications revolution."

2. Peter Beckman (1984, 325ff), in a fascinating book, classifies the postwar bipolar system as beginning in 1975, before which the world remained a monopolar system, in which the United States was the sole superpower, as measured by a complex combination of criteria. But in this book, we follow the conventional use of the term "Cold War bipolarity" to refer, loosely, to the system that prevailed in the post–World War II era ending in 1990.

3. In Hsiung 1997 (33f), I have defined "systemic values" as of a higher genre than norms in the sense that they define what the strategic "game" is that nations play within an international system, whereas norms define the rules of conduct guiding the behavior of nations in playing out the "game" of their mutual relations.

4. Kaplan (1957, 149f) defines "values" cryptically as "objectives of a system," which to him are "values for the system." But he does not use "systemic values" as I do here.

5. There is no consensus on the definition of "world order." For the range of different meanings assigned to the term, see Hoffman 1968 (esp. chapter. 1) and Kim 1983 (chapter 3).

6. In world order studies, values, norms, and structure are usually considered as decisive components (cf. Kim 1983, 22–27). They also determine transformation from one system to another. But in our discussion here, we subsume norms under "systemic values" and consider norms a natural derivative of the "game" of international relations circumscribed by these systemic values. Furthermore, we also assume that norms are dependent on the concerns of nations. Hence, we pose no separate subquestion for norms per se. The three subquestions raised here cover broadly systemic values, concerns of nations, and structure (or power configuration).

7. Later on, we will see that in the geoeconomic age, the role of ideology will lose its importance enjoyed in a geopolitical game. Systemic values may,

in addition, assume a similar function as ideology before the arrival of the geoeconomic age.

8. Cf. Gross 1969 (25ff).

9. Cf. Kyun-won Kim 1970 on the new order that the French Revolution brought to the international system. Also see Samuel S. Kim 1983 (31).

10. There are, in addition to independence, two alternative outcomes to former colonies of Western powers: absorption into the administrative structure of the metropolis, such as the French colonies of Guyane, Reunion Island, Martinique, Guadeloupe, and Montserrat, and British Guyana (Hintjens 1995), and reversion to their previous motherland, like that of Hong Kong (a former British colony) and Macao (a former Portuguese colony) to China (Hsiung 2000). The over 60 total here does not include such colonies as India, Burma, Singapore, and the Dutch East Indies (Indonesia), among others, that became independent shortly after World War II but before 1960.

11. Domestically, in the 2000 U.S. presidential campaign, for example, both the Republican and Democratic candidates fought for the mantle of being the arch-advocate for the well-being of the lower- and middle-income people, when they offered solutions, respectively, to better utilize the Social Security funds and to build retirement accounts through government intervention and patronage. In Africa, a campaign for "African renaissance" was reportedly afoot in which leaders would no longer tolerate despots or ignore the cries of the weak and oppressed (*New York Times,* June 19, 2000: p. 18). On the international front, the land-locked nations, who traditionally were at the mercy of their neighbors for access to the sea, have, since the 1982 Law of the Sea Convention acquired the guaranteed and unprecedented right of transit to and from the sea through the territories of neighboring states. In the United Nations, the "right to development" (GA Res.41/128) and the "right to adequate food" (E/CN.4/Sub.2/1987/23) of the less developed nations are considered to be their human rights. See discussion in Hsiung 1993a (172–173). The trend is continuing.

12. During the 2000 G-7 meeting in Japan, a group of African presidents poignantly reminded the heads of the most industrialized countries that they should not forget the world's poorest nations when they were deliberating speeding debt relief for Russia. *New York Times,* July 21, 2000, p. 8.

13. In the United Nations Human Rights Commission, for example, many European members have tended to take a more moderate stand than the United States. And at the U.S.-sponsored conference on democracy held in Warsaw, in late June 2000, France refused to sign a declaration sought by the U.S. State Department because the French did not believe that democracy could be "imposed" as well as because of their alleged opposition to Pax Americana, or U.S. hegemony (*New York Times,* June 28, 2000: 11).

14. "Asem" stands for the Asia-European Meeting (1996), in Bangkok, which yielded the first formal agreements to seal cooperation, in various

forms, between Asia and Europe (Hsiung 1997, 206). Since there were two follow-up meetings, in 1998 and 2000, the first meeting is retroactively renamed Asem–1.

15. For example, in Singer and Widlavsky (1993, 24), there is a discussion of "the new world of geo-economic conflict," but "geo-economic" is not defined.

16. Of the two parts in this definition of geoeconomics, the first part (macrolevel) may find echoes in the globalization literature (e.g., Mittelman 1996), which, nonetheless, has nothing to say on the microlevel.

17. See "Japan to Mend China Ties While World Eyes the Gulf," *Japan Times Weekly* (September 24–30, 1990): 1.

18. The wide connotations of ideology range from a "science of ideas" (de Tracy 1826, 3) to "a configuration of ideas and attitudes in which the elements are bound by some form of constraint or function interdependence" (Converse 1964). In the IR field, in contrast to comparative politics, what is most decisive is the nature of the relationship among ideologies of constituent units (states in the system) rather than the character of ideologies themselves.

19. In 1995, a trade war between the United States and Japan was averted almost at the last minute.

20. For a discussion of global warming, for example, as an environmental issue that deserves attention on the international agenda, see Sebenius 1991.

21. For an incomplete listing of these global environmental conventions, see World Resources Institute, *World Resources 1992–1993* (New York: Oxford University Press, 1992), 358–361.

22. The United States and the Soviet Union enjoyed clear military superiority over other European states and all non-European states throughout the Cold War; hence they formed the two poles of both the global and European systems. After the Cold War, the United States can remain a pole in Europe only if it retains the capacity to project significant military power into Central Europe.

23. This part of the discussion is based on, but expanded from, a keynote speech I gave at the Workshop on Twenty-First Century World Order & the Asia Pacific, held at Lingnan University, Hong Kong, April 26–28, 2000.

24. The five previous international systems Binnendijk identified are: (1) The Treaty of Utrecht to Waterloo; (2) Congress of Vienna to the Crimean War; (3) the rise of Germany to World War I; (4) the interwar period (1918–1939); and (5) the Cold War period.

25. A "hegemonic war" is defined by Gilpin (1981, 15) as one that determines which state or states will be dominant and govern the system.

26. Contrary to the balance-of-power theory, the power-transition theory holds that evidence from 1860–1975 shows that preponderance (in the hands of a dominant power), not parity, is the best guarantee of peace. See Organski and Kugler 1980.

27. Full text in Notter 1949, 595–606.
28. Beginning the year after Pearl Harbor, these unequal treaties were abrogated one after another through negotiations, as China was fighting on the side of the Allied powers. China also unilaterally abrogated its unequal Shimonoseki Treaty, signed with Japan in 1895, under which China ceded Taiwan and Korea to Japan.
29. For the background of the post-1947 IES, see Spero and Hart 1997 and Jackson 1997.
30. Statistics compiled by myself, based on a number of sources, e.g., the World Bank, UNDP, and the Overseas Development Council. The percentages show increases over time, for example, 79 percent in the 1970s increased to 86 percent in the 1990s, etc.
31. Quoted in "The Wealth of Nations," in *U.S. News & World Report,* May 4, 1992, p. 54.
32. Address by President Jiang Zemin of China at the Millennium Heads of States Meeting, United Nations, September 6, 2000, in *Renmin ribao* (People's Daily), September 7, 2000, 1.
33. This is a book about international relations and world order in the twenty-first century, and this chapter addresses the question of the emergent world order. Domestic developments are relevant only to the extent that they concern or complement developments on the international plane.
34. For an exposition of the U.S. penchant to resort to forcible interventionism abroad, see Louis Henkin et al., *Right v. Might: International Law and the Use of Force,* 2nd ed. (New York: Council on Foreign Relations Press, 1991).
35. At a meeting in China in 1998 commemorating the five hundredth anniversary of the landing in India by the Portuguese explorer Vasco Da Gama, it was decided that China should plan for the celebration, in 2005, of the six hundredth anniversary of the start of the Chinese explorer Zheng He's seafaring expeditions that began in 1405. See LIU Dacai, "Zheng He's Historic Exploits and Chinese Maritime History," *zhongguo pinglun* (China Review) (Hong Kong), no. 37 (January 2001): 38–41.
36. I am relying on an article by Xu Kuangdi, Mayor of Shanghai, published in New Prospective Quarterly (a journal published by UC-Berkeley), cited in an article in *Qiao Bao* (China Press), a Chinese-language newspaper in New York, January 18 2000, 3. Also, Kenneth Scott Latourette, *The Chinese: Their History and Culture* (New York: Macmillan Co., 1964), 228–229. For details, see *Hai-yang fa-chan-shi lun-chi* ([China's] Maritime Development History), a series published by Academica Sinica (Lukang, Taiwan).
37. See "Red Scare," *Far Eastern Economic Review,* October 12, 2000: 28–29.
38. For pioneering studies of China's record of complying with international law, see Luke Lee 1969 and Hsiung 1972.
39. While the Bay of Pigs is a concrete example of U.S. war efforts directed at Cuba, the suit brought by Nicaragua before the International Court of Justice (ICJ) in 1985, a case in which Nicaragua won, is a best evidence

of U.S. resort to force, including mining the Nicaragua Harbor and arming the anti-Sandinista contras, in attempts to destabilize the leftist government in Nicaragua. See ICJ judgment of June 27, 1986, in the Case Concerning the Military and Paramilitary Activities in and Against Nicaragua (Nicaragua v. United States of America, Merits), *1986 ICJ Report*, 14.

40. At the Sino-Africa Forum held in Beijing, October 10, 2000, Chinese President Jiang Zemin urged the establishment, at the turn of a new millennium, of a "new international political and economic order" that would support the equitable development of the poor nations and bridge the vast gap between them and the wealthy nations; *Qiao Bao* (China Press), October 10, 2000, p. 2.

REFERENCES

Albrecht-Carrie, Rene. 1958. *A Diplomatic History of Europe Since the Congress of Vienna.* New York: Harper & Row.

Axworthy, Lloyd. 1999. NATO's new security vocation. *NATO Review* (Winter): 8–11.

Binnendijk, Hans. 1999. Back to bipolarity? *Strategic Forum* (May). Published by the Institute for National Strategic Studies, National Defense University.

Brown, Lester, et al., eds. 2000. *State of the World.* A Worldwatch Institute Report on Progress toward a Sustainable Society. New York: W.W. Norton.

Bull, Hedley. 1995. *The Anarchical Society: A Study of Order in World Politics.* Reprint, New York: Columbia University Press.

Chen, Po-chih. 2000. Analysis of the state of Japan-China trade relations. *Mainland China Studies* (Taipei) 43, no.2: 79–108.

Chen, Xun-wu. 1997. Justice as a constellation of fairness, harmony, and Righteousness. *Journal of Chinese Philosophy* 24, no.4:497–519.

China Institute. 1956. *China and the United Nations.* New York: Manhattan Press.

Converse, Philip E. 1964. The nature of belief systems in mass publics. In *Ideology and Discontent,* edited by David E. Apter. New York: Free Press.

De Tracy, Destutt. 1826. *Elements d'ideologie.* Bruxelles; cited in Kim 1970, xvi.

Dos Santos, Theotonio. 1970. The structure of dependence. *American Economic Review* 60 (May): 231ff.

Emmanuel, Arghiri. 1972. *Unequal Exchange: A Study of Imperialism of Trade.* New York: Monthly Review Press.

Frank, Andre Gunder. 1970. The development of underdevelopment. In *Imperialism and Underdevelopment: A Reader,* edited by Robert I Rhodes. New York: Monthly Review Press.

French, Hilary. 2000. Coping with ecological globalization. In Brown 2000, 184–202.

George, Alexander, ed. 1991. *Western State Terrorism.* New York: Routledge.

Gilpin, Robert. 1981. *War and Change in World Politics.* New York: Cambridge University Press.

Gray, Colin S. 1977. *The Geopolitics of the Nuclear Era.* New York: Crane, Russak & Co.

Grieco, Joseph M. 1990. *Cooperation Among Nations: Europe, America, and Non-Tariff Barriers to Trade.* Ithaca, NY: Cornell University Press.

Gross, Leo. 1969. The peace of Westphalia, 1648–1948. Reproduced in *International Law in the Twentieth Century,* edited by Leo Gross. New York: Appleton-Century-Crofts. The article, like others in the volume, was first published in the *American Journal of International Law.*

Hart, Jeffrey. 1976. Three approaches to the measurement of power in international relations. *International Organization* 30, no.2 (spring).

Henry, Ryan and C. Edward Peartree, eds. 1998. *The Information Revolution and International Security.* Washington, D.C.: CSIS Press.

Herz, John H. 1962. *International Politics in the Atomic Age.* New York: Columbia University Press.

Hinsley, F. H. 1967. *Power and Pursuit of Peace: History and Practice in the History of Relations Between States.* Cambridge, England: Cambridge University Press.

Hintjens, Helen M. 1995. *Alternatives to Independence.* Brookfield, VT: Dartmouth Publishing Co.

Hoffman, Stanley, ed. 1968. *Conditions of World Order.* Boston: Houghton Mifflin.

Holsti, K. J. 1995. *International Politics: A Framework for Analysis,* 7th ed. Englewood Cliffs, NJ: Prentice-Hall.

Hsiung, James C. 1972. *Law & Policy in China's Foreign Relations: A Study of Attitude and Practice.* New York: Columbia University Press.

———.1991. The post–Cold War world order and the gulf crisis. *Asian Affairs* 18, no.1 (spring): 31–41.

———.1993a. Human rights and international relations: Morality, law, and politics. In *Human Rights of Migrant Workers,* edited by Graziano Battistella. Quezon City, Philippines: Scalabini Migration Center, 170–188.

———, ed. 1993b. *Asia Pacific in the New World Politics.* Boulder, CO: Lynne Rienner.

———.1997. *Anarchy and Order: the Interplay of Politics and Law in International Relations.* Boulder, CO: Lynne Rienner.

———, ed. 2000. *Hong Kong the Super Paradox.* New York: St. Martin's Press. One chapter by Liu Bolong is on Macao.

Hughes, Barry B. 1997. *Continuity and Change in World Politics: Competing Perspective,* 3rd ed. Upper Saddle River, NJ: Prentice-Hall.

Hunter, Robert E. 1992. The United States in a new era. In *U.S. Foreign Policy After the Cold War,* edited by Brad Roberts. Cambridge, MA: MIT Press, 3–18.

Jackson, John H. 1997. *The World Trading System: Law and Policy of International Economic Relations.* Cambridge, MA: MIT Press.

Jervis, Robert. 1991/92. The future of world politics: Will it resemble the past? *International Security* 16, no.3 (winter):39–73.

Kaplan, Morton A. 1957. *System and Process in International Politics.* New York: John Wiley & Sons.

Keohane, Robert and Joseph Nye. 1977. *Power and Interdependence.* Boston: Little, Brown.

Kim, Kyun-won. 1970. *Revolution and the International System.* New York: New York University Press.

Kim, Samuel S. 1983. *The Quest for a Just World Order.* Boulder, CO: Westview Press.

Kim, Samuel S., ed. 2000. *East Asia and Globalization.* Lanham, MD: Rowman & Littlefield.

Kurdrle, Robert T. 1999. Three types of globalization: Communication, market, and direct. In Raimo Vayrynen, ed. 1999, 3–24.

Lauren, Paul Gordon, ed. 1979. *Diplomacy: New Approaches in History, Theory, and Policy.* New York: Free Press.

Layne, Christopher. 1993. The unipolar illusion: Why new great powers will rise. *International Security* 17, no.4 (spring):5–51.

Lee, Luke T. 1969. *China and International Agreements: A Study of Compliance.* Leyden, Netherlands: A. W. Sijthoff.

Linder, Staffan B. 1986. *The Pacific Century: Economic and Political Consequences of Asian-Pacific Dynamism.* Stanford, CA: Stanford University Press.

Liska, George. 1963. Continuity and change in international systems. *World Politics* 16:118–136.

Mazur, Jay. 2000. Labor's new internationalism, *Foreign Affairs.* 79, no. 1 (January-February):79–93.

Mearsheimer, John J. 1990. Back to the future: Instability in Europe after the Cold War. *International Security* 15, no.1: 5–56.

Mittelman, James H., ed. 1996. *Globalization: Critical Reflections.* Boulder, CO: Lynne Rienner.

Morgenthau, Hans J. 1985. *Politics Among Nations,* 6th ed., rev. by Kenneth Thompson. New York: Alfred A. Knopf.

Morrison, Wayne M. 1998. China's economic conditions. In *CRS issue brief.* Washington, D.C.: Congressional Research Service.

Mortimer, Edward and Robert Fine, eds., 1999. *People, Nation, and States: The Meaning of Ethnicity and Nationalism.* London: I.B. Tauris.

Notter, Harley. 1949. *Postwar Foreign Policy Preparation.* Washington, D.C.: U.S. Department of State.

Nye, Joseph S. 1999. Redefining NATO mission in the information age. *NATO Review* (winter):12–15.

Organski, A. F. K. 1986. *World Politics.* New York: Alfred A. Knopf.

———and Jack Kugler. 1980. *The War Ledger.* Chicago: University of Chicago Press.

Peerenboom, Randall. 1990. Confucian justice: Achieving a human society. *International Philosophical Quarterly.* 30, no.1:17–32.

Perry, William J. 2000. Security and stability in the Asia-Pacific region. *PacNet NEWSLETTER,* no. 18 (May 5, 2000), Washington, D.C.: Center for Strategic and International Studies.

Pirages, Dennis. 1978. *Global Ecopolitics: The New Context for International Relations.* North Scituate, MA: Duxbury Press.

Rawls, John. 1971. *A Theory of Justice.* Cambridge, MS: Belknap Press.

Renner, Michael. 1996. *Fighting for Survival: Environmental Decline, Social Conflict, and the New Age of Insecurity.* New York: W. W. Norton.

Ross, Robert S. 1999. The geography of peace: East Asia in the twenty-first century. *International Security.* 23, no.4 (spring):81–118.

Russett, Bruce, Harvey Starr, and David Kinsella. 2000. *World Politics: The Menu for Choice,* 6th ed. Boston: Bedford/St. Martin's Press.

Sabrosky, Alan Ned, ed. 1985. *Polarity and War: The Changing Structure of International Conflict.* Boulder, CO: Westview Press.

Schwartz, Benjamin I. 1968. The Chinese perception of world order, past and present. In *The Chinese World Order,* edited by John K. Fairbank. Cambridge, MA: Harvard University Press.

Sebenius, James K. 1991. Designing negotiations toward a new regime: The case of global warming. In *International Security.* 15, no.4 (spring):110–148.

Segal, Gerald. 1999. Does China matter? *Foreign Affairs.* 78, no.5:24–36.

Singer, Max and Aaron Wildavsky. 1993. *The Real World Order: Zones of Peace And Zones of Turmoil.* Chatham, NJ: Chatham House Publishers.

Smith, Woodruff D. 1986. *The Ideological Origins of Nazi Imperialism.* New York: Oxford University Press.

Spero, Joan E. and Jiffrey A. Hart. 1997. *The Politics of International Economic Relations.* 5th ed. New York: St. Martin's Press.

Spkyman, Nicholas. 1944. *The Geography of the Peace.* New York: Harcourt Brace.

Strausz-Hupe, Robert. 1972. *Geopolitics, the Struggle for Peace and Power.* Reprint, New York: Arno.

Sutter, Robert. 1991. China's view of the new world order: Possible implications for Sino-U.S. relations. Congressional research service report, 91–665F, September 11, 1991. Washington, D.C.

Tammen, Ronald L., et al. 2000. *Power Transitions: Strategies for the 21ˢᵗ Century.* New York: Seven Bridges Press.

Tung, William L. 1970. *China and the Powers: The Impact of and Reaction to Unequal Treaties.* Dobbs Ferry, N.Y.: Oceana Publications.

UNDP 1993. Human development report. The United Nations Development Program, as cited in UNA-USA 1999, p. 102.

UNDP 1998. UNDP today: Introducing the organization. Cited in UNA-USA 1999, p. 106.

UNA-USA 1999. *A Global Agenda: Issues Before the 54ᵗʰ General Assembly of The United Nations.* An annual publication of the United Nations Association of the United States of America. Lanham, MD: Rowman & Littlefield Publishers.

Van Ness, Peter. 2000. Globalization and security in East Asia. In Kim, ed. 2000, 255–276.

Vayrynen, Raimo, ed. 1999. *Globalization and Global Governance.* Lanhm, MD: Rowman & Littlefield.

Wallerstein, Immanuel. 1979. *The Capitalist World Economy.* Cambridge, England: Cambridge University Press.

Waltz, Kenneth N. 1979. *Theory of International Politics.* Reading, MA: Addison-Wesley Publishing Co.

———. 1993. The emerging structure of international politics. In *International Security.* 18, no.2 (fall): 44–79.

Ward, Michael Don, ed. 1992. *The New Geopolitics.* Philadelphia: Gordon & Breach.

Weiss, Thomas et al. 1997. *The United Nations and Changing World Politics*. 2d ed. Boulder, CO: Westview Press.

Wolfensohn, James D. 2000. Coalitions for change. *International Studies Review* (Seoul, Korea). 2, no.2:5–14. The article was originally the President's Address to the annual meeting of the Board of Governors, the World Bank Group and the IMF, September 28, 1999.

Wolfers, Arnold. 1962. *Discord and Collaboration*. Baltimore, MD: Johns Hopkins University Press.

World Bank. 1997. *China 2020. Development Challenges in the New Century*. Washington, D.C.: International Bank of Reconstruction and Development.

CHAPTER 2

GLOBALIZATION AND ITS MEANINGS FOR WORLD ORDER: A DISCOURSE IN CONCEPTUAL RETHINKING

STEVE CHAN

Globalization has recently become a popular buzz word. From classrooms, board rooms, and press rooms to the Lincoln Mall of Washington, D.C., and the streets of Seattle, it has acquired a variety of competing and indeed conflicting connotations and denotations. This cacophony confuses sensible discourse. Whereas reasonable people can hold different opinions, one can hardly make any progress toward empirical understanding or normative debate without some necessary conceptual clarification.

Webster's dictionary defines "globalization" as the act or process "to make worldwide in scope and application." One is therefore reminded, first of all, about the geographic coverage of the globalization phenomenon. If the concept of "globalization" stands for anything, it should indicate an extension in physical scope. Second, Webster's definition calls attention to general conformity to some common standard or norm. Presumably, when people refer to "globalization," they have in mind a convergence in popular expectations and practices, in customary application, if you will. Third, in addition to scope and application, there is the scale factor, by which we mean an intensification of the amount of cross-border interaction. Whether in the case of the movement of money, goods, people, or ideas, what distinguishes the era of "globalization" from its predecessors includes an increase in the sheer volume of transnational transactions. This increase would be less interesting if not for the fact that it also raises the sensitivity and vulnerability of traditional authorities to events and developments outside their formal jurisdiction. One often hears "globalization" spoken as a force or process that diminishes the ability of national governments and local communities to set their own agenda and control their own fate. Fourth, and finally, "globalization" is often used to point to rising issue connectivity. To cite just one example, corporate executives tend to justify foreign trade and investment in the name of promoting human rights abroad, whereas their critics often cite deleterious environmental consequences. Living in a small world apparently implies tighter and more immediate feedback across issue areas.

Accordingly, quite aside from its substantive content, such as economic interdependence, cultural homogenization, and political convergence, globalization as a concept suggests five analytic components as just suggested (i.e., physical extension, normative standardization, scale intensification, rising sensitivity and vulnerability, and issue linkage). As I will argue in the following discussion, the application of these analytic components to observed reality remains quite unclear and even highly contentious on both empirical and normative grounds. Thus, for example, has the information revolution spread to the poorer nations in Africa or, for that matter, the poorer families in America? Have Asians come to share the values of Western-style liberal democracy? Has the volume of interaction in fact risen sharply between Latin America and the Middle East? Have the Western oil-consuming nations become more or less vulnerable to energy shortages brought on by their foreign suppliers? Have foreign investment and trade enhanced mass welfare in post-communist Eastern and Central Europe? The accuracy of globalization as a empirical description and its desirability as a normative statement very much hinge on answers to questions such as these.

To the extent that globalization refers to some sort of cross-border transfer of tangible or intangible items (e.g., business culture, democratic principles, cultural icons), there must be a source and a target for such activity. One is therefore prompted to ask about the identity of the initiator and recipient, and the terms of exchange characterizing their relationship. As the following discussion argues, globalization is after all not an anonymous force or a neutral process that is the work of some invisible hand. Its fundamental purpose and consequence is the redistribution of values, wealth, status, and influence. In this redistribution, some actors (companies, sectors, classes, countries) are in a stronger bargaining position than others. Some are price makers, whereas others are price takers. To be explicit, the process of making "worldwide in scope and application" is a highly uneven one. Moreover, the volume of actual cross-border interaction among actors has risen for only some but not for all dyads. Many groups and regions are bypassed and assigned to "benign neglect" (such as Africa, in the case of genocide and AIDS). Simply put, actors are also differentially prepared to cope with external shocks (such as chronic debt crises and bouts with the high price of imported energy or grain) and to bear the burden of subsequent "adjustments" (such as in the case of the victims of "austerity programs" and economic "shock therapies"). And issue linkage tends to operate asymmetrically (such as the U.S. debate on using trade as a leverage for political change in China).

These comments naturally bring us to the notion of world order, a topic discussed by James Hsiung in the previous chapter. Without being tedious, this concept has three distinct connotations. First, it can refer to normative standards for organizing the global community. As such, one can speak of ordering principles that are widely accepted as reasonable and legitimate. Second, order can also mean stability and the opposite of chaos or anarchy. One can of course have stability without justice, such as when a political order is enforced by authoritarianism or colonialism. Finally, "order" can be a synonym of "command." This meaning points to the differential capacity of actors (be they individuals, corporations, classes, or states) to impose the rules of the game and dictate the terms of exchange. Order in this sense may or may not entail legitimate authority, but it certainly implies hegemonic capacity or market dominance (such as alleged by the U.S. government in its antitrust litigation against Microsoft).

The remainder of this essay elaborates on these themes, albeit with a substantive focus on the question "Can Asia Pacific escape from the impact of globalization?"

WHAT GLOBALIZATION?

There seems to be plenty of evidence pointing to "globalization." From Francis Fukuyama's (1992) philosophic celebration of the demise of totalitarian ideologies and the triumph of liberal ideals to Samuel Huntington's (1991) historical analysis of the "third wave," there is a growing literature that shows the increasing popularity of democratic principles and institutions in the world. The breakdown of trade and investment barriers and the concomitant rise of international capital and multinational corporations provide seemingly indisputable evidence of economic interdependence and globalization. "Sovereignty at bay" (Vernon, 1971) appeals to many public officials and private citizens, as an apt description of the political and economic reality that they have to address, for better or worse. Few who suffered through East Asia's recent financial turmoil will doubt the impact of international capital, both in the form of invest-ment funds and foreign debts, on their country's macroeconomic perfor-mance and their personal or corporate asset values (Jomo, 1999). Likewise, recent foreign interventions in Kosovo, Haiti, and Iraq should convince even the most skeptical observers that international conven-tions and norms regarding aggression, ethnic cleansing, and human rights increasingly challenge the Westphalian tradition that upholds each state's assertion of exclusive domestic jurisdiction. And, of course, we are told that advances in information technology and modern telecommunica-tions have made the world "a smaller place." As inhabitants of this "global village," we increasingly share the same thoughts, values, and habits in what is known as cultural convergence. Yet bothersome reservations re-main. Available statistics provide compelling evidence that the economic distance between the developed and underdeveloped economies and that between the privileged and disadvantaged classes are increasing rather than diminishing. The Matthew principle—the rich get richer, the poor poorer—underscores not only the widening income gap but also mount-ing discrepancies in life chances (such as access to education, health care and, yes, personal computers and the Internet).

From this perspective, globalization seems to be more of a code word for the expanded opportunities of the more affluent segments of national and international society. To those who are less fortunate (such as those poor Indonesians and Mexicans who had to bear the brunt of austerity programs), the same processes look more like a "race to the bottom." Just as economic disparities and differences in life chances are not diminish-ing for the people of the world, one may also question whether the world has reached the "end of history" for contending political ideologies. That various authoritarian regimes have met their demise does not in itself constitute proof that the relevant mass publics or elite circles have as-similated the democratic ethos. Although many countries have adopted formally democratic institutions in recent years, it remains quite prob-lematic whether their political culture has undergone a concomitant change to promote and secure those civic values and political norms (e.g., social trust, civic mindedness, norms of diffused reciprocity, tolerance for dissent) that are critical for consolidating and sustaining democratic pol-itics. Just recall that even in an established democracy like the United States, voters have been known to reject the idea of affirmative action for minorities and equal-rights protection for homosexuals.

Accordingly, democratization as a globalization process, as the term is commonly used, seems to refer more to the wider geographic spread of certain forms of government and less to the deeper cultural transforma-tion of the relevant polities. As such, the political reforms of the recently proclaimed democracies in Eastern Europe and Latin America are fragile and vulnerable to reversal. There are ominous signs of political alienation and cynicism among the established democracies. The United States, for example, has suffered a sharp and persistent decline in the social capital and civic ethos necessary for securing democracy (Putnam 1995).

Naturally, there is also the highly contentious matter of whether ideals such as liberal democracy are truly universal values shared by all people, or whether they are in fact parochial concerns shaped by different historical circumstances and perhaps employed to disguise and advance one's national interests. It does seem, however, that many proponents of liberal democracy as a globalization force tend to be more concerned about the protection of people's negative rights that is, their right to be free from government interference and oppression than about their positive rights, that is, the proposition that people everywhere are entitled to be free from the deprivations caused by hunger, disease, and poverty. A concern for procedural rights is often not matched by a comparable interest in substantive rights in distributive justice, if you will.

Normative agreement or objection aside, the description of democratization as a globalization process seems unwise and unwarranted because it is likely to give short shrift to the crosscurrents pointing to the "clash of civilizations" (Huntington 1993). Islamic fundamentalism, Asian Confucianism, African tribalism, and the revival of ethnic and religious animosity in Eastern Europe belie the suggestion of universal values and political convergence. It is often difficult to tell whether the "globalists" are advancing an ideal or offering a description or prediction, a distinction between "ought" and "is" that is often overlooked.

There is of course a great deal of evidence suggesting certain convergence of pop culture. Children in Western Europe have increasing access to Netscape and CNN, those in Eastern Europe learn English at school, those in China are attracted to Coca-Cola and McDonald's, those in Latin America form fan clubs for Star Trek and Star Wars, and Michael Jackson and Michael Jordan become cultural icons for African kids living in even very remote villages. One tends, however, to confuse rather than clarify matters when one refers to these phenomena as forces of globalization when they in fact represent signs of America's cultural hegemony and its radiation. It is also a bit disingenuous to showcase the Kosovo military campaign, which was conducted by a Western alliance that sought deliberately to bypass the authority of the United Nations, as a cause advancing globalization and "world order." Likewise, one wonders what analytical gains and losses follow when one attributes to international capital or international agencies such as the International Monetary Fund and the World Bank prominent roles as agents representing or promoting globalization, when one country is clearly dominant in its command of the relevant financial, institutional, and ideological assets and in its control of the collective agenda. This one country is the same one whose currency (the greenback) intrudes into nearly all countries to prevail, as if national boundaries do not matter.

The question can be put in another way. What value-added does one gain when one replaces a state-centric view of international relations with a view that assigns particular importance to forces that are supposedly beyond the authority and power of states, forces that are in some sense supposed to bring all the inhabitants of the world closer together, whether figuratively or literally? One engages in "concept stretching" when one combines a variety of heterogeneous phenomena and calls them by the same name (Sartori 1970). One may choose to subsume under the concept of political participation such acts as voting, making campaign contributions, attending rallies, writing to officials, protesting, rioting, plotting a coup d'état, and joining a revolutionary war. But do the gains in connotative coverage justify the loss in denotative precision?

Globalization as a concept implies the operation of powerful, impersonal, even natural, forces that are somehow independent of human agency. It also often implies some inevitable outcome regardless of our personal or collective preferences. As such, this perspective can shape subtly but profoundly the nature of not only academic scholarship but also social commentary and political discourse. Is one really to assume that the forces of globalization have nothing to do with statist agendas? Or is the truth of the matter closer to the other way around, that is, that "globalization" forces are to a substantial degree produced by the actions and policies of states; and the consequent pulling and hauling are the very substance of interstate relations and what statecraft is all about? Would it be more realistic to expect that states in fact try to promote, bend, or forestall the forces of globalization even though, obviously, some states are better at it than others? Is it not a big part of this game, if not the entire point, to shift onto others the burden of adjustment? Moreover, does not the nebulous term "globalization" hide what is really going on, namely, a redistributive process that affects values, power, income, status, and life chances, a process whose consequences are hardly neutral for all concerned. Calling it "globalization" tends to direct attention away from questions about national, corporate, and personal interests and responsibilities.

WHICH ASIA PACIFIC?

Asia Pacific of course encompasses a large geographic area with diverse cultures and economies. If one defines Asia Pacific by qualifications for membership in the Asia Pacific Economic Cooperation forum (APEC), one would include the United States, Canada, Australia, and even Chile and Russia. Most people, however, appear to have a narrower focus in mind when they refer to Asia Pacific. The larger Northeast Asian countries China, Japan, and Korea loom large in their conception.

If by "globalization" one means the increased flow of commerce, tourism, and ideas, these countries have become more involved in such exchanges over time. Indeed, given their faster economic expansion, both the Northeast and Southeast Asian countries have scored higher rates of increase in cross-border transactions, whether they are measured in trade volume, jet travel, or study abroad, in comparison with the slower-moving and even stagnant economies. There is hardly any surprise in discovering that over time most Asia Pacific societies and economies have become more "open" to foreign discourse, although the degree of "openness" naturally varies from country to country (e.g., Burma versus Thailand).

Openness defined in terms of the extent of one's foreign involvement, however, does not quite get at the problem at hand which, as implied earlier, requires judgments about differential capacity to shape and influence the terms of exchange. Some states are favored to be price makers while others are seemingly destined for the role of price takers. Some states are better equipped to resist foreign dependency and penetration, while others appear to be far less prepared for such challenge. Finally, some may find ongoing trends to be rather congenial, given their existing values or comparative advantages, while others are more likely to perceive these trends as discouraging and even threatening for the opposite reasons. An evolving situation may play into the strengths of some while forcing others to bear the burden of adjustment.

All of this goes to say that as a region encompassing tremendous heterogeneity, the Asia Pacific countries are positioned differently to address or adapt to the so-called forces of globalization. Thus, Hong Kong and Singapore, to cite two obvious examples, are better prepared to take advantage of the liberalization of national financial regimes than Burma or Vietnam. Japan is better able to create and control production chains across national boundaries than China. And Australia and New Zealand will find the promotion of liberal democracy and respect for human rights less disconcerting than, say, Indonesia.

To rephrase the preceding remarks, one may say that countries have different comparative advantages, or that they occupy different niches in the world political economy, or that they suffer from different degrees of sensitivity or vulnerability to external shocks. Alternatively, one may wish to argue that some states command greater cultural appeal or political reach so that they are in a better position to use their "soft power" (Nye

1990) to co-opt others. Similarly, some states—because of their larger or more autarchic economy, the homogeneity of their society, the consensus characterizing their elites, the cohesion among their bureaucrats, or, in short, their greater political capacity and social resilience—are better able to resist foreign political penetration and cultural domination than others. Therefore, while most indigenous people fell victim to colonialism by the end of the nineteenth century, a few did not. Although English, French, and Spanish have become the dominant language in large parts of Africa and America, they hardly enjoy the same status in China and Japan as they do, say, in Malaysia, Morocco, and Mexico, respectively.

All things being equal, the larger economies are more self-sufficient. Given its sheer physical size, China has less need for foreign trade than, say, Singapore. China's much larger domestic market makes a policy of import substitution more feasible and less costly. Conversely, for Singapore an export-oriented policy is not a matter of virtue but rather one of necessity. Differences in their tangible endowments expand the menu for choice for some and constrain the policy options available to others (Russett and Starr 1996). Small countries like Singapore are more exposed to external influences and can do less to protect themselves against the unwanted effects of such exposure. They are therefore both more sensitive and vulnerable to the forces of globalization.

Although size is certainly not everything, it makes the price of foreign attempts at assimilation, not to mention conquest, prohibitively costly. It is difficult to imagine in today's world of "trading nations" (Rosecrance 1986) that anyone would want to follow Japan's disastrous example of seeking to seize physical control of China as it did during the first half of the twentieth century. China, Indonesia, and Russia offer three examples of "too big to swallow." Security in their case need not come from an ability to project offensive force; their sheer mass deters any would-be aggressor by raising the prospect of protracted quagmire. From this perspective, these countries are in a better position to resist foreign intervention in the name of professed global norms such as democracy, human rights, and collective defense. No one is going to mistake these countries for Haiti, Kuwait, or Kosovo.

Long history often comes with size. Longevity also has certain advantages. Here again, not all Asia Pacific countries are alike. Some are relatively recent creations of Europeans, whereas others have long traditions, deep cultures, and established identification. Foreign fads and fashions would have an easier time gaining "cultural hegemony" in places where the local institutions are of recent vintage and subject to contestation by different communities. Therefore, one would expect a marked difference in popular adoption of Western ideas and practices between, say, Japan and Malaysia or China and the Philippines. These countries accordingly differ sharply in their susceptibility to external cultural influences.

WHICH EXTERNAL FORCES?

It should not be difficult to undertake empirical analyses seeking to determine the extent to which countries are sensitive to external developments. Indeed, much such research has been carried out to show how a country's arms spending "stimulates" other countries' arms spending. Likewise, other statistical studies demonstrate the degree to which the currency values, interests rates, or stock assets of one country rise or fall in tandem with the price fluctuations in foreign capital markets (Chinn and Dooley 1997; Frankel 1993). There are still other analyses demonstrating "contagion effects," such as when coups d'état or democratic changes in one country "diffuse" to its neighbors. These studies suggest that the appropriate analytic question is not so much *whether* one can escape from globalization influences but rather how much one is subject to such influences, to which kind of influences, and from whom. As alluded to earlier, "globalization" is sometimes a euphemism for the soft power of hegemons or would-be hegemons. The cultural reach of these countries is reflected in the extent to which others adopt or emulate their ethos and institutions. To what extent have others assimilated the outlook, habit, and values of the United States, Japan, and China? In a fundamental sense, competition for national influence revolves around the export of one's model of government, business ethos, technical standards, and cultural practices. Whose ideas and institutions do others follow or adopt? Hegemony in Gramsci's (1971) sense very much requires and implies the power to shape or reshape others according to or in one's image. A hegemon's cultural reach is therefore in part reflected by its ability to recruit others to subscribe to its ideology and to accept its institutions as their own.

Fajnzylber (1990) argued that due to their very different histories and cultures, the United States and Japan presented to their follower-nations two very different models of development. In the United States most firms have had an inward-looking tradition. Until relatively recently, their primary concern has been production to satisfy a large domestic market. Exports tended to be of secondary importance. Moreover, an abundance of natural resources has historically meant that much of the exports were in primary commodities (e.g., grain, cotton). The country's popular ethos professes profound misgivings about "big government" and places a high value on individual freedom, exuberant consumerism, and equality of opportunity (coexisting with an acceptance of pronounced socioeconomic inequality in actual distributive outcome). Public policy as well as mass culture tend to encourage consumption at the expense of savings.

In contrast, the core of Confucian economic philosophy advocates "consume less, save more" and admonishes that the growth of a country's consumption must be kept within the limits of its productivity gain. The interests of Japanese producers have generally been favored at the expense of consumers. There has also been a much higher level of popular support for government intervention in the marketplace. The state is seen as a guardian of public trust and common welfare against particularistic interests. In fact, an ingenious system has seemingly evolved in which "patronage politics" is limited to sectors not involved in international trade, such as agriculture and construction, while technocratic control over policy-making about major industries has been protected (Calder, 1988). Moreover, Japanese firms have always been outward-looking. Foreign exports are the central mission rather than a subsidiary concern of corporate executives. Being poor in natural resources and saddled with a relatively large population, manufactures with high added value are Japan's chief exports.

Concomitantly, cultural norms in Japan emphasize the virtues of group conformity, interpersonal collaboration, collective responsibility, and social integration at the expense of personal liberty. They also encourage frugality, savings, and distributive justice. Thus, Japan features more austere consumption patterns, higher rates of capital formation, and greater equity in income distribution than the United States. Its public and private sectors both espouse fiscal conservatism.

Fajnzylber (1990) claimed that the Latin American and East Asian countries have been incorporated, respectively, into the U.S. and Japanese spheres of formal and informal colonialism. This incorporation has influenced the peripheral countries' domestic patterns of authority, production, consumption, and interest alignment, patterns that have in turn influenced profoundly their subsequent developmental possibilities. In Latin America, the relevant historical legacies and dense interactions with the United States have produced (1) a preference for producing for the domestic market, (2) high consumption proclivities by the urban rich, and (3) a heavy reliance on cash crops and minerals for export revenues. These tendencies have in turn led to an emphasis on import-substitution industrialization, and on foreign debts and budgetary deficits as a way of financing both public and private consumption, especially ostentatious consumption of luxurious imports by a small elite. These tendencies also foster an unequal distribution of income and a collective complacency (due to "easy" revenues from selling natural resources), creating vested interests that make graduation from commodity exports more problematic. Conversely, the newly-industrializing East Asian countries have followed the Japanese model, which inclined them to pursue overseas businesses, practice fiscal conservatism, refrain from "exuberant" consumption, and stress social integration (or "harmony").

Fajnzylber's account shows that what usually passes for globalization forces are hardly impersonal processes that somehow materialize mysteriously. Instead, these forces often have definite national origins and promote specific social, economic, and political arrangements that work to the benefit of some and the disadvantage of others. These forces often become part of "deep" social structures, embedding themselves as entrenched interests and established institutions. They "steer" subsequent courses of events, making certain public policies and developmental paths more likely and attractive and other historical possibilities less so. The question "Can Asia Pacific escape the impact of globalization?" poses the challenge directly. At issue is the menu for choice available to the countries in this region. To what extent is this menu being expanded or constricted? That is, do national leaders have sufficient autonomy to select among alternative strategies or are they severely constrained by "globalization" forces (and the domestic institutions shaped and fostered by these forces) in making this selection?

PATTERNS OF "SOFT" HEGEMONY

An initial probe to study the similarities and differences in the "profiles" of national political economies in the Asian Pacific region offered some evidence congruent with Fajnzylber's observations. Chan and Clark (1992) found distinct patterns of national "followership" of the American and Japanese models of development. They undertook a cluster analysis of the countries in this region, using aggregate data that were intended to capture some key aspects of their respective political economies. The variables used for this analysis included, for example, the rate of domestic savings, the rate of exports, the degree of equity in income distribution, and the level of consumption on "transport and communication."

The last variable was supposed to reflect a country's spending on personal motor vehicles and, as such, it provides a measure of its consumption habit for luxury goods in the context of the developing world. Fajnzylber (1990, 338) reported that although South Korea had become the leading auto exporter among the developing countries, its per capita ownership of motor vehicles was only one-tenth to one-fifteenth of that of Latin American countries of comparable economic size.

The cluster analysis by Chan and Clark (1992, 42) shows that if the major Asia Pacific countries (except China) were forced into two clusters, one of them would consist of Japan, South Korea, Taiwan, and Hong Kong and the remaining countries would belong to the other group. If three clusters were allowed, Indonesia would separate to become a class by itself. If the countries were allowed to break into four groups, the United States and the Philippines would become yet another separate category, and so on and so forth. As the number of clusters increases, finer and finer distinctions among the countries are being drawn. When there are only two clusters, the most general typologies are being offered. And at that most general level, the pattern revealed by the cluster analysis seems to make intuitive sense in terms of putative "memberships" in the U.S. and Japanese cultural "camps."

The specific placement of individual countries also seems to make some intuitive sense. As one might have guessed, the Philippines, a former U.S. and Spanish colony, has followed the American model most closely. As already noted, it and the United States formed a distinct cluster when countries were allowed to form four groups. With its traditional hacienda culture, agricultural exports (sugar and coconut), Catholicism, extended patronage system, and skewed socioeconomic distribution, the Philippines is also the most Latin American of the Asian countries (Hawes 1987). Imitation of the "American way of life," from pop art to political campaigns, has gone the farthest in the Philippines in comparison to its regional neighbors. Although, in various ways, the political economies of Thailand and Singapore also exhibit features of the American model, the extent of this replication is much more limited in these countries than in the Philippines.

Also congruent with one's expectations, Taiwan and South Korea, two former Japanese colonies, follow most closely the Japanese model of development in terms of their patterns of economic production, consumption, and distribution. Hong Kong also belongs to this group, sharing with the other two a profile consisting of a large manufacturing sector, a heavy reliance on the export of consumer products, a high savings rate, a low tendency for luxurious purchases (especially for privately-owned vehicles), and a comparatively egalitarian system of income distribution.

Below the most general dichotomous categories, the other APEC countries, such as Indonesia, Singapore, Malaysia, Australia, and Thailand, "belonged" to neither the U.S. nor the Japanese cultural sphere. That is, their national profiles are more difficult to typecast, as they do not consistently feature those attributes exemplified by either the U.S. or the Japanese political economies, according to Fajnzylber. Indonesia presents an especially interesting and, among the countries studied, distinct case. As a relatively low-income oil-exporting country with a heavy emphasis on import substitution, the military-dominated government (until recently) in Djakarta presented a model of political economy that is substantially different from the other countries in Asia Pacific.

Interestingly, adoption of another country's model of political economy does not necessarily imply popular adoration of this country (Reich et al. 1997). The most notable example pertains to South Korea. Although public opinion in this country tends to present a rather negative image of Japan (Hastings and Hastings, 1996), its political and economic institutions have been deeply influenced by the legacy of Japanese colonialism (Cumings 1984). Moreover, South Korea's elite ethos as well as popular culture continue to be influenced by Japan. Among the Asia Pacific countries, South Korea is most similar to Japan in its macropolitical economy. Thus, in this instance, popular sentiments do not necessarily reflect accurately Japan's soft power: Sentimental affinity and institutional affinity do not correspond in this case. Yet, hegemons need not be loved; the durability of their influence depends instead on the extent to which their ideologies and institutions become deeply embedded in the "follower" nations. This co-optation can take place in the absence of the latter's conscious awareness and, in the South Korea case just mentioned, apparently in the face of actual overt public (and possibly, elite) hostility directed against the hegemon.

That sentimental and institutional affinities need not correspond seems also to apply to some other cases. The mass public in Indonesia, Malaysia, and Thailand tend to hold generally favorable impressions of the United States (Hastings and Hastings 1996). These favorable sentiments, however, appear not to have produced behavioral patterns that mimic the American model. An interesting question then is whether popular sentiments are a leading or lagging indicator of aggregate behavior or institutional adoption, or does their relationship imply reciprocal causality.

What about China? Due to a lack of comparable data, this country was not included in the cluster analysis undertaken by Chan and Clark (1992). However, future analysis can easily seek to incorporate it. Chinese culture, of course, has many similarities with Japanese culture. Yet, there are some differences as well. For example, China features "patriarchal Confucianism," which is distinct from the "feudal Confucianism" practiced in Japan and Korea. Although the latter two countries share many of the central values of Chinese Confucianism, such as strong group loyalties, respect for authority, concern with achievement, and a high premium placed on education, feudalism forced the Japanese and Koreans to work and fight together in large groups that extended beyond kinship lines.

This cultural legacy, for example, promotes cooperation in the large corporate structures that distinguish the Japanese and Korean economies from the Chinese ones, where small firms are much more prominent. Indeed, one of the most salient features of Hong Kong's and Taiwan's economies is their decentralized structure in contrast to the dominance of giant corporate conglomerates in Japan and especially South Korea. The vitality and opportunism of small and even medium-size enterprises in Hong Kong and Taiwan, almost all family owned and operated, have led to their being characterized as "guerrilla capitalists" (Lam and Lee, 1992). Thus, the number and centrality of such small-scale businesses engaging in "flexible manufacturing" can be used as one measure of the Chinese model of development. The network of overseas Chinese involved in such entrepreneurial activities, as in Southeast Asia, offers another example of the forces of globalization.

Another feature that is distinctive of the capitalist variants of the Chinese model is the rather aloof and even uneasy relationship between the government and businesses. The latter have been more skeptical and guarded against a predatory state and, unlike Japan and South Korea, close coordination between the public and private sectors is less prevalent. Accordingly, various measures of a state's "embeddedness" in society (Evans 1995) should show a lower level for societies with larger Chinese influence.

Future research could incorporate these variables as well as others, such as the extent of budgetary deficits, the amount of education expenditures, the longevity of ruling coalitions, and public attitudes toward antitrust regulations and political dissidence, to assess the relative influence of U.S., Japanese, and Chinese soft power. As demonstrated some time ago by Bruce Russett (1967), this general approach to political ecology can yield meaningful and revealing maps of international regions and their memberships, which are defined as much by physical location and distance as by cultural, ideological, and institutional affinities.

CONCLUSION

I have questioned the analytic utility of the concept of globalization. To what extent does this concept promise to illuminate rather than to obfuscate? Are we stretching this concept to include so many different phenomena that it loses empirical precision? By using this term, are we implicitly treating the relevant trends and processes as if they represent impersonal forces that somehow unfold naturally in the absence of human agency and partisan agendas? The term suggests that we are somehow all subject to some universal homogenization. It detracts attention from the question of which actors initiate, promote, and benefit from such forces, and which actors are on the receiving end of these forces and must bear most of the burden of adjusting to them. In short, what analytic value-added does the concept of globalization offer us compared to a traditional understanding of statecraft?

It is of course a truism that states are becoming more sensitive to each other's policies. This is so simply because they engage in more external activities than before. It is quite a different matter, however, to determine whether they have become more vulnerable to each other's policies. Vulnerability, defined as the net effects of other's actions on a state after the state has undertaken measures to minimize the impact of these actions (Keohane and Nye 1977), differs sharply across states. Some states command tremendous resources to protect themselves against the unwanted consequences of others' actions while others possess little means to resist foreign encroachment.

This encroachment is most effective when it is successful in co-opting the target's people and institutions. Put more positively from the point of view of the would-be hegemons, it exemplifies these states' soft power, cultural appeal, or political reach. Such influence far exceeds in its importance other more tangible or quantifiable indicators such as currency-exchange rates, trade balance, investment flows, and even military interventions. The influence of soft power comes from its control over ideas and institutions. From the perspective of the developing states, it embodies the legacies of past encounters with foreign interests. That foreign ideas and institutions continue to exercise a profound and pervasive influence even after direct, overt foreign control has been discontinued constitutes, after all, the main theoretical insight and policy implication of those whose writings stress neocolonialism. Foreign-inspired interests, ideologies, and institutions are the basis for hegemonic control. And, as alluded to earlier in my cluster analytic illustration, these inherited interests, ideologies, and institutions continue to determine a country's developmental path. Once launched on such a path, certain alternatives become more difficult and perhaps impossible to undertake or even imagine. It is in this sense that the power to co-opt (rather than to coerce) can be so influential, as it helps to set the "follower" nations' developmental trajectory, define their policy agenda, and shape their feasible options. Globalization and national attempts to control its effects (if not to escape from its forces entirely) document what is, after all, the "stuff" of international relations.

REFERENCES

Calder, Kent E. 1988. *Crisis and Compensation: Public Policy and Political Stability in Japan, 1949–1986.* Princeton, NJ: Princeton University Press.

Chan, Steve and Cal Clark. 1992. The rise of the East Asian NICs: Confucian capitalism, status mobility, and developmental legacy. In *The Evolving Pacific Basin in the Global Political Economy: Domestic and International Linkages,* edited by Cal Clark and Steve Chan. Boulder, CO: Lynne Rienner.

Chinn, Menzie D. and Michael Dooley. 1997. Asia Pacific capital markets: Integration and implications for economic activity. In *Regionalism Versus Multilateral Trade Arrangements,* edited by Takatoshi Ito and Anne O. Krueger. Chicago: University of Chicago Press.

Cumings, Bruce. 1984. The origins and development of the Northeast Asian political economy: Industrial sectors, product cycle, and political consequences." *International Organization* 38: 1–40.

Evans, Peter B. 1995. *Embedded Autonomy: States and Industrial Transformation.* Princeton, NJ: Princeton University Press.

Fajnzylber. Fernando. 1990. The United States and Japan as models of industrialization. In *Manufacturing Miracles: Paths of Industrialization in East Asia,* edited by Gary Gereffi and Donald Wyman. Princeton, NJ: Princeton University Press.

Frankel, Jeffrey A. 1993. Is Japan creating a yen bloc in East Asia and the Pacific? In *Regionalism and Rivalry: Japan and the United States in Pacific Asia,* edited by Jeffrey A. Frankel and Miles Kahler. Chicago: University of Chicago Press.

Fukuyama, Francis. 1992. *The End of History and the Last Man.* New York: Free Press.

Gramsci, Antonio. 1971. *Selections from the Prison Notebooks of Antonio Gramsci.* New York: International Publishers. These selected writings by the former leader of the Italian Communist Party were translated by Quentin Hoare and Geoffrey Norwell Smith.

Hastings, E. H. and P. K. Hastings, eds. 1996. *Index to International Public Opinion, 1994–1995.* Westport, CT: Greenwood.

Hawes, Gary. 1987. *The Philippine State and the Marcos Regime: The Politics of Export.* Ithaca, NY: Cornell University Press.

Huntington, Samuel P. 1993. The clash of civilizations? *Foreign Affairs,* 72: 22–49.

———. 1991. *The Third Wave: Democratization in the Late Twentieth Century.* Norman, OK: University of Oklahoma Press.

Jomo, K. S., ed. 1999. *Tigers in Trouble: Financial Governance, Liberalism and Crises in East Asia.* New York: St. Martin's Press.

Keohane, Robert O. and Joseph S. Nye, Jr. 1977. *Power and Interdependence: World Politics in Transition.* Boston: Little, Brown.

Lam, K. K. Danny, and Ian Lee. 1992. Guerrilla capitalism and the limits of statist theory. In Cal Clark and Steve Chan, eds. 1992.

Nye, Joseph S. Jr. 1990. *Bound to Lead: The Changing Nature of American Power.* New York: Basic Books.

Putnam, Robert D. 1995. Bowling alone: America's declining social capital. *Journal of Democracy.* 6 (1995): 65–78.

Reich, Simon, Steve Chan, and Davis B. Bobrow. 1997. Exploring cultural power and hegemony in the Asia-Pacific. Paper presented at the annual meeting of the International Studies Association, Toronto.

Rosecrance, Richard. 1986. *The Rise of the Trading State: Commerce and Conquest in the Modern World.* New York: Basic Books.

Russett, Bruce M. 1967. *International Regions and the International System: A Study of Political Ecology*. Chicago: Rand McNally.

———and Harvey Starr. 1996. *World Politics: Menu for Choice*. 5th ed. New York: W. H. Freeman.

Sartori, Giovanni. 1970. Concept misformation in comparative politics. *American Political Science Review*. 64: 1033–53.

Vernon, Raymond. 1971. *Sovereignty at Bay: The Multinational Spread of U.S. Enterprises*. New York: Basic Books.

PART II

THE REGIONAL PERSPECTIVE

CHAPTER 3

THE ASIA PACIFIC REGION: CHALLENGES IN THE NEW ERA

JAMES C. HSIUNG

IDENTITY AND RISE OF THE REGION

"Asia Pacific" is a term that has gained increasing acceptance only since the mid-twentieth century. When the Portuguese first came to the area in the fifteenth century, Asia was only a geographical term. Other Europeans came during the late eighteenth through nineteenth centuries, in a scramble to establish colonies of their own in various parts of Asia, from the Middle East through the Indian subcontinent, to today's Southeast Asia (Borthwick 1992, 77–118). U.S. interest in the Pacific began after 1898, when the Philippines was ceded to it after the Spanish-American War. The Pacific came to journalistic prominence only after Pearl Harbor in 1941.

Until the end of World War II, the vast Asian Pacific region only had three independent states, including two major powers, China and Japan, plus a legendary Thailand, ever nimble at the game of keeping off powerful predators coming to its door. The rest were European colonies except for Taiwan and the Korean peninsula, which were under Japanese colonial rule. During the war, the Japanese had briefly occupied the European colonies, from Indochina to Malaya to the Dutch East Indies, displacing their former colonial rulers when the latter were preoccupied with their own war effort back home. Following Japan's defeat in the war, the returning Western colonial masters were confronted with a totally different political ecology, a new militant nationalism that had only been heightened by the brutal interlude of Japanese occupation—a force destined to shape developments in the ensuing years.

By wartime Allied agreement, defeated Japan relinquished its control of both Korea and Taiwan. While the latter was returned to motherland China, the Korean peninsula drifted toward a division into two separate entities across the 38th parallel, the line separating Soviet and American occupation forces in the north and south, respectively. This development set an example for some of the Western colonies, who sought and obtained emancipation from colonial rule, setting in motion a process that was to culminate in the eventual independence of all the region's colonies in the following decades. At the initiative of the United States, the Philippines was also freed, and it gained statehood in 1946 (Lach and Wehrle 1975, 1–9; Hsiung 1993, 214).

The United States came to Asia Pacific not only as the proconsul in occupied Japan (1945–1952) but also as the big brother in the entire region, replacing the Europeans (and the Japanese) in influence. U.S. contacts expanded as its security involvement spread and business in the region flourished. The wars in Korea and Vietnam, moreover, brought thousands of U.S. citizens as well as troops across the Pacific Ocean to East Asia (Borthwick 1992, 212–240). Parenthetically, by comparison, Germany's defeat did not result in as heavy a U.S. turnout in Europe; the U.S. military presence there was no comparison to its presence in Asia Pacific (Muller and Schweigler 1992).

The region's claim to U.S. and global attention was tied to two developments over time. In the first place, while the twentieth century was defined by three global wars (the two world wars and the Cold War), the United States in the last half-century fought three hot wars across the Pacific, including the Pacific War (1941–1945) with Japan, and the Korean and Vietnam wars. A rarely appreciated consequence, however, was that these landmark events in the Pacific helped shape or reshape events elsewhere, even dictating U.S. strategic thinking in their wake. One example is the impact of the Korean War on global politics. As one writer (Jervis 1980) put it, without the Korean War, many of the characteristics associated with the Cold War—for example, high defense budgets, a militarized NATO, intense Sino-U.S. hostility followed by Washington's post–1972 China-card playing, and U.S. security commitments throughout the world—probably would not have developed the way they did. From the Vietnam war, furthermore, the United States learned the lesson never again to engage in prolonged land warfare in far-off places (Bennet and Stam 1998).

Secondly, the other basis of the region's claim to worldwide attention, until the Asian financial crisis of 1997–1999, was the consistent, rapid annual growth rates of the region's economies, hovering in the 6–9 percent range over nearly three decades. At the rate of 7 percent annual growth, double that of the older industrial countries, an economy doubles in a decade (cf. Linder 1986, 14). This phenomenal growth record, spreading from the original eight high-performance economies[1] to other parts of the region, prompted a wide range of respectable analysts (Linder 1986; McCord 1991; Borthwick 1992; World Bank 1993) to pronounce the coming century to be the "Pacific Century."

But after the Asian financial crisis broke out in July 1997, sending the region's economies in nose dives, no more such optimism was heard again. In a matter of weeks, once-vibrant economies and their strong currencies witnessed a meltdown. The severity can be appreciated only in comparative perspective. During the Great Depression of 1929–1932, the asset value of Standard & Poor's 500 fell by 87 percent. During the Asian financial crisis, the asset value crash ranged from 75 to 85 percent in South Korea, Indonesia, Malaysia, and Thailand.[2]

Some of the Asian nations had to turn to the lender of last resort, the International Monetary Fund (IMF), for assistance. Almost immediately, a swarm of sarcastic laments and gloating denunciations greeted the temporary misfortune besetting the Asian tigers. The former optimists and "apologists" for the Asian miracle were shut up. Instead, all that could be heard was the "I told you so" refrain from Western commentators who apparently had bottled-up contempt for the Asian tigers all along. Among the Western media and community of economists, there was a chorus of voices of despair, even ridicule, but not a single word of sympathy, let alone a cool-headed plea for suspending final judgment until more was known about what happened. Christopher Patten (1999), the last British Governor of Hong Kong before its return to China in 1997, could hardly wait to rub it in with a petulant, in a way self-serving, book celebrating "that all the tigers are skinned and stuffed."

Instead of consolation, there were ready-made condolences. Condemnation superseded commiseration and compassion, contrary to the tenets of basic human decency on such occasions of other people's sorrows. Like firemen, the IMF was called in to help. But, unlike firemen, IMF was in no hurry to fight the fire on the scene; instead, it took time to point accusing fingers at the architecture of the house and the furniture arrangement.[3]

Despite IMF's initial gloomy forecasts that it would take years, if not decades, before the region could fully recover and stand on its feet again, reports by early 1999 showed encouraging signs of recovery even among the five worst-hit economies, Thailand, Indonesia, Korea, Malaysia, and the Philippines, although the first two were trailing behind the rest.[4] China enjoyed a sturdy 7–8 percent GDP growth in 1998–1999. Hong Kong, after a hard struggle up from its steep decline, pulled back to a 3.1 percent growth but registered a whopping 14.3 percent during the first quarter of 2000, although it was not back to where it had been before the crisis.[5] Singapore was holding out relatively well during the crisis. Its economic growth, at a respectable 5.5 percent in 1999, was expected to increase to 6.7 percent in 2000. According to an independent outside survey, Singapore was rated to have the best investment environment in Asia, and given a no. 5 ranking on a worldwide list for the years 2000–2004, moving up from its own previous no. 6 ranking for 1995–1999.[6] The World Bank's report *East Asia: Recovery and Beyond,* prepared and completed in 1999, was sold out in no time when it came out in early 2000. By the time of this writing, the only country of uncertainty is Japan, with its banking system remaining in disarray. But, Japan is another story; its banking system problem was largely independent of the region's financial contagion, as we will see below.

In early May 2000, the investment bank Salomon Smith Barney raised its full-year forecast for Asia's regional growth in 2000 to 6.9 percent, from 6.7 percent. But scarcely three weeks later, Salomon raised it again, to 7.1 percent (*New York Times,* 27 May 2000, p. 1). China even achieved an 8.2 percent GDP growth in the first half of 2000.[7] What is confounding to skeptics is that the impressive recovery hardly, if at all, came about as a result of the drastic domestic structural reforms that the critics (including the IMF) said had to be undertaken, or at the cost of draconian austerity programs, although an unusually strong U.S. economy was a contributing factor. This raises a serious question as to whether the real causes of the crisis were internal (i.e., domestic structural failings), as initially alleged in many external premature assessments.

While economic or financial analysis per se is not a charge for this chapter (it is a main concern for chapter 11, by Lok Sang Ho), what concerns us here is the lessons we can draw from the crisis, including what the region's countries have done in reaction. For, as we will see, they help to highlight how well the region can sustain the impact of globalization and, equally, they will throw light on the ticklish question of the future of "Asian values" and the Asian model of development. I say "ticklish" because the *Economist* (July 25, 1998), echoing many other acerbic Western skeptics, already gleefully carried an obituary for the death of "Asian values." Answers to these questions eventually hold the key to whether the tigers were indeed "skinned and stuffed," as Christopher Patten had wished, and even to whether there after all is going to be a Pacific Century, despite the detour. To these questions we shall now turn.

LESSONS FROM THE FINANCIAL CRISIS

To fix the blame for the crisis is not our intent. Our ultimate concern is to see what should make us wiser on the question of development in the global age. The inherent lessons, we hope, will offer some relevance to other regions as well.

Methodologically, in order to determine what is a real "cure" good for the time ahead, we need to examine the issue of causality, or what the true decisive causes of the crisis were. Only after that will we know whether the remedial responses of the region's economies are adequate for their own protection in the long run. The answer is essential to our ability to foresee what lies ahead for Asia Pacific. In getting to that final answer, however, we have to cut through the mountain of complex details surrounding what had transpired.[8]

In my introductory chapter above, I reasoned *inductively* in endeavoring to arrive at a "contour" of the ultimate world order that is likely to emerge in the new century. I proceeded from the specific to the general, beginning with parcels of facts drawn to the three subquestions raised. From the emerging separate answers, we were able to derive a set of generalizations that together ultimately round out an overall picture. Here, however, I would take the opposite tack, to spare my readers the multitude of detailed, often tedious facts surrounding what happened, when, and where. Instead, I will focus on the "whys," to the extent that I can derive them from a prior scrutiny of the crucial data on my part. (This previously done research is not chronicled here.) This discussion will touch on only those data that are absolutely necessary for demonstrating how I arrived at the conclusions I did. Then, I will move on to the responses by the region's nations, in order to see what the future may hold for the Asia Pacific under the crush of globalization. I hasten to add, nonetheless, that one commonality shared by these two approaches, one inductive and the other deductive, is that in both I am guided by the rule of parsimony. The final aim is the reporting of the findings, although I am conscious of my obligation to reveal how my inquiry has led me to the findings.[9] I have no intention of getting myself into the Guinness Book of Records for having given the longest, most convoluted, blow-by-blow review of the Asian financial crisis in its entirety.

ORIGINS OF THE FINANCIAL CRISIS

To put the Asian financial crisis in proper perspective, let us bear in mind that it came amidst a series of financial crises in the world, beginning with the exchange rate shocks that rocked Western Europe in 1992 and 1993. This was followed by the banking and currency crises in Mexico in 1994–1995. The Asian crisis of 1997–1998 was the next to come, sending repercussions to Russia and Latin America promptly in August 1998. By the early fall of 1998, stock markets around the world had tumbled to levels not seen in a full year. In particular, emerging markets suffered the most, in the face of sudden flights of speculative capital, while investors were writing off billions of dollars in losses (Kapstein 1998; Kahler 1998).

The ultimate backdrop for this series of financial crises is, however ironically, what is often described as the "triumph of global capitalism," dating from the collapse of Soviet power and the end of the Cold War, when, as I showed in chapter 1, a new age of geoeconomics was ushered in. With globalized capitalism unfolding, trade and capital flows were increasing at a faster rate than world product. Because of the dizzying pace at which financial markets were being globalized, the volume of private capital flows to developing countries rose more than 500 percent—from U.S.$42 billion in 1990 to U.S.$256 billion in 1997. While world trade grew by 5 percent annually, private capital flow expanded by nearly 30 percent a year (World Bank 1998, 4). Propelling this expansion was an aggressive search for ever higher returns to capital. As stock markets were blooming, countries around the world were liberalizing, privatizing, and deregulating at the urging of international financial institutions, both public and private (Kapstein 1998, 355).

Liberalization meant opening up a country's domestic stock and assets markets, in turn creating a vulnerability to both hot money flows (known as the "casino syndrome") and manipulations by professional international speculators (e.g., behemoth hedge funds). It follows that with varying degrees of liberalization, nations incurred varying degrees of vulnerability to both these hazards (de Brito 1999). This truism was borne out during the Asian crisis, as the most indebted nations (i.e., those most heavily affected by the casino effect), like Thailand and Korea, were the worst hit. The Asian region's heavy debt burden, paradoxically, was a testimony to its economic success in attracting the wide attention of international institutions that had money to lend or that were otherwise looking for opportunities to invest (Makin 1999).

Against this background, it is self-apparent that no one single factor, such as the most favored "crony capitalism" thesis,[10] can adequately explain the genesis of the Asian crisis across the board. Crony capitalism (such as poor corporate governance, lack of transparency in the financial section, or outright corruption), an internal flaw by definition, was found in certain countries, like Thailand, the Philippines, and Korea, but not uniformly in others, and certainly not in Hong Kong (Huang 1998; Sung 1997). Yet, no economy was spared by the financial contagion of 1997–1998.

Instead, a combination of at least three factors provides a more convincing explanation for the crisis plaguing the region as a whole. They are: (1) heavy foreign debt burden, (2) attacks by international speculators,[11] and (3) loss of control by governments, due to either laxity of laws and discipline or premature liberalization without due safeguard. Hence, Thailand, with a short-term, private-sector, foreign debt burden equivalent to 50 percent of its GDP, was the first domino to fall (Lemco and MacDonald 1999, 434). Devaluation of the Thai baht sent rippling effects throughout the region, affecting all its members, especially Korea, which was similarly ridden with huge short-term foreign debts. The rest was a story of chain reactions, likewise typical of a globalized economy.

One thing led to another. The Thai devaluation prompted a competitive round of devaluations of other currencies (spreading from Indonesia to Korea, Malaysia, and the Philippines).[12] Hiking of interest rates by banks (to shore up the local currency and to prevent bank runs) only created hardships for the local economy, leading to reduced exports and drying up of the country's foreign exchange reserves (except in China). Symptomatic of complex interdependence, economic slump in one country spilled over to other countries in the entire region, adding to their own economic woes. According to Jeffrey Winters (1998, 422), a combination of three elements produced the explosive volatility and chain reaction that rocked Asia, namely: (1) the so-called "funnel effect," arising from the fact that a small number (in fact, just about 100 or so) of international fund managers made microlevel decisions about which countries and companies in emerging markets would receive the investments that they were entrusted, by hundreds of millions of independent investors and institutional investors, to make; (2) the intense pressures the fund managers had to labor under; and (3) the generally poor quality of the information feeding into the microlevel decision-making calculus of the fund managers. While this complex point may be too technical for the average reader, the important thing is that all three elements are external, not internal, to each country hit by the crisis. Again, they confirm that the alleged domestic structural flaws of the Asian economies were not the decisive causes of the crisis, as many critics had initially alleged. Rather, external factors (i.e., tied to globalized capitalism) were decisive and controlling.

Other than "crony capitalism," which in itself, as we have noted, has limited explanatory power across the region, two other faults usually attributed to the internal structure of the Asian economies were: overborrowing and a corrupt banking system. I would argue that both these, in their own ways, are likewise tied to external sources. First, overborrowing from foreign capital sources, usually in the form of loans denominated in the U.S. dollar, creating a crushing debt burden (as in the cases of Thailand and Korea), was in the final analysis due to the casino effect that came with globalization. The only way a government could be faulted in the circumstances is that its control over borrowing by public and private end users was inadequate, hence, a monetary policy mismanagement. If this was the case, then the logical solution would be strengthening the control over borrowing. Second, while poorly-regulated financial sectors may be a true flaw in some countries, domestic banking reform alone may not solve the whole problem. Take the Japanese banking system for example. Much venom has been spilled over its faults. One commonly mentioned sin of the Japanese banking system is its nonperforming loans, estimated to be $660 billion (Lorne Johnson 1998, 124). Yet as Alvin So notes (in chapter 4), the influx of foreign loans that came inundating the Japanese economy, once liberalization in the 1980s had opened the floodgates,[13] created economic woes unknown before. The consequential dependence of Japanese companies on foreign capital, which reduced their dependence on domestic banks, in turn weakened the latter's monitoring function on corporate finance. If this is true, then the source of the alleged laxity of the Japanese banking system is not simply an internal problem. And, in that sense, the solution may not be entirely within Japan's grasp. The logical solution, if only partial, should therefore begin with strengthening control over corporate borrowing from the global financial markets as well.

In addition, I might add, the Japanese banks' trouble could also be traced back to Tokyo's deregulation in the 1980s, under pressures from the G-7 and following the 1985 Plaza Accord. Despite its supposed virtues, deregulation not only just opened the Japanese capital market to global capital inflows. It also greatly enhanced equity financing by the so-called "non-banks" (e.g., major manufacturing firms) for Japan's medium and small enterprises, which could not turn to foreign capital markets. And in the process, this change robbed the banks of their core loan market, shrinking it to a third of its previous level by the end of the 1980s. As Owuala (1999, 667) points out, the ensuing competition forced the banks to "engage in speculative lending in property and stocks for survival." The collapse of both property and stock prices at the beginning of the 1990s, he adds, "left on the trail a huge volume of nonperforming assets in many banks." If indeed this was the case, then Japan would need to moderate its unguarded banking deregulation (!) as well as to tighten control over borrowing from the international financial market. Both would go against the counsels usually heard in comments from Western economists about Japan's "nepotic" banking system!

RESPONSES BY THE REGION'S ECONOMIES

In these instances, the logical deduction from the problems encountered invariably pointed to the key word "control." Indeed, resort to capital control is exactly what the region's economies did in reacting to the crisis. Malaysia, which had been among the most open economies on the capital account, went furthest in re-introducing capital controls. Beginning in August 1998, the exchange controls removed the Malaysia ringgit from international currency trading. The new system, modeled after China's, makes the ringgit convertible on the current account, as before, but not on the capital account. It thus prevents the buying of foreign exchange for speculative purposes. Holders of offshore ringgit accounts had in one month's time, September 1 to October 1, to repatriate their ringgits, after which repatriation would be illegal. Thus, contrary to fears of capital flight, imposition of exchange controls yielded a short-term, debt-free capital inflow (Wade 1998, 367; World Bank 2000, 32f)).

In Hong Kong, the government intervened to fend off imminent attacks on both the Heng Seng Index futures of the local stock market and the foreign-exchange market. The immediate purpose was to ease the pressure on the Hong Kong dollar, which is pegged to the U.S. dollar. On a single day, 14 August 1998, the SAR government bought about 6 percent of the stock market, infusing enormous amounts of cash and acquiring a government stake in the private sector (including shares of 13 leading companies). Despite criticisms that the act contravened Hong Kong's laissez faire tradition, the intervention pushed up the Heng Seng Index by 564 points, a rise of 8.5 percent. The rally had immediate global impact, for instance, on the London and New York stock exchanges (Kueh 2000, 249).

In Taiwan, the policy response was to insulate the New Taiwan (NT) dollar, by barring foreign short-term investors while encouraging local investors. In a measure allowing the authorities to control demand for the currency, central bank approval was required for inflows of funds destined for the stock market. The offshore market in NT dollars was also closed. In addition, the government established four stabilization funds, one of them alone totaling U.S.$16.3 billion, designed to stave off any turbulence, beyond a certain level, in the stock market driven by external attacks by foreign speculators (*New York Times,* 4 March 2000, p. 10).

South Korea, where some capital account restrictions had been in place on the convertibility of the won, likewise became much more interventionist, although the government did not move to impose the Malaysian-type exchange controls. In the financial sector, the government moved fast to buy up bad loans from the banks and forced small banks to merge with larger ones (Wade 1998, 368f). The government adopted tighter monetary and fiscal policies and accepted slower growth to keep inflation below 5 percent and the current account deficit below one percent of GDP (Sikorski 1999, 120). Like elsewhere, these were measures taken with a view to enhancing government controls, not the structural reforms that Western critics had demanded.[14] Even the debt rollovers that Korea negotiated in early 1998 were a form of capital control (Krugman 2000, xi).

Throughout the region, Thailand was the only exception in that its government did not institute similar capital controls, for the simple reason that, after having used up nearly all of its foreign reserves in its 1997 futile defense of the baht, the country had no reserves left to defend. Also, it was entirely dependent on the IMF standby facility (Wade 1998, 369).

As a perceptive commentator (Wade 1998, 369–370) has noted, these financial controls, while going against the teachings of laissez faire economics and, equally, against the counsels of globalization spokespersons, were needed for two reasons: (1) to protect against excessive inflows of foreign capital, especially short-term loans (i.e., the casino effects); and, more important, (2) to make the fairly open economies in the Asian region "less vulnerable to the whims and stampedes of portfolio and hedge fund managers, and to reestablish stable growth" following the whirlwind financial crisis.

LESSONS FROM THE ASIAN FINANCIAL CRISIS: A SUMMING UP

From the above discussion, we can summarize the lessons that can be drawn from the way the crisis hit the region, the responses delivered by the region's members in self-defense, and the final outcomes, as follows:

1. Those countries whose government, as a matter of routine policy, maintained some form of control over the currency and stock markets fared considerably better under attack during the crisis. In addition to mainland China and Taiwan, Hong Kong has a U.S. dollar peg policy, instituted since 1983.[15] The peg is a blessing when the economy has sufficient foreign reserves to back it up, although it can turn into a curse without such backup, as happened to Thailand in 1997.[16] Likewise, Singapore has a system pegged to a basket of currencies including the U.S. dollar, which has served the country well in fending off attacks on the Singaporean dollar by external currency speculators.

2. No singular factor can explain the origin of the crisis befalling the Asian economies, certainly not "crony capitalism" or any single-factor theory fixated on domestic causes alone. As we have seen, the crisis came following a series of similar attacks elsewhere, all of them occasioned by the phenomenon known as "globalized capital." Between the two competing explanations—the "endogenous

thesis," which sees the crisis as resulting from the domestic structural flaws of the Asian economies, and the opposing "exogenous thesis," which ascribes the crisis to external causes, or spin-offs of globalized capital—we know from hindsight that the latter thesis has more explanatory power.[17] (A combination of both, though, would offer an explanation above reproach.) The most convincing evidence to ponder is that the region's unexpected fast recovery has been achieved, as we have seen, largely without the Draconian domestic reform or drastic austerity programs that adherents to the endogenous thesis had deemed necessary.

3. The region's speedy[18] recovery seems to be directly correlated to the re-establishment or strengthening of capital controls, which in conjunction with a concomitant ability to maintain price stability and high savings despite hardships, have proven to work well. Inherent in this success, nevertheless, are two additional revealing lessons: (1) that commensurate safeguard is as important as openness if a modern developing economy should hope to maintain sustained development without exposing itself to the risks of "globalized capitalism" (McCleary 1999, 36), and (2) that overreliance on currency control alone will not work without the attendant support of sound economic fundamentals, such that realistic price stability and un-sagging savings (hence, recapitalization) can be maintained.

4. China emerged from the crisis with a clearly impressive performance record. Despite repeated forecasts to the contrary, its renminbi has stood steady and strong, and it was able to chalk up continuing impressive growth rates of 7–8 percent in 1997–1998, when most other Asian economies had minus growth. The secrets for the Chinese triumph are its huge domestic market and its purposefully safeguarded liberalization. While the former condition cannot easily be duplicated elsewhere, the latter element serves to confirm the view cited above that liberalization without corresponding safeguard may subject one's economy to such risks as the casino effects (hot money inflows) from globalized capital. In an attempt to map the "post-crisis landscape," Gangmao Wang (1999) grouped all East and Southeast Asian economies under four "tiers," as gauged by their comparative standing in terms of five economic indexes.[19] In this new classification, Singapore, Taiwan, Hong Kong, and mainland China constitute Tier One, in what Wang terms as the "Chinese language economic circle." Japan is relegated to Tier Two, which also includes South Korea. Placed in Tier Three are Thailand, Malaysia, and the Philippines. All the rest (Indonesia,

Vietnam, Cambodia, and Burma) are in the last group, or Tier Four. If China's progressive liberalization and economic restructuring are on track and its growth rate is maintained, Wang adds (6), "the post-crisis era could see a reversal of roles between Japan and China as the next economic superpower in Asia, in terms of economic size and strength." More, this is to happen "despite the current Japanese [economic] dominance in the region" (3).

In spite of all the lingering skepticism (Sender 2000, 52), the statistics cited above invariably point to the conclusion that by late 1999 the Asian Pacific countries had survived the attack of the financial crisis and the economic downturn that came with it. Prompt recovery, to varying degrees, was reported in all countries. Detractors were quick to jump at the few instances of relapses in such economies as the Philippines, Taiwan, and South Korea during the months of 2000. But even the usually cynical *Economist* (October 28, 2000, p. 71) had to admit that such relapses were prompted by domestic political difficulties. In the Philippines, for example, President Estrada was facing a debilitating impeachment fight (*Asiaweek,* October 27, 2000, 23–26). In Taiwan, the new government of President Chen Shui-bian of the Democratic Progressive Party (DPP), which in the March presidential election drove out the Kuomingtang (KMT) Party after over 50 years in power, was dragging the island down the lane of a constitutional crisis at home and, externally, into a war of nerves with mainland China because of Chen's and DPP's separatist conviction (*FEER,* October 19, 2000, 16–19). South Korea was beset with labor problems, in the wake of its recent democratization (*FEER,* December 7, 2000, pp. 16–20). Notwithstanding these political upheavals, the pattern of Asia's prompt recovery from the financial crisis of 1997–1998, as described above, can be maintained as a whole. The only exception is Japan. Nevertheless, like the speedy recovery of these other countries, even Japan's continuing lackluster economic performance offers a challenge to conventional wisdom. Analysts in the West, including the IMF, usually saw increases in accountability (or greater democracy in the political system) as an important part of the recipe for Asian recovery. In Japan, the Liberal Democratic Party (LDP), which had stayed in power for 38 straight years since 1955, lost its majority control of the lower house of the Diet (parliament) for the first time in 1993. The collapse of LDP loosened the grip on power by the postwar triumvirate made up of the LDP, the Zaikai (big business and finance industry) and the Japanese bureaucracy.[20] Despite the resultant increase in political accountability, Japan's economy did not improve from the doldrums it had been in since 1989. Ironically, it was not until the LDP had once again regained control of the Diet in 1996 that the economy began to show signs of moving forward. (Similarly, despite KMT's ouster in Taiwan, as noted above, which registered a giant step forward in Taiwan's journey to democracy, the increased democracy has paradoxically sent the economy and stock market tumbling down since the new government of the opposition DPP took power in May 2000.)

Hence, the ultimate lesson to be learned from the Asian encounter with the financial crisis is that theories conceived, even tested, in the West may not have the same explanatory or predictive power when applied to the Asian locale. As was also seen above, even the pet Western theory that domestic causes (i.e., built-in structural-cultural flaws and ills) alone brought on the Asian crisis is subject to serious doubt and warrants a thorough review from hindsight. In a direction that orthodox Western economists would call socialistic, a bailout solution first embraced by South Korea and later by China, in which the government bought over bad-debt enterprises, seems to have worked.[21] Regardless of one's ideological stand on the merit (or lack thereof) of such a socialistic measure in either instance, the point worth noting here is that solutions as such would probably not have crossed the minds of those schooled in orthodox Western economics. The inevitable question it poses for these commentators, therefore, is: To what extent was this "blind spot" accountable for their underestimation of the Asian nations' ability to weather the storm and recover the way they did? By extension, could there be other "blind spots" that may have accounted for their diagnosis as to the causes of the crisis (i.e., the "endogenous thesis") that has by now proven misdirected or one-sided? Even Paul Krugman, who had been the foremost advocate of the internal-flaws thesis—that Asians got punished for their own sins—has, two years after his initial finger-pointing, recanted in his latest book (Krugman 2000).[22]

No wonder, as Alvin So notes in the next chapter, Asian nations have looked to "Asianization" as a preferred way to get out of the jam and to preclude future crises. A move in this direction was the proposed creation of an Asian Monetary Fund as a mechanism to combat external currency speculators. Initially proposed by Japan, the fund, with contributions from Asian nations, would work as a war chest to cope with currency speculation and capital flight. The scheme would convert the Asian Development Bank (ADB), the slated administrator, into a lender of last resort,[23] a function delegated to the International Monetary Fund (IMF) under the original Bretton Woods system. Although it failed to be adopted because of strong U.S. objection, the proposal nevertheless typified an Asian proclivity to pool together resources to combat the buffeting impact of the kind of globalization promoted by the IMF and the

World Bank. Another move borne of a similar Asian collective initiative was the proposed creation of an early warning system against future financial attacks, known informally as the "regional surveillance system" accountable to the ASEAN Secretariat[24] (also reported in chapter 7 by Greg Felker below).

Fred Bergsten (2000) has noted a new Asian regionalism on the rise in that the ten ASEAN members and three Northeast Asian nations, China, Korea, and Japan, are quietly fashioning a host of new regional arrangements to look after their financial and trade interests, in that order. The ASEAN+3 has announced a region-wide system of currency swaps to help them deal with future Asian crises. In Bergsten's view, given the impetus of this development, the world is becoming a truly three-bloc configuration, with the EU and North America as the two other dominant systems. "Not only global economic relationships, but political ones too," he added, "will turn on the direction these agreements take—and on how the United States, and others outside the region, decide to respond to them" (23). The ASEAN+3 formula was first hatched by Malaysian Prime Minister Mahathir a decade ago. But nothing happened, largely because of U.S. objection, until now. The fact that the same group of nations, as Dr. Mahathir first envisioned, has had its summit every year and has held regular meetings of its finance ministers since 1997, means the new Asian regionalism, as embraced by the ASEAN+3, is now unstoppable. Structurally, Bergsten notes, this grouping is starting to look like the G-7, the group of the seven most industrialized countries headed by the United States. And, it has become the most active regional grouping outside Europe, although it has yet to move toward integration after the fashion of the European Union. The important thing is that ASEAN+3 has the potential of upstaging the Asia Pacific Economic Cooperation (APEC) forum, which had been Washington's hope for circumventing Dr. Mahathir's original proposed East Asian Economic Group (EAEG).

This move toward a renewed Asian regionalism, in a nutshell, is surging ahead at a speed and in a way that would not have been possible before 1997. Hence, in retrospect, the financial crisis of 1997–1998 was like a blessing in disguise (but a woe to the international currency speculators).[25] For it meant that Asian nations are now better equipped to deal with external currency attacks than before. It remains to be seen, though, how this new development is going to deflect the impact of globalization[26] or even to affect U.S. influence in the region.

Nevertheless, it can be concluded that the Asian region, reacting from its encounter with the recent financial attack, is now better poised to take care of its collective economic security (a dictate of geoeconomics) by region-wide collective action. Should another crisis erupt, it will not be caught by surprise again.

ASIAN VALUES: A POST-CRISIS REVIEW

Many observers, as already noted, would love to write off "Asian values" for the sake of self-assurance that the Asian Pacific nations, despite their economic growths, would not last without following more faithfully in the footsteps of the West, from values to institutions to the managerial modus operandi, and even to eating habits.[27] Our question here is: Assuming all Asians consume McDonald's and ingest Coca Cola with due diligence, does it necessarily follow that they must have exactly the same institutions and the same operating style, or even dream the same dreams, before they can "survive," let alone become competitive with the West? Hence, the question of "Asian values" bears re-examination in light of the recent crisis. But in so doing, we have to make some fine differentiations on a number of crucial issues, if ever we are going to pierce through the many myths surrounding the subject as it is handled in the usual discourses.

First, "Asian values" and the Asian model of development should be kept distinct. In fact, oblivious to the distinction, many commentators loathe to Asian values, which they hold to be inimical to democracy, are led to denouncing the Asian model of development as well. This confusion, as we shall see below, is unwarranted.

Second, Asian values do not fall into a monolithic order. There can be, and are, as many different versions of Asian values as there are nations in the region. What are usually called "Asian values" are in fact equated with the virtues allegedly extolled by the Singaporeans, or the Singapore School.[28] But the irony is that the Singaporeans were originally raising a genuine epistemological question as to whether Asian values and liberal-democratic values should be dichotomized, a question that inscrutably raised the specter of the rise of conservatism in Asia. This specter, as Richard Robinson (1996, xv) points out, aroused fears in the West that conservatism might tilt the global balance against liberalism and skew the ideological contest within Western societies. Hence, the debate on Asian values got shunted into a polemical battle waged by self-designated defenders of liberal democracy. So, we need to keep in mind this differentiation between debate and polemics.

Third, the true spirit of liberal democracy and the views held by its self-designated defenders may not be exactly the same. For instance, an essential hallmark of true liberal democracy is tolerance of diversity and pluralism, but its self-designated defenders are obviously not so tolerant of the Singaporean dissent.[29] By the same token, a fine distinction should be made between Confucianism and Asian values, although the two have often been equated together. Strictly speaking, they are not the same. In regard to the former, besides, there is "patriarchal Confucianism," as found in Chinese-predominant societies (such as Singapore and Taiwan, outside of China itself) and "feudal Confucianism," as practiced in Korea and Japan—a distinction enunciated in Steve Chan's chapter 2 above.

Fourth, even if we accept Confucianism as a short-hand label for "Asian values" to denote in abstract something found in common among the east and southeast Asian nations, we have to distinguish between the Confucian culture as developed in China, on the one hand, and the Confucian-imbued Asian values as generally attributed to those other contemporary Asian nations, on the other hand. In China's long history, Confucianization meant the rise of learning and acquired knowledge, a noninheritable achievement, as a criterion of social mobility, replacing wealth as a measure of all things. This crucial shift not only led to the creation of a system governed by the learned literocrats (in effect, an "epistemocracy") but also to the tempering of brute political power by Confucian humanism and a Confucian censorial system (Creel 1953, 39–44; and Hucker 1965, 50–76). Even the emperor had to bow to the teachings of Confucius. The hereditary nobility in government was replaced by a cadre of plebeians recruited through the *keju* regimes, humankind's first civil service system. Shortly after Confucianism was adopted as the national ethos by Emperor Wu of the Han Dynasty in 136 B.C., it was possible for Kung Sun-hung (or Gong Sunhong, d. 121 B.C.) to be the first commoner to become Prime Minister, setting a precedent for all the following imperial governments (Hsiung 1985, 7–9). Critics should ask themselves: When was the first time plebeians were able to reach such heights in the West?

Confucianism as a short-hand label for modern "Asian values," as attributed to the Singaporean school, consists mainly of the following attributes: (1) respect for authority, (2) strong families, (3) reverence for education, (4) hard work, (5) frugality, (6) teamwork, and (7) a balance between the individual's interests and those of society (David Hitchcock 1994, 2). If this inventory embodies "Asian values" in the running dispute, one wonders what is it that Western critics find so repugnant. Some of the attributes (e.g., hard work, frugality), in fact, are consistent with Max Weber's Protestant work ethic. The value laid on teamwork agrees with a principle in modern business and industrial management. Some of the others (respect for authority and familism) are supportive of political and social stability, a sine qua non for development.[30] The stress on education, more particularly, is exactly what is needed for today's high-tech society, in which "knowledge economy" is the rising star of tomor-row.[31] Already, Gilbert Rozman (1992, 312) has put his stamp of approval on the stress on education: "The increasingly knowledge-based manage-ment of pre-modern East Asian societies was to prove beneficial for their modern development."

In view of the above, the fuss about Asian values, it seems, is not really about the alleged inherent faults of their Confucian content. Rather, harking back to the point Robinson made above, it is because Asian val-ues have unfortunately been implicated in a polemical war in the West between the self-designated liberal-democracy defenders and the chal-lengers from a rising school that has caught fire on communitarian thought. While the buried roots of communitarian thought in the West go very far back, even to Socrates' polis and Rousseau's general will, as Markate Daly (1994) has documented, the self-designated defenders of liberal democracy, whose focus is on the rights and freedom of the indi-vidual, have great fears that the Confucian legacy, with its inherent em-phasis on collective will of the community, will further erode their own support both at home and abroad.[32] The Asian financial crisis, therefore, afforded them a gratuitous opportunity to pull off a fusillade in their vain attempt to kill off Asian values, the target of their fears, for good. Hence, without waiting for the death certificate, the *Economist,* quite typically, was already running an obituary for Asian values in jubilation, as noted above. Alas, it boomeranged.

THE ASIAN MODEL OF DEVELOPMENT

To make sense of this discussion, we have to make a prior distinction be-tween the so-called "Asian model of development," which in shorthand means largely the "developmental state" model (White 1988), on the one hand, and the "Asian values" that made the model work successfully, on the other. The story about the former is well known, and there is a pro-lific literature on the Asian model of development (Belassa et al. 1982; Berger and Hsiao 1986; Fei, Ranis and Kuo 1979; Hofheinz and Calder 1982; McCord 1991; Rabushka 1987; and Wei 1992, to name just a few). And, how it actually worked, reflecting the role and utility of the "Asian values" in practice, was also explored in numerous studies (Chan and Clark 1992; Lam and Lee 1992; Vogel 1979; Johnson 1982; Gold 1986; Tai 1989, etc.). However, the origin of the developmental state in Asia is an understudied subject. It is even more intriguing why the region has such a concentration of so many "developmental states."

The exact meaning of the term "developmental state" has shifted over time, and it also varies in the writings by neoclassical economists (and the

World Bank) and by political scientists (i.e., political-economy experts), respectively. The first group saw the Asian economic "miracles" as mainly the work of the miracle of the market or market-conforming policies of a state intervening in economic development (e.g., World Bank 1993). The second group, on the other hand, focused on the intervening role of the state per se, which set the corporate goal of development and initiated measures, even mobilizing societal forces, to achieve it (Amsden 1989), in what could be called a forced march to modernity. There seems to be a consensus that the so-called "developmental state" model first appeared in postwar Japan (Johnson 1982) but later spread to other Asian nations. The widely accepted "flying geese" paradigm, which visualizes Japan to be flying at the head of a V-shaped formation with other Asian economies following right behind (Okita 1986, 26), seems also to confirm this sequential relationship in the spread of the model. If this is true, the next question is: What accounts for the rise of the developmental state model in postwar Japan, in the first place?

Existing evidence suggests two origins of the Japanese developmental state: first, Japan's economic mobilization during the Pacific War (Dower 1994), and second, the onset of the Cold War after 1947 (Cummings 1987, 61–63). The combination of these two origins solves the puzzle about many things regarding the Japanese developmental-state model. During the war, according to Dower, Japan experienced a second industrial revolution (following Meiji), in which capital and the banking structure were consolidated. Small and medium-sized enterprises were integrated into subcontracting networks that revolved around large industrial conglomerates (anticipating the postwar *keiretsu*).[33] And the industrial work force was stabilized through prohibitions on unauthorized job changes and a seniority-based wage system. Japan's postwar dynamism, in Dower's view, is an extension of its wartime mobilization.[34]

If not for the early onset of the Cold War, the Allied program aimed at dismantling Japan's prewar *zaibatsu* as well as at exterminating war criminals at the Tokyo Trials would have run its full course unabridged. The unexpected premature disruption of the program by the United States in 1948 due to the onset of the Cold War,[35] however, left in place not only the material base of the postwar *zaikai*, but, more important, the power of the bureaucracy in engineering Japan's economic strategies and supervising their implementation in a state-guided growth system. Typical of this transformation was the switchover of the wartime Ministry of Munitions to the all-important Ministry of International Trade and Industry (MITI), which has acted as the leading state sector in the postwar Japanese economy, directly responsible for its rapid economic growth (Johnson 1982, 157–197; Johnson 1995).[36]

From Japan, the "developmental state" model spread to other Asian countries, whose interest in the model was fired by the rapid Japanese economic recovery and growth, with the result that nearly all Asian countries have adopted more or less the same system and programs (Johnson 1981, 9–18; Amsden 1989; White 1988). Hence the dense concentration of so many "developmental states" in the Asian region. It goes without saying that for its part, China's version of a developmental state came about independently, drawing on its Leninist one-party state origins, though modified by the wide-ranging post-Mao reforms.

Returning to the original context of this discussion, the important point to keep in mind is that the genesis of the "Asian model of development," to reiterate, was not due to Asian values or Confucian culture. So, if the recent financial crisis should call into question the Asian model of development (though it did not), Asian values should not be dragged down by guilt of association, simply because the association is tenuous. And, how much more true when, as we have seen, the primary causes of the crisis were not internal so much as external. Thus, as is shown here, the diagnosis of the causality of the Asian financial crisis is absolutely crucial not only for its own sake but because of its far-reaching ramifications. It holds the key to important questions such as the survival of the Asian model of development and the fate of Asian values.

To say this is to point out that polemical critics of both "Asian values" and the Asian developmental model are not above suspicion as to their motivation, particularly in their repeated attempt to pin the origin of the recent financial crisis exclusively on the (alleged but specious) internal cultural-structural ills of the Asian countries when material evidence suggests otherwise. Since this point is at the heart of the overriding concern of this book—twenty-first century world order and the Asia Pacific region—it is why we should subject it to meticulous scrutiny at the risk of hair splitting, as we have done.

In sum, viewing it from hindsight after the recent financial crisis, we should take due cognizance that, contrary to the teachings of laissez faire, the way the Asian nations got themselves out of the jam so promptly was through more, not less, intervention by the state. Besides the capital controls imposed by government in the countries mentioned above, there is additional proof in a few instances that the government's role in the economy has increased in the wake of the crisis. For example, bank restructuring in Japan, as well as in Indonesia, South Korea, and Malaysia, is extending state ownership and control in the financial sector. Japan's U.S.$500 billion rescue package for its banks will result in subscribing banks agreeing to stringent government monitoring and even nationalization (Sikorski 1999, 126). With IMF blessing, the Indonesian government has nationalized nearly all formerly private banks, including the largest, Bank Central Asia. The Thai government, besides, now runs 6 of the nation's 15 banks and nearly all of its 60-odd finance companies (127).

Like that for Asian values, any obituary on the demise of the Asian developmental-state model is premature. In fact, as Sikorski (1999) points out, the model of "Asian capitalism," instead of being discredited, was part of the solution in bringing about financial development and change. And, because of it, the high-performance Asian economies can be expected to proceed, in the World Bank's (2000, 14) words, "from recovery to a new era of high growth." They have only learned how to better manage global financial flows. In the decades ahead, there is no prospect in sight that the Asian nations will abandon their state-guided growth system, a model further strengthened after the crisis, in furthering their economic security in the new age of geoeconomics.

COMPREHENSIVE SECURITY IN ASIA PACIFIC

"Comprehensive security," as discussed in chapter 1, means the extension of national security (in the traditional sense) to other issue areas such as economic security, environmental security, and human security. The question of economic security was already covered in our preceding discussion of the region's financial crisis and the related issues that came up in its context. In the present section, we will address environmental security and human security in the region. Then in the next section, we will return to issues of security of the traditional genre (or national defense interests).

ENVIRONMENTAL SECURITY

Although our discussions are as a whole focused on the East and Southeast Asian nations, the Asian Pacific region, strictly speaking, is much broader in the geographical expanse it covers. Hence, a few words about the Pacific basin[37] are in order. Geographically, the Pacific region is vast. It is the world's largest ocean, studded by thousands of islands, grouped into about 30 different political territories. The Pacific islands are usually associated with high levels of "biophysical vulnerability," or the potential for loss from natural hazards, environmental variability, and change. One of the most widely popularized environmental threats to the region is contamination from nuclear waste dumping and weapons testing. The testing of thermonuclear weapons in the region began in 1946 (AVISO Issue No.1, 1998, 5).

During the Cold War and well into the postcolonial period, the Pacific region remained of strategic military significance to the United States. It is of continuing strategic importance in terms of access to transport lanes, seabed resources, the fisheries, and other natural resources. Conflicts over resources and the environment may in fact intensify due to an expanding interest from Asian governments and private companies offshore (Anthony 1990).

For our purpose, three noticeable issue areas warrant special mention on the environmental security of the Asia Pacific region at large, namely: (1) threats of sea-level rises, caused by global warming, to the archipelagic and island states plus the littoral states with long coastlines; (2) future of shared resources; and (3) recurrent forest fires.

First, except for landlocked Laos, most of the countries in East and Southeast Asia are surrounded by the ocean; Indonesia and the Philippines are archipelagic states.[38] Japan is made up of four major islands plus other lesser islands. Singapore is a tiny island city-state. China, Malaysia, Vietnam, and, to a lesser extent, Cambodia and Thailand, have long coastlines. On a global scale, our ecosystem's climate temperature is steadily rising, as the result of increased concentrations of carbon dioxide and other gases trapped in the atmosphere. The threatened rises in the sea levels due to global warming, therefore, pose particular hazards for the entire Asia Pacific region. According to experts, a doubling of today's atmospheric concentrations of the trapped gases could raise average global temperatures by 1.5 to 4.5 degrees centigrade (or 2 to 9 degrees Fahrenheit). Such increases could raise sea levels by about one to one and a half feet by the year 2050.[39] Another study projects an increase in sea levels by as much as one meter by the year 2100 (Wigley 1999). It is mind-boggling to imagine the effects on residents and businesses near the shorelines in these archipelagic and littoral states, and in such other places as Japan, Singapore, and Hong Kong, resulting from the consequential flooding and intrusion of salt water into estuaries and groundwater, not to mention the inundation of beaches and water-front properties! Infectious diseases, from the dengue epidemic to bird flu, which haunted Hong Kong during 1998, the latter causing a million chickens to be slaughtered, were additional grave reminders of environmental degradation and, more important, that the environment could be a real threat to the region's security. As if these were not enough, the return of the nipah virus in 1999 killed more than 100 people and led to the slaughter of over a million of pigs both in peninsula Malaysia and—much more worrisomely—in the Borneo state of Sarawak,[40] about 400 miles across the South China Sea.

Second, disputes over control of shared resources (such as shared water of international rivers) may lead to conflict, while renewal of resources (for example, fish stocks) may be depleted as a result of conflict. In the larger Asia Pacific region, I can think of at least three separate areas of shared resources, one of which is the South China sea, with its rich fishing grounds and oil and gas deposits. The other two are the international Mekong River and the sea lanes connecting Northeast Asia, through the Taiwan Strait, the South China Sea, and various "choke points" in Southeast Asia, to the Indian Ocean and points beyond.[41] Of the three, the salience of the sea lanes is tied to the region's 60 percent dependence on Middle Eastern oil. A mitigating circumstance, though, is China's deliberate reliance on oil and gas supplies from Central Asia in addition to its own vast resources in Xinjiang under development. The South China Sea is the best known hotbed of disputes, ostensibly because two internationally-contested outlying island groups are located in its waters. The Paracels are claimed by Vietnam and China, which have fought two wars over the islands (in 1974 and again in 1988). To the Spratlys, the other outlying island group, seven parties, including China, Vietnam, Malaysia, Indonesia, Brunei, the Philippines, and Taiwan, have laid overlapping claims (Hsiung 1993, 15 and 83).

While much of the existing literature on disputes in the South China Sea approaches them from the geostrategic point of view, I would like, in the present context, to call attention to the contested shared resources as a crucial factor behind the disputes. For instance, an occasion for Sino-Vietnamese disputes was the announced signing by China of an agreement with Creston Energy Co., a Denver-based U.S. company, for oil exploration (*New York Times,* June 18, 1992, p. 8) in the South China Sea. Immediately, the Vietnamese Foreign Ministry issued a statement denouncing the move as contravening Vietnamese sovereignty, because Vietnam also lays claim to the same area covered by the Chinese agreement (Shee Poon Kim 1994, 67). Another instance was the dispute arising from Malaysia's arrest of four Taiwanese fishing vessels for illegal fishing in its waters in August 1988 (Yu 1991–1992, 138). In these and other cases, if disputes as such should lead to armed conflicts, they would likely inflict irreparable damages to the contested shared resources involved, hence breaching environmental security.

The long, meandering stretch of land traversed by the Mekong River is an area where potential disputes may lead to similar consequences. The Mekong runs a course of 2,600 miles, from southern China through Myanmar (Burma), Laos, Thailand, Cambodia, to Vietnam, where it exits into the South China Sea. And, conflict potential is especially high where the river forms the border between Myanmar and western Laos, and later between Laos and Thailand. From the ecopolitical point of view, that belt is the site of potential future conflicts. For it is home to 230 million people, many living in poverty. Already, the ASEAN has a developmental project known as the Greater Mekong Sub-region (GMS) program with over 100 "priority projects," including the construction of highway and railway links and dozens of hydroelectric dams on the Mekong and its tributaries, at a projected cost of up to $1 billion (*The Economist,* September 7, 1996, 31f).

For China, the Mekong offers a link with Southeast Asia and a chance to develop Yunnan, one of its poorer provinces. But for the poorer countries, GMS offers a dream of prosperity, although the poorest of all, Laos, is rightfully the most cautious, ever fearful that its natural wealth will be carved up by overbearing neighbors. The potential for both mutual benefit and suspicion is seen most clearly in the ASEAN plans for the river itself. While the river affords much hope for hydroelectric power generation, those with the biggest demand for electricity are not necessarily those that have the biggest hydroelectric potential. For instance, Thailand has the greatest need for electricity but the least hydroelectric potential (See chart in *The Economist,* 1996, 32). Many environmentalists, already horrified, warn of problems ranging from the intrusion of salt water into the delta to the loss of fish and rare mammals. China, thus far, is damming the main stream of the Mekong. The anxiety of the downstream countries is clearly understandable. If disputes over sharing of water resources and control of water pollution along the Mekong river, as elsewhere, cannot be peacefully worked out by its riparian states, conflict is a most likely staple in the relations among the nations involved.

A possible solution to these and other similar disputes involving shared resources and environmental control, nevertheless, is to follow a precedent set by China and Vietnam in 1993. In October of that year, the two countries reached an agreement whereby they pledged to suspend, without prejudice, their respective claims to the Paracel Islands in the interest of joint peaceful exploration of its resources (*China Daily,* 21 October 1993; Shee Poon Kim 1994, 79). Conceivably, the same formula could be used in the resolution of disputes over the Spratlys and other sites such as the oil-rich Tiayoyutai/Senkaku island, a long-standing source of friction between Japan and China.

Third, while air pollution such as that caused by industrial waste, tailpipe emissions, and the like is a universal problem, the Asian region has had more than its share of the problem. In Hong Kong, one of Asia's richest cities, for example, wealth has begotten waste, and lots of it—on an average day, about 16,000 tons of garbage go to landfills. Another 1.5 million tons of sewage, enough to fill 1,000 Olympic-size swimming pools, spill into Victoria Harbor. Diesel-powered taxis and trucks rumble through the city's streets, leaving pedestrians cupping hands over mouths, trying not to inhale the air. Polluted air as such is blamed for 2,000 premature deaths a year. "Some in Hong Kong Are Fed Up With Smog," ran a headline in the *Asian Wall Street Journal Weekly*.[42] What is true of Hong Kong is also true of other cities in the region. Yet, as if this were not enough, a forest and land fire in Indonesia, started in mid-1997, kept burning and smoldering for over a year. It finally burned out in East Kalimantan in May 1998, but not before it had scorched at least 500,000 hectares (1.4 billion acres) of land. For the whole year, the haze not only blanketed vast areas of East Kalimantan but reached far-off points in Malaysia, Singapore, the Philippines, and other parts of Southeast Asia (Schindler 2000; IFFN No. 19, 3).

Details of these fires need not concern us except that Indonesia's apparent inability to prevent and control the wildfires, even with fire-fighting equipment donated by the international community, is a source of worry for its neighbors. The same causes and neglect were said to be responsible for earlier, recurrent fires in the country, in 1986, 1991, and 1994. And, these wildfires have been almost always human-caused, such as those resulting from agricultural conversion burns (to prepare land for pulp wood and oil palm plantations), logging operations, and even arson (IFFM 2000). Thus, for their own good, Southeast Asian nations have one more incentive to cooperate among themselves: to help Indonesia find a permanent solution, including the installation of an early warning system and training of competent fire-fighting crews, besides the updating of fire-fighting equipment.

HUMAN SECURITY

Unlike certain other parts of the world, the Asia Pacific region has only remote memories of Kosovo-type genocidal conflicts. No similar attacks on human security, of the kind found in Serbia, Burundi, and Rwanda (besides Kosovo), were heard of in the last decade. But it remains sadly true that Cambodia (briefly known as Kampuchia) during the Pol Pot regime, 1975–79, was the first state after the end of World War II to commit war crimes against its own people. In four years' time, Pol Pot's Khmer Rouge regime was credited with having slaughtered three million people, or one third of its population, approaching half of the estimated six million victims of the Holocaust, over 12 years (1933–1945). While the Nazis killed Jews in Germany, Pol Pot killed his own kin—his fellow Cambodians. The dire magnitude of the Cambodian genocidal crimes remains unparalleled, in peacetime, anywhere in the world. A greater tragedy is that perhaps because these heinous crimes against humanity were committed in Asia, they have never received the same amount of worldwide attention as did the ethnic cleansing in Bosnia and Kosovo, not to mention the Holocaust in Nazi Germany. Like the World War II atrocities and crimes against humanity committed by the Japanese army in Asia (cf. Harris 1994), these heinous crimes in Pol Pot's Cambodia have received far less condemnation in the West.

In a report by United Nations Development Programme (1998), poverty is named a basic source of human insecurity in developing countries, as represented by a few indicators, such as: (1) deprivation of basic consumption needs, including basic sanitation; (2) poor or no access to clean water; (3) children not attending school; (4) insufficient dietary energy and protein; and (5) lack of motorized transport, telecommunications, and modern energy. Fortunately for the Asian region, none of these is a wide-spread problem. But, the region has a few problems of its own, notably: income inequality, aging, racial conflicts, cross-boundary drug trafficking, and the plight of women's rights, which we will discuss separately below.

While no in-depth comparative studies of income inequality across the region is known to me, the problem as a whole seems more pronounced in the more wealthy countries. For instance, in Singapore, according to a government survey released in May 2000, monthly household income for the bottom 10 percent of the population fell to S$133 (or $76.87 in U.S. money) in 1999 from S$258 (or U.S.$149.13) the previous year. At the same time, the richest 20 percent of households made 18 times what was earned by the poorest 20 percent—up from 15 times in 1998 (*FEER* 2000, 24). Hong Kong is not much better. While it is too early to assess the situation in the three years following the territory's return to Chinese sovereignty in 1997, available data for previous years under British colonial rule showed a gloomy picture almost as bad as Singapore. During 1976–1991, the top 10 percent of the population in Hong Kong earned eight times as much as the bottom 10 percent. And the gap was widening, instead of narrowing. Over the ten-year period of 1986–1996, the top 20 percent of wage earners sported a hefty 60 percent increase in income. The bottom 20 percent of all wage earners, on the other hand, had only a 20 percent pay rise (Lui 1997, 60; table 3.5). Neoclassical economic historians argue that income inequality often increases in the early stages of industrialization but that structural changes resulting from the transition will eventually lead to a more equitable distribution of income. The question is how long this transition is going to be before the assumed self-correcting mechanism will even out the gross inequities. For during the indefinite transition, the continuing, and often widening, income gaps pose a dire problem for human security.

Aging is a universal problem in the Asia Pacific. In China, for example, a People's University study shows that by mid-twenty-first century, one-fifth of the population will be 60 years old or above, while octogenarians will total 80 million, or seven times the number in the year 2000 (*Qiao Bao* [the China Press, New York], 20 October 2000, p. 5). The honor of having the most serious aging problem falls on Japan, however. Aggregate data show that Japan is aging faster than any other nation in the world. With 17 percent of the population aged at 65 or over, including 7 percent in the 75 or above group, it has the highest percentage of elderly in population.[43] Before 2010, one in every five Japanese will be a senior citizen. In 2050, the figure will increase to one in three (Japan Insight 2000, data P-1). Not only does this graying phenomenon create a nasty caring problem for the elderly and an increasing burden on the country's old-age welfare programs. But it has created a serious labor shortage that Japan has had to grapple with, forcing it to confront the once taboo option of importing labor from abroad. Despite Japan's traditional xenophobic immigration policy, more and more business executives are calling on the government to open up the country to foreign workers. In a shocking report released in early 2000, the United Nations projected that Japan would need to import 609,000 immigrants a year to maintain its 1995 working-age population level of 87.2 million through 2050. If Japan follows the advice, the report says, 30 percent of the country's population would be immigrants or descendents of immigrants by mid-century (Kanabayashi 2000).

Racial conflicts, as a source of human insecurity, have a long history in Southeast Asia. While the area is a multiracial community, the major division is between the Malays and the Chinese in many countries. In fact, most ex-colonial countries in the area bear a continuing grudge against their colonial heritage for the introduction of the Chinese into the Malay world. In the nineteenth century, Chinese were imported by the colonial rulers for coolie labor into their Malay-populated colonies. In a strange twist of history, descendents of these early Chinese coolies now dominate the economy in many of the postcolonial Asian countries (Antolik 1990, 11f). Bicommunal conflicts rocked the first years of the postcolonial Singapore, and the underlying animosity between the Chinese and the Malays was a cause for its short-lived federation with Malaya to form the new Malaysia during 1963–1965 (Lee Kuan Yew 1998). In the neighboring Malaysia, riots and clashes between the Malay majority and the Chinese minority during 1969–1971 even triggered a brief period of martial law (Antolik, 29). The jitters created by these conflicts have intimidated the Chinese in Singapore ever since, although they make up 76.4 percent of the local population, as compared to Malays' 14.9 percent. The timid

Chinese majority in Singapore are keenly aware that they are besieged by a sea of Malays in neighboring countries, from Malaysia and Indonesia to the Philippines.

The most gruesome of recurrent racial attacks on the Chinese minority was found in Indonesia. During the riots of May 13–15, 1998, which broke out following a shoot-out by security forces, killing four students during an antigovernment demonstration at Trsakti University in Jakarta, initial reports only touched on the looting and destruction of properties against the ethnic Chinese minority. The horrifying atrocities committed against them were not known until weeks later, after the Joint Fact-Finding Team (TGPF) concluded its report. The Chinese, who make up a bare 4 percent of the Indonesian population, were blamed for "not repaying the community" with their wealth. The TGPF report showed the following ethnic Chinese casualty list:

- Many among the 1,198 people murdered (including 27 shot) and 31 missing;
- 40 shopping centers burned;
- 4,083 shops burned;
- 1,026 houses burned; and
- 168 girls and women raped.

Most rape victims, from age 9 to 55, were savagely gang-raped in public, often in front of their own families. About 20 of them died after their miseries: Some were killed by their tormentors; some died of injuries afterwards; and some committed suicide. Mounting evidence suggests that the riots, originally believed to be spontaneous outbursts, were masterminded to deliberately target the ethnic Chinese, with complicity by elements of the security forces (see YRC 1998). Reports alleged that ethnic Chinese women raped in the riots were victims of organized sexual attacks. So, also, were the killing and sacking of the Chinese and their properties the result of racially motivated assaults (CNN.com 1998).

If their numerical minority combined with their success in the local economy was indeed the ultimate source of grief for the ethnic Chinese in Indonesia, the same symbiosis is repeated elsewhere, in Malaysia, Thailand, the Philippines, etc. However, in Indonesia, the trouble for the Chinese minority was further complicated by the dubious role of the military, which was implicated in the 1998 riots and, more specifically, in the way the riots turned on their allegedly targeted victims in Jakarta, as later in East Timor and Aceh.[44] Admittedly, Indonesia is a country simultaneously plagued by sectarian violence, separatist movements, and political disarray complicated by an autonomous military. So, the racial problem confronting the ethnic Chinese there may be peculiarly acute. It remains true that only in Malaysia, among all the Malay-dominant Asian countries, was the Chinese minority able to secure an agreement on "power sharing" with the local ethnic majority (Antolik 1990, 30). Barring future similar developments elsewhere, racial conflicts similar to those that erupted in Indonesia in 1998 can be expected to recur, though not necessarily to the same degree of violence and destruction. I wish to point out, nonetheless, that any racial conflict, even if the ethnic Chinese should be the alleged targeted victim, will claim a gratuitous additional toll on other groups, including some members of the ethnic majority who happen to be in harm's way. In this sense, racial conflicts as such are a real, though occasional, harrying challenge to human security in Asian Pacific countries with a largely "bicommunal" make-up in their population.

Illicit drug trafficking is another source of human insecurity haunting the Asian region. The production and consumption of narcotic substances has a long history in East Asia. But several disturbing new developments have forced narcotics trafficking onto the regional security agenda for the first time (Dupont 1999).[45] First, once primarily a producer of heroin shipped to other parts of the world, East Asia has itself become a major heroin consumer and an emerging market for a new class of designer drugs such as "ice" and "ecstasy." Drug dependency in countries with no record of drug addiction in recent decades (e.g., China and Vietnam) is rising on an alarming rate. Secondly, narcotics trafficking is a new multibillion-dollar business in East Asia; it was probably the only enterprise not affected by the recent economic crisis. Drug money is distorting regional economies and exacerbating corruption and political instability.

In contrast to Latin America, noted for its illicit trade in cocaine, East Asia thrives in the heroin trade. Some 90 percent of the world's heroin hails from the Golden Triangle (Burma, Thailand, and Laos) and the Gold Crescent (Afghanistan, Iran, and Pakistan), although the latter is, geographically speaking, in South and Southwest Asia (Dupont, 437). The Golden Triangle region, which also accounts for 65 percent of all illicitly produced opium, sustains a heroine industry conservatively estimated to be worth at least U.S.$160 billion annually. This figure, incidentally, is four times the value of the world's total arms trade (438). Until the late 1980s, virtually all the heroin from the region went to the United States or other non-Asian markets. But today, much of it is destined for East Asia, where the number of addicts is on a continuing sharp rise.

While attention has been, though properly, directed to the effects of drug trafficking on the political stability (government integrity), social fabric, and economic well-being of the region, I wish, nevertheless, to stress the crushing blow to human security that stems from drug addiction. One only needs to heed to what happened to the Chinese nation. In 1773, the British took over the lead in opium trade from the Portuguese, when the East India Company established a monopoly of opium cultivation. Backed by the superior power at London's command, the British, who began by smuggling, were soon able to force an open opium trade down China's throat, enforced by two wars (1839 and 1856). American opium traders also cashed in on the lucrative trade.[46] Opium addiction spread throughout China like a prairie fire. The consequence was devastating.[47]

In short, China, which in 1800 was still a first-rate power accounting for 33 percent of the world manufacturing output, much larger than the U.S. share of world GDP today,[48] was reduced to a helpless weakling at the mercy of the outside world after opium addiction began to take root, even among the top echelons of society. Foreign powers forced their way into China and helped themselves to one concession after another from an already decrepit system under Manchu rule. China even lost control of its own customs autonomy to the British, not to mention the various slices of territory it had to cede to foreign powers under coercion—for instance, Hong Kong to Britain; Annam (today's Indochina) to France; Korea and Taiwan to Japan; a territory totaling 600,000 square miles (or eleven times the size of New York state) in Manchuria to Russia, etc. In addition, China had to pay huge indemnities after each defeat in the wars imposed by the powers that came practicing "gunboat diplomacy." In one instance alone, after China was defeated in the 1894–1895 war, the penalty payment was 200,000,000 taels of silver to Japan, in addition to cession of territories. Foreign powers also claimed extraterritorial consular jurisdiction in the scattered foreign settlements within China (principally in Shanghai), where Chinese laws could not reach. The end result was not only the collapse of the traditional imperial order, but that the Chinese nation had to endure for over a century and a half the scourge of emaciated health and, in serious cases, warped psyche. The international disrepute and contempt in which the Chinese nation was held, in the meantime, remotely anticipated a future militant Communist regime to surge to power—with a vengeance (cf. Houn 1973, ch. 1). The bottom line is that during the part of the history just recounted, the Chinese nation suffered from the endless assault of opium inflows from the world drug trade, which denied them their human security and chances for human development.

The sad thing is that though the old ex-systemic opium pushers (backed by the naked power of their government) are gone for good, they are replaced by the indigenous private drug traders in Asia today. The drug market has only expanded. One positive development, though, is that China and the United States are joining hands in the fight against illicit drug trafficking in the region. For a few years, Chinese and U.S. law-enforcement agencies have occasionally cooperated to stop contraband drug shipments. On June 19, 2000, the two countries signed an agreement to step up cooperation in the fight against illegal drugs, especially heroin and methamphetamine (*New York Times,* June 20, 2000, p. 11). Until such efforts become region-wide and have proven effective in stopping the drug trade, the widespread narcotics trafficking—and the drug dependency it helps to cultivate—will remain a horrific source of human insecurity in the Asia Pacific. Beyond the immediate step of international cooperation in interdicting the drug supplies, there is more work ahead in the rehabilitation of the addicts, which requires redoubled efforts by national governments in the region.

Other items on the agenda of enhancing human security and human development in the region are: empowerment of the people, wider democratization, and women's rights, which are in a way interrelated. Space will allow me only to touch on one of these items, the state of women's rights in Asian nations.

Contrary to the assumptions of the detractors of Confucian values, the worst case of women's rights is found in no other country than Japan, whose culture is predominantly Shinto-influenced and only residually Confucian. In fact, its Confucian content is probably the lowest among East and Southeast Asian nations. In Japan, the privileges of manhood are deeply entrenched still, more so than elsewhere in the region. In the job market, men are hired with the general assumption that they will build careers with their companies, women are typically separated into one of two categories—that is, *ippan shoku* (miscellaneous workers) and *sogo shoku* (a career track). The miscellaneous female workers, still legion in every Japanese ministry and large company, are typically in their 20s and dress in company uniforms or in smart clothing of their own. They smilingly direct visitors to their appointments and serve tea to guests. Some may do clerical work, sales, or accounting. But they will rarely rise above this lowly status and enter career tracks largely reserved for males.[49] Despite the passage of a landmark antidiscrimination law in 1985 and its reinforcement in 1999 with amendments that include sanctions against sexual harassment, many Japanese companies still maintain the separate-track personnel management system described above.

In a rare break with tradition, 23 women were elected members of the lower house of the Diet 1996. But the fact is that in a 1995 international survey of the proportion of women in parliaments in 161 countries, Japan ranked one hundred forty-fifth, with only 2.3 percent of the seats in the more influential lower house being occupied by women. Even with the 23 added in 1996, boosting woman representation to 4.37 percent, Japan ranked only around one hundred and twenty-first.[50] To say that women have a long way to go in Japanese politics is tantamount to saying that women's rights are still lagging far behind men's.

Similar problems confront women's rights elsewhere in the region, but they may not necessarily all result from the indigenous culture of the localities involved. In some cases, the problems may be traced back to an unfinished chapter in their colonial legacy. One of the two last places to exit from Western colonial rule in the region is Hong Kong, which may offer an example. In this former British colony, sexual discrimination against women continued to exist even after the New Territories ordinance that deprived women of land inheritance rights was amended in 1994 under the departing colonial government. According to an authority on the subject (Wu 1995, 194), the practices of discrimination against women resulting from the lack of equal opportunity protection by law—that is, practices that have been abolished in other Chinese societies—were "frozen in time by colonial ordinances" in Hong Kong. In addition to sexual discrimination, I might mention the long-standing colonial policy of tolerating concubinage as one of the things "frozen" in time. And, even after the enactment of the Bill of Rights, under the British post-1989 campaign to democratize on the verge of their 1997 departure, there were 50 existing laws that were inconsistent with the International Covenant for Civil and Political Rights, to which Hong Kong became a party as a British colony. Whatever was not rectified under the outgoing British colonial government devolved upon the post-handover government of the Hong Kong Special Administrative Region (SAR), after July 1, 1997.

But the thing is that, pending the final undoing of the injustices, the responsibility for the vestigial restrictions on these rights, including the rights of women, was on the SAR government's back. During the first year after Hong Kong was returned to China, the United Nations was already questioning the SAR government on its human-rights record. The list of 29 queries raised by a UN working group concerned exactly Hong Kong's failure to comply with the Convention on the Elimination of All Forms of Discrimination Against Women. Specifically, the list included women's land inheritance rights in the New Territories and the participation of women in politics and the public sector, which are part of the dark side of unmitigated, though often neglected, legacies from the long British colonial rule (Hsiung 2000, 318f).

Regardless of their origins, native culture, or vestiges of colonial neglect, such injustices against women's rights are a palpable challenge to a very real part of human security in the region.

PEACE AND SECURITY IN THE REGION

A NON-UNILINEAR REVIEW NEEDED

In order to have a truly sensible discussion of security of the traditional genre in the Asia Pacific region, we need be aware of two distinct perspectives. One is the usual unilinear view, seeing all things as having sprung from the same root substance and as following the same path. The other perspective, which questions this blind faith in the mono-genesis and uni-directionality of all things in all times and places is, in essence, anti-unilinear. For illustration, a metaphor may be found in the field of evolution theory. According to its adherents, the Darwinian model of evolution, which benefited from the method of classification pioneered by the great Swedish biologist Linnaeus, is supposedly applicable to all species in all cases. On the other hand, an alternative evolutionary paradigm is offered by Alfred Wallace, a contemporary of Darwin's, who exemplified the anti-unilinear view. The paradigm of this process is found in the giraffe, which, by reaching upward over a long period of time, somehow willed itself to lengthen its neck. The relevant lesson gained from this paradigm of acquired traits, despite the controversy and challenge mounted by its critics, is that one should always be keen on looking for an alternative explanation. In Wallace's case, the alternative explanation offered is something not reducible to the lottery of heredity or to the cruel vagaries of the environment, which are held to be the only truth that matters in the unilinear view (Iyer 1984, p.3). The skepticism inherent in this moral both represents and holds the key to a non-unilinear approach.

What is true of natural science is true of social science. As will be shown below, the non-unilinear perspective holds the potential of opening to us an alternative vista on developments in the Asian region that may reveal a categorically different meaning for crucial matters relating to the quest of peace and security.

Besides, I shall add the element of differences in "time horizons" (as shown below) as a distinguishing feature for the two perspectives just mentioned. Realization of this oft-neglected point will help sensitize us to the strategic utility of a non-unilinear discourse on the subject under review.

As Paul Bracken (2000, 147) notes, the year 1998 may look the same on the calendar to all nations on earth, but its meaning may be vastly different to them. For Asia, the year 1998 represented the five hundredth anniversary of Vasco da Gama's landing in India, an event that opened the West's infamous inroads in the region, a history that the West would rather have the world forget, just to save Western powers the embarrassment. Instead, he adds, the West spent the 1990s celebrating its victory in the Cold War. The new epoch, in this view, marked the spread of a Western form of triumphant globalization, a linking of economics and cultures; and in it "American values and norms would spread to countries who would willingly embrace the superior ways that gave the United States the world's greatest military force as well as the world's richest economy" (148).

The trouble with this view, Bracken cautions, is that "the post–Cold War era never came to Asia. It was a Western conceit." Without using the term "non-unilinear," Bracken suggests an alternative line of interpretation that holds that Asia and the West do not live in the same historical time zones (my term) and, hence, have different time horizons.[51] The very term "post–Cold War era," he notes, presumes that the U.S.-Soviet struggle was the central event of our time and that its end marked a completely new beginning for the entire world. But the Cold War was not a world war; and in Asia, the Cold War was not merely different from that in Europe; it was also less important, observes Bracken, adding: "The central motor of Asia's history in the twentieth century was *postcolonialism,* the efforts of China, Vietnam, India, Iran, and others to create viable nation-states after the long period of foreign rule" or foreign dominations in China's case (148, emphasis added).

To carry Bracken's thought one step further, we may say that throughout the East and Southeast Asian region, the second half of the century just past ushered in a new era in which, with the rare exception of Japan, all nations—both the newly independent states and China and Thailand (the only two other independent Asian states before the end of World War II)—share a jubilance over the demise of colonial rule or, as in the Chinese case, the end of Western "imperialist" dominance. Postcolonial nationalism and the tasks of state- and nation-building that go along with it, in contrast to the technology-led search for power in the West, lie at the heart of all social and political pursuits in postcolonial Asia[52] and underscore all security concerns as well. In modern China, the prime mover is its peculiar nationalism, *rekindled* following the collapse of the traditional order at home and the departure of foreign domination[53] and further abetted under Communist rule; and its tasks are state and nation *rebuilding.* For the Chinese nation, the overwhelming question is whether China's national independence and territorial integrity can be upheld against any more encroachments after a century and a half of prostration at the hands of foreign powers.

All this contrasts with the Western belief that nationalism is passe in an era in which sovereignty in the Westphalian state-centric system is being eroded in favor of the rise of the individual and the mounting importance of nonsovereign actors. To people living in the Western historical time zone, and looking through the Western time-horizon lenses, a bewilderment is why, with few exceptions, Asian state-building fueled by postcolonial or rekindled nationalism has produced political institutions that are too strong for their liking. Even worse, this state-building drive is often accompanied by a high degree of assertiveness, even militancy. An extreme example was Sukarno's Indonesia with its *konfrontasi* policy, going to war with Malaysia in 1963–1966 (Antolik, 1990, 18f).

But in comparable times of history (another "time zone"), let us recall, the end of medieval bondage in Europe ushered in a period of state absolutism both on the continent and in Tudor England (under the rule of Henry VII, Henry VIII, and Elizabeth). And, the Napoleonic wars followed, not preceded, the French Revolution, in the wake of which French nationalism took flight.[54] The Japanese military adventures abroad in the early decades of the twentieth century, likewise, came in the wake of a nationalistic upsurge that began with the Meiji Reform dynamism of the late nineteenth century (cf. Mansfield and Snyder 1995, 85f).

Other examples of assertiveness powered by nationalism, though of the rekindled sort, were China's armed conflicts with the Soviet Union over Zhenbao/Damansky Island (1969), and with Vietnam (1974 and 1988) and the Philippines (1995) over the outlying islands in the South China Sea. But rather than acts of calculated expansionism, as is often assumed in the West, these instances of nationalistic spurt were in defense of self-perceived sovereign territorial interests (China's participation in the Korean War was at the behest of Stalin[55]). So is the Taiwan issue in the same category, as we shall see below. So, too, does postcolonial nationalism provide a grammar for understanding the developments across contemporary Southeast Asia, as Benedict Anderson (1998) has shown in his expert comparative study that covers both domestic politics and international situations such as East Timor.

Even the Korean anomaly over the past half a century can be understood in the same context, in that the peninsula is saddled with what may be called "one nationalism, but two states." Postcolonial Korean nationalism, which surged following the peninsula's emancipation from the clutch of Japanese colonial rule at the end of World War II, cries out for national reunification. But by a twist of history beyond their control, two Korean states were created by international forces directed from Moscow and Washington (Kim and Cho 1976). Hence, in this sense, the Korean War (1950–1953) was a foolhardy crash attempt, with Stalin's blessings, by North Korea's Kim Il-Sung to reunify the peninsula by force, waged in desperation because of U.S. military support for South

Korea. While unrelenting tension continued on the peninsula ever since the Armistice of 1953, it was Korean nationalism that eventually proved to be the healer, after the relentless passage of time. Precisely because both Koreas shared the same nationalistic sentiments, it was possible for just a handshake and three hours of talks in Pyongyang, on June 15, 2000, between President Kim Dae Jung of South Korea and Kim Jong Il, who succeeded his father as North Korea's paramount leader in 1994, to reach a broad agreement on reconciliation in 50 years hence (*New York Times,* June 15, 2000, p. 1).

What about the North Korean nuclear missile threat? Yes, that, too, can fit into this postcolonial nationalism thesis. Two reasons are behind North Korea's nuclear program. First, until withdrawn in 1991, the United States had tactical nuclear weapons in South Korea, posing what Pyongyang perceived as a threat that must be responded to in kind, although the country's resources were stretched to the breaking point.[56] Second, in a distorted logic, the North Koreans claim their missile force is directed against Japan, the target of the nationalistic ire of all Koreans. Despite their ideological differences, both South Korea and North Korea share a strong resentment against Japan for the atrocities they had endured under its colonial rule during 1910–1945. For instance, the plight of the "comfort women," an issue concerning wartime Japanese army brothels using abducted Korean (as well as other Asian) young women as sex slaves, is the one issue that readily rallies both Koreas on the same side against the Japanese. When the North Koreans tested their guided missile in August 1998, by design it flew over the airspace of Japan. One wonders, though, other than venting a pent-up nationalistic fury, what constructive purpose this ostentatious act of intimidation would serve. Indeed, it has only boomeranged, as it galvanized the Japanese into seeking anti-missile help from the United States, which resulted in pumping U.S.$8.5 million into joint research on developing a joint theatre missile defense (TMD) system.[57] But who says nationalism is not blind at times?

However, unlike the Napoleonic wars (1796–1815) and Japanese overseas adventures of the 1930s through 1940s, which were expansionist strikes, or, in blunt language, naked acts of aggression, these Asian postcolonial conflicts just mentioned were localized wars fought with the limited goal of safeguarding one's territorial rights under challenge. North Korea's missile program may arguably be an exception, even though to what extent it is a prelude to a premeditated aggression of a kind resembling the Napoleonic wars or Japan's Pacific War is not so clear. The nationalist force propelling the latter two, earlier instances of armed adventures abroad, it bears noting, was decidedly different from the postcolonial nationalism that underscored the localized Asian conflicts just mentioned. Parenthetically, the Vietnam War was an extension into Asian territory of the otherwise extraneous Cold War between the two superpowers, hence an exception, although the unanticipated valor with which the North Vietnamese fought to final victory, against all odds, probably reflected the power released by a fierce postcolonial nationalism that stemmed from Vietnam's emancipation from French colonial rule. It remains true that in no case did we find that postcolonial nationalism in contemporary Asia Pacific powered any outright aggression like Saddam Hussein's invasion and annexation of Kuwait in 1990.

Below, I am going to argue that, to the total neglect of the depth and implications of the force of postcolonial nationalism in the region, Washington tends to treat the kind of occasional flashes of Asian postcolonial nationalism as sinister acts of aggression. The consequential U.S. overreaction has led to a "security dilemma," or the spiral of an escalating arms race, with the typical result that every state ends up less secure than before.

Understanding this point holds the key to knowing what to make of the region's international relations (including its members' bilateral relations with the United States) and, above all, the peace and security issues concerning both the region and the United States.

When viewed in the alternative light (a non-unilinear view) just suggested, everything takes on a new meaning. For instance, the habitual list of the remaining "flash points" in the east Asian region, as assessed from the U.S. point of view, includes: the Korean Peninsula, the South China Sea, and the Taiwan Strait. To Washington, these are geopolitical challenges to U.S. security interests in Asia in the post–Cold War era. But from the time horizon of postcolonial nationalism, all three cases look differently. We have already addressed the first two of the three flash points above; let us next turn to the Taiwan Strait situation.

The Taiwan issue, in the final analysis, is one that figures prominently in the collective Chinese urge for national integration and reunification, a cherished goal of their rekindled nationalism. Rightly or wrongly, the question is wrapped up in China's apprehensions about perceived external forces bent on promoting separatism in Tibet, Xinjiang, and Taiwan.[58] Seen from mainland Chinese nationalistic lenses, Taiwan became a bastion of a contending Chinese regime (the Republic of China) in 1949, after Chiang Kai-shek's government lost the civil war on the mainland and withdrew to the island, which it had recovered, only four years before, from Japan per wartime Allied agreement.

During Deng Xioaping's lifetime, three places claimed by China remained to be reunited with the mainland, Hong Kong, Macao, and Taiwan. In rapid succession, however, Hong Kong and Macao were returned to Chinese sovereignty in the last years of the twentieth century (1997 and 1999), from under long foreign colonial rule of the British and the Portuguese, respectively. Taiwan, in Beijing's view, is the last piece of "lost" territory yet to be brought back under the sovereign umbrella of all China. Although the island was returned in 1945 to China under Chiang Kai-shek's government, the Communist regime in Beijing, installed in 1949 after it chased out the Chiang Kai-shek government from the mainland, has never been able to set foot on it. Hence, Beijing's emphasis on acceptance of the "one China" principle as a prior condition for any peaceful deals with Taiwan's increasingly recalcitrant authorities.

The United States, per its own Taiwan Relations Act (TRA) of 1979, is under a self-imposed obligation to help in the defense of Taiwan's security against any external attempt to change the island's existing status by force. Washington, thus, is perceived by Beijing to be blocking China's bid to reunite with the island, because the U.S. protective shield by itself could, and does, give aid and comfort to separatist forces seeking Taiwan's secession from the "one China" orbit. At the time of President Richard M. Nixon's historic visit to China in 1972, "all Chinese on either side of the Taiwan Strait maintain that there is but one China and that Taiwan is a part of China," to which position the United States did not object, or so declared the U.S. side in the Shanghai Communiqué. This document, which Nixon signed while in China, and the next communiqué, dated December 15, 1978, announcing the normalization of Sino-U.S. relations, during the Carter Administration, had an identical commitment to the "one China" principle. And, the principle was embraced as the first premise in the TRA as well. The U.S. expectation was that the Taiwan problem was to be settled by the Chinese themselves through peaceful means.

What has changed since then is that Taiwan's own commitment to the "one China" principle has come under question ever since its President, Lee Teng-hui, in a surprising statement on July 9, 1999, described Taiwan's relations with mainland China as "state to state," in what has come to be known as the maverick "two states" theory. From Beijing's standpoint, the situation was getting even worse after an opposition candidate, Chen Shui-bian, was elected Taiwan's new President on March 18, 2000. Chen's party, the Democratic Progressive Party (DPP), has a standing platform seeking Taiwan's separatist independence from China. Hence, his election cast a pall over cross-strait relations, as Beijing threatened to resort to force if Taiwan should spurn the peaceful negotiations route that would be possible only under the one-China principle and opt for a separatist course.

The latest confrontation across the Taiwan Strait presents a dilemma for the United States, caught between its TRA-mandated obligations to look after Taiwan's security and its reluctance to be dragged into an armed conflict with China for the sake of Taiwan. Washington's fears were, thus far, singularly fixated on Beijing's militant stance and likely action on Taiwan. The other side of the coin, however, is that the chances of the United States being dragged into an unwanted war with mainland China could likewise be precipitated by Taiwan if its new president, counting on his island's support on Capitol Hill and under the TRA, should play a calculated game of brinkmanship. In mid-July 2000, for example, a squadron of Taiwan's airforce fighters sneaked into mainland China airspace under the cover of night, only to withdraw when met by mainland PLA airforce interceptors.[59] While the incident was denied by Taipei, it jived with Taiwan's new strategy of "extra-territorial (i.e., outside the island) warfare" that President Chen's brain trust had crafted, which ordains carrying the war to enemy territory (i.e., the Chinese mainland).[60]

But the bottom line is that the Chinese on both sides of the Taiwan Strait are in control of their own destiny. Taiwan's own nativist nationalism, first fanned by its emancipation from Japanese colonial rule, has received a new fillip from its belated democratization drive, begun in 1986. If democratic theory is to be trusted, democratizing regimes, as distinct from either existing democracies or autocracies, are by far the most war-prone, and their increased war-proneness is the highest during the tenth year of democratization (Mansfield and Snyder 1995). In Taiwan's history since 1945, the only time that it came closest to a hot war with the mainland was in 1996, or ten years after its democratization drive began.[61] If its new government should misconstrue its electoral mandate from the March 2000 election as one supporting the DPP's policy of seeking Taiwan's separatist independence (in fact, Chen received only 36.9 percent of the vote), it could invite catastrophe. The forces of "postcolonial" nationalism in China are still riding high,[62] and there seems to be no way that Beijing's leaders could sit idly by if and when Taiwan should choose to openly sever its political umbilical chord with mainland China.

Should the United States, in the ensuing Taiwan Strait conflict, intervene for the island's sake as if the one-China premise embraced by the TRA had not changed, it would only be a misstep with catastrophic consequences. The outcome of a direct U.S. war, possibly a nuclear one, with mainland China fought for Taiwan's sake would please no one, not even the Taiwanese, if it meant being caught in a nuclear "crossfire." Should that happen, the culprit would be a failure in statesmanship on Washington's part, for having mistaken a Chinese national reunification coup, staged as a last resort, for an assumed act of aggression against a faithful U.S. client (Taiwan). It would also demonstrate the confusion of a quixotic Taiwanese separatist venture—an avoidable risk-taking—for an alleged journey to freedom, as Taiwan's lobby on Capitol Hill likes to trumpet. If that nightmare should come true, it would offer one more piece of evidence why on matters of peace and security in the Asia Pacific, the West's unilinear conception of a post–Cold War technology-led search for naked power should not be transposed by sheer faith.

A Security Dilemma in East Asia and Beyond

The theory of security dilemma is usually applied from a unilinear perspective. But in our discussion here, I will show that its truthfulness is only further complicated by looking across different historical time zones, as each side reacts from its own disparate time horizon. This is exactly what happens in U.S. security relations in Asia—including South Asia and East Asia, and possibly beyond.

Before proceeding any further, let me explain briefly, for the uninitiated, what is meant by "security dilemma." In conditions of anarchy (i.e., absence of a world government), states must rely on their own means to protect their security and independence. In doing so, however, their search for security becomes a cause of insecurity for others. As each state arms itself against its overbearing neighbors, or to cope with the perceived threats of "rogue" states (now called "states of concern"), the latter respond in kind by increasing their own armaments as they see fit. An arms race ensues from the competitive round of arms buildup thus set in motion. This "security dilemma," a term coined by John Herz (1950, 157–180), can be best summed up in two truisms: (1) one state's security may mean another state's insecurity; and (2) the state whose initial arms buildup at time-1 set off the competitive round of arms buildups may find itself, at time-n, less secure than before.

In Northeast Asia, for instance, the presence of U.S. tactical missiles, until their removal in 1991, provided a rationale, rightly or wrongly, for the North Koreans to develop their own nuclear weapons in protecting their own security, as noted above. But as a latecomer and given its limited resources, North Korea had to do what Microsoft, a late starter in its own right, has done in competing with IBM, the world's undisputed computer giant. Instead of competing on the same grounds of hardware and circuits, on which IBM is unbeatable, Microsoft chose to shift to software and bits, in which IBM's vaunted competencies were much thinner. In fact, IBM's advantage, its lead in technology, actually worked against it, serving to channel corporate energies into varying existing hardware while not even recognizing the new danger until it was too late (Bracken 2000, 151). Likewise, instead of competing for better tanks and airplanes, let alone inter-continental ballistic missiles (ICBMs)—all of them America's long suit—North Korea, like other "rogues," chose to develop weapons of mass destruction (WMD) and the ballistic missiles to deliver them. If developing an arsenal as such makes North Korea a "rogue" state, then there are now at least eight of them in Asia. Israel, Syria, Iraq (if ever it escapes UN sanctions), Iran, Pakistan, India, China, and North Korea are all reorienting their militaries from infantry to disruptive technologies. Looking at the geographical distribution of this list of eight, one wonders why to many in Washington the powder kegs are not so much in the Middle East and South Asia, as in Northeast Asia!

Since the Vietnam War, U.S. strategy eschews involvement in land warfare in a far-off place, which might risk loss of public support at home if the war drags on and battle deaths mount (Scott and Stam 1998). Instead, there has been a shift toward reliance on air strikes with smart bombs that can be used in operations of short duration involving low human casualties, such as in Desert Storm over Iraq in 1991 and Kosovo in 1999. This shift makes the United States overwhelmingly dependent on overseas forward bases, such as Saudi Arabia and Italy in the two campaigns, respectively.

From the time horizon of the "rogue states," it only makes sense for them to develop a formidable ballistic missile force in their counterstrategy, because foreign forward bases are America's Achilles' heel. Ballistic missiles would make these bases, once symbols of U.S. power, virtual hostages to missile attack (Bracken 2000, 153). It is as though the "rogue states" are playing Microsoft to America's IBM. And, like Microsoft, they will have an edge for as long as Washington does not change its "mainframe" strategy.

In order not to let this Asian ballistic missile and WMD strategy trump the West's technological lead in military showdowns, Washington's reflex is to reach for antiballistic defense. But since Washington will never be able to protect its allies, South Korea, Japan, or Saudi Arabia, without also protecting itself, a Theatre Missile Defense (TMD) system must be supported by a National Missile Defense (NMD) system.[63] Typical of the security dilemma syndrome, however, the target states at which the TMD system is implicitly or explicitly aimed are actually served notice by Washington that they, regardless of their independent will, have no choice but to step up their own ballistic missile program to counter the TMD challenge. Since in developing its TMD system the United States risks violating the 1972 Anti-Ballistic Missile Treaty unless Russia gives its concurrence, something President Vladimir Putin has refused to grant, Washington has no moral ground to demand that India, Iran, China, and North Korea scrap their respective ballistic missile programs and stop proliferation (Bracken 2000, 154).

From the U.S. time horizon, the whole idea of a missile defense system is conceived out of a need to protect American troops and interests in Asia as well as to shield the continental United States. The irony is that it violates a critical requirement in nuclear deterrence, that neither side, in mirror image, be denied the capability to deter a preemptive strike.[64] The side that has a fool-proof shield system has a decided advantage of launching a preemptive strike with impunity, because the opponent's retaliatory second strike will fail to inflict the expected pain and damage, the surety of which is the necessary guarantee against a first strike in the first place. Thus far, China and Russia, supported by the five Central Asian states, have vigorously lodged their opposition to the TMD idea (*New York Times,* July 19, 2000, p. 6). At the G-8 foreign ministers meeting, held in Okinawa while the annual G-8 Meeting was going on, all but the U.S. Secretary of State were opposed to the deployment of the TMD system (*Japan Times Weekly,* July 22, 2000, p. 4). So have many independent analysts dissented on the same ground. For one, Greg May (2000, 1), assistant director of the conservative think tank Nixon Center, points out that the TMD system does more than arouse Chinese suspicion that the United States is more interested in solidifying its absolute strategic advantage than in achieving meaningful arms control, thus freeing China to step up its own military armaments. In addition, by the rumored likelihood that Taiwan may participate in the TMD or otherwise receive its protection, it also unnecessarily alarms China that gratuitous encouragement from the U.S. protective shield may egg Taiwan on in fearless pursuit of a divergent course of no return. This prospect will make the goal of reunification all the more elusive and, worse, may force China to consider preemptive strikes against Taiwan to stop its separatist drift before it is too late[65]—strikes that the United States seeks to avert in the first place.

What is more, just as the TMD offers powerful incentives for China, among others, to expand its military capability, including upgrading its missile force and acquiring an anti-carrier missile capability,[66] China's move could prompt India and Pakistan, both of which have detonated their nuclear devices recently, to do likewise (Hiebert and Lawrence 2000, 17).

The ultimate irony is that the United States, which was the first one to commit its superior technology into building a most modern, hopefully invincible, military arsenal, designed to assure maximum security to

both itself and its allies, will paradoxically find itself less secure than before at time-n, after the ensuing round of competitive arms races. This
outcome becomes all the more true because the alleged "rogue states,"
and others that feel likewise threatened, choose to play Microsoft to
America's IBM position. Since this competitive round of induced arms
buildup is anticipated by the security dilemma theory, hence preventable,
the question remains: Why does all this paradox come to pass regardless?
The answer lies in Washington's uncontrollable urge for global supremacy, which is understandably an irresistible temptation. As Bracken
(2000, 155) notes, in Asia today, aside from Japan,[67] no Asian country
has yet mounted a technological military challenge to the West. But if the
United States continues to press forward with its overbearing military
expansions, NMD and TMD and what have you, the world can expect
more such challenges in return in the future, which may not be confined
to the Asian region alone. The ultimate irony is that the real source of instability in the Asian region does not rest in the ballistic missile buildup
of the "rogue states" but ultimately in what has caused the competitive
round of the missile-buildup race to go forward in the first place. Such is
the truth of a security dilemma!

CONCLUSION

In this chapter, we have traced the modern rise to global prominence of
the Asia Pacific from its centuries-old obscurity as a region. Its impressive economic success, reaching miraculous proportions, became a common object of envy for many in other regions. Some Western analysts
trained in orthodox neoclassical economics may have had an ax to grind
about the East Asian "developmental state" model. But a wide range of
other analysts had, on the basis of the high performance of the Asian
economies, forecast that the twenty-first century would be the Pacific
Century.

The financial crisis of 1997–1998 brought chaos to the health of the
Asian economies, whose miraculous success had defied the law of laissez
faire. The crisis also gave critics a gratuitous occasion to mount their
sniper attacks on the Asian model itself. The meanest of them all, substituting momentary wishful thinking for stark reality, gleefully trumpeted that all Asian Tigers were "skinned and stuffed." Some visceral
cynics readily ran obituaries on the death of Asian values. But the irony
is that, against all dire Western predictions, including those of the IMF,
which had foreseen years of struggle ahead before the region could ever
stand back on its own feet again, recovery was both comparatively speedy
and widespread. By early 1999, impressive growths were reported even

among the five worst hit countries. History has mercilessly made fun of these "people of little faith" in Asian values.

We have also noted that the Asian region has emerged stronger, certainly better prepared to ward off future attacks from turbulence in the global capital markets. One common measure taken by almost all Asian nations was the adoption of more, not less, control of their financial and assets markets, contrary to the counsels of the globalization advocates, including the IMF. The crisis has shown that unsafeguarded liberalization, or naked openness to the flows of globalized capital, is the best recipe for placing one's own fate at the mercy of the "casino effects" of hot money moving in and out, as well as the willful manipulation by international profiteers. We have also seen that the crisis was not really caused by deep-seated internal structural-cultural defects, as had initially been speculated. Even Paul Krugman, the foremost critic whose early bold castigation of the Asian model predated the crisis and who at the beginning of the crisis had diagnosed internal flaws as the culprit for the financial attack that sent the region's robust economies diving nose down, had to recant openly by 1999. He did so with courage and disarming honesty.

We have also discussed various aspects of "comprehensive security" and noted that the region shares a lot in common with the global scene, but that it also has its own idiosyncratic problems, such as recurrent forest fires in Indonesia both as a health hazard and an environmental scourge, and the rise in drug trafficking, threatening the human security of the region. To this can be added the little-noticed trouble of piracy, which is both a growing barrier to maritime trade and a threat to human security (Dillion 2000), and is unparalleled elsewhere. While the aging problem is universal in the region, as elsewhere, the severity of it in Japan is the most acute on a world scale.[68]

In addition, our discussion extended to security of the traditional genre. This, in our view, is a subject that can be comprehended fully only if one adopts a non-unilinear perspective on the region. In this regard, we have proposed the thesis that the region's peace and security issues be placed in the larger context of postcolonial nationalism, with the exception of Japan, which was itself a colonial power before the end of World War II. We have noted that state-building and sensitivity about sovereign territorial rights (and in China's case, the tasks are state rebuilding and national integration and reunification, after having resurfaced from over a century and half of Western domination) may explain most of what has transpired both domestically and in external relations. State-building, which has bred a habitual proclivity for strong governments at home, is basically an inward-looking enterprise. The inward-looking bent thus created may explain, in addition, why there have been scanty efforts to build region-wide institutions like NATO, the Western European Union (WEU), and the Organization of Security and Cooperation in Europe (OSCE), not to mention the European Union (EU), in Europe since the end of World War II. As is shown in chapters 6 and 7 below, the ASEAN and APEC are no comparison. There is obviously no commonly felt need for such security institutions as have been found in Europe, precisely because all conflicts in the region have been localized flare-ups associated with, and typical of, the postcolonial nationalistic concerns in defense of sovereign territorial rights, not outright acts or threats of aggression such as those posed by the Soviet bloc in Europe during the Cold War. Even the Taiwan Strait problem, potentially the most explosive issue affecting the security of all nations in East and Southeast Asia (Lee Kuan Yew 2000, 16), fits into the category of post-colonial national reunification—if "postcolonial" in the case of China means after the end of domination in Asia by external colonial powers (in 1895 Taiwan was ceded by a coerced China to Japan, and remained as a Japanese colony until 1945).

The discussion of postcolonial nationalism points to certain conclusions: First, the conflicts due to postcolonial reflexes, as mentioned above, are not of a category on a par with hegemonic wars (i.e., wars that determine which state or states will be dominant and will govern the system).[69] Even the strong governments that have emerged from the post-colonial state-building in the region do not approach the totalitarian proportions of Nazi Germany or Stalinist Soviet Union, much less exhibit their expansive obsession in foreign policy. The reason for this is, to reiterate, that postcolonial governments are preoccupied with the inward-looking enterprise of state- and nation-building (or rebuilding); they are, as a whole, not externally directed, unless provoked. Even the Communist regime in China has not proven much different, as has been shown in its history since 1949. Under Mao, China was riveted on domestic ideological campaigns, no matter how abominable they may have been; and since Deng, China has been preoccupied with its domestic economic reform and development. Foreign involvement was almost an aberration under Mao and has been justified largely by its linkage to domestic economic growth since Deng.

Secondly, however, if there is anything to this postcolonial thesis, Japan should be seen differently. We have noted that Japan has become more assertive in recent years, to the alarm of the region's other nations that have experienced Japanese aggression and atrocities during World War II.[70] And, since at least 1995, many Japanese, especially in Okinawa, have unabashedly agitated against the United States in their unreserved opposition to the continuing presence of U.S. troops on Japanese bases.[71] To the extent that these are indicative of a renewed nationalism of sorts, it is nationalism of a revanchist variation, directed mainly against the United States, the victor in the Pacific War that had inflicted on Japan the disgrace of defeat and unconditional surrender. Revanchism is different from the postcolonial nationalism of the rest of the region. Since this topic deserves a separate book, I will not say anything more except to suggest that those who are truly concerned with peace and security in East Asia in the new century should look into how revanchist assertiveness differs from postcolonial nationalist assertiveness. The first puzzle to crack is the steady inordinate increases in Japanese annual defense budgets, which since the end of the Cold War in 1990 have remained the world's third highest, or over three times that of the Chinese,[72] despite the fact that China has a territory 25 times bigger to defend and has 10 times as much population. The next puzzle is the rising support in Japan for amending, possibly removing, the renunciation-of-war clause (Article 9) of the Japanese postwar Constitution imposed by the U.S. Occupationaires.[73]

In addition, the last section in this chapter dealt with a peculiar security dilemma that is both explicable and avoidable. Explicable because it is a natural outcome of a mutual misreading of intentions between actors in two disparate time zones. It is avoidable because if our security managers were alert to the inherent different nature of postcolonial conflicts and pursuits, in contradistinction to the ordinary expansionist acts in the quest of glory and power, their strategic response would probably have been different, thus obviating the vicious spiral of the arms buildup that has resulted. We have argued that both China's urge for reunification with Taiwan and North Korea's past foolhardy attempt to reunify the Korean peninsula by force are typical flashes, or outbursts, of postcolonial nationalism. All this is different from what has motivated aggressive ventures like Germany's in both world wars and Japan's in the Pacific War (1941–1945), which really began in 1931, if the China phase of the Kwantung Army's overseas adventures is counted. Coming to grips with this convoluted reality requires, in the final analysis, both a non-unilinear perspective and a firm grasp of Asian history and culture beyond the restaurant level, which can come only through methodical comparisons across disparate time horizons.

NOTES

1. The eight include the four NIE's (Korea, Taiwan, Hong Kong, and Singapore), ASEAN-3 (Thailand, Malaysia, and Indonesia), among members of

the Association of Southeast Asian Nations, and China. See the World Bank 1993, 1.

2. Cf. Prybyla 2000, 70.

3. Criticisms of the IMF bail-out behavior during the crisis were widespread. See, for example, Feldstein 1998; Calomiris 1998, and Vasquez 1998. Even the World Bank came out criticizing the IMF's response, which among other things made bank interest hikes a condition for IMF bail-out to countries in trouble. *Xinbao* [Hong Kong Economic Journal], 4 December 1998, 8. The high-interest requirement caused many small and medium-sized companies to go bankrupt, making the economic meltdown worse.

4. See ADB 2000.

5. See Lu Jiang, "Hong Kong's Economy in the Three Years Since Reversion," *The Mirror Monthly,* no. 276 (July 2000): 15. But in a private communication, Lok-sang Ho, who is also a contributor to this volume, expressed his apprehension about the continuing "weakened growth" of Hong Kong, because it was mainly export-led.

6. The survey, conducted by an arm of the *Economist* in London, was reported in the *World Journal* (a Chinese-language newspaper in New York), May 15, 2000, p. D2.

7. *Renmin ribao* (People's Daily), overseas edition, July 25, 2000, p. 2.

8. Of the many extant studies I know, the one by a group headed by Karyiu Wong (1999) provides detailed chronologies for seven economies in the region (Thailand, Malaysia, Indonesia, South Korea, Taiwan, Hong Kong, and Japan) and "country reports" for five (Indonesia, Hong Kong, Malaysia, Japan, and Taiwan). Another study by Giancarlo Corsetti, et al. (1998), offers analyses on nine members of the region, including China and the Philippines, which are not covered by Wong, but not Japan, which is addressed by Wong.

9. For a relatively reliable account of what happened leading to the crisis and what lay ahead for developing countries after the crisis, see World Bank 1998/1999.

10. For a most representative articulation of the "crony capitalism" thesis, see Dittmer 1999.

11. Although they raided in the dark, in the absence of international rules of regulation, what happened in Thailand was a typical example. International institutional speculators (e.g., hedge funds), pulling together their resources, bought the local currency (the baht) short in huge volumes and then dumped it on the market when the government's low reserves rendered it unable to defend the currency. When the currency fell, the speculators made a kill and ran with their money.

12. Cf. World Bank 1998/1999, 71, table 215.

13. Following the 1985 Plaza Accords. See Lorne Johnson 1998, 117.

14. The Korean government, in a change of heart, did allow more open access to domestic markets by foreign banks and insurance companies. But

it at the same time required improvement in corporate and state disclosure to increase the transparency of the financial system, so as to upgrade government's ability to control such matters as overborrowing, a crucial cause for Korea's succumbing to the financial contagion. See Sikorski 1999, 120.

15. The dollar peg was introduced in August 1983 in an atmosphere of political crisis, shortly after Sino-UK negotiations started on the return of Hong Kong to China, to shore up confidence in the Hong Kong dollar. The peg fixed the conversion rate of HK$7.8 to the dollar.

16. By July 2, 1997, the Thai government had spent a staggering U.S.$23 billion, or practically all of its foreign reserves, buying baht in a vain attempt to maintain the dollar peg, but to no avail. Hence, devaluation of the baht was the only resort. In the Thai case, the dollar appreciation was a decisive factor when the peg went from a blessing to a curse. See Winters 1998, 421.

17. During the height of the crisis, Asian analysts emphasized external factors, such as speculation by mammoth international hedge funds, while outside commentators tended to blame it on endogenous causes. For a more balanced view, see Asia Development Research Forum (ADRF) Hong Kong meeting, 18–19 May 1998, *Summary of Discussions,* a copy of which is in my personal files. Selected readings for the conference could be sourced from the Asia Crisis Home page Web site of Nouriel Roubini: http://www.stern.nyu.edu/- nroubini/asia/AsiaHomepage.html. Also see Montes 1998. In view of the declaration of war by George Soros's Quantum Fund on Hong Kong's financial market (*South China Morning Post,* 28 August 1998, p. l), it would be hard to maintain that the region's financial crisis was solely brought on by domestic woes, however.

18. It is necessary to note that the recovery was "speedy" relative to forecasts by the IMF and other sources that had seen years, even decades, before the region could stand back on its feet again. I would also add that in the midst of recovery reports, not every country recovered at the same rate and speed. Thailand and Indonesia, for instance, were among the tardier recovering economies. I am thankful to David Denoon, my colleague at New York University, for this point.

19. The five indexes are: GDP growth rate, interest rate, inflation rate, external debt to GDP ratio, and the exchange rate.

20. On the postwar Japanese triumvirate, see Tsurutani 1977, 71ff.

21. See "A Mine Full of Possibilities," *Far Eastern Economic Review* (13 July 2000): 62.

22. I owe a debt to Dr. Xiangdong Wei, in the Department of Economics, Lingnan University, Hong Kong, for this information, including how the international hedge funds operated.

23. As reported in "Asian Monetary Fund a Step Closer," *The Nation,* a Thai independent online news and information service; at: wysiwyg://17/http://www./-nationmultimedia.com/new/05aa06.shtml.

24. As reported in *New York Times,* May 1, 2000, Special Advertising Supplement on Malaysia, p. 8.
25. In the wake of the crisis, Asian nations seem more disposed to cooperation over competition than before. Malaysia and Singapore, for instance, were prepared to bury their old hatchets and redirect their usually rocky relationship over the past three decades, because they both saw advantage in working together to fend off future attacks by international financial predators. See "Bridge Over Troubled Waters," *Far Eastern Economic Review* (October 5, 2000): 26.
26. For a discussion that the world that emerges from the crisis will likely be different from that which entered the crisis, see Dan Ciuriac 1999, esp. p. 70. For a general discussion of globalization and the Asia Pacific, see Kris Olds et al. 1999.
27. The Heritage Foundation, for example, in a Backgrounder (No. 1150, dated 5 December 1997), branded the "Asian miracle" a mirage and declared the IMF bailout would not work. So, in effect, the Asian success model was finished.
28. Eric Jones, "Asia's Fate: A Response to the Singapore School," *The National Interest,* 35 (spring 1994):18–28. In parts of this discussion, I am relying on Subramaniam 2000.
29. In the Singaporean view, Western liberal democracy is only one variant, among many, of democratic systems of government. See Kausikan 1998, 17.
30. To what extent Indonesia suffers from social instability because its culture is not Confucian is a moot question bordering on racism. But it would be tantalizing to ask whether there is any correlation between Indonesia's lack of social stability and its lagging behind other Asian nations in economic development.
31. Cf. Subramaniam 2000, 24.
32. Defenders of liberal democracy consider communitarianism to be the culprit for what they call "illiberal democracy." See Fox 1997, 561; and in general Bell 1996, and Zakaria 1997.
33. For a fascinating exposition of the postwar *keiretsu* system in the Japanese business and finance community, see Michael Gerlach 1992.
34. Everything Ezra Vogel (1979) described about postwar Japanese system seems to be a replica of Dower's wartime Japan.
35. This is not to mention the remnants of the war criminals who escaped punishment with the early termination of the Tokyo Trials. Some of them, such as Shintaro Iishihara, ex-Dietman and Governor of Tokyo, rejected repentance and continued to deny that Japan's wartime crimes, from the Rape of Nanking (when over 300,000 Chinese civilians were massacred in two weeks by the Japanese Kwantung Army) to biological warfare in China to the Comfort Women offenses against many Asian victim nations of Japanese aggression, had ever happened. For an independent account of Japanese wartime biological warfare in China, see

Sheldon Harris, *Factories of Death: Japanese Biological Warfare, 1932–45, and the American Cover-Up* (London and New York: Routledge, 1994).

36. In fact, the reforms imposed by the U.S. Occupation helped to further strengthen the power of the Japanese bureaucracy, after they had removed powerful politicians tainted with the war guilt, smashed the military, dispossessed the landlords, and crushed the labor movement. On the strengthening of the Japanese bureaucracy's power under U.S. occupation, see Yanaga 1964, 307ff.

37. In our usage, the term "Asia Pacific" refers mainly to countries in East Asia and Southeast Asia, though it occasionally extends to actors on the eastern half of the Pacific Rim, principally North America. We follow the usual usage of the "Pacific Basin," when reference is made to the tiny island states, ranging from Fiji, Tonga, to Papua New Guinea, that dot the Pacific Ocean, although occasionally we may extend the concept to include the Pacific Rim.

38. An "archipelagic state" is defined in Article 46 of the 1982 Law of the Sea Treaty as "a State constituted wholly by one or more archipelagos and may include other islands."

39. Data available from the Intergovernmental Panel on Climate Change (IPCC), an international scientific body, cited in Porter 1995, 219. See also Lester Brown et al. 2000, 6.

40. Simon Elegant, "The Virus That Wouldn't Die," in *Far Eastern Economic Review* (17 August 2000): 16–17.

41. While sea lanes as such were considered a matter of security in the military sense during the Cold War, especially in view of the threats posed by the Soviet Pacific Fleet, I tend to treat them as a collective good shared by all east and southeast Asian nations, as they are a vital "lifeline" in that they are indispensable to uninterrupted supplies of badly needed oil supplies from the Middle East. For a discussion of the Asian Pacific sea lanes in the context of military security, see Ko and Shaw 1983.

42. Peter Wonacott, *Asian Wall Street Journal Weekly*, July 3–9, 2000, p. 1.

43. By comparison, 10 percent of China's 1.2 billion population is over the age of 60.

44. For a commentary on the dubious role played by the Indonesian army, see "Jakarta Must Strike a Delicate Military Balance," by Barry Wain in the *Asian Wall Street Journal Weekly*, June 26–July 2, 2000, p. 17.

45. At a Steering Committee meeting, held in Canberra, Australia on 10 December 1996, the Council for Security Cooperation in the Asia Pacific (CSCAP) decided to establish a study group on transnational crime, to consider the security implications for the region of transnational crime, including drug trafficking. See Dupont 1999, 435, n. 6.

46. See Immanuel C. Y. Hsu, *The Rise of Modern China* (New York: Oxford University Press, 1970), 215–217.

47. Cf. Allison Jamieson, "Global Drug Trafficking," *Conflict Studies* 234 (September, 1990): 1–2.

48. Please consult my discussion of this point in chapter 1 above. See also Segal 1999, 25; and Frank 1998, 111–117.

49. Howard W. French, "Women Win a Battle, but Job Bias Still Rules Japan," *New York Times,* February 26, 2000, p. 3.

50. Sheryl WuDunn, "In a House Ruled by Men, 23 Women Break in," *New York Times,* October 26, 1996, p. ll.

51. The idea of "time horizons" is developed in Arthur Stein 1990. But the idea that different peoples may live in different "time zones" of history is mine.

52. For many Asian countries, political institutionalization was the main task of state-building in the postcolonial era. Cf. Robert A. Scalapino et al., *Asian Political Institutionalization* (Berkeley, CA: Institute of East Asian Studies, University of California, 1986).

53. In his revolutionary program called *San Min Chu I* (the "Three Principles of the People"), Sun Yat-sen, the founding father of Republican China (in 1912) listed nationalism first and foremost. He explained that the Chinese, who had long since gone beyond the stage of ethnic nationalism to a peculiar culturalism (i.e., whoever embraced Chinese culture would be accepted as legitimate by the Chinese, including the Manhu rulers). Hence, he argued, the Chinese needed to rearm themselves with rekindled nationalism if they were going to confront the tasks of national reconstruction at home and of fighting "imperialist" inroads from abroad. See C. Martin Wilbur, *Sun Yat-sen: Frustrated Patriot* (New York: Columbia University Press, 1976), 197–208.

54. For a classic work on the philosophical foundations of nationalism, the impact of the French Revolution on nationalism and politics in Europe, and the appeal of nationalism throughout the world, see Elie Kedourie, *Nationalism,* rev. ed. (New York: Praeger, 1960).

55. In his monumental study on China's entry into the Korean war, Whiting (1960, 45) finds no "direct evidence" of the Chinese participation in the decision for the North Korean invasion of South Korea, which was "planned and directed by the Soviet Union."

56. In the wake of the Pyongyang summit, North Korea vowed to continue with its nuclear program and declared that, when threatened by a hostile United States with "thousands of missiles," the North Koreans cannot stop developing missiles. *New York Times,* July 13, 2000, p. 13.

57. In view of this almost predictable Japanese reaction, the North Korean act would make sense only if it was an impulsive venting of pent-up nationalistic frustrations against the Japanese that boomeranged. Cf. "Japan: At Very Long Last a Right Step (15 January 1999)," *Asia Times on Line,* January 19 1999. Available at: http://www.atimes.com/editor/AA19BaO1.html.

58. Based on interviews with top Chinese leaders, including Deng Xiaoping, with whom I had a six-hour audience, 29 July 1987, at his Beidahe summer resort.

59. "A Near-Dog Fight across the Taiwan Strait," in *Yazhou zhoukan* [Chinese Asia Week], a Hong Kong publication, issue of August 28–September 3,

2000, quoting a report carried in *Jiefangjun Bao* [People's Liberation Army Daily], 12 August 2000.

60. For a discussion of Taiwan's strategy of carrying war to the enemy's territory, see commentary by Chen Fang-yu in *Straits Review Monthly* (Taipei), no. 117 (September 2000): 25f.

61. Cf. Hsiung 1998.

62. Over 90 percent of the people polled in mainland China, in any survey in recent months, have supported the use of force by Beijing to stop Taiwan's separatist drift. Accordingly, one of the three Chinese "missions for the new century," adopted at the 5th session of the 15th Central Committee of the Chinese Communist Party, on October 11, 2000, is to complete the "national reunification" of China; *Remin ribao,* October 12, 2000, p. 1. 63. For a cogent analysis of ballistic missile defense, the proliferation of ballistic missiles, and the U.S. policy in response, see Denoon 1995.

64. Cf. Lawrence Freedman 1983.

65. Cf. "Study Said to Find U.S. Missile Shield Might Incite China," *New York Times,* August 10, 2000, p. 1.

66. China has repeatedly sworn off developing or acquiring an aircraft carrier, but is reportedly interested in acquiring an anti-carrier missile force. This is an apparent reaction to the March 1996 experience, when at the height of a Taiwan Strait crisis, two U.S. carrier battle groups cruised through the Strait in an ostensible demonstration of support for Taiwan.

67. This can be gauged by the epochal rise in Japanese annual defense expenditures, which since 1991 have been the world's second largest, at the rate of U.S.$40–50 billion, or three to four times those of China. Cf. statistics in *The Military Balance, 2000–2001,* a publication of the International Institute of Strategic Studies (London).

68. For details, see Phillips 2000.

69. See definition of "hegemonic war" in Gilpin 1981, 15.

70. When Japan made a bid for a permanent seat on the UN Security Council in the early 1990s, not a single Asian state supported it.

71. Cf. "Okinawa's Patience Runs Out," *The Economist* (28 October 1995): 33. Also, "Yankee Go Home?" in *Far East Economic Review* (10 August 2000): 20.

72. According to *The Military Balance: 2000–2001,* published by the London-based International Institute of Strategic Studies (IISS), Japan's defense budget for 2000 was U.S.$45.6 billion, as compared with China's U.S.$14.5 billion for the same year.

73. "Japan's Constitution: A Call to Arms," *The Economist,* (27 February 1999): 21f.

References

ADB 2000—see "Asian Development Bank. 2000" below.

Amsden, Alice H. 1989. *Asia's Next Giant: South Korea and Late Industrialization.* New York: Oxford University Press.

Anderson, Benedict. 1998. *The Spectre of Comparisons: Nationalism, Southeast Asia, and the World.* London: Verso.

Anthony, J. 1990. Conflict over natural resources in the Pacific. In *Conflict Over Natural Resources in South-East Asia and the Pacific,* edited by L. Ghee and M. Valencia. New York and Singapore: Oxford University Press.

Antolik, Michael. 1990. *ASEAN and the Diplomacy of Accommodation.* Armonk, N.Y.: M. E. Sharpe.

Asian Development Bank (ADB). 2000. *Asian Recovery Report 2000,* a semi-annual review of Asia's recovery from the crisis that began in July 1997; Available at: http://aric.adb.org/exteral/arr2000/arr.htm.

AVISO Issue No. 1, 1998. Environmental change, vulnerability, and security in the Pacific. Online publication series of the Global Environmental Change and Human Security Project, sponsored by the U.S. Agency for International Development, University of Michigan, Woodrow Wilson Center, and Canadian International Development Agency; available at: http://www.gechs.org/aviso.

Belassa, B., et al. 1982. *Development Strategies in Semi-Industrial Economies.* Baltimore, MD: Johns Hopkins University Press.

Bell, Daniel, et al., eds. 1996. *Towards Illiberal Democracy in Pacific Asia.* Oxford and New York: St. Martin's Press.

Bennet, D. Scott, and Alan C. Stam, III. 1998. The declining advantage of democracy: A combined model of war outcomes and duration. *Journal of Conflict Resolution* 42, no.2:344–366.

Berger, Peter and Michael Hsiao, eds. 1986. *In Search of East Asian Developmental Model.* New Brunswick, NJ: Transaction Books.

Bergsten, Fred. 2000. East Asian regionalism: Towards a tripartite world. *The Economist* (15 July 2000): 23–26.

Borthwick, Mark. 1992. *The Pacific Century.* Boulder, CO: Westview Press.

Bracken, Paul. 2000. The second nuclear age. *Foreign Affairs* 79, no.1:145–156.

Brown, Lester, et al. 2000. Challenges of the new century. In *State of the World 2000,* edited by Lester Brown, Christopher Flavin, and Hilary French. New York: W. W. Norton & Co. Annual report of the World Watch Institute.

Calomiris, Charles W. 1998. The IMF's imprudent role as lender of last resort. *Cato Journal,* 17, no.3.

Chan, Steve and Cal Clark. 1992. The Rise of the East Asian NICs: Confucian capitalism, status mobility, and developmental legacy. In *The Evolving Pacific Basin in the Global Political Economy: Domestic and International Linkages,* edited by Steve Chana and Cal Clark. Boulder, CO: Lynne Rienner, pp. 27–48.

Ciuriak, Dan. 1999. The Asia crisis: The challenge to conventional wisdom. *The American Asian Review* 17, no.1:61–102.

CNN.com. 1998. Reports allege organized raping during Indonesian riots. At website: http://www.cnn.com/WORLD/asiapcf/9806/28/indonesia.apes/.

Corsetti, Giancarlo, Paolo Pesenti, and Nonriel Roubini. 1998. *What Caused the Asian Currency and Financial Crisis? Part I: A Macroeconomic Overview.* Paper available through the coauthors: (1) corsett@econ.yale.edu; (2) paolo.posenti@ny.frb.org; and (3) nroubin@stern.nyu.edu.

Creel, H. G. 1953. *Chinese Thought: From Confucius to Mao Tse-tung.* New York: Mentor Books.

Cummings, Bruce. 1987. The origins and development of the northeast Asian political economy: Industrial sectors, product cycles, and political consequences. In *The Political Economy of the New Asian Industrialism,* edited by Frederick Deyo. Ithaca, NY: Cornell University Press.

Daly, Markate. 1994. *Communitarianism: A New Public Ethics.* Belmont, CA: Wadsworth Publishing Co.

de Brito, Jose Brandao. 1999. The anatomy of the East Asian crisis: An alternative model of currency crises. Paper presented at the International Conference on the Challenges of Globalization, October 21–22, 1999, Bangkok, Thailand. Available through tobeas@bbrito.freeserve.co.uk.

Delven, Ben. "Lion's share," *Far Eastern Economic Review* (August 3, 2000): 24.

Denoon, David B. H. 1995. *Ballistic Missile Defense in the Post–Cold War Era.* Boulder, CO: Westview Press.

Diamond, Larry and Marc F. Plattner. 1998. *Democracy in East Asia.* Baltimore, MD: Johns Hopkins University Press.

Dillion, Dana. 2000. Piracy in Asia: A growing barrier to maritime trade. *Backgrounder* no. 1379 (22 June 2000). Washington, D.C.: Heritage Foundation.

Dittmer, Lowell. 1999. Globalization and the Asian financial crisis. *Asian Perspective,* 23:45–64.

Dower, John W. 1994. *Japan in Peace and War.* New York: New Press.

Dupont, Alan. 1999. Transnational crime, drugs, and security in East Asia. *Asian Survey,* 39, no.3:433–455.

Fei, John, Gustav Ranis, and Shirley Kuo. 1979. *Growth with Equity.* New York: Oxford University Press.

Feldstein, Martin. 1998. The IMF's errors. *Foreign Affairs,* 77, no.2 (March/April): 20–33

Fox, Russell Arben. 1997. Confucian and communitarian responses to liberal democracy. *Review of Politics,* 59, no.3 (summer):561–592.

Frank, Andre Gunder. 1998. *Re-Orient: Global Economy in the Asian Age.* Berkeley, CA: University of California Press.

Freedman, Lawrence. 1983. *The Evolution of Nuclear Strategy.* New York: St. Martin's Press.

Gerlach, Michael L. 1992. *Alliance Capitalism: The Social Organization of Japanese Business.* Berkeley, CA: University of California Press.

Gilpin, Robert. 1981. *War & Change in World Politics.* London and New York: Cambridge University Press.

Gold, Thomas B. 1986. *State and Society in the Taiwan Miracle.* Armonk, NY: M. E. Sharpe.

Harris, Sheldon H. 1994. *Factories of Death: Japanese Biological Warfare, 1932–45, and the American Cover-up.* London and New York: Routledge.

Herz, John. 1950. Idealist internationalism. *World Politics,* 2, no.2:157–180.

Hiebert, Murray and Susan Lawrence. A call to arms: America's missile defense program could unleash an Asian arms race. *Far Eastern Economic Review* (August 3, 2000): 16–17.

Hitchcock, David I. 1994. *Asian Values and the United States: How Much Conflict?* Washington, D.C.: Center for Strategic and International Studies.

Hofheinz, Roy and Kent Calder. 1982. *The Eastasia Edge.* New York: Basic Books.

Houn, Franklin W. 1973. *A Short History of Chinese Communism.* Englewood Cliffs: NJ: Prentice-Hall, Inc.

Hsiung, James C., ed. 2000. *Hong Kong the Super Paradox: Life after Return to China.* New York: St. Martin's Press.

———. 1998. Taiwan's democratization and its implications for international relations theory. *Tamkang Journal of International Affairs* (Taipei) 3, no.1:51–75.

———. 1985. *Human Rights in East Asia: A Cultural Perspective.* New York: Paragon House Publishers.

———, ed. 1993. *Asia Pacific in the New World Politics.* Boulder, CO: Lynne Rienner.

Huang, Zhilien. 1998. The unexpected opportunity for Hong Kong's new genre of enterprises in the midst of the East Asian financial crisis. *Haixia pinlun* [Straits Review] (Taipei), no. 86 (February): 44–6.

Hucker, Charles O. 1965. Confucianism and the Chinese censorial system. In *Confucianism and Chinese Civilization,* edited by Mary Wright. New York: Atheneum; first published by Stanford University Press in 1959.

IFFM. 2000. Background on the Indonesian fire problem. Information made available by the Indonesian Forest Fire Management, at: http:///www.iffm.or.id/background.html.

IFFN No. 19. Transboundary haze pollution in Southeast Asia. Report by Daniel Murdiyarso, Program Head, BIOTROP-GCTE, Southeast Asian Impacts Centre, Bogor, Indonesia.

Iyer, Raghavan. 1984. Spirit, mind, and matter. *Hermes* (September), sourced from website: http://theosophy.org/tlodocs.

Japan Insight 2000. Population aging and longevity: Today Japanese men and women have the longest life expectancies in the world. Sourced from website: http://www/jinjapan.org/insight/html.

Jervis, Robert. 1980. The impact of the Korean War on the Cold War. *Journal of Conflict Resolution,* 24, no.4 (December):563–592.

Johnson, Chalmers. 1995. *Japan: Who Governs? The Rise of the Developmental State.* New York: W.W. Norton.

———. 1982. *MITI and the Japanese Miracle: The Growth of Industrial Policy: 1925–1975.* Stanford, CA: The Stanford University Press

———. 1981. Introduction—The Taiwan Model. In *Contemporary Republic of China: The Taiwan Experience, 1950–1980,* edited by James C. Hsiung. New York: Praeger Special Studies, pp. 9–18.

Johnson, Lorne D. 1998. Explaining the economic slowdown in Japan. In *The Asian crisis: What has happened and why?* edited by Kar-yiu Wong. Department of Economics, University of Washington. Available at: http://weber.u.washington.edu/~karyiu.1

Kahler, Miles, ed. 1998. *Capital Flows and Financial Crises.* Ithaca, NY: Cornell University Press.

Kanabayashi, Masayoshi. 2000. Immigration attitudes shift: Economic realities may force the door open. *Asian Wall Street Journal Weekly* (May 29-June 4, 2000): p. 10. The UN projections cited are available in: Replacement migration: Is it a solution to declining and aging populations? Available at website: wysiwyg://19/http://russia.shaps.hawaii.edu/.

Kapstein, Ethan B. 1998. Global rules for global finance. *Current History* 97, no.622 (November):355–360.

Kausikan, Bilahari. 1998. The "Asian values" debate: A view from Singapore. In Diamond and Plattner 1998, pp. 17–27.

Kim, Se-jin, and Chang-hyun Cho, eds. 1976. *Korea: A Divided Nation.* Silver Spring, MD: The Research Institute on Korean Affairs.

Kim, Shee Poon. 1994. See Shee, Poon Kim 1994, below.

Ko, Tun-hwa and Yu-ming Shaw, eds. 1983. *Sea Lane Security in the Pacific Basin.* Taipei: Asia and the World Institute.

Krugman, Paul. 2000. *The Return of Depression Economics.* New York: W.W. Norton.

Kueh, Y. Y. 2000. Weathering the Asian financial storm in Hong Kong. In Hsiung 2000, pp. 235–264.

Lach, Donald and Edmund Wherle. 1975. *International Politics in East Asia Since World War II.* New York: Praeger.

Lam, Danny and Ian Lee. 1992. Guerrilla capitalism and the limits of statist theory: Comparing the Chinese NICs. In *The Evolving Pacific Basin in the Global Political Economy,* edited by Steve Chan and Cal Clark. Boulder, CO: Lynne Rienner, 1992, pp. 107–124.

Lee Kuan Yew. 2000. The cruel game. An interview published in *Far Eastern Economic Review* (June 8, 2000):16–17.

———. 1998. *The Singapore Story: Memoirs of Lee Kuan Yew.* New York: Simon and Schuster.

Lemco, Jonathan and Scott B. MacDonald. 1999. Is Asian financial crisis over?" *Current History* 98, no.632 (December):433–437.

Linder, Staffan B. 1986. *The Pacific Century: Economic and Political Consequences of Asia-Pacific Dynamism.* Stanford, CA: Stanford University Press.

Lui, Samuel Hon Kwong. 1997. *Income Inequality and Economic Development.* Hong Kong: City University Press.

McCleary, William A. 1999. Three globalization issues: An overview. Paper delivered at the International Conference on the Challenges of Globalization, October 21–22, 1999. Bangkok, Thailand.

McCord, William. 1991. *The Dawn of the Pacific Century: Implications for Three Worlds of Development.* New Brunswick, NJ: Transaction Publishers.

Makin, Tony. 1999. Preventing financial crises in East Asia. *Asian Survey,* 39, no. 4:668–678.

Mansfield, Edward and Jack Snyder. 1995. Democratization and war. *Foreign Affairs,* 74, no.3:79–89.

May, Greg. 2000. Reality check: Beijing must factor into missile defense education. Nixon Center E-Mail Bulletin, June 9, 2000. Available on website: http://www.nixoncenter.org/publication/Reality%20Check/.

Montes, Manuel F. 1998. *The Currency Crisis in Southeast Asia.* Singapore: Institute of Southeast Asian Studies.

Muller, Steven and Gebhard Schweigler, eds. 1992. *From Occupation to Cooperation.* New York: W.W. Norton. Okita, Saburo. 1986. Pacific development and its implications for the world economy. In *The Pacific Basin: New Challenges for the United States,* edited by James Morley. New York: Academy of Political Science, pp. 23–34.

Olds, Chris, Peter Dicken, Philip F. Kelly, Lily Kong, and Henry Wai-chung Yeung, eds. 1999. *Globalization and the Asia Pacific.* London and New York: Routledge.

Owuala, Sunday I. 1999. Banking crisis, reforms, and the availability of credit to Japanese small and medium enterprises: A research note. *Asian Survey* 39, no.4:656–667.

Patten, Christopher. 1999. *East and West: China, Power, and the Future of Asia.* New York: Times Books.

Phillips, David R. 2000. *Aging in the Asia Pacific.* 2d ed. London and New York: Routledge.

Porter, Gareth. 1995. Environmental security as a national security issue. *Current History,* 94, (May) 592.

Prybyla, Jan S. 2000. China and Taiwan, a comparative study of economic problems in the Asian financial crisis. *The American Asian Review* 18, no.4:69–114.

Rabushka, Alvin. 1987. *The New China.* Boulder, CO: Westview Press.

Robinson, Richard, ed. 1996. *Pathway to Asia: The Politics of Engagement.* London: Allen and Unwin.

Rozman, Gilbert. 1992. The Confucian faces of capitalism. In Borthwick 1992, pp. 310–322.

Schindler, Ludwig. 2000. Fire management in Indonesia-quo vadis? Paper given at the "International Cross Sectoral Forum on Forest Fire Management in Southeast Asia," December 8–9, 1998, Jakarta. Available at: http://www.iffm.or.id/itto.html.

Scott, Bennet D. and Alan C. Stam, III. 1998. The declining advantage of democracy: A combined model of war outcomes and duration. *Journal of Conflict Resolution* 42, no.2:344–366.

Segal, Gerald. 1999. Does China matter? In *Foreign Affairs,* 78, 5:24–36.

Sender, Henry. A false dawn. *Far Eastern Economic Review* (July 27, 2000): 16–20.

Shee, Poon Kim. 1994. China's changing policies toward the South China Sea. *The American Asian Review* 12, no.4 (winter).

Sikorski, Douglas. 1999. The financial crisis in Southeast Asia and South Korea: Issues of political economy. *Global Economic Review* (Seoul) 28, no.1:117–129.

Stein, Arthur A. 1990. *Why Nations Cooperate: Circumstance and Choice in International Relations.* Ithaca, N.Y.: Cornell University Press.

Subramaniam, Surain. 2000. The Asian values debate: Implications for the spread of liberal democracy. *Asian Affairs* 27, no.1(spring):19–36.

Sung, Chen-chao. 1997. The economic and political implications of the Asia Pacific regional financial crisis. *Haixia pinlun* [Straits Review] (Taipei) 82:12–15.

Tai, Hung-chao, ed. 1989. *Confucianism and Economic Development: An Oriental Alternative?* Washington, D.C.: Washington Institute for Values in Public Policy.

Tsurutani, Taketsugu. 1977. *Political Change in Japan.* New York: David Mackay.

UNDP. 1998. *Human Development Report 1998.* New York: United Nations Development Program.

Vasquez, Ian. 1998. Why the IMF should not intervene. Summary of comments presented at the Conference on the Asian Crisis and the Reform of the Monetary System. Fundacion Dialogos, February 25, 1998, Madrid, Spain. Available at: http://www.Cato.org/speechew/sp-iv22598.html.

Vogel, Ezra F. 1979. *Japan as Number One: Lessons for America.* Cambridge, MA: Harvard University Press.

Wade, Robert. 1998. The Asian crisis and the global economy: Causes, consequences, and cure. *Current History* 97, no.622 (November): 361–373.

Wang, Gangmao. 1999. Post-crisis economic landscape: Re-takeoff and integration of East Asian economies. Paper delivered at the International Conference on the Challenges of Globalization, 21–22 October 1999, Bangkok, Thailand. Available at: fbawkm@nus.edu.sg.

Wei, Wou. 1992. *Capitalism, A Chinese Version: Guiding a Market Economy in Taiwan.* Columbus, OH: East Asian Studies Center, Ohio State University.

White, Gary, ed. 1988. *Developmental State in East Asia.* New York: St. Martin's Press.

Whiting, Allen S. 1960. *China Crosses the Yalu: The Decision to Enter the Korean War.* Stanford, CA: Stanford University Press

Wigley, Tom M. L. 1999. *The Science of Climate Change: Global and U.S. Perspective.* Arlington, VA: Pew Center on Global Climate Change.

Winters, Jeffrey A. 1998. Asia and the "magic" of the marketplace. *Current History* 97, no.623:418–425.

Wong, Kar-yiu, ed. *The Asian Crisis: What Has Happened and Why?* Available at: http://weber.u.washington.edu/~karyiu.

World Bank. 1993. *The East Asian Miracle: Economic Growth and Public Policy.* New York and London: Oxford University Press.

———. 1998. *East Asia: The Road to Recovery.* Washington, D.C.: The International Bank of Reconstruction and Development.

———. 1998/1999. *Global Economic Prospects and the Developing Countries.* Washington, D.C.: International Bank of Reconstruction & Development.

———. 2000. *East Asia: Recovery and Beyond.* Washington, D.C: International Bank of Reconstruction and Development.

Wu, Anna. 1995. Hong Kong should have equal opportunities legislation and a human rights commission. In *Human Rights and Chinese Values,* edited by Michael Davis. London: Oxford University Press.

Yanaga, Chitoshi. 1964. *Japanese People and Politics.* New York: John Wiley and Sons (Science Editions).

YRC (Yellow Ribbon Campaign). 1998. Final report of the joint fact-finding team (TGPF). Sourced from website: wysiwyg://31/http://www.geocities.com/Tokyo/Palace/2313/.

Yu, Peter. 1991–1992. Issues on the South China Sea: A case study. In *Chinese Yearbook* (Taipei), 11:138–200.

Zakaria, Freed. 1997. The rise of illiberal democracy. *Foreign Affairs* 76, no.6: (November/December):22–43.

CHAPTER 4

THE "GLOBALIZATION PROJECT"[1] AND EAST ASIA: AN OPPORTUNITY OR A TRAP?

ALVIN Y. SO

THE GLOBALIZATION PROJECT

Over the past two decades, globalization has become a buzz word and a growth industry. Globalization has become the theme of journals' special issues, publishers' book series, and conferences on development and area studies. The studies of globalization generally focus on the intensification of linkages in the world economy. The term "globalization" is defined as the increasing scale and importance of exchanges of people, products, services, capital, and ideas across international borders (Dittmer 1999, 46). Due to recent advances in technology, communication, and transportation, global mobility at the end of the twentieth century is said to be unprecedented in speed, range, density, and accessibility. Take, for example, the globalization of finance. In 1998, some U.S.$1.2 trillion changed hands daily in foreign exchange markets, six times the amount of a decade ago (Dittmer 1999, 46). Following this logic, studies of globalization argue that social and economic processes now function at a predominantly global level and nation-states are no longer decision-makers but decision-takers.

Instead of studying the intensification of linkages in the world-economy, however, this chapter perceives globalization as a developmental project. The focus here is on what Philip McMichael (1996) calls the "Globalization Project," that is, how globalization has become a new model of development for the Third World countries. The proponents of the globalization project are the global agencies such as the

International Monetary Fund (IMF), the World Bank, the United States, and transnational corporations. The globalization project was articulated in the 1980s, in the light of the failure of both the national import-substitution model in the Third World countries and the command economy model in the socialist countries. The newly industrializing countries (NICs) are held up as exemplars of the new strategy of the globalization project because development now means successful participation in the world-economy.

As McMichael (1996, 148–176) points out, the globalization project has proposed the following policies to promote development:

- *Market liberalization and deregulation.* In order to enhance its competitiveness in the world economy, developing countries must liberalize their market and eliminate inefficient regulations. Instead of erecting trade barriers to promote import-substitution, developing countries should promote export-led growth and industrialization and welcome foreign investment.
- *The comparative advantage axiom.* The development strategy of the globalization project depends on the world market rather than the domestic market for its stimulus. This strategy assumes that national prosperity derives from specialization in those forms of economic activities in which a country does best. Thus, the slogan is: "Find your niche in the global marketplace," and specialization is the path to economic prosperity.
- *Restructuring and democratization of the state.* In order to accomplish the above goals, it is necessary to restructure the state, such as decentralizing central authority, downsizing the bureaucracy, reducing state subsidies, and selling public enterprises. Also, in order to make the state more responsive to global market forces, a Third World country must democratize and uphold human rights standards.
- *Global governance.* Third World states face a new world order in which global institutions [such as the World Bank, the IMF, the G-7 group, the United Nations, and the World Trade Organization (WTO)] have assumed a more active governing role. The leverage of global governance includes debt and bailout, universal credit rating, human rights regimes, environmental regimes, trade dispute settlement mechanisms, and military threats.

In the eyes of its proponents, the globalization project would provide a new opportunity for the Third World countries. Although the short-term agonies of globalization are many, it is believed that in the long run globalization will be highly beneficial to development. Thus, Dittmer

(1999, 46) remarks that "globalization offers opportunities for generating both high profits for multinational corporations and more rapid economic growth for host nations." Besides, globalization is taken as an irreversible process. Once globalization has started, it cannot be stopped and will have profound implications for Third World development.

For the critics of the globalization project, however, the project represents what amounts to a trap rather than an opportunity for development. The globalization project is seen as promoting only the interests of the global agencies and institutions, even at the expense of local and national interests. McMichael (1996, 181–208), for example, argues that globalization has led to a global labor surplus. As the world market becomes more consequential, firms have to undertake technical upgrading, relocation to cheaper labor zones, and constant product innovation. All these competitive strategies, taken together, undermine the stability of the labor markets. Labor redundancy arises. At the beginning of the 1990s, as many as 80 million people were estimated to be living as migrant laborers around the world. In addition, not only is wage employment contracting, but wage labor is also showing a trend where jobs become part-time and impermanent. Finally, the globalization project has brought on a legitimacy crisis, should the regime show either indifference or incapacity to help, in the face of a breakdown of the existing social welfare institutions in the market ambience. Disillusioned citizens, repressed workers, and neglected rural communities have demanded the opening of their political systems. Many social movements—ranging from labor, environmental, feminist, to fundamentalist movements—have emerged to challenge the globalization project.

Is the globalization project, in reality, an opportunity or a trap for Third World countries? This chapter attempts to examine how the globalization project was introduced to East Asia during the 1970s, how globalization was said to have created an East Asian economic miracle up to the mid-1990s, how the Asian financial crisis in the late 1990s has led to a reinterpretation of the globalization project, and finally how East Asia has developed its own brand of regionalization to meet the challenges of globalization.

PROMOTING THE GLOBALIZATION PROJECT IN EAST ASIA

CHINA

At first glance, East Asia seemed to be quite receptive to the globalization project over the past two decades. The Chinese government, for instance, has tried very hard to promote marketization. In the countryside, communes were dismantled. Peasant families were given plots of land to cultivate, and they were responsible for their own gains and losses. They were also encouraged to sell their products to rural markets and seek work in nearby township enterprises. In the cities, urban youth were encouraged to engage in petty trading and industrial activities, while state-owned and collective enterprises were asked to contract out their unprofitable operations to private enterprises. Many government officials resigned and set up their own private enterprises.

At the same time, the Chinese government developed an open-door policy toward foreign investment through the establishment of special economic zones (SEZs) and the opening of coastal cities and delta areas. The CCP wanted to attract large-scale, high-tech, capital investments from transnational corporations. The preferred form of operation was "joint-venture" between the Chinese government and transnational corporations, so that Chinese managers could acquire advanced technology, Western management know-how, and information about world-market conditions from their foreign partners. It was hoped that these joint-venture projects would invigorate aging state-owned enterprises, raise industrial production to levels comparable to those of the core states, help Chinese industries to break into the world market, and earn the needed foreign currency through export-industrialization. In order to attract foreign investments, special privileges such as inexpensive factory sites, preferential tax rates, low wages, and tariff exemptions were granted to transnational corporations.

In order to improve the competitiveness of the state-owned enterprises at the global market, the Chinese government put forward the following enterprise reforms: Reducing excess labor in the state-owned enterprises and gradually instituting a contract system in place of lifetime employment; introduction of a labor market; reduction of the state workers' benefits and a widening of the wage gap by abolishing the national eight-scale wage structure; separation of Party and administration by investing the manager with more power, and forcing enterprises to be responsible for their own gains and losses. On the shop floor, work discipline was tightened, and welfare socialism could not longer be taken for granted. Thus, state-owned enterprises began to hire temporary rural immigrants (with no job security and no benefits) on an increasing scale in order to save costs.

In the mid-1990s, the Chinese government decided to "hold onto the big and let go of the small" state-owned enterprises, a process that eventually would shrink the once-dominant state sector to a few important industries such as communications, public utilities, and heavy industries. Rallying to the central government's call, city and provincial authorities plunged into a frenzy of public auctions and backroom deals.

On the political front, there were signs that China was also moving toward political liberalization. The Chinese government released political prisoners like Wei Jingsheng and Wang Dan, much to Washington's delight. President Clinton was allowed to address Chinese TV viewers live on his chosen theme of human rights. In the same spirit, Beijing also said it would sign the United Nations' Covenant on Civil and Political Rights. At the societal level, there were press and think-tank debates on human rights and the expansion of democratic village elections. At the 15th Party Congress, Jiang Zemin even talked of introducing elections for the township government, the lowest level of the formal government hierarchy. Reforms in the legal system were also taking hold; for instance, the Administrative Litigation Law allowed citizens to sue government officials, a first in China's long history.

South Korea

Like China, South Korea also seems to have embraced the globalization project. The Korean interpretation of globalization, where economic restructuring is central, relies on a perception of external challenge and historical necessity (Gills and Gills 1999, 203). An external environment increasingly characterized by demands for market opening, technological innovation, and increased capital mobility requires national adjustments in order to sustain global competitiveness.

Such a conception of globalization has led the South Korean government to propose a wide range of reforms, including transparency of transactions, fair competition, financial deregulation, tax reform, industrial relations reform, and political and administrative reform. The *chaebol* (giant corporate network) was to be downsized and prepared for competition on a level-playing field, both domestic and international. Society was to be reformed and democratized, allowing more scope for citizen participation and inclusion. The best example of this comprehensive approach was the Globalization Commission (Segyehwa Ch'ujin Wiwonhoe), which was established by President Kim Young Sam in January 1995 (Gills and Gills 1999, 201). Thus, South Korea was undergoing a transition to both democracy and a liberal free market system in the 1990s.

Japan

It seems that Japan was also pushed by the globalization project to accelerate market opening and economic liberalization. When Japan's merchandise trade surplus began to swell from U.S.$7 billion in 1980 to over U.S.$30 billion in 1984, the Reagan Administration championed the idea of "fair trade" and sought to open up the supposedly closed Japanese market to U.S. exports. In numerous negotiations, American trade negotiators tried to force concessions from Japan in a wide range of areas, including reduction of import quotas, relaxation of import certification rules, abolition of tobacco monopoly, and admission of American lawyers. In 1985, the U.S. government unveiled the "Market-Oriented, Sector-Specific" (MOSS) approach to addressing specific barriers in specific markets, such as telecommunications, medical equipment, pharmaceutical, electronics, and forest products.

Again in 1985, the United States reached the Plaza Accord with other major industrial powers (the Group of Five) to engineer a devaluation of the dollar in order to reduce the growing U.S. trade deficit. After the concerted action of the Group of Five, the yen dropped sharply from 237 yens to the dollar in 1985 to 128 yens to the dollar in 1988 (Chiu and So 1996).

Under pressure from the globalization project, the Japanese government started the liberalization of finance in the early 1980s. As government regulations on finance were lifted, corporations began to raise capital through equity financing, by issuing bonds and stocks at both domestic and global markets. That reduced their dependence on the Japanese main banks, weakening the monitoring function of the main banks on corporate finance.

GLOBALIZATION AS AN OPPORTUNITY FOR EAST ASIAN DEVELOPMENT

Up to the mid-1990s, the globalization project was seen as having created a golden opportunity for East Asian development. The East Asian Newly Industrializing Economies (NIEs) were said to represent a new model of export-led industrialization in the Third World countries. Export to the global market contributed to resource allocation according to comparative advantage, helped the East Asian NIEs overcome the limitations of their small domestic markets, and provided the "carrot and stick" of competition. The East Asian NIEs adopted such export policies because of their stable incentive system, limited government intervention, and reliance on private capital (Balassa 1988).

Furthermore, East Asia was the focus of the World Bank's 1993 publication, *The East Asian Miracle,* which told the story of how Asian nations had, since 1960, grown faster than all other regions of the world. Between 1980 and 1995 their pace of growth accelerated to a rate nearly three times that of the world economy. The World Bank appraised the Asian model with great enthusiasm for its market-friendly policy, macroeconomic stability and export growth, economic growth with a relatively high level of equity, well developed human and physical capital, and efficient capital allocation and productivity change (World Bank 1993; Dittmer 1999, 49).

However, no sooner was the globalization project declared to be a success in East Asia than the Asian financial crisis erupted in 1997.

THE ASIAN FINANCIAL CRISIS
AND THE COMPETING EXPLANATIONS

THE ASIAN FINANCIAL CRISIS

The Asian financial crisis started in early 1997, when a leading Korean conglomerate named Hanbo Steel declared bankruptcy in January and a big Thai finance company named Samprasong Land missed its February deadline for foreign debt payment. Then the financial crisis spread to Indonesia, Malaysia, Hong Kong SAR, and other economies. The key manifestations of the crisis were plummeting currencies and real estate prices, failing banks, massive layoffs, a wholesale flight of foreign capital, labor strikes, public demonstrations, and civil unrest. Charles Wolf (1999, p.8) gives the following figures on the economic magnitude of the Asian financial crisis: The percentage declines in *currency value* from June 1997 to August 1998 were: −80 percent for Indonesia, −40 percent for Malaysia, −40 percent for Thailand, −32 percent for South Korea, −20 percent for Japan, 0 percent in Hong Kong, −20 percent for Taiwan, and 0 percent for China. The percent changes in own-currency value of *stock market capitalizations* were: −41 percent in Indonesia, −69 percent in Malaysia, −56 percent in Thailand, −45 percent in Korea, −25 percent in Japan, −49 percent in Hong Kong, −12 percent in Taiwan, and −16 percent in China.

We need to examine both the figures of stock markets and the currency because the decline in own-currency value market capitalization can further be reduced by the decline in currency value. For example, the 41 percent decline in Indonesia's own-currency market capitalization meant that a stock that was worth 100 rupiahs in June 1997 was worth about 59 rupiahs in August 1998. Because the value of the rupiah also decreased by about 80 percent against the dollar, the dollar equivalence of the 59 rupiahs fell by another 80 percent. That is, in August 1998, the asset originally worth 100 rupiahs retained only 12 percent $[(1.00−0.41) \times (1.00−0.80)]$ of the dollar value it had in June 1997. Charles Wolf further estimates that looking at the average of all the Asian territories, an Asian asset worth 100 dollars in June 1997 was worth only 25 dollars in August 1998 (Wolf 1999, 8).

THE EXPLANATION BY
THE GLOBALIZATION PROJECT

Why did the Asian financial crisis occur? The IMF held that the Asian financial crisis was created by the failure to control large payment deficits, the explosion in property and financial markets, the misman- aged exchange rate regimes, the rapidly expanding financial system that was poorly regulated, and the unwillingness to act decisively once confi- dence was lost (Kapur 1998).

Dittmer (1999, 52) agreed that the financial crisis arose because of overinvestment, disregard of profits, and the subordination of competi- tion to corporate interests in Asian economies. The culprit was said to be "crony capitalism," typically resulting in excessive investment in unprof- itable or marginal projects. First, being under-regulated and rife with po- litical favoritism, the financial sector tended to overinvest in areas such as property, with the tacit guarantee that the government would bail it out if serious problems developed. Second, the markets lacked adequate information (transparency) about the true financial status of the corpo- rations and the banks. In South Korea, for example, opacity had become so systemic that corrective action came too late and ultimately could not prevent the collapse of market confidence.

The IMF finally was authorized to intervene just days before po- tential bankruptcy in South Korea. This financial "cronyism" and lack of transparency exacerbated capital flight when the balloon was punc- tured: Given the fact that investors knew so little about the financial soundness of the economy, they were liable to exit at the first rumor of trouble.

For the proponent of the globalization project, the best solution to the Asian financial crisis is still more integration into the world market, but with universal rules of transparency applied.

THE EXPLANATION BY CRITICS
OF THE GLOBALIZATION PROJECT

According to critics, the Asian financial crisis shows clearly that the glob- alization project is a trap for Third World development. For the critics (McNally 1998), the Asian financial crisis is not fundamentally about corruption, crony capitalism, or overly regulated markets. Rather, the Asian financial crisis is a product of the globalization project, especially the massive inflow of short-term financial capital into the deregulated Asian markets. Thus, Wade (1999, 41–54) points out that among the Asian countries that were worst hit, all had embraced a radical liberalization of finance. And, these changes created good opportunities for speculations in stock and real estate markets.

For example, under pressure from the global agencies, Japan started liberalization of finance in the early 1980s. As government regulations on finance were lifted, corporations began to raise capital through equity finance by issuing bonds and stocks in both domestic and international markets, as mentioned above. That reduced their dependence on the main banks, seriously weakening the monitoring function of main banks on corporate finance. The Plaza Accord of 1985, another measurement of globalization of finance, resulted in the rapid appreciation of the yen, triggering sharp rises in both stock and real estate prices and the rise of the bubble (see Gao forthcoming). After the bubble burst, the Japanese slump began in the early 1990s with huge collapses in stock and real estate markets. When the depths of the Asian financial crisis fed back to Japan, Japanese output contracted about 1 percent in 1997 and slumped a staggering 5.3 percent in the first quarter of 1998.

In Southeast Asia, private capital flows into Indonesia, Malaysia, the Philippines, South Korea, and Thailand had nearly quintupled between 1990 and 1996, soaring from U.S.$20 billion to U.S.$95 billion per year. As financial capital poured into the region, making it relatively cheap and easy to raise funds, manufacturing and construction firms kept bringing new projects on line. East Asia's economic upswing thus acquired the classical characteristics of a speculative boom. However, by early 1997, some investors bet against the euphoria. They recognized that too many factories, hotels, and highways were being built in the mist of a global over-capacity. Quietly at first, they withdrew from new investment projects in Asia. They pulled cash out of stock markets; they dumped Asian currencies. Once kick-started, the process snowballed. Whereas private capital flowed into East Asia up to 1996, this region experienced in 1997 a net outflow of private capital to the tune of U.S.$20 billion (McNally 1998, 5).

Thus, the critics argue that, as a result of the globalization project, East Asia experienced soaring poverty, unemployment, malnutrition, devastation of the natural environment, food riots, student demonstrations for democracy, and growing militancy among the workers against layoffs.

RETHINKING THE OPPORTUNITY/TRAP ANALYSIS

It seems that both the proponents and the critics of the globalization project have not provided a fully adequate analysis of East Asian development. Although the proponents have exaggerated the developmental potential of the globalization project, the critics have also overstated the harmful consequences of the Asian financial crisis.

MEDIOCRE CRISIS

Even at the height of the Asian financial crisis, not all East Asian countries were equally infected by the "Asian flu." In 1998, the real GDP
growth in China was a respectable 7.8 percent and that in Taiwan was 4.9
percent. Also, it is ironic that before the critics of the globalization project published their books on the Asian financial crisis, the crisis had already subsided. While no analyst predicted the abrupt eruption of the
Asian financial crisis in 1997, no one foresaw its quick ending either. By
1999, most Asian countries already registered a modest growth of their
real GDP. In a reversal of its earlier gloom, the IMF predicted that there
will be a strong growth of real GDP in the Asian economies in 2000
(Kim 1999, 36).

For example, South Korea's real GDP growth rate for 1999 was estimated at 10 percent in early December 1999, up from −5.8 percent in
1998. The Korean won soared to a two-year high against the U.S. dollar
(at 1,140 won per dollar) in mid-December 1999, up from nearly 2,000
won per dollar at the peak of the Asian financial crisis in December 1997.
The trade surplus is also widening ($2.17 billion for October 1999), and
foreign direct investment in the first ten months of 1999 rose 83 percent
to a record $10.25 billion from a year earlier. The four largest *chaebols* are
on track to meet the government's end-of-the-year targets for debt reduction, having pared debts and solid assets (Kim 1999, 37; Gills and
Gills 1999, 223).

In this respect, it seems that the Asian financial crisis is far from
being a turning point for Asian development, leading to economic decline and bankruptcy. Instead, using a term of the stock market, the
Asian financial crisis looks more like a correction of the Asian economy
than a great reversal.

PARTIAL GLOBALIZATION

Aside from the wrong prediction on the seriousness of the Asian financial crisis, the globalization literature also has presented a misleading picture that East Asian countries have wholeheartedly embraced
the globalization project. Although East Asia has intensified its linkages with the world economy at the end of the twentieth century, it has
not fully endorsed the globalization project's market liberalization and
deregulation policies, democratization programs, and the norm of
world governance.

For example, the Asian crisis has rekindled the debate in China on
how fast it should open its market to foreign competition. In late Sep-

tember 1998, the Chinese government moved to raise barriers to imports from the United States, to impose wide-ranging currency controls aimed at stemming the flight of capital, to counter deflationary trends by imposing price controls, to deprive foreign investors of majority control over joint ventures in the retail and insurance sectors, and to restrict foreign participation in the telecom sector. In addition, the Chinese government in the fall of 1998 also raised the value-added tax rebates—the standard Value Added Tax (VAT) rate is 17 percent—for key exports several times last year as export momentum slowed, triggering outcries that China was unfairly subsidizing overseas sales. Underground publications criticized China's eagerness to join the World Trade Organization, with one proclaiming that "it is still far too early for China to lift protective barriers." Meanwhile, bureaucrats in powerful ministries said WTO membership would destroy China's unproductive state enterprises and shatter its fragile banks. It is interesting to see how the Chinese officials will handle the WTO demands over the next few years (*Chinese Business Review,* January 14, 1999).

In addition, the Asian crisis, with the attendant slow economic growth, increasing unemployment, and the erosion of regime legitimacy in its wake, prompted the Chinese government to adopt a hardline policy toward political dissent. In December 1998, the Chinese government smashed the nascent China Democratic Party and arrested its organizers, who were veteran dissidents. Fearing that the China Democratic Party would politicize worker complaints, the Chinese government sentenced three party organizers to, respectively, 11-, 12-, and 13-year jail terms. A few days later, a veteran labor activist, Zhang Shanguang, was sentenced to 10 years in prison for telling the U.S.-government-funded Radio Free Asia about protests among farmers, to air their complaints about high taxes and corrupt officials. These sentences were reported in the *People's Daily,* the official presses in China, sending a loud message to the political activists that the government would not tolerate anyone taking advantage of the prevailing conditions to organize politically (*Washington Post,* 21 January 1999).

Japan, too, has contested the globalization project. Gao's (forthcoming) paper asks: "Why has globalization not brought about a radical reform in the Japanese economic institutions?" His answer is that in Japan, globalization is perceived as the cause rather than the rescue for the bubble economy; the big bang of the finance industry is blamed for driving the economy into a liquidity trap; the assertion for a universal model of market economy conflicts with the strong desire for national identity; and the efficiency principle in liberalization is contested by the widely shared belief in economic equality.

It seems that several Asian economies were able to avoid the dramatic harmful consequences of the Asian financial crisis because they were only partially committed to the globalization project. As Pempel (1999, 10) points out, whether an Asian country was able to be immune to the financial crisis depended on how little it was "plugged in" to the global capital markets. East Asian countries, such as China (and, to a certain extent, Taiwan), had only minimum connection to the global capital grid because they retained restrictions over capital flows, foreign trade, and currency convertibility that were among the most severe in the region. As a consequence of such insulation, these economies were largely immune to short-term property and stock bubbles, currency speculations, and "hot money" outflows.

The crucial question, then, is: What explains East Asia's ability to resist the globalization project? In the next section, it will be pointed out that geopolitical origins of strong developmental states and the timing of the globalization project have helped to explain the East Asian path of development.

Why Was East Asia Able to Resist the Globalization Project?

Geopolitical Origins of the Strong Developmental State Model

After World War II, the United States replaced Great Britain as the new hegemonic power of the world, leading to an unprecedented expansion (the upward phase) of the capitalist world economy. In response to the threat of communism, the United States divided East Asia into two opposing spheres: (1) A communist bloc, which was composed of mainland China, North Korea, and the Soviet Union. (The United States tried its best to contain the spread of communism in East Asia.) (2) Japan, which the United States designated as a critical element in a U.S.-led East Asian order. Later, in the Korean War, South Korea and Taiwan were included in this U.S.-led anticommunist front as well. The U.S. patronage of capitalist allies and its assault on communist foes in East Asia had a profound impact on the contour of development in this region.

For example, the Korean War, U.S. economic blockage, and China's forced withdrawal from the world-economy in the 1950s influenced socialist China to adopt a Leninist model for state-building to confront the "imperialist enemies" from without and the "counterrevolutionaries" from within. This Leninist party-state was all powerful in that it extended both vertically and horizontally to every sphere in the Chinese society. Vertically, the Leninist party-state was the first Chinese government that was able to exert its political control all the way down to village, family, and individual levels. Horizontally, there was a great expansion of state functions. The Leninist state did not just collect taxes and keep social order but also oversaw such functions as education, health care, marriage, culture, economic policy, etc. After 1978, in the post-Mao era, although the CCP was no longer Leninist in ideology, it still inherited a strong Leninist state machinery to carry out its modernization policy, as called for by Deng Xiaoping.

In order to build a strong Japan that could contain the spread of communism in East Asia, antitrust reforms of the zaibatsu were halted; reparation programs were terminated; and labor militancy and strikes were quickly suppressed. It was this sudden reverse course of U.S. occupation policies in the late 1940s that laid the foundation for a strong developmental state in Japan. The reforms imposed by the United States during its occupation of Japan increased the power of the bureaucrats vis-a-vis other political groups, as U.S. reforms helped remove influential politicians, smashed the military, dispossessed the landlords, and crushed the labor movement. Thereafter, the Japanese state was empowered to formulate independent industrial and financial policies to promote development.

In addition, in order to rebuild the Japanese economy after the damage of World War II, the United States opened its huge domestic market for Japanese products as well as provided aid, loans, and procurement to promote Japanese development. Moreover, the U.S. government tolerated a closure of the Japanese economy to foreign enterprise, thus providing a crucial breathing space for Japanese corporations to recuperate from their World War II wounds.

Like Japan, Taiwan and South Korea were also blessed by the Cold War. Military tensions in the East Asian region justified the actions of the Taiwanese and Korean authoritarian states in building up the military, banning labor unions and strikes, and suspending democratic elections. Moreover, U.S. foreign aid to South Korea averaged 39.7 percent of the government budget and 65 percent of total investment during the period of 1953 through 1961. In Taiwan, U.S. aid financed 95 percent of its trade deficit in the 1950s; and, through foreign savings, it almost totaled 40 percent of gross domestic capital formation (Cummings 1987). As a result, U.S. aid not only helped solve the economic problems of these Asian states in the 1950s (such as alleviating huge government budget deficits, financing investment, and paying for imports) but it also presented the states with powerful tools with which to intervene in the economy, enforce compliance in the private sector, and build up a strong military for defense. The United States was also willing to open its own market to them while tolerating their continued discrimination against dollar exports.

THE TIMING OF THE ARRIVAL OF THE GLOBALIZATION PROJECT

By the late 1970s, strong developmental states and robust economies thus had already been firmly established in East Asia as a result of the American anticommunist project during the Cold War. Japan quickly recovered from its defeat in World War II to emerge as an economic power in the Asian region. China possessed a strong Leninist state ready to launch the "Four Modernizations" program (i.e., modernization in industry, agriculture, defense, and science and technology) after the turmoil of the Cultural Revolution. South Korea, Taiwan, and Hong Kong became NIEs engaging in export-industrialization.

It was under such conditions that the globalization project was introduced into East Asia. The introduction came during a period in which East Asian economies were at their upward phase, when their exports and industrialization were expanding by leaps and bounds. Since the East Asian states achieved their economic success without having had to adopt such policies as market liberalization, deregulation, democratization, and global governance, they certainly looked upon the globalization project with suspicion. Why should they adopt the globalization project if they could do without it during their rapid development from the 1950s to the 1970s? Moreover, as strong developmental states, they also had the capacity to deal with challenges from the globalization project, such as selectively introducing some measures (like cutting down some tariffs) to satisfy the demands of the global agencies while firmly rejecting other measures that would be harmful to their national interests.

The globalization project was also introduced during a period in which the United States began to change its policy from anti-communism to peaceful coexistence in the Asian region. The 1970s saw U.S. withdrawal from Indochina and the U.S.–China diplomatic breakthrough. Burdened by huge military expenses, humiliated by defeat in the Vietnam War, the United States saw its industrial, commercial, and financial supremacy being increasingly challenged by rival core powers, prompting the rise of protectionism in the United States. Thus, the United States in the 1980s was no longer willing to trade access to the American market for foreign policy favors from the East Asian states. From the East Asian states' viewpoint, the U.S. globalization project in the 1980s was highly hypocritical, because the United States wanted other states to liberalize their markets while protecting its own.

Not satisfied with the globalization project, the developmental states in East Asia thus put forward an alternative regionalization project.

THE ASIAN REGIONALIZATION PROJECT

When global agencies such as the IMF began to construct a globalization project in the 1980s, East Asian states responded by putting forward a regionalization project in various forms. Putting the package together, the "Asianization" project" has the following distinctive features: *Network Capitalism, not Marketization.* The crux of East Asian development lies in network capitalism, not liberalization of market or deregulation. For Lever-Tracy and Tracy (1999, 5), the main motor of Asian economic development is Chinese diaspora capitalism, characterized by the horizontal networks of mainly small and medium-sized entrepreneurial family businesses linked transnationally through long-term personal relationships of reputation-based trust. The three legs on which Chinese diaspora capitalism rests are: continuing control by members of entrepreneurial families; a preference for personalized, long-standing, external networks based on trust and often leading to primordial friendship; and a strategy of multiplication and diversification. These attributes have survived and flourished despite stock exchange flotations, professional management, Western education, and the attenuation of patriarchy and of dialect divisions. An unusual degree of similarity and continuity between large and small firms has facilitated rapid social mobility and given each some of the strengths of the other, with small firms able to engage in global operations through transnational networks and those that have grown large still able to enjoy the flexibility derived from personal connections and family control.

While Lever-Tracy and Tracy highlight the networks of small Chinese firms, Hamilton (1999, 53) points out the distinctiveness of the large Japanese firms and networks. Japanese large business groups, composed of tiers of independent firms, were more flexibly organized and more all-encompassing than were their American counterparts. The Japanese groups created horizontal synergies by linking upstream firms that produced intermediate goods (such as steel) to downstream assembly firms that manufactured such things as automobiles. They also created vertical synergies in each area of final production by developing *keiretsu,* vertically tiered hierarchies of firms that constituted "one-set-ism," the principle of self-sufficient production systems. To make this economic organization work as a self-sustaining system, they situated financial services—banking and insurance—and trading companies at the center of each group. Although these Japanese business networks have strong links with the state, they are examples not of cronyism but of vertical integration carried to its logical conclusion.

REGIONAL INTEGRATION, NOT COMPARATIVE ADVANTAGES

There has been a regionalization of production in East Asia as foreign investment from Japan, South Korea, and Taiwan became increasingly important throughout the 1980s and the 1990s in underwriting development in Southeast Asia. Dicken and Yeung (1999, 117) point out that "regionalizing strategies are significantly more powerful than globalizing strategies among such [Asian] firms."

For example, while Japanese FDI decreased by nearly 40 percent overall between 1989 and 1994, investment in members of the Association of Southeast Asian Nations (ASEAN) grew by 17.7 percent. Most Japanese firms continue to extend their linkages and production networks into East and Southeast Asia despite the economic decline in Japan in the 1990s, creating extremely complex intra-regional production chains and networks. This aspect can be seen from the rapid growth in imports of consumer goods into Japan from Japanese-owned factories in Asia. Between 1992 and 1996, imports from foreign subsidiaries rose from 4 to 14 percent of imports overall. While almost everything made by Japanese companies in the United States was sold locally, a growing proportion of the products of their Asian subsidiaries were imported into Japan (Higgott 1999, 95).

An example of this regional production process can be seen in the case of Jinbao, a calculator factory in Thailand (Bernard and Ravenhill 1995). In Jinbao, the innovation behind the product, the brand name, and the marketing are Japanese. All key components for the calculators are also imported from Japan. All procurement and administration are controlled from Taipei, and the management of the plant is Taiwanese. The labor is Thai. Output from the plant is exclusively for export. In international trade data, Jinbao's production is recorded as Thai exports of electronic goods. To purchasers at the other end the products appear to be Japanese. The direct foreign investment statistics indicate a Taiwanese investment.

According to Dicken and Yeung (1999, 119–120), the Asian firms adopt a regional integration strategy because the Asia Pacific region has been a growth region since the late 1970s. Many countries in the region have either emerging markets or relatively low costs of production. The regional market and production location thus provide an opportunity for Asian firms to grow and establish their market position. In addition, the barriers—social, cultural, and political—to establishing a significant presence in North America and European markets are substantial. The Asian firms have yet to develop capacity to compete with transnational corporations on their "home turf."

There is a "flying geese" ideology to justify the regionalizing developmental strategy of Asian firms. In this perspective, the Japanese firms played the lead position in the East Asian region because they had the most advanced level of technology sophistication. Ranked behind Japan in a spreading "V" of decreasing levels of technical sophistication are first the NIEs (Hong Kong, Singapore, South Korea, and Taiwan) and then the Southeast Asian states (Malaysia, Thailand, Indonesia, and the Philippines). The "geese" behind Japan, it is argued, will learn from the progress of those up ahead, move up the product cycle, and eventually close the technological gap.

ASIAN VALUES, NOT WESTERN DEMOCRATIZATION

The culturalists argue that what the successful East Asian economies have in common is their Confucian tradition. Confucianism placed the family as the paramount institution within society, which led to the emergence of family entrepreneurship in East Asia. Furthermore, Confucianism shaped a new pattern of personal corporate management different from the West's rational, bureaucratic management. Finally, Confucianism glorified the established authority of the better-educated and rationalized their claims of superiority on the basis that they possessed specialized wisdom (e.g., Rozman 1992).

In addition, Confucian paternalism provides the political stability that is needed for rapid industrialization. Asian distaste for open criticism of authority, their fear of upsetting the solidarity of the community, and the knowledge that any violation of the community's rules of propriety will lead to ostracism all combine to limit the appeal of Western democracy and social movements. Due to the Confucian emphasis on harmony and the demand for consensus, adversarial relationships are muted, and critics are taught the benefits of conformity. Deyo (1989) also points out that labor peace in the Asian NIEs is generally attributed to the political culture, which stresses hierarchy, cooperation, a preference for mediation to confrontation, industriousness, deference to elders, and, most important, the subordination of individual to family, group, and state.

Regional Cooperation,
Not Global Governance

Regions are socially constructed as much as they are determined histori-cally, geographically, or economically. In order to promote the globaliza-tion project, Washington engineered the inauguration of APEC (Asia Pacific Economic Cooperation) forum. With the United States as its leader, the APEC includes non-Asian states such as Canada, Chile, Mex-ico, Australia, New Zealand, as well as Asian states (Japan, China, Hong Kong, Singapore, South Korea, Taiwan, Indonesia, Malaysia, the Philip-pines, Thailand, Papua New Guinea, and Brunei). The formation of the APEC enabled the United States to address major economic issues and disputes in the Asia-Pacific region. In 1993, the United States tried to transform APEC into an Asia-Pacific economic community to foster free trade and to forge close trade and investment ties in the region.

However, some Asian states have reservations regarding the transfor-mation of APEC from a consultative forum to a regional trade bloc that would discriminate against non-member countries. Mahathir Mohamad, the Prime Minister of Malaysia, was particularly vocal toward APEC: "We don't want APEC to become a structure community and we don't want it to become a trade bloc. We don't want APEC to overshadow ASEAN nor do we want to see APEC being dominated by powerful members. Every-one should be equal" (*The Australian,* September 19, 1994, p.2).

The APEC forum in Seattle in 1993, in fact, triggered off a new epoch of Asian solidarity between China and ASEAN vis-à-vis the challenge from the United States. As an alternative to APEC, there was support for the formation of an alternative EAEC (East Asian Economic Caucus). Qian Qichen, former Chinese Foreign Minister, explains: "East Asian countries are confronted with certain challenges and problems. It is there-fore useful for them to conduct dialogue, consultation, and coordination on questions of common concern" (*ASEAN Digest* Jan/Feb. 1994, p.13).

Asianization as a Resistance Movement

The above Asianization project provides a medium for Asian states to develop an "Asian regional approach" to problem solving in the region. It also is a means to enhance the bargaining power of Asian Pacific states within wider global contexts, with the hope of projecting Asian voices into the wider global context.

Thus, Asianization can be interpreted as an Asian resistance to the globalization project. For example, Asian Confucian values could be seen as a means to resist the hegemony of Washington's "Asia-Pacific" democratic discursive strategy and a protest to the superiority of unguarded liberalism in the globalization project.

Asianization has also increased the tension between East Asian states and the global agencies such as the IMF and the United States. At the beginning of the Asian financial crisis, for instance, the main donors for the initial financial adjustment package to rescue the Thai economy in late 1997 were Japan ($4 billion), South Korea and Taiwan ($2 billion each) and Hong Kong SAR and the PRC ($1 billion each). These economies were attempting to consolidate their regional positions in both an economic and political fashion. Conversely, not only did the United States refuse to support the above Asian rescue package, but it also opposed regional calls to set up a Japan-led $100 billion "Asian only" bailout. This generated considerable regional resentment toward Washington, which in turn galvanized the United States and the IMF into strongly reasserting their position that adjustment funds not under the direct or indirect control of the IMF might not be "properly used." Asian states may take, digest, and implement the IMF's bailout package. However, the bailout package seems increasingly problematic to the Asian states, because it appears to provide the IMF with an opportunity to further pry open East Asian economies, paving the way for globalization agencies to make inroads into the Asian banking sector and the Asian market (Higgott 1999, 103–4).

CONCLUSION

The globalization project—which emphasizes market liberalization, democratization, the ideology of comparative advantage, and global governance—has been put forward by such global agencies as the IMF and the United States since the 1980s. Although the proponents argue that this project will provide a golden opportunity for Third World development, its critics charge that the globalization project is a trap because it has led to global labor surplus, marginalization of the workforce, and legitimization crises in the Third World.

At first glance, it seems that East Asia had embraced the globalization project, as China pushed for marketization, deregulation, and democratization, South Korea set up the Globalization Commission, and Japan liberalized its regulation on finance. Up to the mid-1990s, the globalization project was seen to have created an East Asian economic miracle. However, the critics argued that the globalization project was harmful for Asian development, as shown by the eruption of the Asian financial crisis. For the critics, it was the radical liberalization of finance that laid the basis for speculations in stock, real estate markets, and currency markets in the 1990s.

In contrast to the arguments in the globalization literature, this chapter argues that the critics have overstated the seriousness of the Asian financial crisis, because the crisis was of short duration and failed to reverse the growth dynamics of East Asia. On the other hand, the advocates of the globalization project have also erred by failing to point out that East Asian states have successfully resisted the globalization project.

Why was East Asia able to resist the globalization project? This is because, due to geopolitical considerations during the Cold War, the United States had nurtured strong development states in the East Asian region, which have survived beyond the end of the Cold War. It is also because the globalization project was introduced during the period in which East Asia was in the upward phase of the world economy. Thus, the developmental states in East Asia had the capacity to formulate an alternative "Asianization" project to challenge the globalization project. The Asianization project calls for network capitalism instead of marketization, emphasizes regional economic integration rather than comparative advantage, stresses Asian Confucian values as compared to Western democratic ideals, and opts for regional cooperation to avoid global governance. Of course, Asianization does not mean that Asian states will withdraw (or be isolated) from the world economy. Rather, Asianization is a resistance mechanism to the globalization project, aimed at promoting the bargaining power of the Asian states in the global arena.

What are the future prospects of the Asianization project? It is likely that the dynamics of Asianization will continue in the early twenty-first century. When East Asia has fully recovered in the near future from the economic downturn caused by the Asian financial crisis of the late 1990s, Asian business networks will play a more prominent role in promoting regional economic integration, and Asian states will work more closely with one another in designing a collective approach to the emergent problems in the region.

However, there is a limit to how far the Asianization project can go forward. The East Asian region is still under the dual economic domination of the United States and Japan, and is still under a unilateral American security network. Lingering suspicions remain from World War II, such that other Asian states view Japanese regional power with alarm. Also, China and Taiwan have not reached a common ground to solve their differences over the national reunification issue, nor has China developed close enough economic and political ties with Japan. In addition, the regional ties linking the East Asian region have remained largely commercial, and there is very little institutionalization of political authority. As such, it seems that Asianization has yet to emerge as a full-blown project to challenge the globalization project in the early twenty-first century.

NOTES

1. "Globalization project," used here for the first time, is in quotation marks to denote a developmental project first proposed for the Third World countries by global agencies such as the IMF and the World Bank as well as the United States and transnational corporations. The term was given by Philip McMichael (1996). Quotation marks will not be used in the rest of the chapter.

REFERENCES

Balassa, Bela. 1988. The lessons of East Asian development: An overview. Supplement to *Economic Development and Cultural Change* 36,no.3:S273-S290.

Bernard, Mitchell and John Ravenhill. 1995. Beyond product cycles & flying geese. *World Politics*. 47:171–209.

Chiu, Stephen and Alvin Y. So. 1996. Will Japan become the next hegemon in the world economy? *Contemporary Development Analysis* 1: 27–52.

Cummings, Bruce. 1987. The origins and development of the Northeast Asian political economy: Industrial sectors, product cycles, and political consequences. In *The Political Economy of the New Asian Industrialism,* edited by Frederic Deyo. Ithaca: Cornell University Press.

Deyo, Frederic. 1989. *Beneath the Miracle: Labor Subordination in the New Asian Industrialism.* Berkeley: University of California Press.

Dicken, Peter and Henry Wai-Chung Yeung. 1999. Investing in the future: East and Southeast Asian firms in the global economy. In *Globalization and the Asia-Pacific,* edited by Kris Olds, Peter Dicken, Philip F. Kelly, Lily Kong, and Henry W.C. Yeung. London: Routledge.

Dittmer, Lowell. 1999. Globalization and the Asian financial crisis. *Asian Perspective* 23: 45–64.

Gao, Bai. Forthcoming. Globalization and ideology: The competing images of the contemporary Japanese system in the 1990s. *International Sociology.*

Gills, Barry K. and Dong-Sook S. Gills. 1999. South Korea and globalization: The rise to globalism? *Asian Perspective* 23: 199–228.

Hamilton, Gary. 1999. Asian business network in transition. In *The Politics of the Asian Economic Crisis,* edited by T. J. Pempel. Ithaca: Cornell University Press.

Higgott, Richard. 1999. The political economy of globalisation in East Asia: the Salience of "region building." In *Globalization and the Asia-Pacific,* edited by Kris Olds, Peter Dicken, Philip F. Kelly, Lily Kong, and Henry W.C. Yeung. London: Routledge.

Kapur, D. 1998. The IMF: A cure or a curse? *Foreign Policy* III: 114–126.

Kim, Samuel. 1999. East Asia and globalization: Challenges and responses. *Asian Perspective* 23: 5–44.

Lever-Tracy, Constance and Noel Tracy. 1999. The three faces of capitalism and the Asian crisis. *Bulletin of Concerned Asian Scholars* 31,no.3: 3–16.

McMichael, Philip. 1996. *Development and Social Change.* Pine Forge Press.

McNally, David. 1998. Globalization on trial: Crisis and class struggle in East Asia. *Monthly Review* 50,no.4:1–14.

Pempel, T.J. 1999. "Introduction." Pp.1–16 in *The Politics of the Asian Economic Crisis,* edited by T. J. Pempel. Ithaca: Cornell University Press.

Rozman, Gilbert. 1992. The Confucian faces of capitalism. In *Pacific Century,* edited by Mark Borthwick. Boulder: Westview Press.

Wade, Robert. 1999. The coming fight over capital flows. *Foreign Policy* 113: 41–54.

Wolf, Charles. 1999. Three systems surrounded by crisis. In *The Chinese Economy: A New Scenario, A Conference Report,* edited by Murray Weidenbaum and Harvey Sicherman. Philadelphia: Foreign Policy Research Institute.

The World Bank. 1993. *The East Asian Miracle.* New York: Oxford University Press.

PART III

INTER-REGIONAL AND INTRA-REGIONAL TIES IN THE NEW ERA

CHAPTER 5

EUROPE AND THE ASIA PACIFIC: TWO REGIONS IN SEARCH OF A RELATIONSHIP

BRIAN BRIDGES

Globalization, driven by corporate entrepreneurship and international communication advances, is undoubtedly intensifying worldwide interconnectedness,[1] but it cannot totally eliminate either the legacies of history or the realities of geographical and cultural distance. Certainly not in the case of Europe and the Asia Pacific, two regions whose relationship during the twentieth century suffered from the vagaries of both mutual antagonism and mutual neglect. The relationship moved from exploitative, informal, and formal colonization through the traumas of decolonization and reduced contact to the often far-from-creative tension derived from competitive commerce.[2] In the past two decades, the relationship has been dominated by the business of doing business, and, although political and security concerns did begin to grow slowly in importance as the Cold War wound down, they have failed to displace economics as the central element of the relationship. In sum, the relationship has remained a distant, irregular, and lopsided one. This chapter examines the prospects for the two regions in terms of developing their inter-regional relationship and their respective roles in the changing global order.

Two caveats are in order. First, the difficulties of defining Europe and Asia (or the Asia Pacific) both geographically and metaphorically have been rightly pointed out.[3] For the purposes of this chapter, discussion will focus primarily on the existing 15 West European members of the European Union (EU) and the north-east and south-east Asian states roughly encompassed by an arc from Japan to Burma (Myanmar).

Secondly, generalization for the sake of conciseness by using terms such as "Europeans" and "Asians" should not obscure the fact that very different views do exist within the informed elites, let alone the peoples, covered by these terms.

In thinking about the future of the Europe–Asia Pacific inter-regional relationship in this new century and the setting of that relationship within the broader global order, a number of variables come into play. The first relates to the discourse and practice of regionalism—what kind of Europe and what kind of Asia are emerging in the face of globalization? The second revolves around how the United States sees its interrelationship with these two regions. The third is based on the political will and commitment to the inter-regional dialogue—primarily but not exclusively the Asia-Europe Meeting (ASEM) process—and the relevance of noncommercial areas of interest within that dialogue. The final, admittedly more short-term, factor is the lingering aftermath—and the perceived lessons—of the Asian financial crisis.

THINKING REGIONALLY: EUROPE'S DILEMMA

Social, economic, and technical change and the emergence of trends towards greater regionalization and globalization have both complicated the structures underlying the global order and undermined, but not totally destroyed, the autonomy of national governments. However, the linkages between the international, regional, national, and indeed local remain strong. Within that context, the debate about regionalism, or regionalization, and globalization has become multifaceted, particularly as scholars have moved away from conceptualizations that focus exclusively on the economic dimensions.[4] Regionalization has been cast as both a factor encouraging eventual globalization and as an obstacle, or diversion, along that road. In order to address the issue, it is necessary to understand the dynamics of the regional experiments in both Europe and the Asia Pacific.

What kind of Europe is emerging at the beginning of this new century? The EU has, of course, developed a long way from the vision of the founding fathers, who set out, back in the 1950s, to build a new Europe through a process of economic integration worked out within the framework set by Soviet hostility and U.S. sponsorship.[5] When progress began to founder through what has been characterized as "Eurosclerosis"—a hardening of the arteries of European dynamism and flexibility—attempts were made from the mid-1980s to initiate and then to complete the move to a single internal market by the end of 1992.[6] The immediate objective was to resuscitate the European economy by removing obstacles within the European Community to the free flow of goods, services, and labor, but, because of sensitivities among national governments and peoples, the likely ultimate goal—political as well as economic union—remained implied rather than clearly articulated. The working out of the 1992 process, of course, was to be complicated by the profound political and sociocultural changes that occurred in Eastern Europe at the end of the 1980s.

Since the late 1990s, however, European policy-makers have been forced to address more urgently a long-standing dilemma—whether to enlarge the community further, whether to deepen its functions, or even whether to try to attempt to do both—in the context of where Europe really wants to go to and how Europe relates to the changing global order. The EU has had a certain magnetic appeal for other European states, but the last three members to join the EU, in 1995, were broadly comparable with the existing members in levels of economic development and political structures. Much more difficult to manage will be the almost certain entry of the former communist countries of Central and Eastern Europe—and Turkey—over the coming decade or so; some of the new aspirants could gain admission in 2002–2003. Enlargement cannot be completely divorced from deepening, not least because without substantial institutional reform in the near future, policy-making in an EU of 25 to 30 members will grind to a halt.

Since the mid-1990s deepening has found expression in two key aspects: the move to economic and monetary union (EMU), which took a significant step forward in January 1999 with the introduction of the single currency, the euro, for 11 of the current 15 members (now known as the "Eurozone"), and the aspiration for a common foreign and security policy (CFSP). While monetary union is not, of course, political union, EMU naturally introduces a new set of constraints on policy-making and as such represents a crucial step on the way to greater integration. It is an economic project designed to bring net economic benefits (European businessmen are broadly optimistic on this point, while ordinary citizens are more sceptical), but it will also bring political benefits, particularly in reducing uncertainty and suspicion among members and more generally in enhancing Europe's status in the international arena.

Even though the EU has gradually extended its competence from purely economic policy matters to some aspects of political and even security affairs, it is not yet a full-fledged actor in the international arena. EU decision-making processes involve not just the European Commission and member governments but also European and national parliaments and a wide range of sub-state organizations; this makes the EU into a kind of multiple coalition system and inevitably detracts from external policy consistency. Individual member countries not only develop their own relationships with their Asian Pacific counterparts but on particular issues exhibit cross-cutting tendencies that undermine European coherence. The move toward CFSP is intended to reduce, even eliminate, such problems. One of the four main stated aims of the EU's 1997 Amsterdam Treaty, in itself an attempt to consolidate and amplify certain aspects of the earlier 1993 Maastricht Treaty, was to give Europe a stronger voice in international affairs. However, as one official EU publication frankly acknowledged, it would be naive to think that a few amendments to the texts on European cooperation in this area would, as if by magic, cause Europe to speak with a single voice and send the world a coherent message.[7] Nonetheless, an active debate is now underway within Europe about the roles that the EU can play in the global management of "soft" and "hard" political and security issues. The striking characteristics of this debate are the degree of convergence that is beginning to occur among EU member countries and the extent to which the focus of this convergence is moving toward more, rather than less, activism in global crisis management.[8]

The ambivalence with which the Asians viewed the earlier stages of the European experiment was neatly encapsulated in one of the *Far Eastern Economic Review* front covers back in May 1988: "Europe: Asia's Friend or Foe?" On occasions, the EU has been watched with skepticism, particularly when the Europeans seemed incapable of living up to their rhetoric, such as in the first half of the 1980s or even in the mid-1990s. Others were suspicious, concerned that moves such as the 1992 process would only lead to a "Fortress Europe" that would be more protectionist against Asian products and services. Yet others sought inspiration from the ideals and practice of European regionalism in order to spur the development of regional cooperation concepts in the Asia Pacific in the 1960s or even as a form of "countermodel" in later decades. It should also be noted that some of the Asian Pacific initiatives for security-related organizations in the early post–Cold War period explicitly drew on European models, though not so much the EU per se as other intra-European bodies such as the Conference for Security and Cooperation in Europe.

The evolutionary process of the EU in the early twenty-first century does have important implications for the Asia Pacific. First, the speed and ease of the enlargement program. A prolonged and difficult enlargement process, with existing members arguing over budgetary and institutional reforms, would cause disillusion not just among the waiting applicants but also across the watching wider world, including the Asia Pacific. An introspective Europe, preoccupied with the problems of managing the transition to full membership of the Central and Eastern European states, may neither wish nor feel the need to be engaged in the

Asia Pacific region. But a successfully enlarged and more confident EU might be more willing to act as a "civilian superpower" with a heightened role in world order.

Second, the tendency for the "euro" to act as a barometer of Europe's economic health and perceived status in the world. Sensitized to currency issues by the Asian financial crisis, Asians have seen the arrival of the euro as providing an opportunity to diversify away from dependence on the almighty U.S. dollar. Many states in the region are slowly increasing their foreign currency reserve holdings of European currencies in the new form of the euro, although it has to be admitted that the euro performance in terms of its exchange rate against the U.S. dollar up to the time of this writing has been disappointing.

Finally, the greater propensity for Europe to act as one in external relations. Asian Pacific states, like other external partners of the EU, are certainly well aware that the EU, especially through the European Commission, has been functioning in an increasingly coherent manner in economic relations with them, but they also invariably note that it has yet to adopt a coordinated political and security posture. In the four major security "crises" in the Asia Pacific region in the 1990s—the Cambodian crisis up to 1993, the North Korean nuclear weapon crisis of 1993–1994, the Taiwan straits crisis of 1995–1996, and the East Timor crisis of 1999—European involvement was limited to either financial contributions, such as in the Korean Energy Development Organization set up to solve the North Korean nuclear problem, or limited personnel contribution by individual countries operating under the UN flag, such as in Cambodia and East Timor. However, the steady progress that the EU has been making during 2000 toward creating a new EU-controlled "rapid reaction force" with capabilities to operate "out of area" (a concept still geographically vague but that might in due course be extended to include Asia) suggests that in the longer term there might well be an enhanced and coordinated defence and security role for the EU in the Asian Pacific region.

ASIA PACIFIC REGIONAL COOPERATION

By comparison with the European integration process, the Asian Pacific experience has both been more laggardly and more multilayered, with more varied examples of regional and subregional cooperation. There is also a difference in kind between the European model, which is built on a highly institutionalized, highly legalistic form of supranationality, with "integration" as an ostensible target, involving countries that share a relative homogeneous cultural background, and the Asian experience so far, which involves a much more culturally diverse set of countries and that has tended to informality, relied on minimal amounts of either institutionalization or national sovereignty derogation, and deployed a rhetoric that emphasizes "cooperation" and "open regionalism."

Although the concept of broad Asian Pacific regional cooperation can be dated back to the Pan-Asian ideas of the early part of the twentieth century or the Japanese wartime "Greater East Asia Co-Prosperity Sphere," it was the mid-1960s that saw the first flowering of regionalist ideas within the Asian Pacific region. The subsequent history of the development of Asian Pacific regionalism, through academic and business-led initiatives to the founding of the intergovernmental Asia Pacific Economic Cooperation (APEC) forum in 1989, and the counterproposal of an East Asian Economic Grouping, has been well covered by scholars and practitioners.[9] It is important here, however, to note that the Asia Pacific encompasses a huge variety of countries that differ from each other in terms of political systems, resource endowments, and economic development levels, as well as ethnic, religious, and cultural backgrounds. This in turn has led to a desire to approach regional "community"-building through a process of gradual, step-by-step consensus formation. One by-product of this has been the emergence of different conceptions of the region and regional cooperative organizations, which have yet to be fused into a single over-arching entity such as the EU in Europe.

What do these varying types and varying degrees of economic cooperation mean for the Europeans? Much of the early debate in the 1970s and 1980s in Europe about Asian Pacific cooperation and integration was colored by the stuttering in the European integration experience and the apparently embryonic and extremely rudimentary nature of the early Asian Pacific experiments. Even ASEAN (the Association of South-East Asian Nations), with which the Europeans came into frequent contact from the late 1970s, was seen as having by, comparison with the European Community's record, only a very limited degree of success in promoting intra-ASEAN regional economic cooperation, let alone integration. Even through the 1990s Europeans noted that trade and investment promotion delegations from individual ASEAN countries visiting Europe would stress the comparative advantages of their own particular national economic environment and would rarely, if ever, mention the ASEAN dimension. Altogether this led to a European tendency to at best underestimate the Asian Pacific cooperation movement and to at worst dismiss it as a nonstarter.

This rather jaundiced view of Asian Pacific economic cooperation undoubtedly colored early European views of the APEC process too, particularly as Europe was by then committed to its own much more advanced 1992 process. However, by 1993 a more sinister view of APEC emerged among Europeans as the Americans moved first to upgrade APEC activities with the first annual leaders' summit and then proceeded to use APEC as a tool to beat the EU, quite successfully, during the closing stages of the Uruguay Round of the General Agreement of Tariffs and Trade (GATT) negotiations. As encapsulated in the words of one senior French policy researcher, some people in Europe began to see APEC as a "war machine" that, when linked with the emerging NAFTA (North American Free Trade Agreement), would act as a means of "economically encircling" Europe.[10] After the 1993 Seattle APEC summit, the EU's policy response to the revamped APEC was to request opportunities for dialogue with the organization, but a distinct coolness amongst APEC members to such an idea, coupled with the emergence of new opportunities for inter-regional dialogue with at least most of the Asian members of APEC through the ASEM process, meant that formal links between the EU and APEC have not been created. Since 1997, moreover, the perception among Europeans that APEC was becoming bogged down with its own problems as it tried to move down the road toward deepening and that as an organization it had proved singularly unable to cope with the Asian financial crisis dampened EU enthusiasm for pushing for any kind of formal dialogue with APEC. The predominant European perceptions of Asian Pacific regionalism, therefore, changed from skepticism in the 1970s and 1980s to suspicion in the early/mid-1990s and back again to skepticism by the end of the 1990s.

For both Europe and the Asia Pacific, however, the continuing debates about regionalization and globalization are going to be affected by differences between informed elites and ordinary citizens over the conceptualizations and practical realities of these ideas. Political and economic elites might continue to advocate the benefits of both regionalization and globalization, but resistance at the popular level, founded on concerns about the distribution of gains between rich and poor countries and within single countries and nurtured by attendant feelings of marginalization, has certainly not disappeared and, if anything, is on the increase. The series of protests outside international economic meetings around the world since late 1999 and the Danish people's vote in September 2000 against joining the EU "eurozone" are both manifestations of such unhappiness. The need to address these popular concerns is shared by political and economic leaders in both Europe and the Asia Pacific.

TRILATERALISM AND THE U.S. FACTOR

The Euro-Asian relationship does not exist in a vacuum. It is inevitably affected by the interlinkages with the United States, which appears to be both in and out of the Asia Pacific; outside geographically and culturally, but inside economically, politically, and strategically. For both Europe and the Asia Pacific countries, the relationship with the United States was, and still is, more important than their relationship with each other. To use once again that well-worn metaphor about the triangle, it has been a skewed triangle, with the Euro-Asian side of the triangle far weaker than the other two sides. Historically, both Europeans and Asians have found it difficult to live with and live without the United States. Fears that the United States might move to the extremes of either isolationism and protectionism, on the one hand, or interventionism and bullying, on the other, have persisted. These perceptions have provided the Europeans and the Asians with not only reasons for comparing notes about how to cope with the mood swings of the Americans, but also reticence at times about risking upsetting the Americans too much. This is what one European scholar has aptly described as "the shackles of timidity."[11]

Back in the 1970s, as the Trilateral Commission was launched, Europe, the United States, and Japan seemed to be the three poles of the nonsocialist industrialized world economy, and there seemed to be grounds for expecting trilateralism to emerge in a more formal intergovernmental context. That has not occurred. In the subsequent decades, Europe or the EU, North America or NAFTA, and the Asian Pacific region as a whole rather than Japan alone have, through growing economic interdependence and corporate globalization, become closer together, but this has not produced a regularized or institutionalized contact. Neither the Group of Eight (as the original Group of Seven Economic Summit has now become) nor the Organization for Economic Cooperation and Development (OECD) has provided a substitute mechanism.

In trade and investment terms, the interlinkages around the triangle have often resulted in shifting two-against-one tactical coalitions on particular sectoral issues and occasionally, as seen in the concluding stages of the GATT Uruguay Round, on broader issues. However, the propensity of the Europeans and the Asians to work together effectively against the United States on economic issues has been low and therefore nonthreatening (this view seems to extend to ASEM as an organization also[12]). In the security field, too, the sole remaining superpower has tended to dominate the triangle, especially given the particular though differing natures of the U.S. alliance systems with both Western Europe and key allies in the Asia Pacific and the embryonic character of Euro-Asian security links. Undoubtedly, the close economic and security linkages of both Western Europe and the Asia Pacific with the United States mean that changes in U.S. domestic politics in so far as they affect U.S. foreign economic and security policy, will inevitably reverberate significantly in these two regions. Neither the Europeans nor the Asians can afford to ignore the Americans.

Talking to or Past Each Other?

In the past, Euro-Asian inter-regional dialogue was hampered by the diversities and complexities of the organizations and institutional practices developing in each of the two regions; consequently, pre-ASEM the dialogue was extremely muted. Even the EU-ASEAN (Association of Southeast Asian Nations) dialogue, which was formalized as early as 1978, covered only one part of the Asian Pacific region. During the 1990s, regular dialogue mechanisms were also established between the EU and certain individual Asian Pacific states such as Japan, South Korea, and finally China, but there too, progress, as with the longer-running EU-ASEAN dialogue, tended to be uneven and unexciting.

The feeling that something was missing in the Euro-Asian relationship was around for some time, but not until the mid-1990s was region-to-region interaction seen as a realistic cure. ASEM, the result of a Singaporean initiative to strengthen the third leg of the so-called Europe-Asia-America triangle at the inter-regional level, contains the 15 EU members plus the European Commission with the 7 older members of ASEAN plus China, Japan, and South Korea.[13] The European representatives had gone into the first ASEM in Bangkok in 1996 on the defensive in the face of Asian economic triumphalism, but at ASEM-2 in London in 1998 it was the Asians who were looking battered. Although the ASEM-2 initiatives, to create a trust fund and provide technical assistance programs, were small beer compared to the totality of the financial problems then facing the Asia Pacific region, they did at least pass on the message that Europe was not about to desert Asia.[14] As economic recovery appeared in the Asian Pacific region, it was possible for both sides to go into ASEM-3, in Seoul in October 2000, in a more balanced mood—or closer to the equality preached, but more apparent than real, in the two previous meetings. Apart from the specific declaration supporting peace on the Korean peninsula, which was inevitably a preoccupation of the host country, the main focus of ASEM-3 was on consolidating the dialogue process, with a new cooperation framework document being approved.[15]

But where does ASEM go from here? ASEM has so far resisted both widening and deepening, but it is facing pressures, particularly from the wider Asia and Pacific area, to include more members and, given the European predilection for institutionalization, to agree to at least a modest degree of deepening. However, with anything up to 20 applicants from

Europe and Asia wishing to join, ASEM-3 set out criteria and mechanisms for membership that are designed to make expansion limited and slow-moving. The meeting also eschewed any formal institutionalization, preferring instead to focus on intensifying dialogues at various levels and in more sectors. Moreover, it remains true that, as a senior EU official forecast on the eve of ASEM-2, although ASEM will be a useful inter-regional forum for sending political signals and for the concerting of efforts, the end results of ASEM will often depend upon implementation at the bilateral level.[16] ASEM has gone through the initial getting-to-know-one-another stage, but if it is to have a lengthy life, then it does have to move on to more substantial and constructive dialogue. This means searching for areas of common ground and interest not just in the economic arena but also in the politico-security and civic-cultural dimensions.

In the run-up to the ASEM 3 meeting, officials from both sides identified and began to stress increasingly the "soft" dimensions of security or what can also be described as "comprehensive security,"[17] where there was clearly going to be a greater degree of consensus than on either the more purely military aspects of security or sensitive political topics such as human rights. This coming together derived from the growing awareness that there are no national solutions to such transnational problems and that both regions indeed do share a similar agenda in this respect. Issues such as environmental pollution, changes in weather patterns, drug-trafficking, smuggling of illegal immigrants, information technology security (cyberwarfare), communicable diseases and food security are impossible to solve within one country, or even one region. These areas of functional cooperation in what has been deemed the "public order" dimension of globalization[18] are likely to increasingly provide the motivation for inter-regional dialogue and can help to bring it real substance and value. Judging from the positive but nonetheless modest results of the Seoul summit meeting, ASEM, like APEC, clearly has its limitations. It will survive (further meetings in 2002 and 2004 were agreed upon), but these new areas of exchange and cooperation are the key to whether ASEM raises its profile to be a forum of priority for policy-makers in both continents. However, the heightened salience of these new issues among not just the informed elites but also among ordinary people suggests that ASEM will be increasingly forced to address these issues in a timely and concrete manner.

Life after the Asian Financial Crisis

The Asian financial crisis was as much of a surprise to the Europeans as it was to the Asians. Malaysia's prime minister, Dr. Mahathir Mohamad, was not alone in lamenting that "the economic turmoil . . . reduced the

[Asian] tigers to whimpering kittens."[19] Initial European relief and even smugness that, despite past Asian pronouncements about the superiority of the Asian way of doing things, the Asians were human after all, were transformed into a realization that the financial instability in Asia could not but have an influence on Europe. Trade balances turned sharply negative, investment flows declined, and European banks, heavily exposed in lending to Asian companies, suffered losses.[20] The psychological transmission mechanisms of international financial markets have not always been well understood, but at the very least, as the Bank of International Settlements has noted, the crisis in the Asia Pacific served as a "painful reminder" that the interconnections between global markets were becoming increasingly complex.[21] To many within the Asia Pacific region, the crisis was interpreted as a negative result of globalization, with particular blame being laid at the door of international speculators who were cast as being allied with Western countries keen to further open up Asian markets. However, the obvious unpreparedness of the Europeans—and the Americans—for the severity and spread of the Asian financial crisis, the longer-term benefits for the West from the post-financial crisis restructuring of Asian Pacific economies seem to have been more accidental than intended.

After two years of suffering, moreover, most of the Asian tigers are beginning to show their claws again. South Korea was in the van of the recovery, recording 10 percent growth in 1999, but, even though none could come close to equalling that record, all the affected Asian Pacific nations managed to get back into positive growth. Just as it was misleading during the days of the Asian "economic miracle" to describe the whole region as one of untrammelled dynamism, so too is it premature now to typecast the region as being ready and able to "scale new heights." Even the much- heralded "New Economy" boom seems to be in danger of bursting in some places and regional economists are warning against excessive optimism and talking about the potential danger of another slowdown in economic growth, especially if oil prices remain high.

Two particular side-effects of the Asian financial crisis are of importance here. First, as Richard Higgott presciently argued, the net effect of the Asian financial crisis has been to increase interest in East Asian, as opposed to Pacific-wide, regionalism.[22] Certainly, Asian disillusionment with the 1997 and 1998 APEC meetings' results, ambivalence about the American role in the Asian financial crisis, and preliminary intra-regional discussions about reducing dependence on the mighty U.S. dollar as the first step to what might lead to an "Asian currency" or at the very least an "Asian monetary fund" suggest that the Asians may well be turning in on themselves, or at least trying to redefine themselves in contradistinction to the Americans. It is still in the early days, but already it begins to look like an annual summit meeting of the ASEAN-10 and the Japanese, Chinese, and South Korean leaders, with great potential. At the November 1999 Manila summit of these 13 countries, for instance, calls were made by the host President Joseph Estrada for an East Asian common market, one East Asian currency, and one East Asian community."[23] All this suggests at the very least a greater awareness of and interest in thinking through issues relating to an East Asian (as opposed to an Asian Pacific or pan-Asian[24]) regional identity or consciousness which may ultimately be more satisfying for the East Asian elites.

Second, the ongoing process within Europe of reassessing the relative importance of the two Asian giants, Japan and China, was reinforced. For almost three decades until the mid-1990s Japan had remained the primary focus of Europe's Asia policy, predominantly because of the economic challenge but also because there gradually developed some hopes, largely unfulfilled about the eventuality of Japan playing a more internationalist political and security role. However, the prolonged Japanese economic slowdown since the early 1990s and the intra-EU process of rethinking policies towards Asia as a whole in 1994–1995[25] inevitably began to dilute Japan's stature. The Hong Kong handover and, more substantially, the Asian financial crisis, from which China emerged relatively unscathed, combined with the perceived failure of Japan to get its house in order, have meant that in both geopolitical and geoeconomic terms China is coming to replace Japan as the centerpiece of Europe's Asia policy.[26] Moreover, signs of China's growing nationalism, its more belligerent tone toward Taiwan, and the tempting commercial prospects aroused by its imminent entry into the World Trade Organization will only serve to further concentrate European minds on China's relative weight.

INTER-REGIONALISM AND GLOBALIZATION

Governments, companies, and peoples are striving to cope with the continuing changes in international society and international order. The end of the Cold War provoked extensive discussion about a new international security architecture; similarly the Asian financial crisis has led to widespread discussions about a new international financial architecture. The earlier debate on security has not been resolved satisfactorily and the "new world order" has yet to arrive. In a similar fashion, the more recent debate on global financial governance has yet to reach a conclusion and, indeed, as recovery appears across the Asian Pacific region, may also tend to fall by the wayside. Global structures can, therefore, be expected to remain unsatisfactory. In such circumstances, it may well be that regions—and regional organizations—will have an enhanced relevance.

Against this background, how is the inter-regional relationship between Europe and the Asia Pacific likely to develop? In the short-term, this "third side" of the international triangle, which of course also includes North America, is unlikely to be significantly strengthened. The only real forum for inter-regional dialogue, ASEM, will no doubt continue to exist, but without taking on any pretensions about being able to stimulate a quantum leap in the inter-regional linkages. The definition of the inter-regional relationship will remain closer to working partnership than to community. Both Europe and the Asia Pacific can be expected to be preoccupied with a certain amount of introspection, as the EU absorbs its many aspirants and as the Asia Pacific tries to decide whether it wants to be East Asian or not. For both regions the relationship with the United States will continue to have higher political salience than the linkages with each other.

For the informed elites of both Europe and the Asia Pacific, a closer relationship between the two regions is seen as desirable, but, admittedly, not absolutely essential. Neither intermittent security crises nor the Asian financial crisis have fundamentally altered that premise. Nonetheless, the longer-term processes of globalization—such as greater corporate interpenetration, faster information flows, and spreading ecological and social concerns—can be expected to heighten the importance of exploring whether and how the inter-regional relationship might be both broadened and made more rounded. The recovery from the Asian financial crisis has shown that the Asia Pacific cannot be counted out and that there is, if anything, a greater need for Europeans to "think Asian." Europe's process of reinventing itself should make Asians aware that is also worth "thinking European."

NOTES

1. Samuel S. Kim defines globalization as "a set of processes of stretching and intensifying worldwide interconnectedness in all aspects of human relations and transaction—economic, social, cultural, environmental, political, diplomatic, and security—such that events, decisions, and activities in one part of the world have immediate consequences for individuals, groups, and states in other parts of the world." See "Korea and Globalization (*Segyehwa*): A Framework for Analysis," in Samuel. S. Kim, *Korea's Globalization* (Cambridge: Cambridge University Press, 2000), 18.
2. On the Europe-Asia relationship in the twentieth century, see Hans Maull, Gerald Segal and Jusuf Wanandi, eds., *Europe and the Asia Pacific* (London: Routledge, 1998); Brian Bridges, *Europe and the Challenge of the*

Asia Pacific: Change, Continuity and Crisis (Cheltenham: Edward Elgar, 1999); and Christopher Dent, *The European Union and East Asia: An Economic Relationship* (London: Routledge, 1999).

3. Pekka Korhonen, "Monopolizing Asia: the Politics of a Metaphor." *Pacific Review* 10. no.3 (1997):347–365

4. For a stimulating discussion, see Richard Higgott, "The Political Economy of Globalization in East Asia: The Salience of 'Region Building,'" in Kris Olds et al., *Globalisation and the Asia-Pacific: Contested Territories,* (London: Routledge, 1999), 91–106.

5. See William Wallace, *The Transformation of Western Europe* (London: Pinter, 1990).

6. Dennis Swann, *European Economic Integration: The Common Market, European Union and Beyond* (Cheltenham: Edward Elgar, 1996), 38–39.

7. European Commission, *Amsterdam: A New Treaty for Europe* (Brussels: Directorate-General for Information, 1997), 10. After EU member states publicly adopted different positions about recognizing North Korea on the eve of the ASEM 3 Summit, the European Commission President Romano Prodidrily observed: "This is not a positive fact but it is not unusual. It is progress if there are only two positions instead of five." Deutsche Press-Agentur report, October 20, 2000, available at: http://web.lexis-nexis.com/universe/do . . .&mid5=632cu31344 1c09579d4905- dd9e6de2db. Henry Kissinger's old complaint about not knowing the telephone number for Europe still holds good; but then what is the telephone number for Asia?

8. See, for example, the contributions in Francois Heisbourg, *European Defence: Making It Work* (Paris: Western European Union Institute for Security Studies, 2000).

9. See M. Dutta, *Economic Regionalization in the Asia-Pacific* (Cheltenham: Edward Elgar, 1999); Stuart Harris, "Varieties of Pacific Economic Cooperation," *Pacific Review* 4, no.4 (1991):301–11; and Donald Hellmann and Kenneth Pyle, eds., *From APEC to Xanadu: Creating a Viable Community in the Post–Cold War Pacific* (New York: M.E. Sharpe, 1997).

10. *Nikkei Weekly,* 11 April 1994.

11. Leo Schmit, "Reflections from the ASEM Bowl in China," *IIAS Newsletter.* November 1999.

12. Davis Bobrow, "The US and ASEM: Why the Hegemon Didn't Bark?" *Pacific Review* 12, no.1 (1999):103–128. However, in the run-up to ASEM 3, various officials did hint that the United States and its international posture would be a topic of active concern among participants.

13. David Camroux and Christian Lechervy, "Close Encounter of a Third Kind? The Inaugural Asia-Europe Meeting of March 1996," *Pacific Review* 9, no.3: 442–453.

14. Brian Bridges, *Europe,* 185–188. See also comments by various contributors to "The ASEM III Summit" special issue of *Asian Affairs* (Hong Kong), no.13 (Autumn 2000); and Yeo Lay Hwee, "ASEM: Looking Back, Looking Forward," *Contemporary Southeast Asia* (April 2000): 113–144.

15. *Chairman's Statement of the Third Asia-Europe Meeting, Seoul, 20—21 October 2000; Asia-Europe Cooperation Framework 2000.* Issued by Ministry of Foreign Affairs, Republic of Korea, Seoul, Korea. Available at: http://www.asem3.org/english/index01.html

16. Percy Westerlund, "Strengthening Euro-Asian Relations: ASEM as a Catalyst," in *ASEM: A Window of Opportunity,* edited by Wim Stokhof and Paul van der Velde (London: Kegan Paul International, 1999), 25.

17. For a detailed elaboration of the term "comprehensive security" as covering economic, environmental, and human security, see chapter 1. ASEM background documents do not use that terminology, but see the Asia-Europe Vision Group's report, *For a Better Tomorrow: Asia-Europe Partnership in the 21st Century* (1999) and, in particular, the European Commission's Working Document, *Perspectives and Priorities for the ASEM Process into the New Decade* [COM2000(241), 18 April 2000], which argued for making enhanced cooperation on "soft security" and the "new security issues" a specific ASEM priority. Available at: http://europa.eu.int/comm/external relations/asem/asem process/work grp2000.htm.

18. Keith Suter, "People Power," *The World Today,* October 2000, 13.

19. *Straits Times,* 3 March 1998.

20. Brian Bridges, "Europe and the Asian Financial Crisis," *Asian Survey* (May-June 1999): 456—67. According to my own calculations from International Monetary Fund data, the EU trade deficit with the Asia Pacific in 1997 was around 40 percent larger than in 1996 and soared by a further 93 percent in 1998.

21. Bank for International Settlements, "Quarterly commentary and statistics on recent developments in international banking and financial markets: press summary," Basle: 9 March 1998. Available at: http://www.bis.org/press/p980309.htm.

22. Richard Higgott, "Shared Response to the Market Shocks?" *The World Today* (January 1998): 6.

23. *South China Morning Post,* 29 November 1999.

24. Malaysian Prime Minister Mahathir, speaking in October 2000, made it clear, when he called for setting up an "Asian Association for Development," that South Asia was excluded from his particular vision: "Asians cannot come together the way Europeans can come together. Asia must accept it is a divided continent. Accepting this, it must plan its future as separate sub-continents, growing according to its special comparative advantages and at different paces." *New Straits Times,* 30 October 2000.

25. The EU adopted an "Asia strategy" policy paper in 1994 and then followed up with a series of papers clarifying policies toward individual Asian countries or subregions.

26. The head of the EU office in Hong Kong, Etienne Reuter, neatly expressed this European view: "China has become a protagonist of stability, advising and assisting countries in the region; Japan is perceived as having an economy that weakens and political institutions that resist reform." *Hongkong Standard,* 11 June 1998.

CHAPTER 6

REGIONAL TRADE AND SECURITY ARRANGEMENTS IN THE ASIA PACIFIC AND THE WESTERN HEMISPHERE IN COMPARATIVE PERSPECTIVE

RICHARD FEINBERG[1]

INTRODUCTION

Free trade areas are to the contemporary world what military alliances were during the Cold War years: expressions of commitments and interrelationships that transcend their formal documentation. For example, United States relations with Japan and South Korea were much deeper and diverse than the military commitments made in the respective security pacts. Today, free trade areas, such as the Association of Southeast Asian Nations (ASEAN), the North American Free Trade Area (NAFTA), and the European Union, imply obligations and benefits on an agenda of mutual concerns that are much more far-reaching than the mere reduction of barriers to the movement of commodities and capital.

Today, free trade areas typically express an intention to consolidate and deepen the variety of existing ties—commercial, political, diplomatic, and perhaps even military—between societies. The initiation of the two trading arrangements analyzed here—the Asia Pacific Economic Cooperation (APEC) forum and the Free Trade Area of the Americas (FTAA)—came about as the result of a myriad of causalities, many beyond the purely commercial. In the minds of many of their progenitors and creators, APEC's Bogor Declaration of free trade and investment and the Western Hemisphere's free trade commitment are but steps toward bold visions of more prosperous and secure regional communities of nations and peoples.

Both APEC and the FTAA are significant as economic forums. APEC members, now totaling 21 economies, account for about one half of world output and 42 percent of global trade.[2] Including North America, Japan, and China, and with the addition of Russia, APEC encompasses the world's main power centers exclusive of Europe. The FTAA initiative covers the entire Western Hemisphere (except Cuba) and about 38 percent of the global product. Both APEC and the FTAA have declared their intentions to realize region-wide free trade by specific target dates and to promote liberal investment rules.

But both APEC and the FTAA are part of larger regional community-building projects with important geopolitical overtones. In the economic arena, these two trading arrangements are accompanied by a multitude of economic development initiatives, including programs aimed at building human and infrastructure capacity to adjust to globalization, spreading the benefits of growth more widely, and fostering a more sustainable development. In APEC, the trade and investment agenda is accompanied by an array of economic and technical assistance programs designed to prepare members for further liberalization. In the Western Hemisphere, from its inception, the FTAA has been imbedded in the broader process of the summits of the Americas (Miami, 1994; Santiago, 1998; Quebec, scheduled for April, 2001). Free trade is just part—albeit a critical part—of the comprehensive economic, social, and political mandates issued at the Americas' summits. The summit declarations proclaim that free trade, democracy promotion, economic integration, and poverty alleviation are mutually consistent and supportive goals. Thus, we can speak of the FTAA cum summitry to underscore how the trade initiative is deeply imbedded on a much broader hemispheric agenda.

Both the Asia Pacific and the Western Hemisphere free trade initiatives are governed by decision-making processes capped by summit meetings of heads of state and government—visible signals that interests beyond those of trade ministers are at stake. The geopolitical agendas on the minds of these leaders may be part and parcel of the formal multilateral agenda or may be reserved for private bilateral sessions. In the Western Hemisphere, political issues were on the summit agenda from the outset, and the defense and security items on the summit agenda have been expanding ever since. APEC has been much more circumspect about tackling security issues as part of the formal agenda. Yet, in both regions, many participants hope that enhanced economic interdependence and integration into global markets will dampen historic animosities, facilitate cooperation on the new security agenda (nonproliferation, illegal immigration, communicable diseases, international crime, and narcotics trafficking), and improve the overall security environment. One does not have to be a crude economic determinist to imagine positive spillovers from economic cooperation into strategic comity.

This comparative study of APEC and the FTAA has several purposes. The fates of these two regional integration experiments are inexorably linked: They both gained momentum at the same historical moment, and both enterprises will be strongly affected by future developments at the global level, including progress or lack thereof in the WTO. In addition, senior policy-makers in the key member countries link the two processes in their calculations; the actual and perceived progress in one regional effort will continue to influence policy initiatives in the other. A number of Western Hemisphere countries are also members of APEC, including the NAFTA partners—the United States, Canada and Mexico—as well as Chile and Peru. Finally, comparative studies allow for valuable cross-pollination through the discovery and sharing of experiences and "best practices."

This chapter will first consider factors—both common and unique—behind the formation of APEC and the FTAA cum summitry. It will then analyze the centerpiece of both experiments, namely their proposed trade regimes. In examining the trade regimes, the study will compare the principles and objectives adopted by each regime, bargaining forum and modalities, institutional structures (ministerials, working groups, secretariats), information flow (monitoring feedback and analysis), administrative arrangements, issue scope, and allowances made for differing levels of development and size among countries.

Since APEC and the FTAA cum summitry are not just about trade, this chapter will compare and contrast their non-trade economic and social agenda, including economic and technical cooperation (APEC), and poverty alleviation and modernization of the state (FTAA), as well as treatment of environmental protection and labor rights. Finally, the chapter will also consider the handling of diplomatic and security matters.

ORIGINS

The emergence of both APEC and the FTAA in the late 1980s and early 1990s can be located in system-altering shifts in global political economy. That is, both can be explained in part by trends in the international security system, in the evolution of private markets and firm behavior, in cross-border alliances among like-minded elites, and in the growing influence of transnational epistemic communities that shared relevant ideas and policy initiatives (table 6.1). But too often analyses of the origins of these groupings (Aggarwal 1994); Soesastro 1994) fail to take sufficient note of the glaring presence, in each of these spheres, of countervailing forces opposed to strong regionalism. In the ensuing struggle between forces in favor and opposed to APEC and the FTAA, at critical moments the outcomes were influenced by nonstructural forces, such as chance events that forced decisions, and by leadership choices made in the face of politically feasible alternative paths. In fact, such circumstantial and subjective elements have been important in the formation of both APEC and the FTAA.

At the same time, the precise manner in which broad historical forces acted upon the Asia Pacific and the Western Hemisphere naturally depended upon the unique characteristics of each region. The interaction between common external or systemic variables and local conditions account for the substantial similarities as well as the great differences between the two regional formations.

The Formation of APEC

The creation of APEC in 1989, and its critical elevation from ministerial to heads of state level in 1993, is generally explained in terms of several variables or levels of analysis: international systemic change, state-level interests, private markets, and the power of ideas.

The bipolar world of the Cold War, it is often alleged—with its division of the globe into two hostile military blocs—left little room for important initiatives by second tier powers or by groups of developing countries (Camilleri 1994; Keohane 1984). Supposedly, secondary powers or coalitions felt too weak to act or feared that one of the superpowers would constrain their ambitions. This argument, however, may be overstated. The United States not only tolerated but encouraged economic integration in Western Europe, in part because it felt that a stronger Western Europe served as a bulwark against Soviet expansion (Kahler 1994). The United States also favored ASEAN on security grounds: By banding together, South East Asian nations could better resist aggression by the communist states of North Vietnam and China, as well as bolster themselves against communist-led internal subversion. The United States generally tolerated and at times even endorsed Latin American regional integration efforts (for example, at the 1967 Punta del Este hemispheric summit). However, the United States did have reservations about the economic development models of import substitution industrialization (ISI) being pursued by some ASEAN and some Latin American nations—an approach that was en-

Table 6.1 Origins of APEC and the FTAA

Variable	APEC	FTAA
International system	Fading of north-south divide Fading of socialism-capitalism schism	Fading of north-south divide
State interests	Leadership by Japan, Australia, Indonesia But: ASEAN ambivalence; divisions within U.S. government	Leadership by Argentina, Chile, Canada Latin Americans bandwagoning on NAFTA But: Brazilian ambivalence; Mexican preference for NAFTA exclusivity; divisions within U.S. government
Private markets	Increase in intra-regional trade and investment flows But: protectionist sectors	Increase in intra-regional trade and investment flows But: protectionist sectors
Regional precursors	ASEAN, ANZCER But: no precedents for broad regional cooperation	NAFTA, CACM, CARICOM, Andean Pact, MERCOSUR, OAS, IDB
Conceptual ideas	Pacific Community ideal Export orientation replacing ISI But: "Asia for Asians"; nationalisms; cultural/political heterogeneity; globalism as the best	Western Hemisphere ideal Open market orientation replacing OSI But: Latin American nationalisms; U.S. skepticism; globalism as the best
Influential individuals	Eminent Persons Group White House officials Robert Hawke	White House officials
Circumstances	1993 Seattle meeting Uruguay Round endgame	Gore's post-NAFTA address, Miami Summit of the Americas; APEC initiative

Abbreviations: Association of Southeast Asian Nations (ASEAN); North American Free Trade Agreement (NAFTA); Australia-New Zealand Closer Economic Relations (ANZCER); Central American Common Market (CACM); Southern Common Market (MERCOSUR); Organization of American States (OAS); Inter-American Development Bank (IDB); import substitution industrialization (ISI).

shrined in some regional integration pacts. ISI was often wrapped in an anti-U.S. rhetoric and prejudiced the interests of some U.S. traders and investors. Differences over economic development strategies, rather than objections to regionalism per se, and contrasting perceptions regarding the impact of the international economic system on national development opportunities drove a wedge between industrial and developing nations, between North and South.

In the years after World War II, no major power from within Asia was capable of providing the local leadership required to catalyze regionalism. China was enfeebled by civil war (1940s) and isolated by its Cultural Revolution (1966–1976). Still recovering from its military defeat and psychological humiliation, Japan was too weakened to play a leadership role. It was this debilitation, and the memories of Japan's aggression, rather than Cold War bipolarity, that prevented Japan from leading a regional integration movement in the post-war years (Kahler 1994, 20). Japan's security dependence on the United States was not, per se, the critical inhibiting factor; indeed, Japan remained militarily dependent upon the U.S. security guarantee in the 1980s when it seized a leadership role in promoting regional cooperation.

The Cold War years were not conducive to regional cooperation in Asia. But this regional fragmentation was due less to bipolarity than to local divisions arising from historical memories, ideological cleavages, and North-South tensions. It was more factors operating at the regional level, rather than shifts at the international systemic level, that postponed the emergence of APEC.

By the late 1980s, each of these barriers to regional cooperation was falling. Memories of past conflicts were fading and communist-capitalist and North-South cleavages were closing. The ASEAN model of economic development was shifting from ISI to export-led growth linked to foreign investment. Japan had not only recovered from military defeat but was experiencing rapid technology-driven growth and spectacular export success. Its firms were investing heavily in ASEAN nations as well as in North America. It was poised to assume a leadership role in the region (Funabashi 1995). In Oceania, Australia, having adopted a more outward-oriented growth model, was taking a new interest in its Asian neighborhood (Ravenhill 1998; Terada 1999).

The post–Cold War geopolitics permitted but did not guarantee the emergence of formal, inter-governmental regional cooperation in Asia. The decision to create APEC was also influenced by economic variables—particularly the growing interests of firms in regional markets, and governments in facilitating the movement of trade and capital. With the adaptation of export-oriented strategies, and the reduction in trade barriers in many countries, intra-regional trade boomed in the 1980s and early 1990s, outpacing the region's trade with the rest of the world (table 6.2). After the 1985 Plaza Accord made Japanese exports less competitive, intra-regional investment also soared, most notably of Japanese firms in ASEAN markets. These market developments created domestic political pressures, in Japan but also throughout the region, for governments to further reduce barriers to economic exchange and to create regional policy bodies to facilitate such exchange (Busch and Milner 1994). For the Japanese government, regional cooperation to promote market opening had benefits for Japanese investors and traders; for ASEAN, regional cooperation held the promise of additional international investment, as well as readier access for exports, by domestic and internationally owned firms, to Japanese and other regional markets (Akashi 1997).

Regional economic integration was being market driven, and trade and investment barriers were falling through unilateral liberalizations being undertaken as part of profound national economic reform programs, creating fertile conditions for more formal integration efforts. But whereas private-sector dynamics were paving the road for regional cooperation, the role of ideas in the formation of APEC should not be ignored (Aggarwal 1994; Higgott 1998). Policy-oriented intellectuals had long been arguing for the economic and strategic advantages of deeper regional ties (Drysdale and Garnaut 1993; Soesastro 1994). Since the late 1960s, the Japanese-supported Pacific Trade and Development Conference (PAFTAD) had been convening policy intellectuals to debate a series of regional economic issues and to search for ways for transnational collaboration. During the 1980s, the influence of policy intellectuals had found embodiment in the Pacific Economic Cooperation Council (PECC), a tripartite business, academic, and government forum organized to catalyze regional cooperation; its Trade Policy Forum pooled the talents of trade experts to study regional integration proposals. There was a considerable overlap in the key personalities in PAFTAD and PECC, as they grew to form a transnational epistemic community of policy-oriented experts advocating closer regional ties throughout the Asia Pacific (Woods 1993).

Yet, the formation of APEC was not inevitable. There were still serious geopolitical and ideological obstacles to regional cooperation. Japanese-Chinese rivalry continued, imbedded in geography and history. Some ASEAN leaders remained wary of the motives of bigger powers and feared that a larger regional organization might swallow up, distort, or dilute the importance of their subregional trading arrangements (SRTAs) (Plummer 1998). Moreover, while states were opening their economies to international trade and investment, they were far from being in full agreement regarding optimal development models. These are among the enduring reasons why multilateralism has never thrived in the region.

Indeed, there was no consensus definition of the region (Higgott 1994; Dirlik 1992). One definition of Asia would include the Indian subcontinent but exclude the Western Hemisphere. The Asia Pacific concept included North America and perhaps the Pacific littoral of South America. Then there was the thorny question of whether Russia was a Pacific or essentially European power.

As it contemplated a leadership role in forming a regional arrangement, the Japanese government was divided on the desirability of U.S. participation (Terada 1999). To exclude the United States meant a stronger profile for Japan, but also risked frightening some Asian nations and offending Washington. For its part, the United States feared being left out of a regional institution (Baker 1995,609). The United States wanted to participate to reaffirm its presence in Asia, to gain from any economic liberalization, and perhaps to preempt any Japanese bid for a separate leadership. If there was to be an Asian prosperity sphere, this time the United States wanted to be on the inside. But in the United States as elsewhere, there were differing views with regard to the value and potential for regional cooperation, and its possible adverse implications for existing global initiatives (Funabashi 1995, 80–84; Bhagwati 1993).

The decision by APEC to pursue free and open trade, while an attractive goal for a commercially-oriented regional organization, was not a foregone conclusion..The actual decision was heavily influenced by the recommendations of its appointed Eminent Persons Group (EPG). Led by a highly effective policy entrepreneur, C. Fred Bergsten, the EPG issued strongly-worded reports advocating free and open trade in the Asia Pacific (Eminent Persons Group 1994) that served as intellectual catalysts and provided a set of coherent ideas to APEC (Funabashi 1995, 141). If APEC was a forum in search of an agenda, the EPG filled that vacuum and helped to coalesce opinion around a bold vision.

At least several governments were hesitant to accept the EPG's very ambitious goals, but the targets were distant enough in the future, and the process was sufficiently couched in consensual and voluntary terms, that governments relaxed their reservations. Moreover, in the enthusiasm of the moment, and barraged by the forcefulness of the EPG's arguments, laggards felt compelled to go along with the emerging consensus.

Had APEC not been elevated to leaders meetings, it may have lacked the initiative to seize the EPG's offering. Yet, the elevation of APEC from rather pedestrian, constrained ministerials to high-profile summits was a very circumstantial occurrence. The groundbreaking 1993 Seattle Leaders Meeting was not the result of a planned or negotiated process (Aggarwal and Morrison 1994, 19, fn.30), but rather stemmed from several coincidences: that it happened to be the U.S. turn to host the 1993 APEC ministerial, that a new U.S. president had taken office in Washington, that this new president was open to fresh international

Table 6.2 Intra-Regional as Compared with Worldwide Trade Growth

| | West Hemisphere Region | | | APEC | | | |
	Intra-Regional Trade	Worldwide	Ratio of Trade Growth: Intra-Regional/Worldwide	Intra-Regional Trade	Worldwide	Ratio of Trade Growth: Intra-Regional/Worldwide	Total World Trade
1985/1980	15%	11%	1.36	39%	20%	1.95	-4%
1990/1985	47%	53%	0.89	84%	73%	1.15	86%
1995/1990	73%	55%	1.33	82%	70%	1.17	48%
1997/1995	27%	21%	1.29	0%	42%	0.00	9%

Trade Growth of West Hemisphere

Trade Growth of APEC

Source: IMF, Direction of Trade Statistics Yearbook, various issues

initiatives, and that a few well-placed senior White House officials (notably Bowman Cutter, deputy director of the newly created National Economic Council, and Sandra Kristoff, National Security Council senior director for Asian Affairs) so advised their president.

There was considerable opposition to the idea of an APEC summit within the U.S. bureaucracy—from Europeanists and trade globalists, from those who oppose summits because they increase the power of the White House as against cabinet agencies (such as the Treasury), and from some domestic and political advisers who guard the President's calendar. The pro-Summit White House officials circumvented routine bureaucratic decision-making channels, which tend to institutionalize inertia and veto new ideas, by taking the summit idea directly to President Clinton and by inserting it into presidential speeches (Funabashi 1995, 80–81). The pro-APEC contingent took advantage of the youth of the administration. Typically there is more fluidity in decision-making early in an administration, before bureaucratic routines are firmly set and when individuals may take advantage of personal ties to senior officials that may predate government service.

As with the decision to convene the first Summit of the Americas (taken in late November 1993), the decision to transform APEC into a leadership forum was largely internal to the U.S. government. The White House decided to take advantage of its privileges as host and of its inherent power. The Asian and Western Hemisphere partners were informed that Seattle was being elevated from a ministerial to a leaders meeting either with very short notice prior to public announcement or after the fact.

One argument for hoisting the APEC flag was to spur the Europeans into making enough concessions to conclude the Uruguay Round. Through APEC, the United States signaled to the Europeans that it harbored an alternative trade strategy should they block progress in the GATT/WTO. This instrumental objective was achieved but was inherently short-lived and self-liquidating. Taken by itself, it would suggest that U.S. interest in APEC would flag once the Uruguay Round was over.

In sum, in the late 1980s geopolitical shifts facilitated but did not make inevitable the formation of formal, intergovernmental regional cooperation mechanisms in the Asia Pacific. Dynamic private markets stimulated on-going regional liberalization, but the continuation of this self-reinforcing process did not require an additional layer of official decision-making. Moreover, there were strong counterforces—in local cultures and history, among some globalists and protectionists, and within official circles in key countries (Higgott 1994). The formation of APEC, therefore, far from being inevitable, was a matter of policy choice and leadership decisions influenced by circumstantial events and personalities. The specific content of APEC's institutional formation and policy agenda—annual summits and the creation of regional free trade—was even less structurally predetermined.

To complete the argument, let us imagine a feasible counterfactual. Different decisions might have left APEC at the ministerial level. APEC might have turned aside the more radical notions of its Eminent Persons Group, agreeing instead to focus on less controversial and perhaps more realistic commercial measures such as trade facilitation and sectoral cooperation. There would have been no Bogor Declaration. Also, a ministerial-led arrangement would probably have generated a less wide-ranging agenda for development assistance. Indeed, even now there are observers who consider this scenario a better fit, a more stable equilibrium more reflective of the balance of forces in the Asia Pacific.

THE FREE TRADE AREA OF THE AMERICAS

As with the Asia Pacific, during the Cold War it is not clear that bipolarity itself was the critical factor in suppressing regional cooperation in the Western Hemisphere. On the contrary, the struggle with the Soviet Union was an incentive for regional cooperation, as epitomized in the Kennedy era Alliance for Progress. At the height of the Cold War, in 1967 a Western Hemisphere summit at Punta del Este agreed on the formation of a free trade area—but one that included Latin American nations only. The United States supported the initiative and acquiesced to its own exclusion. At that time, a hemisphere-wide free trade association (FTA) was unthinkable. In the Western Hemisphere as in Asia during the 1960s, a region-wide FTA would have been inconsistent with North-South divisions and with the ISI model in vogue among developing countries. No doubt, had the idea of a hemispheric FTA been tabled, some in the United States would have questioned its consistency with global trade governance; however, it should be noted that earlier in the decade the United States had promoted the creation of a regional development bank, the Inter-American Development Bank (IDB), after it felt comfortable that it would complement and not conflict with the globalist Bretton Woods institutions.

During the 1980s, as in Asia, shifts were occurring in national development strategies and in private markets, which created more favorable conditions for Hemispheric economic cooperation. Under pressure from external debt, Latin American nations began to abandon ISI strategies, to liberalize their domestic markets and unilaterally to open their economies to international trade and investment—trends accelerated by reinvigorated or new subregional integration pacts. For their part, U.S. firms, through direct investment, strategic alliances, and intrafirm trade, increased their presence in Latin American markets. Within the Western Hemisphere, intra-regional trade grew by 47 percent from 1985–1990 and by another 73 percent from 1990–1995 (table 6.2). This market-driven integration interacted in a virtuous cycle with government liberalization policies, and together they changed the economic landscape of the region.

Latin American interest in regional integration also obeyed certain political and dynamic motives (Devlin and French-Davis 1999; Corrales and Feinberg 1999). Notwithstanding histories of national conflict and rivalries, centripetal forces of a common heritage and culture from time to time gain strength and pull the region together, as occurred during the early 1990s. In addition, a free trade agreement with the United States could serve to signal to investors, domestic and international, that the authorities were committed to market-oriented reforms. In an act of self-bondage, local authorities could lock themselves into reform policies through international agreements, thereby raising the domestic costs to altering course and increasing the confidence of investors that the region would not revert to ISI populism.

In 1990, in a dramatic policy shift, the Mexican government proposed the creation of a FTA with the United States—an initiative that President George Bush accepted. That same year, the Andean presidents urged Bush to consider deeper economic engagement in the region (Feinberg 1997, 39–52). Consequently, the United States announced the Enterprise for the Americas Initiative (AEI), the forerunner of the FTAA. The AEI comprised a multilateral fund within the IDB to spur private investment, some bilateral debt relief tied to continued economic reform and free trade agreements with the ultimate goal of a hemisphere-wide free trade system.

Both the Mexican FTA and the AEI were adopted by Bush without allowing for much internal bureaucratic consideration. Bush tasked his Treasury Department to develop the AEI and to prevent harassment by those in the State Department and U.S. Trade Representative's office, who had reputations for opposing regional preferential schemes (Feinberg 1997, 47, fn. 25).

The U.S. Treasury saw the AEI as an instrument for rewarding and legitimizing the "technopols" that were liberalizing Latin American economies and in many cases helping to consolidate democratic regimes (Dominguez 1997). In addition to international legitimacy, external support took the form of multilateral financial and technical assistance. For their part, the economic reformers welcomed this external support in their battles with the beneficiaries of ISI who opposed reform. This international alliance of elites is often overlooked, yet it explains in part the temporal variation with regard to the enthusiasm for regional cooperation and free trade initiatives. When the reform process was still young and fragile, this transnational alliance was highly valued in Latin America, and its importance was recognized in the United States. By the late 1990s, as the reform process was more consolidated in many Latin American countries, it was less in need of dramatic new official initiatives to sustain itself. Thus, paradoxically, the consolidation of reform diluted one of the factors that had stimulated the AEI and FTAA earlier in the decade.

Compared to Asia, in most of Latin America there was less ambivalence toward a region-wide FTA. The Western Hemisphere ideal had a long and venerable history stretching back to the early nineteenth century (Corrales and Feinberg 1999). While hemispheric cooperation always had had its opponents, it enjoyed strong roots in the hemisphere's contiguous geography, common history, and shared cultures and languages (notwithstanding the diversity of indigenous peoples). Certainly compared to the historical, religious, and linguistic heterogeneity of Asia, the Western Hemisphere stands as relatively homogenous.

Similarly, the Western Hemisphere is not plagued by the types of fierce rivalries among powerful states that characterize Asia's geopolitics. In its own hemisphere, the United States is overwhelmingly dominant militarily; it definitively defeated Mexico in the mid-nineteenth century, after which Mexico essentially disarmed. The natural regional hegemon in South America, Brazil, allied with the United States in World War II, has remained under U.S.-led hemispheric security arrangements. The rivalry between Mexico and Brazil for Latin American leadership is muted by U.S. dominance; furthermore, Mexican strategic interests focus primarily on North America while Brazil concentrates primarily on its South American neighborhood. In this sense, the Western Hemisphere benefits from unambiguous and unchallenged hegemonic stability.

Furthermore, whereas ASEAN viewed with suspicion a larger formation involving bigger powers, most of the Latin American subregional trading arrangements welcomed a hemispheric FTAA. They looked forward to easier or more secure access to the region's overwhelmingly largest market (the United States) and a more secure and lucrative environment that could attract foreign investors. (Hufbauer and Schott 1994). Recall that it was the members of the Andean Common Market, in their meeting with President Bush, that spurred the creation of the AEI. From the outset, the five members of the Central American Common Market were enthusiastic about a hemispheric FTAA. Only MERCOSUR (Southern Common Market) demurred; Chile and Argentina were among the main proponents of a hemispheric FTAA, but Brazil was ambivalent. Brazilian strategic thinkers saw a U.S.-led FTAA as challenging Brazil (and MERCOSUR) for leadership in South America, while Sao Paulo's industrialists did not relish unfettered competition from U.S. firms. Brazil's diversified trade patterns also raised questions about the efficiency effects of a hemispheric FTA (Da Motta Vega 1997, Yeats and Erzan 1992).

Whereas, in Asia, multilateral cooperation was an embryonic idea advanced in some private sector and academic circles, the Western Hemisphere already was thickly populated with regional institutions (albeit of varying degrees of effectiveness). Latin America had a long if checkered history of regional and subregional trade pacts, the recent incarnations of which included precise and binding liberalization commitments. Moreover, in the early 1990s, relations between the United States and Latin America were the best in memory, perhaps in history (Corrales and Feinberg 1999). The NAFTA negotiations gave impetus to the idea of hemispheric free trade, and Latin American countries worried that NAFTA gave Mexico preferential access to the huge U.S. market. One network of policy-oriented elites, the Inter-American Dialogue, explicitly urged the NAFTA partners to begin consultations with other hemispheric governments to build NAFTA into a Western Hemisphere trade pact (Inter-American Dialogue 1993). Several signatories of that report shortly assumed senior positions in the new Clinton administration. However, it cannot be said that the AEI, NAFTA, and FTAA were the result of an organized political movement or strong intellectual groundswell.

Rather, it was a particular sequence of events that caused this inchoate feeling of goodwill to be concretized in the aspiration to create a FTAA. In telescoped fashion: U.S. Vice President Al Gore short-circuited opposition to a hemispheric summit within the executive bureaucracy (among many of the same forces that had reservations about elevating APEC to the summit level—globalists, Europeanists, domesticists and, in this case, some who favored attention to Asia over Latin America) and himself asked President Clinton if he could announce a hemispheric summit, in a speech he was to give in Mexico to celebrate NAFTA (Feinberg 1997,55−61). The decision to host a hemispheric summit involved only a few officials, almost all in the White House, and was made within 48 hours. As with the decision to elevate APEC to the summitry level, White House officials took advantage of the relative fluidity in decision-making characteristic of the early days of a new administration and seized upon the circumstantial opportunity presented by a scheduled speech to announce an initiative and thereby preempt opposition.

These activist officials understood that trade would be a centerpiece of the Americas summit. However, not all could foresee that the Latin Americans, wanting to bandwagon on NAFTA, would seize upon the vehicle of the 1994 Summit of the Americas to press the United States for an explicit commitment to an FTAA. Clearly ambivalent, the Clinton administration acceded as the condition for making the U.S.-hosted summit a success. The United States yielded to Latin American pressure for a date certain for completing negotiations for the FTAA only after APEC had set its own date certain and the Latin Americans insisted on equal treatment.

As with APEC, it is possible to imagine a feasible counterfactual. Following the NAFTA accord, the United States could have continued with the Bush administration strategy of lower-level working group meetings with individual or subgroups of countries focusing in a relaxed mode on limited trade and investment issues. A presidential trip to Latin America could have substituted for the summit, thereby depriving the Latin Americans of the opportunity of ganging up on the United States to insist on an FTAA (and substituting a GATT/WTO-style roundtable bargaining model for the Bush administration's hub-and-spoke style). Indeed, such a cautious approach would have been more consistent with the policy path chosen by the Clinton administration during its second term, once anti-FTAA forces reasserted themselves.

Comparative Beginnings

The preceding comparison between the formation of APEC and the FTAA is illuminating in several respects. Common contributing factors emerge: a more relaxed international environment, an ongoing process of market-driven integration, more conducive national development models, and communal region-wide intellectual currents and networks. Among emerging market economies, there was a strong interest in overcoming the old North-South divide and in integrating domestic and international markets (Tussie 1998). Yet, in both regions these currents were not so powerful as to make APEC—with its summits and Bogor Declaration—and the Americas summits—with their FTAA—inevitable.

Both regional integration schemes faced opposition from various bureaucratic factions, private sector interests, and scholarly analysts with contrary ideas. Among regional powers (Japan, China, Brazil), there was the ever-present ambivalence in the face of U.S. power. Among subregional trade arrangements (SRTAs), such as ASEAN and MERCOSUR, there was concern that their integration projects might be overshadowed or even gobbled up by larger, more powerful structures. Some traditional Latin Americanists and Asianists feared that integration projects that included the United States and Canada, and in the APEC case Australia and New Zealand, were a danger to their narrower visions.

In both regions, markets—driven by investor decisions, relative costs, technology—were boosting trade and investment flows, without the benefit from a broad, regional-wide FTA. A formal FTA might serve to codify existing gains, raise the costs to regression, and accelerate further integration—but it was not an obvious precondition for continued progress. Moreover, there were other proven avenues for further liberalization—unilateral acts, subregional pacts, market openings spurred by the Bretton Woods institutions—that did not require a broad regional umbrella. As suggested above, there were feasible alternative outcomes that might have pursued these paths.

Final decisions were dependent upon special—even peculiar—historical circumstances and leadership decisions. In the United States, the openness of President Clinton to new initiatives, the ability of a few senior officials in the early days of an administration to short circuit routine, bureaucratic decision-making procedures, and the use of speech appointments and meetings as decision-forcing events, were special factors of some importance in both cases.

What does it mean to say that an outcome was the result of circumstance or leadership? Can we not locate interests behind the political logic? The argument presented here is that circumstances and leadership produced outcomes that were not readily predictable based purely upon an assessment of the power of competing coalitions of interests. On the contrary, interests opposed to the outcomes were probably dominant—but were trumped by events.

Yet outcomes that do not reflect underlying interests are vulnerable to reversal in future battles. Bold leaders may seek to alter the balance of political forces, for example by strengthening supportive coalitions, by gaining ground in ideological debates, or by weakening or appeasing opposition parties. APEC and the FTAA grew out of just such circumstantial and subjective decisions, and in the absence of concerted leadership, rest on fragile foundations and their futures are therefore far from certain.

Neither APEC (as opposed to APEC summits) nor the FTAA were in the first instance the product of U.S. initiative. On the contrary, the United States—ambivalent at best—was pulled in by initiatives taken by other nations and leaders. These two important regional formations were in their first instance driven by "local" forces, not by the one remaining superpower. This historic truth should give various APEC and

FTAA participants a sense of pride and ownership. But it may also be a serious weakness: As has been demonstrated in recent years, not only does the United States not feel strong ownership of these two regional initiatives but its active participation is hampered by serious domestic opposition to economic cooperation with low-wage areas.

In comparison to APEC, although the FTAA began with less fanfare from the outset it has stood on firmer ground. Asia's latent power rivalries, the region's profound cultural heterogeneity, the ambivalence of ASEAN, the diversity of development levels and models—all worked against the easy elimination of barriers to free trade and investment flows throughout the Asia-Pacific. Whereas for the Western Hemisphere, hegemonic stability, relative cultural homogeneity, the enthusiasm of existing SRTAs (with the partial exception of Brazil), and the convergence of economic models (outside Cuba)—together assembled relatively impressive building blocks for an FTA.

TRADE REGIMES

The APEC and FTAA trade regimes were not conceived of as breaks with the reigning global integration paradigm. Neither was presented as a revolutionary undertaking challenging existing norms. On the contrary, both undertakings were careful to underscore their allegiance to GATT/WTO norms, to proclaim their adherence to "open regionalism," and to label themselves as building blocks—not stumbling blocks—toward freer global trade. They self-consciously "nested" themselves within the dominant international regime (Aggarwal 1994). Fears expressed by some historians and academic economists that such regional trading arrangements (RTAs) might undermine and destroy GATT/WTO globalism were unwarranted, as should have been clear from the spirit, scope, and institutional structures of the two RTAs (Bergsten 1997; Lawrence 1996). It should be noted, however, that APEC and the FTAA use the term "open regionalism" differently (Haggard 1997). For the FTAA, open regionalism suggests a commitment to trade creation and to avoiding new protectionist measures against nonmembers that would promote trade diversion. The region remains open to the global economy, and intra-regional integration is designed to enhance the region's international competitiveness (United Nations Economic Commission for Latin America and the Caribbean/UNECLAC 1994, 6–9). For the FTAA, open regionalism does not mean to imply the extension of trade preferences to nonmembers, nor is the FTAA likely to be open to extrahemispheric nations, at least in the early years. Within APEC, there has been a heated debate

Table 6.3 Comparative Trade Regimes

Topic	APEC	FTAA	Comments
Principles and norms	WTO consistent; open regionalism; non-discrimination; transparency; SRTAs as building blocks; voluntarism; unilateralism; comparability	WTO consistent; open regionalism; non-discrimination; transparency; SRTAs as building blocks; reciprocity; balance	In APEC "open regionalism" includes accession and may mean most-favored-nation (MFN) treatment; FTAA follows "Western" model, APEC experiments with "Asian" informality
Key objectives	Free and open trade and investment	Free trade area	
Negotiating forum	Summits (leaders meetings); ministerials; senior official meetings (SOMs); Committee on Trade and Investment (CTI); working groups	Summits (leaders meetings); ministerials; Trade Negotiations Committee (TNC); negotiating groups	APEC working groups not empowered to negotiate
Negotiating modalities	Individual Action Plans (IAPs); Collective Action Plans (CAPs); Early Voluntary Sectoral Liberalization (EVSL); continuous process; early harvest	Single undertaking; simultaneous process; early harvest	APEC's decentralized gradualism contrasts with FTAA's centralized single undertaking
Oversight of implementation	Self review; peer review; PECC/TPF studies	To be determined	APEC's IAPs create demand for monitoring of implementation
Administrative structures	APEC Secretariat	OAS/IDB/UNECLAC; Tripartite Committee; rotating administrative secretariat	FTAA builds on existing hemisperic institutions

(continues)

Table 6.3 (continued)

Topic	APEC	FTAA	Comments
Issue scope	Comprehensive; issue areas include tariffs and non-tariff barriers, services, agriculture, subsidies, investment, IPR, government procurement, technical barriers, safeguards, rules of origin, anti-dumping, sanitary standards, dispute resolution, competitive policy	Comprehensive; issue areas include tariffs and non-tariff barriers, services, agriculture, investment, IPR, government procurement; rules of origin; Standards, dispute mediation, competition policy; customs procedures, mobility of business persons, Uruguay Round implementation	Strong overlap of scope
Timetables	2010/2020	2005	FTAA timetable is for completion of negotiations; APEC timetable is for implementation
Special treatment for developing/ smaller economies	Flexibility; differential timetables; ecotech	To be determined; technical assistance; infrastructure assistance; poverty alleviation; democratization	APEC links TILF and Ecotech; Americas' summitry issue coverage is comprehensive, linkages are indirect
Stakeholders	Private sector (ABAC); PECC; EPG	Americas Business Forum; Civil Society Committee	Private sector is influential in APEC; NGOs have formal access to FTAA process

Sources: APEC Leaders Declarations, especially the Osaka Action Agenda; Summit of the Americas' Declarations and Plan of Action, Miami, 1994 and Santiago, 1998.
Abbreviations: Intellectual Property Rights (IPR); APEC Business Advisory Council (ABAC); Trade and Investment Liberalization and Facilitation (TILF); Pacific Economic Cooperation Council (PECC); Trade Policy Forum (TPF); Eminent Persons Group (EPG); Non-governmental Organizations (NGOs); Organization of American States (OAS); Inter-American Development Bank (IDB); United Nations Economic Commission for Latin America and the Caribbean (UNECLAC).

over the meaning of "open regionalism," which some take to imply the extension of most-favored-nation treatment to nonmembers—perhaps conditioned upon reciprocity (Bergsten 1997). In its weakest form, APEC open regionalism could mean that APEC is nothing more than a caucus for incubating trade initiatives that would only enter into force upon adoption by the GATT/WTO. Certainly, for APEC open regionalism has meant a willingness to consider accession by new members.

In their selection of issue coverage, both trade regimes were very much reflections of their times. In fact, their issue scopes are remarkably similar and include tariffs and nontariff barriers, services, agriculture, investment, intellectual property rights (IPR), government procurement, rules of origin, dispute settlement, and competition policy (table 6.3). This list includes issues—notably agriculture and services—that were unfinished in the Uruguay Round (the so-called "built in" agenda slated for further negotiations); issues of greatest interest to industrial countries (investment, IPR, government procurement, competition policy); and issues of particular interest to many developing countries (tariffs and nontariff barriers, rules of origin, dispute settlement); as well as more pedestrian issues of general interest (customs procedures). In the case of the FTAA, the list of issues mimicked the chapters in the 1993 NAFTA accord that, at the time, appeared to many observers, especially in the United States, as a template for the FTAA. In some issue areas, such as services, investment, and competition policy, some countries saw opportunities to make advances within these more restricted regional settings that could later be taken up by the WTO.

At the Leaders Meeting in Bogor (Indonesia) in November 1994, APEC set firm dates for achieving the goal of "free and open trade and investment in the Asia-Pacific"—by 2010 for the industrialized economies and 2020 for the developing economies. Coming just weeks prior to the first Summit of the Americas in Miami, Florida, this announcement made it impossible for the United States to continue to resist Latin American pressures to set a target date for the emerging FTAA. The Argentine government sent a sharply worded note to the U.S. State Department: " If the APEC declaration is not balanced with a similar commitment by America, we will have surrendered the priority of U.S. trade initiative to the Pacific." (Feinberg 1997, 137)

Despite appearances, the declared end dates for APEC and the FTAA are in fact identical. FTAA's target date is for the *completion* of negotiations; if one assumes a 15-year phase-in period (as in NAFTA), the FTAA will achieve free trade by 2020—APEC's target date for the completion of its free and open trade goals. In their origins, therefore, APEC and the FTAA were bound by common targets.

In their formative moments, APEC and Western Hemisphere integration positively reinforced each other. Some Asian nations were alarmed by NAFTA and by its potential expansion into an FTAA, and saw APEC as a strategic response that could open markets and perhaps bargain with NAFTA/FTAA. APEC also kept the United States looking toward Asia and promised enhanced access to the world's biggest single market. For its part, the Summit of the Americas and its FTAA offspring were directly inspired by APEC. The decision by APEC leaders at Bogor to realize their free trade vision by a date certain made possible the consensus among leaders at Miami to set a date certain for their own integration project.

Another commonality between the two trade regimes is their relatively weak institutionalization. Their built-in softness is the result of the power of the many forces in both regions aligned against accelerated regional integration. Member states were not prepared to pool sovereignty because they remained uncertain about the prospective impact of more openness and integration upon their various economic and security interests. In particular, the United States resisted the creation of self-willed bureaucracies that might limit its own flexibility; ironically, developing countries in APEC and the FTAA feared that the United States (and in APEC, Japan) could bend any well-endowed regional institution to advance its own interests. In both regional settings, member governments purposefully eschewed creation of a powerful international bureaucracy that might develop a mind of its own. There would be no Bretton Woods or WTO-like regime whose relative autonomy might give it the power and the will to drive policy. There would be no powerful figures—like the managing directors of the IMF, the presidents of the World Bank, or the commissioners of the European Union—who might willfully rally opinion toward a self-selected policy direction.

APEC members did establish a Secretariat in Singapore staffed primarily with officials temporarily borrowed from member states, who therefore owe their primary loyalty not to APEC but to their home bureaucracies. The main functions of the roughly two-dozen professional staff are to serve as a secretariat to organize APEC meetings, collect and circulate documents, and, to a modest degree, monitor APEC implementation. It has little in-house analytical capacity and very modest resources to commission outside expert research. The executive directorship rotates each year to a representative of the country chairing that year's Leadership Meeting, thereby denying continuity or visibility of leadership (Bodde 1997).

In the case of the FTAA, the Western Hemisphere could build upon existing regional institutions with self-identities linked to regional cooperation. The U.S. Trade Representative office (USTR)—which harbored suspicion about the FTAA from the outset—initially feared creating any regional administrative body, out of concern that the Latin Americans might gang up on the United States. In the end, it acquiesced in allowing a role for the Organization of American States (OAS), through its Special Committee on Trade and its new Trade Unit (with the financial support of the Inter-American Development Bank (IDB) and the participation of the UN Economic Commission for Latin America and the Caribbean (UNECLAC). The Miami Summit allowed that the OAS Committee could "assist in the systematization of data in the region and continue its work on studying economic integration arrangements in the Hemisphere, including *brief* comparative descriptions of the obligations in each of the Hemisphere's existing trading agreements" (Summit of the Americas 1994; emphasis added). The U.S. intent was to limit scope for policy research and to proscribe policy advocacy. Six months later, at the trade ministerial in Denver, Colorado, governments reinvigorated a long-standing but dormant Tripartite Committee (OAS, IDB, UNECLAC) and requested that it provide analytical support as requested by the newly minted working groups. Within these international organizations, in the OAS responsibility lies with the Trade Unit, in the IDB with the Department of Integration and Regional Programs, and in ECLAC in its Washington Office. The Tripartite Committee has gradually gained the confidence of governments and has provided useful technical support to the FTAA process.

After the FTAA formally "launched" negotiations in 1998, it established a rotating Administrative Secretariat to backstop the negotiations by handling logistics and documentation. The secretariat was to move among the three cities (Miami, Panama, Mexico City) selected to host the negotiating groups during an 18-month period. Such a ready-made assemblage would be no threat to national trade ministries.

Both APEC and the FTAA created a ministerial-dominated ladder of committees to undertake trade negotiations (FTAA parlance) or discussions and dialogue (APEC-speak). In each case, the dozen or so issues were assigned to separate working groups that reported to a vice ministerial committee (FTAA's Trade Negotiations Committee, or TNC; APEC's Committee on Trade and Investment Committee, or CTI; and Senior Officials Meeting, or SOM). These senior committees in turn reported to trade ministers that met periodically. At the top of this hierarchy stood the annual APEC Leaders Meeting and the occasional Summits of the Americas.

However, if the APEC and FTAA forums were very similar in form, their assigned modalities were starkly different—a reflection of the different regional realities (table 6.1). The modalities of the FTAA were crafted to drive toward the free trade goals by the target date, even while national governments maintained firm control over the negotiating process. At the FTAA's March 1998 ministerial in San Jose, Costa Rica, the issue-oriented Negotiating Groups were assigned specific objectives for negotiation. For example, the working group on market access was tasked a work program to negotiate for the progressive elimination of tariffs and non-tariff barriers, as well as other measures with equivalent effects, which restrict trade between participating countries. All tariffs will be subject to negotiation.

At the FTAA's 1999 ministerial in Toronto, Canada, ministers instructed all of the Negotiating Groups to prepare a draft text of their respective chapters, indicating areas of consensus and placing brackets where agreement could not be reached (Ministerial Declaration of Toronto, 1999). This comprehensive bracketed draft text is to be ready for the 2001 Quebec summit. In recognition of the hemisphere's power structure, the co-chairs of the final round of negotiations will be the United States and Brazil. For Brazil, being in the chair is a source of prestige and power, but it is also a double-edged opportunity. If, as 2005 approaches, the United States decides it prefers a successful conclusion to the talks, it may well be able to rally other hemispheric nations to pressure Brazil to negotiate in good faith. As Brazilian diplomacy typically seeks to exert leadership from the center of a negotiation, Brazil may feel obliged to compromise, possibly at the expense of some of its MERCO-SUR goals. Unlike Japan, which was willing to torpedo the 1998 Early Voluntary Sectoral Liberalization (EVSL) negotiations to protect narrow domestic interests (see below), Brazil is probably too deeply embedded in its regionalist setting to willfully incur such isolation and condemnation.

APEC has adopted a more relaxed and open-ended style appropriate to its less coherent geopolitical, developmental, and cultural characteristics. For example, in contrast to the specific and purposeful FTAA taskings, APEC's Working Group on Tariff and Non-Tariff Measures was asked "*to consider the possibility* of adopting a work program to progress the Osaka Action Agenda objective of progressively reducing non-tariff measures." (APEC Committee on Trade and Investment, 1999; emphasis added). Unlike the FTAA tasking, this very modest agenda was not fitted into a firm schedule of dates and meetings for the production of negotiated texts.

These widely different functions of the respective issue-specific working groups reflect the distinct norms and negotiating modalities that distinguish APEC from the FTAA. The FTAA is more closely nested within GATT/WTO modalities—of bargaining, balanced and specific reciprocity, and a single undertaking. The elites of the major Western Hemisphere countries, including the trade negotiators, are acculturated through education and experience to such realist modes of international bargaining. The willingness to follow such tried-and-true paths indicate a seriousness of intent, or at least the intent to create the possibility of a trade accord, should the major actors be so inclined as the decision point of 2005 approaches.

APEC, on the other hand, may be accused of being either more innovative or less committed to its free trade rhetoric. From the outset, APEC rejected "Western" bargaining methods, preferring instead a more "Asian" informal approach characterized by voluntary measures undertaken as part of a process of "concerted unilateral liberalization." APEC forums make suggestions, but member economies submit their own Individual Action Plans (IAPs)—APEC's core instrument for advancing toward its Bogor goal of " free and open trade and investment." IAPs are of a "rolling nature," commitments are nonbinding, and are revised in a process of "continuing voluntary improvement" (Osaka Action Agenda, 1995). In addition, Collective Action Plans (CAPs) assist integration through the provision of databases and the promotion of enhanced transparency, studies of best practices and possible policy initiatives, and business facilitation.

For example, in the area of investment, countries may select for their IAPs investment-liberalizing and business-facilitating measures from a "master menu" of options developed by an APEC working group (Vancouver Leaders Statement, 1997). APEC was careful to state that this menu of investment measures is not prescriptive and will evolve over time.

IAPs are supposed to be "comprehensive" and "comparable." In the more traditional GATT/WTO bargaining model, comparability is subjectively defined according to the revealed preferences of the bargainers. In APEC, there is no ready measurement of comparability. Any attempt to do so would be further complicated by APEC's allowance for countries to approach the Bogor targets at their own pace and on a "rolling basis," so that some countries may be backloading their IAPs. In the absence of a single undertaking, IAPs harbor both immediate and dynamic components that are inherently difficult to compare and measure.

Most of the IAPs submitted by APEC members have been widely criticized for failing to go beyond what members would have done in any event, in the context of Uruguay Round obligations, subregional accords or in unilateral national programs (Bergsten 1997, 5; Aggarwal and Morrison 1999, 13). Even those analysts who have noted that most APEC members are on track toward meeting their Bogor goals—in the sense that if they maintain their recent liberalization trajectories they will approach free trade by the target dates of 2010/2020—have questioned the contributions of the IAPs. For example, Yamazawa and Urata expressed dismay that "Although APEC economies are supposed to improve their IAPs every year . . . the additions in 1997 and 1998 have turned out to be minimal" (1999, 46). The United States in particular has been criticized for failing to go beyond its Uruguay Round commitments in its IAPs (Lee 1999, 22). To foster better performance on IAPs, APEC has instituted voluntary peer reviews of IAPs by other APEC members, and APEC Senior Officials commissioned PECC's Trade Policy Forum to review the IAPs (PECC 1999). Individual IAPs are now posted on the web page of the APEC Secretariat (http://www.apecsec.org), facilitating private expert studies as well.

Mounting frustration with the IAPs and their voluntarism drove APEC—under U.S. urging—to consider a sectoral approach to trade liberalization. The first such effort bore fruit, when at the 1996 Leaders Meeting APEC agreed to eliminate tariffs in information technology, if a "critical mass" of the full WTO (defined as more than 90 percent of sectoral trade) did so. Such an APEC offer proved impossible for the European Union and others to refuse (Bergsten 1997, 6). Flush with this success in the Information Technology Agreement (ITA), at the Vancouver Leaders Meeting, APEC agreed to consider a process of " early voluntary sectoral liberalization (EVSL)." As a concession to APEC norms, the trade ministers said that EVSL was meant to compliment the IAPs, and that member economies would participate in a "voluntary" basis and according to their own chosen timetable. Nine sectors were selected for discussion: environmental goods and services, fish and fish products, forest products, medical equipment and instruments, energy, toys, gems and jewelry, chemicals, and telecommunications.

Mexico and Chile immediately dissented. From an efficiency perspective, they argued that sectoral liberalization could distort trade, and from a bargaining perspective, that if the "easy" sectors (or sectors of main interest to the industrial countries) were tackled up front, no political will would be left to tackle the remaining sectors. Japan and other APEC members grew increasingly uneasy as the EVSL discussions began to resemble GATT/WTO negotiations, with participants being pressured to sign on to a package deal. It was never entirely clear whether APEC intended to implement any EVSL agreement on its own or wait for accession by a "critical mass" of the full WTO. However, this bridge was never reached: At the 1998 Kuala Lumpur Leaders Meeting, the Japanese government, in response to strong domestic pressures, shocked participants when it flatly refused to accept liberalization in the "sensitive" areas of forestry and fisheries. Other APEC members, however, were relieved to escape a process that looked more concerted than voluntary. Stymied, APEC threw its EVSL initiative into the WTO; it was under consideration during the 1999 Seattle ministerial, the collapse of which left the future of APEC's EVSL initiative murky at best.

If APEC's IAPs have so far proven problematic, and its EVSL initiative was frustrated, APEC may still have contributed toward the goals of freer trade and investment flows. The Common Action Plans (CAPs) have promoted useful business facilitation measures such as customs standardization. More critically, the (unweighted) average tariff rate of APEC member economies has been lowered by almost half between 1988 and 1998—from 15.4 percent to 7.6 percent (Lee 1999, 10). Assigning precise credit for this impressive liberalization process is methodologically impossible, but APEC might claim that it helped to establish an ideological ambiance that encourages domestic liberalizers and in which backsliding—even in the face of the severe 1997–1998 financial crisis and recessions—was constrained (Curtis and Ciuriak 1999; Garnaut 1999). APEC also helped to bridge sociological gaps between public and private sectors and to further expose government officials to the ideas and interests of market-oriented firms.

In summary, the regional free trade projects of APEC and the FTAA were born at the same historical moment, and share a similar agenda of issues and target identical end dates. Both manifest similar organizational characteristics: In neither case have governments yet been willing to pool sovereignty, such that secretariats are highly constrained and national ministries control the negotiations and discussions. But the FTAA has had the advantage of assistance from existing regional organizations.

The greatest difference between the proposed FTAs lies in the clarity of objectives and crispness of negotiating modalities. Swept forward by strong historical currents favoring enhanced cooperation within the Western Hemisphere, the FTAA has the unambiguous goal of a free trade area circumscribed by geography, while its more traditional negotiating modalities mimic those of the GATT/WTO. APEC's concerted voluntarism and its EVLS initiative broke new ground, even if they have yet to yield abundant harvests. The IAPs provide comfort to participants that prefer to set unilaterally their pace of liberalization and may be uneasy engaging in regional forums with countries they still consider unfamiliar or perhaps untrustworthy. These similarities and differences between APEC and the FTAA are readily explained by the separate geopolitical, economic, and cultural realities in which the two trade agreements are embedded.

Both APEC and the FTAA strive to overcome the old North-South divide, as they seek to integrate markets of industrial and developing countries. Yet APEC has allowed developing countries a considerably more relaxed timetable for fulfilling the Bogor goals and has established a broad agenda of trade-related capacity-building initiatives to prepare the poorer nations for further liberalization. In the Western Hemisphere, countries negotiating the FTAA have pledged to "take into account differences in the levels of development" (in the Santiago Plan of Action), but have yet to spell out what this might mean. The FTAA is wrapped within the summits of the Americas, with their broad political and social institution-building agendas, but these initiatives are less directly linked to the capacity to meet trade liberalization goals. Within the Western Hemisphere, "readiness" for the FTAA has been discussed more in terms of macroeconomic stability than in terms of microeconomics or institutional and human capacity. So far both liberalization processes have avoided conferring "special and differential treatment" that might imply different end-obligations for developing countries.

The future of both RTAs will be influenced by developments in the WTO (Granados 1999). APEC received an early boost from a stalemate within the Uruguay Round negotiations, and both APEC and the FTAA may receive more attention in the wake of the collapse of the Seattle WTO ministerial. Alternatively, it is possible that should the WTO eventually succeed in launching a new trade round, energies may be diverted away from regional integration efforts, and countries may hesitate to make "concessions" in regional forums that they would rather reserve for global negotiations. In that case, regional negotiations may still serve as testing grounds for initiatives that may later be channeled into the WTO. But it may also be true that progress in global forums may establish new "floors" for regional negotiations, bringing them that much closer to their ultimate free trade goals.

OTHER ECONOMIC AND
TECHNICAL ASSISTANCE ISSUES

For countries throughout the Asia Pacific and the Western Hemisphere, trade is critical to growth—but trade is an instrument meshed in larger development strategies. The summitry processes in both regions—while having trade as the centerpiece—also encompass a broader development agenda. In APEC, the developing countries have insisted on economic and technical assistance (Ecotech), in part in order to build capacity to undertake economic reforms and to be able to take advantage of the opportunities created by integration into global markets. In the Western

Hemisphere, interstate relations have had a long history of broad political and economic agendas, such that when negotiators were drafting the texts for the Miami summit, it was immediately assumed that political, economic, and social issues would be covered (Feinberg 1997). Indeed, the more controversial trade section was among the last to be negotiated.

In the wake of the collapse of the December 1999 WTO ministerial in Seattle, critics of the WTO are pressing for linkage between trade agreements and such issues as environmental protection and social development. As precedents, the APEC and FTAA trade negotiations are imbedded in broader processes that do include such issues, albeit in constructive ways that eschew negative sanctions.

APEC's Ecotech

In 1995, APEC leaders adopted the Osaka Action Agenda that established the three pillars of APEC activities: trade and investment liberalization, business facilitation and economic and technical cooperation. These have, in effect, been collapsed into two broad spheres of activity: TILF (trade and investment liberalization and facilitation) and Ecotech. The 1996 Manila Action Plan (MAP) compiled members' initial individual action plans (IAPs) and outlined six areas for economic and technical cooperation: developing human capital; fostering safe and efficient capital markets; strengthening economic infrastructure; harnessing technologies of the future; promoting environmentally sustainable growth; and encouraging the growth of small and medium-sized enterprises. By 1998, APEC had underway 274 activities relating to these six priority areas (APEC Senior Officials 1998, 1).

From the outset, TILF and Ecotech were linked in developmental and political terms. The developing countries argued that they required assistance to prepare their economies to compete in global markets. In effect, they were willing to strike a political bargain: They would accept the market-opening TILF agenda of the industrial and some developing economies in return for Ecotech. Some industrial country members, particularly the United States, feared that the LDCs intended to transform APEC into yet another channel for North-South resource transfers; they resisted elevating increasing "development assistance" into a major APEC goal—hence, the coining of a new term, "Ecotech."

The developing countries have repeatedly complained that APEC has dedicated much more attention to TILF than to Ecotech, and that Ecotech has yielded little in the way of additional resources. Occasionally, developing countries have argued against accelerated progress on trade liberalization on the grounds that the industrial countries have not fulfilled their Ecotech pledges. Developing countries seized upon the 1997–1998 financial crisis to underscore their original argument for Ecotech: that without stronger domestic institutions, developing countries were not prepared for the market-opening objectives of TILF. Industrial countries have accepted this conceptual argument, but only Japan has been willing to place significant financial resources behind APEC's Ecotech.

Besides the lack of additional financial resources, independent experts and APEC itself have identified numerous shortcomings with APEC's Ecotech efforts (Ro and Ahn 1997; ABAC 1997; APEC Senior Officials 1998; Elek 1997). Common criticisms include the dilution of efforts across too many issues and projects; duplication of efforts; too few clear goals, milestones and performance criteria; and emphasis on process and meetings as opposed to more tangible results. APEC senior officials noted that "the extent of economies' interest and participation varied widely from one activity to another." (APEC senior officials 1998, 4.) Yet, these shortcomings are not surprising and reflect APEC's self-constrained structure and norms. APEC lacks a strong central administrative structure with the expertise and authority that might design and impose order on a rational work plan. APEC's norms of consensus, cooperation, and dialogue facilitate logrolling and agenda-setting via inclusion of each member's pet initiatives. APEC norms permit the approval of initiatives without clear guidelines and performance criteria that might be used to hold governments accountable. The norms of voluntarism and informality militate against monitoring mechanisms with teeth. When the issue of resources is raised, voluntarism allows the rich countries to wiggle off the hook. The predictable result is a laundry list of admirable goals but with initiatives that generally feature incomplete terms of reference.

Nevertheless, APEC has been active in sustainable development and in certain labor issues. APEC's work on sustainable development has emphasized clean technologies, sustainable cities and the sustainability of the marine environment. Other projects have taken into account the linkages between environmental sustainability and economic growth, food production, energy, population, and poverty reduction. Under these rubric, various APEC forums have generated some 60 projects. The effectiveness of many of these projects has been questioned (Zarsky and Hunter 1997). But the point remains that APEC countries have readily accepted the legitimacy of environmental issues and their relationship to trade and growth, so long as they are approached through positive initiatives that directly target identified problems. There are no negative linkages between TILF and Ecotech—no TILF sanctions in the event of noncompliance with Ecotech.

Most of APEC's labor initiatives occur within the context of human resource development, focusing on labor market development and human resource management. Projects have also examined how workplace safety and health contribute to productivity. However, so far APEC has ducked the debate about the relationship between trade and labor standards, or the impact of trade liberalization on wage levels (Harcourt 1996).

SUMMITRY IN THE WESTERN HEMISPHERE

The action plans for the summits of the Americas have been negotiated as complex, comprehensive grand bargains that codify and promote the agenda for inter-American relations. When Vice President Gore announced his government's invitation to the first post–Cold War hemispheric summit in 1994, he suggested a broad agenda, "to make explicit the convergence of values that is now rapidly taking place in a hemispheric community of democracies: a community increasingly integrated by commercial exchange and shared political values." (Feinberg 1997, 60). The final summit texts were the outcome of a prolonged process of negotiations that bridged the U.S.-Latin American divide, during which plurilateral coalitions lined up behind an array of political, economic, and social initiatives. The final Miami Plan of Action included 23 main initiatives with over 150 action items. Eight initiatives were aimed at "preserving and strengthening the community of democracy in the Americas," for example by augmenting the ability of the OAS to monitor elections and to combat corruption. The 12 initiatives to promote prosperity and to eradicate poverty, in addition to promoting free trade, mirror APEC's Ecotech agenda: capital market development, infrastructure, energy cooperation, cooperation in science and technology, universal access to education and basic health services, and encouragement of microenterprises and small business. The 1998 Santiago summit built on the Miami agenda, giving greater priority to education and adding initiatives on migrant workers, indigenous peoples, judicial administration, municipal administration, and counternarcotics, among others.

As in APEC, the inter-American summits readily embraced sustainable development, and the Miami conference launched three initiatives—to promote sustainable energy use, biodiversity, and pollution prevention. As in APEC, there was no direct link between trade negotiations and environmental practices. When pressed by labor unions, the Clinton administration argued that many of the summit initiatives, directly and indirectly, promoted labor interests: For example, democracy facilitated labor organization, access to education and health built human capital, and economic growth created jobs. At the 1998 Santiago summit, leaders agreed to have their Ministries of Labor address child labor, to promote active labor market policies, and to prove safety and health conditions in the work place. But there was no hint of linking compliance with these pledges to trade. Unimpressed, U.S. organized labor has continued to oppose the FTAA in the absence of explicit linkages between labor practices and trade, including trade sanctions to enforce compliance with labor standards.

As with APEC, there has been criticism that the inter-American summits have often failed to translate words into deeds—that implementation has been uneven at best. The Leadership Council for Inter-American Summitry—a self-appointed "eminent persons group"—found progress on some initiatives, including in the areas of poverty alleviation, health, education, and civil society promotion. Progress on sustainable development issues was judged "modest" (Leadership Council 1999, 11). Overall, this independent assessment found serious flaws in the summitry process, including diffusion of energy among too many initiatives and action items; the frequent absence of measurable goals, timetables, priorities, and accountability; insufficient technical and financial resources; and weak to nonexistent monitoring mechanisms. As with APEC, these flaws are not surprising, and flow from weak institutionalization as well as from a bargaining process that lacks institutional control and strong accountability mechanisms and that promotes logrolling and least-common-denominator laundry lists. At the Santiago summit, an effort was made to correct some of these procedural flaws by strengthening the role of the OAS in the administration of some summit initiatives, and by creating a formal "troika" of countries—past, present and future summit hosts—to work with a Summit Implementation Review Group (SIRG) of officials from foreign ministries to monitor and assess follow-up. A greater effort was made to involve the IDB and World Bank in helping to finance and provide technical assistance to specific initiatives.

In APEC, some developing countries felt that the TILF—Ecotech bargain was not being honored and that they were therefore justified at balking at further APEC-sponsored trade liberalization. In the Western Hemisphere, the dynamic is just the reverse. Some in the United States have resisted further liberalization of the U.S. market partly on the grounds that the Latin American and Caribbean countries have not fulfilled commitments made in the summitry process, in areas of mutual concern such as counternarcotics, judicial reform, corruption, and the environment. In the minds of some U.S. actors, there is an implicit linkage between the broader summit agenda initiatives of greatest interest to the United States and political support for the FTAA. More subtly, lack of rapid progress on such issues tarnishes the image of Latin America in the United States, making it harder to persuade the U.S. Congress and public that they should partner with Latin America in the form of a major free trade accord.

In reviewing these economic and politic issues, it is apparent that both APEC and Western Hemisphere summitry are plagued with implementation and compliance problems that derive from inherent organizational weaknesses. Both organizations need to impose more discipline on their decision-making and build stronger mechanisms for implementing agreements and monitoring compliance. As members gain more confidence in these organizations, they may become more willing to pool some sovereignty, at least in select issue areas. Closer cooperation with private sector organizations and other civil society organizations may provide means for cost-effective implementation and monitoring of some initiatives. Effective partnerships with the regional development banks offer the promise of badly needed financial and technical assistance resources; the IDB has been supportive of some Western Hemisphere summitry initiatives, but the Asian Development Bank has been less engaged in APEC activities.

Both regional organizations have tackled labor and environmental matters. If they can produce a record of accomplishment, they could demonstrate the feasibility of constructively addressing workers' rights and environmental protection in trade-oriented forums where both industrial and developing countries are present.

POLITICAL/SECURITY ISSUES

In their treatment of political and security issues, APEC and Western Hemisphere summitry differ most starkly. The heterogeneity of political systems and the persistent security tensions in the Asia Pacific have caused APEC to exclude political and security issues from its agenda. To the extent that Asian countries are willing to discuss security issues in a regional forum, they have preferred the ASEAN Regional Forum (ARF). Thus, when in an address to a business forum during the Leaders Meeting in Kuala Lumpur in 1998, Vice President Al Gore criticized Malaysia's political regime, most Asian political and business leaders felt that he had violated APEC protocol. Nevertheless, APEC Leaders Meetings do provide occasions for leaders to huddle in bilateral and small-group gatherings where they routinely broach security issues.

In contrast, it was the Latin Americans that insisted that in the Miami Declaration of Principles, the section on democracy precede the section on economics and free trade, on the grounds that politics is the "more noble" concept and trumps economics. (Feinberg 1997, 143). The hemispheric summits have not explicitly excluded nondemocracies from the FTAA, but the Miami summit blessed an initiative that threatens the expulsion from the OAS of countries where democratic order has been interrupted, and Cuba has been excluded from the summitry process and FTAA negotiations. In Miami, many of the Latin American leaders welcomed enhanced international legitimacy for their democracies, and whatever additional assistance they might gather for democratic institution-building. At Santiago, the Latin Americans acknowledged the value of the series of meetings of ministers of defense that the United States had been promoting, to strengthen civilian control over militaries and to promote regional participation in international peacekeeping, among other topics. The Santiago summit also blessed ongoing efforts at regional confidence and security-building measures.

By coincidence, the 1999 APEC Leaders Meeting convened in Auckland, New Zealand, just at the moment when nearby East Timor was being wracked by violence following a referendum to separate from Indonesia. This hot topic was not placed on the formal APEC agenda but was discussed at "informal" meetings and bilaterals among the leaders. The APEC meeting probably contributed to the regional consensus behind, and Indonesian acquiescence to, a UN peacekeeping force for East Timor. It remains to be seen whether this precedent promotes a gradual broadening of the APEC agenda into regional security matters.

So the characteristics of the regional security environment have differentially determined the salience of security issues on the formal agendas of APEC and Western Hemisphere summitry. In both regional arrangements, trade has taken center stage. Yet, in both regions, there is a subtext: that deeper economic integration, willfully promoted by governments and supported by private sectors, will weave webs of mutually beneficial relations that will enhance regional security.

CONCLUSIONS

In the late 1980s and early 1990s, intra-regional tensions were easing, ideological clashes were dimming, and North-South accusations were fading. In their transition from the status of "developing" to "emerging market" economies, countries in Asia and Latin America were opening to global trade and investment flows. But the 1994 decisions at Bogor and Miami to seek free regional trade were not the inevitable outcome of power or economic structures. On closer examination, the evidence reveals that critical decisions on the road to creating these regional trading arrangements were influenced by individuals (i.e., a few key leaders, senior government officials, and policy intellectuals) and by chance—by schedules of meetings and speeches. These details reveal striking parallels behind the launching of the two free trade pledges.

This subtler understanding of history also suggests that the Bogor pledge and the FTAA process may rest on insecure foundations. In fact, more recently counterforces have regrouped and have succeeded in slowing the transformation of official pledges into tangible deeds. Particularly in the larger economies, protectionist forces have pressured their governments to adopt "go slow" approaches. Nevertheless, for a host of reasons, the FTAA would appear to stand on firmer ground than the Bogor Declaration. The Western Hemisphere's common political discourse, relaxed security environment, long history of cooperative enterprises, and geographic unity create relatively favorable conditions for commercial integration. In addition, existing regional institutions are permanent catalysts for pushing members toward cooperative goals. Yet, even in the Western Hemisphere, countervailing forces are powerful enough to render the final outcome uncertain.

Neither of the regional trade arrangements (RTAs) challenges global market integration. Within APEC or FTAA, neither the key industrial nor developing countries that formulated the bloc's norms, goals, and structures sought to break with WTO globalism. Both RTAs are carefully nested within WTO norms, and member countries have purposefully prevented them from developing strong institutions. The APEC and FTAA trade forums have similar vertical structures carefully controlled by national trade ministries. But APEC and the FTAA are governed by different negotiating modalities: The FTAA adheres to WTO-style bargaining, balanced, specific reciprocity and a single undertaking, whereas APEC has followed an "Asian" unilateral voluntarism that appears to be weaker, though suited to APEC's less harmonious geopolitics. IAPs and EVSLs were more innovative but, so far, have yet to yield strong results.

As part of larger regional community-building projects, and designed within processes of periodic summits, the two RTAs are accompanied by a multitude of development initiatives, and, in the case of the Western Hemisphere, explicitly political, prodemocracy goals. Despite some tangible accomplishments, these processes have been frustrated by the inherent logic of weak institutionalization and undisciplined bargaining procedures. Members will have to relax their preference for maximizing their freedom of action and accept some pooling of sovereignty if they are to obtain a greater degree of effective regional cooperation. Some Western Hemisphere initiatives, however, have benefited from structures facilitated by preexisting regional institutions, and by financing from the Inter-American Development Bank. APEC has yet to corral the Asian Development Bank in the same effective manner.

Both processes have broached environmental and labor issues, through constructive initiatives in some cases intended to facilitate trade liberalization, but in no case is noncompliance linked to renewed trade barriers. In the wake of Seattle, as the WTO searches for ways to manage the controversial labor and environment issues, it may find some useful precedents here.

Both regional integration projects will be influenced by global developments such as progress or lack thereof in the WTO, and by the battles between free traders and protectionists in key countries. At the same time, important geopolitical differences between the two regions will keep their political and security agendas separate and will also continue to instill degrees of independent development in their trade agendas. Both RTAs are accompanied by comprehensive development agendas, and both will need to reformulate their development and technical assistance mechanisms to enhance their effectiveness and credibility.

By excluding Cuba, the FTAA implicitly links democracy and free trade, even if the Western Hemisphere has not yet adopted an explicit "democracy clause" (as have MERCOSUR and the European Union) that would expel a member that broke with democratic norms. The heterogeneity of political systems in the Asia Pacific has kept APEC focused on economic matters. Nevertheless, in both regions, closer trade ties may contribute to wider and deeper transnational linkages, a more relaxed geopolitical environment, and, ultimately, to greater regional security.

NOTES

An article version of this chapter appeared as "Comparing Regional Integration in Non-identical Twins: APEC and the FTAA," in *Integration and Trade* vol. 4, no. 10 (January-April 2000): IDB-INTAL, Buenos Aires.

1. For their valuable comments on earlier drafts, the author wishes to thank Vinod Aggarwal, Stephan Haggard. Miles Kahler, and Angela O'Mahony, and for expert research assistance, Xin Wang.
2. When APEC was established in 1989, there were 12 founding members, namely Australia, Brunei Darussalam, Canada, Indonesia, Japan, Republic of Korea, Malaysia, New Zealand, Republic of the Philippines, Singapore, Thailand, and the United States. In 1991, APEC accepted the People's Republic of China, Hong Kong (its designation has been changed to Hong Kong, China since 1 July 1997) and Chinese Taipei. In 1993, Mexico, Papua New Guinea, and Chile were admitted. In 1997,

Peru, Russia, and Vietnam were granted accession. APEC has placed a moratorium on admission of new members.

REFERENCES

ABAC 1997. See APEC Business Advisory Council below. Aggarwal, Vinod. 1994. Comparing regional cooperation efforts in the Asia- Pacific and North America. In *Pacific Cooperation: Building Economic and Security Regimes in the Asia-Pacific Region,* edited by A. Mack and J. Ravenhill. St. Leonards, Australia: Allen & Unwin.

——and Charles Morrison. 1999. APEC as an international institution. Paper presented at the 25th PAFTAD meeting, Osaka.

Akahsi, Yoji. 1997. An ASEAN perspective on APEC. Working Paper No. 240, Kellogg Institute, University of Notre Dame, Notre Dame, Indiana.

APEC Business Advisory Council. 1997. APEC means business: ABAC's call to action. ABAC Report to the APEC Economic Leaders, Vancouver.

APEC International Assessment Network (APIAN). 2000. *Learning From Experience.* Singapore: Institute for Southeast Asian Studies (ISEAS) for APIAN.

APEC Senior Officials.1998. *1998 Report on Economic and Technical Cooperation to the Tenth Ministerial Meeting.* Kuala Lumpur.

Baker, James. 1995. *The Politics of Diplomacy: Revolution, War & Peace, 1989–1992.* New York: G.P. Putnam's Sons.

Bergsten, Fred. 1997. APEC in 1997: Prospects and possible strategies. And Open regionalism. In *Whither APEC? The Progress to Date and Agenda for the Future,* Special Report 9, edited by C. Fred Bergsten. Washington, D.C.: Institute for International Economics.

Bhagwati, Jagdish. 1993. Regionalism and multilateralism: An overview. In *New Dimensions in Regional Integration,* edited by Jaime De Mello and Arvind Panagariya. Cambridge: Cambridge University Press.

Bodde, William. 1997. Managing APEC. In *Whither APEC? The Progress to Date and Agenda for the Future,* edited by C. Fred Bergsten. Washington, D.C.: Institute for International Economics.

Busch, Marc and Helen Milner. 1994. The future of the international trading system: International firms, regionalism, and domestic politics. In *Political Economy and the Changing Global Order,* edited by Richard Stubbs and Geoffrey R. D. Underhill. New York: St. Martin's Press.

Camilleri, Joseph. 1994. The Asia-Pacific in the post-hegemonic world. In *Pacific Cooperation: Building Economic and Security Regimes in the Asia-Pacific Region,* edited by Andrew Mack and John Ravenhill. St. Leonards, Australia: Allen & Unwin.

Corrales, Javier and Richard Feinberg. 1999. Regimes of cooperation in the western hemisphere: Power, interests, and intellectual traditions. *International Studies Quarterly* 43, no.1 (March):1–36.

Curtis, John and Dan Ciuriak. 1999. APEC after 10 years: Performance and prospects. APEC Study Center Consortium Meeting. Auckland.

Da Motta Veiga, Pedro. 1997. MERCOSUR and the construction of the FTAA. *Integration and Trade* [Buenos Aires] 1, no.3.

Devlin, Robert and Ricardo French-Davis. 1999. Towards an evaluation of regional integration in Latin America in the 1990s. *The World Economy* 22. Also Working Paper 2, INTAL/ITD Series. Buenos Aires: IDB-INTAL.

Dirlik, Arif. 1992. The Asia-Pacific idea: Reality and representation in the invention of a regional structure. *Journal of World History* 3, no. 1.

Dominguez, Jorge. 1997. Technopols: Ideas and leaders in freeing politics and markets in Latin America in the 1990s. In *Technopols: Freeing Politics and Markets in Latin America in the 1990s,* edited by Jorge Dominguez. University Park: Pennsylvania State University Press.

Drysdale, Peter and Ross Garnaut. 1993. The Pacific: An application of a general theory of economic integration. In *Pacific Dynamism and the International Economic System,* edited by Fred Bergsten and Marcus Noland. Washington, D.C.: Institute for International Economics.

Elek, Andrew. 1997. An Asia-Pacific model of development cooperation: Promoting economic and technical cooperation through APEC. In *Building an Asia-Pacific Community: Development Cooperation Within APEC,* edited by Andrew Elek. Brisbane: The Foundation for Development Cooperation.

Eminent Persons Group. 1994. *Achieving the APEC Vision: Free and Open Trade in the Asia Pacific.* Singapore: APEC.

Feinberg, Richard. 1997. *Summitry in the Americas: A Progress Report.* Washington, D.C.: Institute for International Economics.

Funabashi, Yoichi. 1995. *Asia Pacific Fusion: Japan's Role in APEC.* Washington, D.C.: Institute for International Economics.

Garnaut, Ross. 1999. APEC ideas and reality: History and prospects. Paperpresented at the 25th Pacific Trade and Development Conference, Osaka.

Granados, Jaime. 1999. *El ALCA y la OMC: Especulaciones en torno a su interaccion.* Serie INTAL-ITD, Documento de Trabajo 4. Buenos Aires: IDB-INTAL.

Haggard, Stephan. 1997. The political economy of regionalism in Asia and the Americas. In *The Political Economy of Regionalism,* edited by Edward Mansfield and Helen Milner. New York: Columbia University Press.

Harcourt, Tim. 1996. *Labor Issue in APEC.* Issue Paper No. 9. Melbourne: Australian APEC Study Center.

Higgott, Richard. 1994. Australia and the Pacific Region: The political economy of "relocation." In *Political Economy and the Changing Global Order,* edited by Richard Stubbs and Geoffrey R. D. Underhill. New York: St. Martin's Press.

———. 1998. The international political economy of regionalism—the Asia-Pacific and Europe Compared. In *Regionalism and Global Economic Integration—Europe, Asia and the Americas,* edited by William D. Coleman and Geoffrey R. D. Underhill. New York: Routledge. 1998.

Hufbauer, Gary and Jeffrey Schott. 1994. *Western Hemisphere Economic Integration.* Washington, D.C.: Institute for International Economics.

Inter-American Dialogue. 1993. *Convergence and Community: the Americas in 1993.* Washington, D.C.: Inter-American Dialogue.

Kahler, Miles. 1994. Institution-building in the Pacific. In *Pacific Cooperation: Building Economic and Security Regimes in the Asia-Pacific Region,* edited by Andrew Mack and John Ravenhill. St. Leonards, Australia: Allen & Unwin.

Keohane, Robert. 1984. *After Hegemony: Cooperation and Discord in the World Economy.* Princeton, NJ: Princeton University Press.

Lawrence, Robert. 1996. *Regionalism, Multilateralism and Deeper Integration.* Washington, D.C.: The Brookings Institution.

Leadership Council for Inter-American Summitry. 1999. *Mastering Summitry: An Evaluation of the Santiago Summit of the Americas and its Aftermath.* Policy Report II. Miami, Florida: the Dante B. Fascell North South Center, University of Miami.

Lee, Honggue. 1999. *An Assessment of APEC's Progress Toward the Bogor Goals: A Political Economy Approach to Tariff Reductions.* KIEP Working Paper 99–19. Seoul: KIEP.

Pacific Economic Cooperation Council (PECC). 1999. *Assessing APEC Individual Action Plans and Their Contribution to APEC's Goals.* Singapore: PECC International Secretariat.

Plummer, Michael. 1998. ASEAN and institutional nesting in the Asia-Pacific: Leading from behind in APEC. In *Asia-Pacific Crossroads: Regime Creation and the Future of APEC,* edited by Vinod Aggarwal and Charles Morrison. New York: St. Martin's Press.

Ravenhill, John. 1998. Australia and APEC. In *Asia-Pacific Crossroads: Regime Creation and the Future of APEC,* edited by Vinod K. Aggarwal and Charles E. Morrison. New York: St. Martin's Press.

Ro, Jaebong and Ahn, Hyungdo. 1997. APEC's EcoTech: Prospects and issues. KIEP Working Paper 97–02. Seoul : KIEP.

Soesastro, Hadi. 1994. Pacific economic cooperation: A historical explanation. In *Indonesian Perspectives on APEC and Regional Cooperation in the Asia Pacific.* Jakarta : Center for Strategic and International Studies.

Summit of the Americas. 1994. Plan of Action. Available at: www.summit-americas.org. It can also be found in Advancing the Miami process: Civil society and the summit of the Americas, edited by Robin Resenberg and Steve Stien. Miami: North-South Center, University of Miami Press (1995):12–27.

Terada, Takashi. 1999. *The Genesis of APEC: Australia-Japan Political Initiatives.* Pacific Economic Paper No. 298. Canberra: Australia-Japan Research Center.

Tussie, Diana. 1998. Globalization and world trade: From multilateralism to regionalism. *Oxford Development Studies* 26, no.1.

United Nations Economic Commission for Latin America and the Caribbean (UNECLAC). 1994. *Open Regionalism in Latin America and the Caribbean.* UNECLAC: Santiago, Chile, January 14.

Woods, Lawrence. 1993. *Asia-Pacific Diplomacy: Nongovernmental Organizations and International Relations.* Vancouver: University of British Columbia Press.

Yamazawa, Ippei and Shujiro Urata. 1999. Trade and investment liberalization and facilitation. Paper presented at the 25th PAFTAD meeting, Osaka.

Yeats, Alexander and Refik Erzan, Refik. 1992. *Free Trade Agreements with the United States: What's in it for Latin America?* Washington, D.C.: World Bank.

Zarsky, Lyuba and Jason Hunter. 1997. Environmental cooperation at APEC: The first five years. *Journal of Environment and Development* 6, no.3 (September).

CHAPTER 7

ASEAN REGIONALISM AND SOUTHEAST ASIA'S SYSTEMIC CHALLENGES

GREG FELKER

Pragmatism and common sense have brought the ASEAN we know into being, but the regional compact must henceforth be reinforced by a commitment to common shared values and ideals.

—Anwar Ibrahim,
former Deputy Prime Minister of Malaysia, 1993

. . . the sudden reversal of fortunes of the region have led many, including some in Southeast Asia itself, to raise questions . . . about the validity of the very idea of ASEAN.

—Rodolfo Severino, Jr., Secretary-General of ASEAN, 1998

You can see the beginning of a unified ASEAN because it can be considered almost as one entity.

—Domingo Siazon, Philippines Foreign Minister, 1999

INTRODUCTION

A few brief years ago, the Association of Southeast Asian Nations (ASEAN) enjoyed growing prestige as perhaps " . . . the most successful case of regionalism outside of Europe" (Buszynski 1997, 555). Following the Cold War's demise, ASEAN broadened its functions, expanded its membership, and pursued a leadership role in Asia's nascent multilateral economic and security forums (Abad 1996; Wah 1995; Mutalib 1997). At the turn of the millennium, however, ASEAN was in disarray, its claims of regional solidarity and diplomatic prowess seemingly discredited. Tensions among its members flared into acrimonious public disputes, while external powers imposed solutions on the region's economic and security crises. Southeast Asian leaders themselves publicly suggested that formidable challenges threatened to unravel ASEAN's regional cohesion and marginalize its members in the global political economy. Pessimistic observers argued that, because of deep-seated flaws in its approach to regionalism, "ASEAN will likely fade into irrelevance. . . ." (Narine 1999, 360).

This chapter argues that ASEAN regionalism retains its core rationales and essential relevance amid both internal strains and structural changes in Asia's international relations. ASEAN will remain a crucial component of Asia's international relations, both as a primary referent for its members' external relations and as a prototype for the conduct of a broader Asian multilateralism. The grouping's recent troubles deflate its claims to a shared security identity and potent extramural influence. Its diplomatic principles are not uniquely effective in surmounting interstate rivalries and power asymmetries through cooperative socialization and consensus decision-making. Instead, the grouping's key strength is precisely its ability to facilitate cooperation, however limited, in diverse areas of common regional interest while bypassing and even partially mitigating conflicting national interests. Notwithstanding its recent difficulties, ASEAN represents a resilient form of regionalism even as Asia's diverse societies enter into deeper and more complex relations of interdependence.

CONFLICTING PERSPECTIVES
ON ASEAN REGIONALISM

ASEAN has become a key empirical referent in debates about the foundations and varieties of regionalism, and its troubles and future prospects thus carry important theoretical implications (Ravenhill 1998). A growing strand of liberal scholarship emphasizes the normative dimension of international order, and in this vein several scholars argue that ASEAN illustrates constructivist theories of international relations (Busse 1999; Khong 1997). The group's continuous dialogues and confidence-building efforts gradually forged a collective regional identity, while its diplomatic norms evolved over time into a common strategic culture (Mak 1998). Acharya (1997) observed that the essence of the "ASEAN Way" lay less in a convergence of ultimate political and economic values than in a set of shared procedural norms that rigorously guarded members' sovereign rights: (1) informality and an aversion to institutionalization; (2) a commitment to continuous consultation without a specific agenda or fixed approach to forging agreement; and (3) a strict consensus decision-rule. The idea that strong regional unity can be built on a shared premise of unqualified national sovereignty appears rather oxymoronic. Yet according to its advocates, these norms gave Southeast Asia's weak states the assurance they needed to embrace multilateral coordination and gradually develop common expectations of mutual benefit and the rudiments of a shared identity.

More conventional neoliberal analyses stress the growth of socioeconomic interdependence as the key driver of ASEAN regionalism. Two decades of rapid growth produced a quantum leap in the flows of goods, information, and people across Southeast Asia and the broader Asia-Pacific region. Unlike similar processes in Europe and North America, economic linkages within ASEAN developed without extensive legal agreements or supranational institutions. ASEAN's integration was thus often described as a "natural" market-led phenomenon. The implication is that economic interdependence itself moved states' policy decisions in a more cooperative direction, rather than the converse (Higgott 1995). Region-wide trends toward economic liberalization and political reform, and the general fading of militarized threats in intramural relations, are cited as evidence of powerful structural imperatives for cooperation.

Mainstream neoliberals were less sanguine, however, about ASEAN's conservative diplomatic philosophy and resistance to institutionalized cooperation (Funston 1998, 1999). In Buszynski's (1997) formulation, ASEAN was a classic expression of "old" regionalism, one aimed at bolstering national sovereignty and governmental power and focused on countering specific external threats, whereas the global trend has been toward "new regionalism," which builds upon shared values, pools sovereign decision-making powers, engages in multiple fields of cooperation simultaneously, and facilitates interactions among diverse social groups as well as government agencies. ASEAN has always avoided negotiating binding treaty agreements beyond its core principles and relied on voluntary cooperation coordinated through informal diplomacy. It has eschewed building formal institutional structures to carry out its activities, instead preferring to conduct multilateral relations through a virtually continuous series of ministerial meetings and technical working groups, capped off by summit meetings that became annual affairs during the 1990s.

The adequacy of ASEAN's state-centered, value-neutral regionalism was increasingly doubted, however, as complex interdependence gave rise to new international political standards, more active civil societies, and mounting pressures for democratic political reform. The interdependence of Southeast Asia's domestic affairs was graphically illustrated during the economic crisis of 1997–1998, when the "contagion effect" transmitted the fallout of poor policy choices in individual countries to the entire region. In this context, the group's informal, consensus-based diplomacy and nonintervention principle often seemed little more than an excuse for shirking responsibility for urgent regional problems, ranging from poor economic governance to the choking haze from Indonesia's forest fires.

Viewed in light of liberal-institutionalist assumptions, therefore, ASEAN's recent malaise is the predictable result of its failure to adapt to basic trends in the international system associated with complex interdependence, including the erosion of the sovereignty principle and the rise of international civil society. The grouping's ambitious post–Cold War agenda was bound to fail unless its leaders modified their aversion to supra-national decision-making and engaged in more substantive negotiation over value-laden socio-economic and political issues. As several authors point out, however, this diagnosis leaves open the prospect for future progress toward greater regional cooperation, particularly since interdependence seemingly leaves little viable alternative (Solingen 1999; Acharya 1999c). Viewed optimistically, ASEAN's recent tribulations appear as a painful but ultimately constructive episode in the region's evolution, a "wake-up call" that constrains its members to renovate both domestic and regional institutions in order to deepen regional cooperation. Insofar as the economic crisis accelerated democratization across the region, moreover, ASEAN's previously instrumental embrace of economic and diplomatic coordination might deepen into a shared commitment to broadly liberal sociopolitical values (Acharya 1998).

Neorealist critics have been similarly skeptical about the efficacy of ASEAN's regionalism. In contrast to liberal-institutionalists, however, they locate the association's weaknesses in two, far less tractable, flaws: deep-seated rivalries and conflicts of interests among its members, and Southeast Asian states' profound weakness, individually and collectively, vis à vis external powers. The dean of scholars on Southeast Asian international relations, Michael Leifer, has long argued that, notwithstanding ASEAN's admirable record in keeping the peace, its members' foreign policies have always remained guided by realist principles of "self-help." Knotty regional issues and bilateral disputes are assiduously excluded from ASEAN's multilateral dialogues.[1] The diplomacy of benign neglect has served adequately in managing conflicts but has largely precluded positive multilateral action to resolve regional problems. ASEAN's defense of state sovereignty, stress on procedural norms over substantive outcomes, and resistance to institutionalized bargaining all point to the tenuousness of regional cohesion (Moller 1998, Narine 1997, 1999). Recent trends have brought intragroup tensions to the fore, as economic crisis, leadership transitions, uneven democratization, and the inclusion of new, economically backward members exacerbate conflicting national perceptions of what degree and types of regional cooperation are desirable.

As for coping with extramural challenges to Southeast Asia's security, ASEAN from its founding rejected the concept of collective security based on explicit defense arrangements, either among its membership or between the association and outside powers. East Asia's stable Cold War power structure allowed ASEAN to maintain a tenuous balance between its aspirations to a coordinated, autonomous regional diplomacy and the reality of its members' dependence on bilateral security guarantees with outside powers, notably the United States.[2] ASEAN's modest successes in coordinating its members' extramural diplomacy reflected overwhelmingly instrumental cooperation against a well-defined external threat in the form of Communist expansionism.[3] As one observer put it, "As an international actor, ASEAN has constituted a community of convenience based on functional considerations rather than a community of shared visions" (Nischalke 2000, 107).

With the Cold War system's sudden collapse, many observers predicted a decline in U.S. capacities and willingness to provide extended deterrent protection, even as China's economic ascent and regional ambitions unsettled several of ASEAN's old and new members (Whiting 1997). Just as at the end of the Second Indochina War, the prospect of a U.S. draw-down prompted ASEAN to enhance its diplomatic coordination. The association launched the Asia-wide ASEAN Regional Forum (ARF) to keep the United States engaged in regional security and to bring China and Japan into a process of confidence-building. Yet neorealists were as skeptical of the new initiative as they had been of the ASEAN's intramural efficacy (Leifer 1996). Indeed, ASEAN members continued to augment, albeit modestly, their bilateral security arrangements with outside powers during the 1990s (Ganesan 2000). From a neorealist viewpoint, then, ASEAN's effort to mobilize collective regional strength in the shifting post–Cold War Asian system was doomed from the start.

Each of these perspectives throws partial light on ASEAN's turbulent fortunes, for as Hsiung (chapter 1) and Muthiah (1998, 645–670) argue, Asia's international relations are shaped both by value changes at the system and unit levels and by the strategic interaction of power and interests within these shifting normative parameters. Yet most of the pessimistic analyses of ASEAN regionalism employ unrealistic standards of regional cohesion and efficacy and overstate the need for a wholesale transformation of the grouping's diplomatic modalities. Fundamental continuities are evident amidst Southeast Asia's turbulent post–Cold War trajectory, and these suggest that, despite its limitations and recent difficulties, ASEAN's brand of regionalism remains not only viable but also vitally relevant to Southeast Asia's fortunes.

Simply put, the intramural and systemic imperatives that have furnished ASEAN's raisons d'être are strengthening, rather than fading, in the evolving Asia-Pacific order. Southeast Asian states' shared syndromes of external dependency and marginality, on the one hand, and internal vulnerability, on the other, explain ASEAN's durability over three decades and remain paramount considerations for the foreseeable future. Just as at its birth, ASEAN operates in an uncertain international environment defined by an ambiguous transition in great-power relations. As a result, bilateral sources of security and patronage are inadequate to its members' needs, and subregional cooperation becomes an indispensable element of each state's external diplomacy. More broadly, the Asia-Pacific region features a growing divergence between geostrategic dynamics, in which China's rising power concerns many in Southeast Asia, and geoeconomic processes, in which Japan and China figure as key partners and potential counterweights to U.S. unilateralism. This pluralization of power structures in the Asia-Pacific reinforces Southeast Asian states' historic desires to use coordinated regional diplomacy to balance their highly unequal bilateral relations with Asia's great powers.

Recent traumas have indeed punctured ASEAN's more expansive claims to a collective identity and uniquely cooperative security culture. Criticisms of ASEAN's conservative, sovereignty-focused diplomatic norms carry weight at a time when globalization is eroding the boundaries between the domestic and international affairs and fostering the growth of social interactions outside the sphere of state-to-state relations. Yet many observers overstate ASEAN's inadequacies in this regard and incorrectly assert the need to reject its regionalization model *in toto* in favor of Western prototypes (Narine 1999). Complex interdependence is often presumed to require national governments to delegate authority to supranational institutions, and in this regard, ASEAN regionalism is often contrasted negatively with arrangements like the EU and NAFTA. Yet the superiority of formal transnational institutions in managing complex interdependence is hardly clear. Like nation-states themselves, international institutions have struggled to cope with the growing scope and complexity of transnational interactions. Such bodies as the EU and the WTO face serious challenges to their bureaucratic decision-making and even to their very legitimacy. Likewise, attempts by the IMF to micromanage institutional reforms in its client states have been notable for their failure.

Regionalism is a process rather than a state of affairs, and ASEAN's region-building project clearly must adapt to changes in its domestic and external environments. The group's insistence on unanimity and its rigid segregation of domestic and international issues is increasingly untenable. More formal bargaining will necessarily augment the group's open-ended consensus-building. Yet its general preference for "concerted unilateralism" over the growth of a formal institutional superstructure may remain the most productive means of fostering cooperation in a diverse region. Other aspects of ASEAN's diplomatic praxis, moreover, remain particularly apposite in the more complex international environment emerging in Asia. The grouping has, from its founding, embraced notions of comprehensive security, in which economic, social, and political concerns are integrated with strategic issues in multilateral dialogue.

ASEAN'S POST–COLD WAR AGENDA

When ASEAN was founded in 1967, its initial prognosis was bleak. Not only did Southeast Asia include a diversity of political regimes and economic structures, but its members also faced numerous territorial disputes, cross-border Communist and ethnic insurgencies, and domestic communal tensions that threatened to spill across national borders.[4] The first ASEAN Summit was held only in 1976 when, in the wake of the Communist-led reunification of Vietnam, the conservative regimes of Southeast Asia met in Bali to build a stronger framework for regional cooperation in the vacuum caused by a feared U.S. withdrawal. The resulting Declaration of ASEAN Concord and Treaty of Amity and Cooperation (TAC) articulated the group's core mission, which was to nurture regional "resilience" (*ketahanan,* in Malay), conceived in terms of twin goals of domestic stabilization and resistance to external threats. Regional cooperation would contribute to these goals by observing two core principles: First, the signatories pledged to observe non-intervention in each other's domestic affairs and to shelve boundary disputes. Second, they agreed to work toward limiting the intrusion of outside powers in the region's affairs, as earlier enshrined in the group's 1971 declaration calling for the creation of a Zone of Peace, Freedom, and Neutrality (ZOPFAN) in Southeast Asia.

The practice of mutual forbearance proved surprisingly effective, enabling Southeast Asian governments to consolidate domestic control and foster economic development. In terms of external diplomacy, ASEAN's newfound cohesion was deployed to counter the Vietnamese occupation of Cambodia, which began in 1979 and lasted for more than a decade. ASEAN's de facto leader, Indonesia, was relatively more concerned with growing Chinese influence than with the Soviet-backed Vietnamese expansionism, but ASEAN united behind Thailand's rigid opposition to any accommodation short of Vietnamese withdrawal. This posture operationalized the Bali Treaty's "front state" principle, which mandated deference to the diplomatic leadership of whichever ASEAN member was most impacted by external events (Moller 1998, 1088).

As it entered the 1990s, ASEAN celebrated its successful management of peaceful internal relations and basked in its growing recognition as a potent diplomatic actor in wider regional affairs. But regional leaders recognized that the sudden collapse of the Cold War, together with the East Asian economic boom and growing economic integration, had decisively altered the international environment in the Asia-Pacific region. They knew that the association was compelled to adapt its diplomatic goals and modalities to remain relevant to a post–Cold War world.

ASEAN's response involved a three-fold effort at organizational change, which, though pursued in typically cautious fashion, was tantamount to a major transformation of the group's scope and mission. The first element was a revitalization of ASEAN's efforts to foster economic cooperation. The founding ASEAN documents emphasized economic, social, and cultural cooperation as primary goals, but a slew of cooperation schemes had achieved little. In the wake of the global recession of the early 1980s, the ASEAN economies moved decisively to open their economies to the boom in foreign direct investment (FDI) from North America, Japan, and the East Asian newly industrialized countries (Bowie and Unger 1997). The vast influx in FDI following the 1985 Plaza Accords created complementary linkages where none had existed before. Multinational corporations (MNCs) created region-spanning corporate networks that distributed different stages of production among multiple Southeast Asian subsidiaries and linked them into an integrated production process (Chen and Drysdale 1995; Borrus et al, 2000). Soon, ASEAN's intra-regional investment and trade volumes began to grow, led by the rise in intrafirm and intraindustry transactions consisting of parts, components, and raw materials destined for assembly and export outside the region.

While regional economic integration owed little to ASEAN's multilateral cooperation schemes, the expansion of the regional manufacturing complex created a powerful incentive to coordinate its members' economic policies so as to bolster the region's continuing attraction to FDI.[5] ASEAN's leaders viewed with concern the potential threats to the liberal global trading system posed by the GATT's troubled Uruguay Round and the rise of economic regionalism in Europe and North America with the advent of the European Single Market and NAFTA in 1992 and 1994, respectively. It was against this backdrop that the Fourth ASEAN Summit in Singapore in 1992 announced the goal of an ASEAN Free-Trade Agreement (AFTA), which set a target date for regional free trade in 2015 and laid out a program for coordinated tariff reductions.

The second pillar of ASEAN's post–Cold War adjustment was a drive to reach out to its former Indochinese rivals and the previously isolationist Myanmar and integrate them into the association. This project was billed as the realization of the vision laid out in ASEAN's founding documents for a united community of all Southeast Asian nations. As with the EU's embrace of its former socialist rivals to the east, there was some concern that widening ASEAN's membership might frustrate efforts to forge a deeper cooperation, particularly since Vietnam, Laos, Cambodia, and Myanmar had inward-looking, radically less-developed economic systems. Yet the dominant view within ASEAN was that their rapid incorporation would serve to accelerate a region-wide convergence of interests in economic development and hasten the fading of historic tensions between Vietnam and its neighbors. On the diplomatic front, moreover, it was felt that ASEAN's collective weight would be strengthened, rather than diluted, by bringing the newcomers into its fold (Hay 1996, Mutalib 1997). Vietnam acceded to the Bali Treaty in 1992 and formally joined ASEAN in 1995. Laos and Myanmar followed in 1997, though Hun Sen's violent coup d'état in Phnom Penh forced a postponement of Cambodia's entry until 1999. ASEAN's forging ahead with expansion in the face of strong criticism from the United States and European Union, particularly in connection with Myanmar, indicated its high level of solidarity and diplomatic confidence.

Third, ASEAN reversed its longstanding opposition to the growth of wider multilateral security and economic frameworks in the Asia-Pacific and instead moved to secure its position within these evolving structures. Southeast Asian states' prior wariness reflected in part their desire to sustain the United States' preeminence in regional security affairs, inasmuch as creating a multilateral Asian security system might hasten the retrenchment of the U.S. forward deployments. More importantly, ASEAN wished to avoid being displaced by larger multilateral frameworks, seeing in proposals for trans-Pacific institutions a potential for losing its own valued cohesion and diplomatic autonomy. At the same time, however, the ASEAN states recognized that their economic and security fortunes had become ever more tightly linked to those of the broader Asia-Pacific. The prospect of declining U.S. commitment to the region and rising Chinese influence meant that the Cold War's "hub-and-spoke" system of U.S. bilateral security agreements would necessarily be augmented by greater initiative and organization among its Asian partners (Acharya 1995, 187–88). ASEAN did not want to leave the initiative to others, who might set expansive agendas at odds with its own preferences for minimal infringements on national sovereignty, or who might embroil ASEAN in alliances that curtailed its ability to deal flexibly with outside powers like China, Japan, and the United States.

Finally, while the United States remained the primary security guarantor for the original ASEAN members, it was also the major focus of their fears that their access to global economic markets might gradually be curtailed. The U.S. shift toward more aggressive unilateralism in international economic affairs from the late 1980s indicated that, with its Cold War strategic motivations fading, it was no longer prepared to fuel East Asia's export miracle without demanding reciprocal trade access and a bigger investment stake in the region's growing market. The United States also began to link its economic diplomacy to its new doctrine of "democratic enlargement," which ASEAN's authoritarian and semi-democratic regimes found worrisome. This element of uncertainty prompted ASEAN and other regional actors to search for multilateral frameworks that might help them to both placate and restrain the "rogue superpower" (Crone 1993).

In the economic realm, therefore, ASEAN embraced the Australian initiative to create an Asia-Pacific Economic Cooperation (APEC) forum, but only after first negotiating in the 1990 Kuching Declaration a collective stance on the terms for its participation. These included an affirmation that APEC's modus operandi would conform to ASEAN's own preference for informal, nonbinding dialogue and consensus-rule decision-making, rather than formal negotiations aimed at binding agreements. Second, ASEAN insisted that APEC would practice "open regionalism," meaning that members could choose to offer all benefits of intra-APEC liberalization to nonmembers, as well. Such a stance was ideologically congenial to the Anglo-American members of APEC, but its significance to ASEAN was that it excluded the possibility that APEC might evolve into an economic bloc that would subordinate its own collective influence or interfere with its economic relations with other parts of the world, such as the EU. When APEC initiated a series of annual summit meetings, ASEAN insisted on the right to have one of its members host every second meeting. Although the grouping's Anglo-American members soon became impatient for more specific, concrete progress toward APEC's declared goal of regional free trade, ASEAN together with Japan successfully resisted pressure to negotiate binding timetables and sectoral liberalization agreements.[6]

In the security field, ASEAN shepherded to fruition a Japanese proposal to create a new multilateral dialogue arrangement, called the ASEAN Regional Forum (ARF). Launched in 1994, the ARF expanded on the annual ASEAN Post-Ministerial Consultations (PMCs) with outside powers. The new forum sought to directly transpose ASEAN's own diplomatic practices to the wider East Asian region (Acharya 1997). In line with ASEAN's intramural diplomacy, the ARF eschewed formal negotiations and binding security commitments in favor of an ongoing and open-ended process of consultation. The group's concept paper projected a gradual progression from confidence-building measures to vaguely specified roles in preventive diplomacy and, at some future date, conflict resolution mechanisms. Rather than seek to resolve knotty problems, the ARF's contribution to a peaceful East Asia was to be achieved through a process of familiarization that might "socialize" the potential rivals, China, the United States, and Japan, to the norms of mutual restraint and positive-sum cooperation for joint economic gain.

A regional security structure led by relatively weak states and encompassing strategic rivals is an anomaly in terms of neorealist theory, since stable multilateral cooperation can come only from a stronger state's hegemonic marshalling of subordinate allies against a common threat. In this regard, ASEAN's leadership of the ARF was seen as testament to the group's use of collective diplomacy to overcome its members' strategic weakness and seize the chance to influence the still-uncertain post–Cold War East Asian security dynamics. While mutual suspicions between China, the United States, and Japan had scuttled other proposals for a new multilateral security structure, ASEAN's leadership was viewed as acceptable to all sides.[7] Not the least significant aspect of the ARF concerned the exercise of ASEAN's "soft power." While realist observers doubted, constructivist scholars took seriously the association's claims that its own security culture, defined in terms of mutually acceptable diplomatic processes, rather than the trading of values based on fixed interests, could influence the course of Asian regional development, just as it had within Southeast Asia. Given the prevailing uncertainty about the shifting balance of power in East Asia, and the fact that the region's great powers were engaged in a complex process of redefining their interests, there was reason to believe that ASEAN's practice of diplomacy-as-socialization might help foster the emergence of a peaceful new order in Asia, transforming the "ASEAN Way" into the "Asian Way" of international relations (Acharya 1997).[8]

ASEAN'S TROUBLED TRANSITION
TO A NEW INTERNATIONAL ERA

ASEAN's ambitious post–Cold War agenda, launched with great optimism at the beginning of the 1990s, encountered severe tests over the course of the decade. ASEAN's faltering initiatives revealed the group's limited capacities for collective problem-solving and the tenuousness of regional unity.

ASEAN AND SOUTHEAST ASIA'S
GEOSTRATEGIC CHALLENGES

ASEAN's bid to project greater collective influence in Asia's post–Cold War international politics shaped the structure and conduct of the region's new multilateral organizations. The grouping's substantive achievements in extramural diplomacy, however, fell short of official rhetoric, as two important cases demonstrate. Southeast Asia's major concern in terms of traditional security affairs was the prospect that China might use its growing military capabilities to challenge the existing regional order and project its influence southwards. The focal point of this concern was the Spratly Islands claimed by China in total and in part by five different ASEAN members.[9] Notwithstanding their own conflicting claims, the ASEAN states presumably shared a stronger common concern with dissuading China from taking an assertive posture with regard to its island claims.[10] The value of a coordinated approach to the Spratlys was all the more salient insofar as the issue focused the broader question of a declining American security commitment. The United States abandoned its Philippine bases in 1991 after having its leases revoked, and while listing freedom of navigation in the South China Sea as one of its core regional interests, indicated that its bilateral security commitments to the Philippines did not extend to disputes over the Spratlys themselves (Simon 1999).

ASEAN's effort to manage the Spratlys began in 1990 with a series of dialogues convened by Jakarta. At the 1992 ASEAN post-ministerial meetings, ASEAN issued a joint declaration of principles for the peaceful resolution of conflicting claims to the islands. China indicated that it might be willing to postpone the question of sovereignty and explore joint development, but soon thereafter passed a law affirming its sovereign claim and issued oil exploration licenses to a U.S. oil company in an area overlapping Vietnamese claims. In 1995, China erected "fishing structures" on Mischief Reef, a mostly-submerged outcropping on the Philippines' continental shelf and a mere 120 kilometers from its shores.

China prevented the issue from being formally debated at the next ARF meeting, yet in informal discussions, ASEAN signaled its dismay to China and followed the meeting with internal discussions aimed at defining a common code of conduct for the region. Whether because of these moves toward greater ASEAN coordination, or simply out of a desire to avoid alarming its interlocutors, China announced at the Third ARF in 1996 that it would ratify the Law of the Sea Treaty and at least discuss the competing claims in a multilateral setting. In 1997 a joint Sino-ASEAN statement called for peaceful resolution of the conflicting claims.

ASEAN's tentative solidarity on the issue, however, decayed significantly in 1998 and 1999. The Philippines discovered that China had significantly expanded its Mischief Reef structures, and soon thereafter arrested Chinese fishermen operating in the area. Rather than registering alarm, other ASEAN claimants to the Spratlys responded by becoming more assertive about their own claims. Malaysia erected its own structures on Philippine-claimed reefs, while Vietnamese soldiers fired upon a Filipino surveillance flight. At their December 1998 summit, ASEAN heads of state agreed to negotiate a code of conduct for the South China Sea. At a November 1999 summit meeting in Manila between ASEAN, Japan, South Korea, and China, the Philippines persuaded ASEAN to endorse a draft text that would forbid the occupation of new reefs and the construction or expansion of structures. Yet the code failed to specify the geographic scope of coverage, since Vietnam insisted that any joint ASEAN position include not only the Spratlys, but also the Paracel islands, in which it had a bilateral dispute with China. ASEAN failed to persuade China to accept the code and instead was left with a vague promise to consider guidelines in the future. In early 2000, China signed a set of bilateral cooperation agreements with the Philippines. At the subsequent ARF meeting in August, however, China again rejected the ASEAN document, but this time proposed its own alternative, which included a ban on military exercises in the area, aimed in part at the Philippines' renewed cooperation with the U.S.

ASEAN's uneven record in the Spratlys dispute highlights the difficulties it faces in mobilizing collective influence to manage extramural security challenges. China's ability to disregard ASEAN's concerns underscores the improbability of using multilateral diplomacy to redress the vast power differentials between its members and the region's heavyweights. Moreover, by extending its diplomatic protocols of consensus-seeking and non-confrontational dialogue to the ARF, ASEAN handicapped its own options for adopting a harder bargaining position and gave China considerable diplomatic flexibility in setting terms of discussion. Finally,

ASEAN's members found it more difficult than in the Cambodia issue in the 1980s to reconcile their differing perceptions of the seriousness of the threat posed by China's encroachment, and their conflicting claims have made it difficult to maintain a united bargaining front. Yet, while collective diplomacy did not succeed in inducing China to commit to a formal cooperation regime, ASEAN's tentative coordination did signal the issue's regional dimensions and ramifications. Given China's desire to expand its influence in Southeast Asia, even partial (and greater latent) regional solidarity had evident deterrent effect. China's reluctant steps to respond to ASEAN's concerns in a multilateral context offers further evidence of the indirect impact of ASEAN regionalism.

ASEAN's credibility as a collective actor in regional security affairs suffered a stark reversal in the East Timor imbroglio in September 1999. ASEAN governments had long backed Indonesia's rejection of international criticism of its behavior in East Timor. They reacted with dismay and concern, therefore, when Indonesian President B. J. Habibie announced in early 1999 that he would allow the United Nations to organize a referendum in East Timor the outcome of which could determine the territory's independence. When the Indonesian military and its militia auxiliaries in East Timor unleashed a scorched-earth campaign of terror after the referendum, ASEAN played no role in the urgent search for a solution but instead offered only pro forma endorsements of Jakarta's right to decide on the question of outside intervention. This failure was particularly acute, given that Indonesia had explicitly offered ASEAN a role, at one point suggesting that it would accept an Asian or ASEAN peacekeeping force, but not one led by outsiders.[11]

The eventual decision to admit an Australian-led intervention force raised fears within ASEAN that Western powers had lost regard for Southeast Asia's strategic value. Malaysia's Prime Minister Mahathir voiced the more conspiratorial notion that the Timor affair represented a deliberate effort by outside powers to weaken or even dismember Indonesia and humble ASEAN. A more realistic concern was that the United States and its allies no longer saw much reason to tread carefully in intervening into the region, or to defer to ASEAN's leadership in the region's security affairs. These fears were inflamed when Australian Premier John Howard told a newspaper interviewer that he saw Australia serving as the U.S. "regional deputy" in security affairs.[12] Again, however, ASEAN's members held diverging views as to the danger of the precedent set by outside intervention, and these prevented ASEAN from influencing the manner in which the affair was resolved. Thailand and the Philippines immediately volunteered to join the Australian-led intervention force, with Malaysia and Singapore adopting a more cautious stance and the Indochinese countries refusing to participate at all.[13] When negotiations began to organize a longer-term United Nations peacekeeping mission to begin in 2000, the UN responded to ASEAN's call for local leadership, but this occasioned further squabbling over who should lead the force. Thailand volunteered but offered to defer to Malaysia, which loudly campaigned for the job. In the end, Timorese objections blocked Malaysia's bid, and the Philippines was given the job. In sum, ASEAN had proved impotent to address the greatest security crisis in its domain in decades. In the words of one observer connected with ASEAN's regional security dialogues, "We should have done something to make ASEAN count. . . . It turned out to be irrelevant."[14] By failing to persuade Indonesia to resolve the crisis or, more realistically, to negotiate the terms for outside actors to participate in its resolution, ASEAN sacrificed its goal of strategic autonomy, which mandated that members work to minimize the overt intrusion of outside powers into the region's affairs.

ASEAN AND SOUTHEAST ASIA'S GEOECONOMIC CHALLENGES

ASEAN's diplomatic status was greatly enhanced in the 1990s by its claim to represent the world's most dynamic economic region. As flows of investment and trade began to bind the Asia-Pacific economies more closely together, Southeast Asian governments sought to work collectively through ASEAN to shape a multilateral governance structure for the broader East Asian political economy. As in security affairs, ASEAN's goals were to engage the wider region on terms that would maximize its collective profile while avoiding becoming either isolated or marginalized by any larger economic grouping. In particular, ASEAN sought to export its own diplomatic preferences for a loosely institutionalized Asia-Pacific economic structure, one that would forestall any major rupture in economic relations between the region's major economies while also restraining their ability to restrict market access or use other leverage to pressure the region's smaller economies. Yet, as in the security realm, ASEAN's post–Cold War strategy encountered severe tests that revealed real limits to its internal cohesion and external influence. Diverging national interests, the lack of a common vision of their external strategic economic interests, and the overwhelming external dependency of the ASEAN economies combined to undermine its bid for a more powerful role in the regional political economy.

ASEAN's geoeconomic diplomacy consisted of two chief elements: the advancement of the ASEAN Free Trade Area (AFTA) and the exertion of collective influence over APEC. As noted earlier, the chief motivation for organizing a free trade region in Southeast Asia was not the growth of intramural trade relations. Instead, AFTA was a calculated strategic response to the formation of regional economic blocs elsewhere in the world, namely North America and Europe. One of its primary purposes was to enhance its attractions as a host for foreign direct investment (FDI) and thereby prevent a diversion of investment flows to Mexico, Eastern Europe, and even China. The chief variable in this strategy's success was the credibility of ASEAN's commitments to allow the free flow of goods and services across the region, even when this jeopardized their respective national industrial strategies. Unlike NAFTA or the EU, however, the AFTA eschewed binding treaty commitments in favor of coordinated voluntary tariff liberalization, thus making credibility harder to achieve. Member governments promised to reduce or eliminate tariffs for specified percentages of each country's total trade line-items, but were each allowed to exempt a list of "strategic" commodities. These exclusions often included sectors of most interest to foreign investors, such as automotives and crucial service sectors like infrastructure and telecommunications. Finally, ASEAN governments did not substantially augment the institutional structure of the Association to manage the process. The ASEAN Secretariat's technical working committees were inadequately equipped to monitor the implementation of liberalization commitments, and no formal dispute resolution process was included in the agreements.

ASEAN initially viewed the establishment of APEC with skepticism. Its members shared an anxiety that the United States and its allies might be able to use the multilateral forum to pressure them to liberalize their economies at an accelerated rate (Nesadurai 1996). A second concern was that the development of a region-wide system of economic rules would inevitably detract from ASEAN's effort to bolster its own status as an economic unit through the AFTA accords. These concerns were articulated most forcefully by Malaysia's Prime Minister Mahathir, who in 1991 proposed an alternative grouping of like-minded Asian political economies, the East Asian Economic Caucus (EAEC), that would link ASEAN to Japan, China, and South Korea while excluding the United States, Canada, Australia, and New Zealand. Mahathir's concept resonated with widespread fears of a world economy decomposing into three self-contained regional blocs. Yet, quite apart from Japan's unwillingness to take the leadership role Malaysia urged on it, other key ASEAN nations rejected any effort to create an Asian regionalism that conflicted with, rather than balanced, their close ties with the United States.

As in the ARF, ASEAN largely succeeded in establishing its own diplomatic norms as the guiding principles of APEC, most notably the concept of "concerted unilateralism" as opposed to a gradual ratcheting up of formal multilateral commitments. It was joined by Japan and China in resisting the U.S. insistence that APEC should begin to set firm timetables, negotiate binding sectoral agreements, and adopt an expanded agenda covering such things as investment rules and trade-in services. While this standoff appeared to represent a modest victory, the Asian economic crisis soon brought a searing test of ASEAN's capacity for positive action in economic affairs. The tremendous power and global scale of the financial forces involved made it unreasonable to expect that ASEAN alone could act in ways that would significantly alter the course of the crisis. Yet the association proved singularly unable to mobilize collective action to address the terms of the crisis, either independently or through the APEC forum, and failed even to mobilize sufficient bargaining power to modify the terms that the International Monetary Fund and the United States set for financial support plans to the region.[15]

ASEAN's initial reaction to the gathering economic storm included efforts to mobilize cooperative actions. In early 1997, the group had initiated a new series of meetings involving Finance and Central Bank officials, and through this mechanism they backed Thailand's temporarily successful defense of the baht in April of that year. When the financial tide soon swamped local governments' reserves and drove them off their currency pegs, Malaysia and Singapore pledged large initial contributions to the bailout packages organized by the IMF for Thailand and Indonesia. In late 1997, Malaysia's Prime Minister Mahathir made a tour of the ASEAN region promoting the idea of using local currencies, rather than the U.S. dollar, to denominate regional trade. The idea was dismissed at the 1997 ASEAN Summit as impractical, given that the region's trade was overwhelmingly dominated by dollar-denominated transactions with outside regions. At the same time, ASEAN issued an official appeal to the world's wealthier economies to implement major reforms to the international financial system.

Not surprisingly, these gestures had very little impact on the rapidly deteriorating regional economy. More importantly, though, ASEAN was unable to strike a credible unified stance with which to negotiate with the IMF and its U.S. backers for even slightly more favorable treatment. In one notable episode, Indonesia attempted to use Singapore's offer of financial credit as a bargaining chip in its negotiations with the IMF. Suharto pledged that half of the promised allocation would go toward propping up the rupiah, rather than the to trade financing that had been initially agreed upon. Singapore was forced to quickly declare that its own support was conditional on Indonesia's signing a deal with the IMF (Narine 1999).[16] Soon, the major ASEAN economies parted ways in their crisis responses. Singapore emphasized its transparent and noncorrupt institutions, the

Philippines advertised the relative solvency of its banking system, and Malaysia insisted repeatedly, "We are not Indonesia" (Funston 1999). Having witnessed the damage to investor confidence done by Suharto's gamesmanship with the IMF, Thailand's new government assiduously courted Western official and financial audiences with pledges to implement market-based reforms. In the midst of these efforts to send reassuring signals and boost global confidence in the region's will to change, Mahathir's inflammatory attacks on Western economic neocolonialism only fed the growing alienation of Malaysia from its neighbors. Singapore, too, earned the ire of both Malaysia and Indonesia, who perceived the city-state as exploiting their distress by allowing traders in its currency and stock exchanges to speculate against their own economies. In an interview in August 1998, Indonesian President Habibie, angered by Lee Kuan Yew's earlier criticism of his selection as Suharto's vice-president, bitingly referred to Singapore as "just a little red dot on the map." When Malaysia imposed capital controls in September 1998, it also declared a Singapore-based, over-the-counter market in Malaysian stocks illegal, freezing hundreds of millions of dollars in shares held by some 180,000 Singaporean (and Malaysian) investors.

The crucial turning point in the struggle for authority over Asia's recovery strategy, however, came early on in the crisis at the November 1997 meeting of APEC Finance Ministers in Manila. Japan had proposed an Asian Monetary Fund as a mechanism to spread liquidity across the region in order to jump-start its battered export machine and ease the pain in its ASEAN clients. The United States rejected the proposal in no uncertain terms, making it clear that it would tolerate no infringement on the IMF's ability to make liquidity support strictly conditional on structural reforms in the afflicted economies. The failure of the AMF proposal was not itself surprising; most likely it was intended (at least in the short run) as a bargaining chip to moderate the IMF-U.S. policy. What is revealing, however, is that this negotiating bid failed decisively, as the United States called Japan's bluff and ASEAN failed to speak with one voice on the idea. The only tangible result of the meeting was the creation of a regional mutual surveillance system, known as the Manila Framework, in which the ASEAN countries pledged to share detailed financial data and practice joint monitoring of the health of the region's banking systems.

Having failed to forge cooperation for collective action in either direct economic measures or in bargaining with the IMF-U.S. complex, ASEAN instead returned to its familiar strategy of seeking to stimulate the interests of foreign investors by renewing pledges for region-wide liberalization. At their December 1998 summit in Hanoi, the ASEAN heads of state launched a Plan of Action, the chief measures of which were the acceleration of the implementation of the target deadline for free trade (among original members) from 2010 to 2003, the harmonization of foreign direct investment rules under the previously announced ASEAN Investment Area, and an agreement on the liberalization of service sectors. These measures were intended as signals that ASEAN's commitment to liberalization had not been reversed by the trauma of severe economic turmoil. Yet, they represented a reformulation of ASEAN's existing approach to regional economic cooperation, based upon voluntary unilateral measures rather than binding regional agreements or supranational institutions for implementing these commitments. As such, their credibility was open to question.[17] In fact, subsequent meetings in 1999 to work out specific plans to accelerate AFTA ran into difficulties, as various governments sought exceptions to the deadlines for strategic sectors, as when Malaysia and the Philippines declared their inability to accelerate their liberalization of auto-sector tariffs.

By the end of 1999, Southeast Asia had entered a rapid economic recovery, driven by the IMF's acquiescence to expansionary fiscal policies and the recovery of demand for Southeast Asia's (now more competitively priced) electronics exports. Yet the crisis had highlighted the congenital weakness of the nascent multilateral framework for economic cooperation in Asia and underscored the continued U.S. veto power over broader institutions, such as the IMF and even the Asian Development Bank, which powerfully constrained Southeast Asia's economic options. In light of these realities, the only possible means of counterbalancing U.S. power was for ASEAN to coordinate more closely with the larger economies of Northeast Asia, Japan, China, and South Korea. In an ironic echo of the Malaysian Prime Minister's earlier, spurned EAEC proposal, ASEAN invited those countries to a summit meeting in Manila in November 1999. The meeting revived ASEAN's earlier predilection for visionary rhetoric, as the "ASEAN+3" issued a communiqué that laid out a long-term goal of an East Asian common market and revived the concept of an Asian Monetary Fund (AMF). In a follow-up Finance Ministers' meeting in Brunei in March 2000, an agreement on an AMF was announced, only to be withdrawn in favor of a more limited plan for the sharing of foreign-exchange reserves.

ASEAN's Membership Enlargement and the Specter of Faction

Even as ASEAN's extramural security and economic initiatives faltered, the crises of the late 1990s also raised questions about whether its internal solidarity had begun to fray. These issues loomed especially large in connection with ASEAN's second major thrust in the 1990s, namely the incorporation of the Indochinese countries and Cambodia into the regional diplomatic community. These four states had experienced a vastly different Cold War history from that of the original ASEAN members and brought into the group far lower levels of economic and social development, much deeper suspicions of global trends of economic and political reform, and distinct perspectives on the region's external security environment.[18] Yet ASEAN had vested a tremendous symbolic investment in the goal of "unifying" the region by bringing all ten states under its wing. It was an article of faith that surmounting the region's own Cold War divisions would enhance ASEAN's quest for greater autonomy from the vicissitudes of great-power manipulation.

Vietnam's transition from bitter foe to a member of the club took place over a remarkably brief five-year period and was seen as adding particular muscle to ASEAN's collective diplomatic strength. In addition to its vast population and potent military, Vietnam had begun to open itself to investment and was touted as the next Southeast Asian tiger. ASEAN's expansion program ran into far more controversy as it began to prepare for the admission of Myanmar. Western powers, led by the United States and the EU, had ostracized the military junta in Myanmar (SLORC) since its bloody suppression of student demonstrations in 1988 and its annulment of an opposition election victory in 1990. They had tried to enlist Southeast Asian countries to join in isolating the country, but ASEAN resisted the pressure and instead avowed a strategy of "cooperative engagement." During this time, Myanmar had turned to China for military support in vanquishing its ethnic insurgencies, a development ASEAN viewed with concern. When Myanmar declared its intention to reform and join the regional economic boom, ASEAN moved quickly to strengthen its economic and diplomatic ties.

To critics within and outside the region, ASEAN's embrace of the Myanmar regime was an illustration of its shallow, elite-centered, and value-neutral definition of regional identity. ASEAN leaders argued that incorporating the country into the region's expanding zone of cooperation and prosperity would hasten the process of economic liberalization and governmental modernization that Myanmar officials had already espoused. Privately, however, several ASEAN members harbored doubts about the wisdom of embracing a regime that appeared so unstable and that was so odious to the international community.[19] Yet the issue soon became embedded in ASEAN's external diplomatic agenda, becoming a key point of contention in several Southeast Asian countries' rhetorical debate with Western countries over issues of democratization, human rights, and "Asian values." When the United States and other countries publicly pressured ASEAN not to admit what they considered to be a rogue state, the organization felt compelled to move forward with the expansion. Myanmar's entry into ASEAN instantly complicated the group's effort to adopt a higher-profile collective role in global affairs. Most notably, the EU refused to agree to move ahead with its new joint multilateral forum with ASEAN if Myanmar had full participation rights. Many observers noted the irony in ASEAN's failure to anticipate the conflict between two of its key projects. In Moller's (1998, 1091) pithy summary, "'If widening its membership had been designed to provide ASEAN with more collective bargaining power, the outcome looked more like the opposite.'"

Cambodia's entry into ASEAN proved to be an equally difficult test. Two weeks before its scheduled admission, co-Premier Hun Sen overthrew his rival Prince Ranarridh, in a violent coup. Already on the defensive over Myanmar and alarmed over the potential for a revival of Cambodia's fading civil war, ASEAN postponed the admission. Hun Sen then proceeded to manipulate the underlying differences of opinion within ASEAN in a bid to swiftly end his international isolation and secure legitimacy for his government. With Malaysia and Vietnam already urging recognition, Hun Sen received a mission by an ASEAN "troika" composed of Indonesia, the Philippines, and Thailand and offered to accept the group's mediation in exchange for swift action on its membership. When this bid failed, Hun Sen loudly declared his willingness to forgo ASEAN membership rather than submit to interference by outside powers. By invoking ASEAN's own hallowed principle of nonintervention against the group's mediation effort, he highlighted the mounting contradictions between the group's advocacy of a rigid sovereignty doctrine and its pursuit of a stronger collective diplomacy.

Besides provoking immediate diplomatic challenges, the admission of ASEAN's new members greatly increased the complexity of the consensus-building required for any action in ASEAN's informal coordination system. The group's founding members had developed considerable skill in negotiating in an almost familial diplomatic style, whereas the new members were unaccustomed even to the confidential form of give-and-take necessary for group cohesion. Many observers feared that, rather than socializing Vietnam and Myanmar into the traditional deference and trust prevailing among the original members, the decision would lead to a factional split between the older, more economically and socially open members and their newer defensive, inward-looking colleagues. Some evidence for this concern emerged when Vietnam took the ASEAN chair in 1998 and began to push for Cambodia's admission at the December Hanoi Summit. When several other members balked,

Vietnam sought to preempt them by making a public announcement of Cambodia's acceptance. The embarrassing confrontation was only resolved by settling on a face-saving interim period before the installation ceremony in April 1999. Fears of ASEAN factionalism were further provoked in November 1999, when Vietnam convened a meeting with Cambodia and Laos to discuss common positions in advance of ASEAN's upcoming summit in Manila. One observer remarked that, "The 'Indochina conclave' is evidence that a caucus of politically closed states is emerging in ASEAN."[20]

Besides the immediate diplomatic fallout, the expansion controversies had created a subtler but even more important challenge to ASEAN's diplomatic agenda. The confrontation with Western powers had forced the group to articulate its approach to regionalism in terms of universal principles and rationales. For the first time, ASEAN's diplomatic culture was explicitly linked to the achievement of specific positive outcomes beyond the maintenance of intramural peace. The principles of nonconfrontational and informal diplomacy were now offered as more effective mechanisms for both conflict resolution and the encouragement of change in Myanmar (Amer 1999). This subjected the group's procedural principles to greater scrutiny and made the "ASEAN Way" vulnerable to criticism should it fail to bring results.

The ASEAN Way Besieged— the Noninterference Principle

Noninterference in its members' domestic affairs has always been one of ASEAN's core diplomatic values. The principle is directly rooted in the group's foundation, which came as a reaction to Sukarno's bid to destabilize his neighbors in pursuit of expanded power for Indonesia. ASEAN's conservative leaders recognized that their common dilemma of weak state structures, complex societies, and internal insurgencies demanded that they refrain from exploiting each other's internal difficulties for short-term gain. In the 1990s, however, growing voices within the region began to argue that the region's growing interdependence and changing values required a new, more substantive basis for international cooperation.

The 1990s actually began with ASEAN seeking to transpose its diplomatic conventions to the domain of its rapidly growing external diplomacy. In parallel with the Asian Values rhetoric emanating from Singapore and Malaysia, the articulation of "The ASEAN Way" transformed the noninterference principle from what was originally a contingent solution for maintaining peace among mutually vulnerable states into an official ideology of international relations. Advocates of Asian Values frequently invoked cultural essentialism to legitimate soft-authoritarian government. Just as often, however, they pointed to the region's economic performance as a more instrumental justification, thus tying Asian Values to objective performance criteria. In the same way, the disputes over Myanmar and Cambodia prompted ASEAN to link its diplomatic protocols to concrete changes in its members' political systems. No longer was noninterference defended on purely intrinsic terms; instead, ASEAN claimed that socialization and mutually-beneficial cooperation would foster economic and political reforms in Myanmar and Indochina. By justifying noninterference on efficacy grounds, ASEAN leaders subjected their diplomatic protocols to empirical criticism.

The noninterference principle and Asian Values ideology never achieved a uniform acceptance across ASEAN. The Philippines, together with Thailand after 1988 (they are the group's only fully democratic states), was more willing to engage the United States' in dialogue on human rights issues.[21] Following Thailand's 1992 coup and popular uprising, that country also began to integrate more liberal concepts into its foreign policy making. While ASEAN's strategic core—Indonesia, Malaysia, and Singapore—remained committed to their restrictive political models, new reformist currents began to emerge as part of the politics of generational change. ASEAN's "second-tier" leaders, such as Anwar Ibrahim and B. J. Habibie, sought to capitalize on a growing thirst for social reform by recasting the Asian values debate and stressing the need for socially responsive government.[22] Partly because they were unable to effect domestic changes prior to assuming leadership, younger leaders like Anwar spent much time building regional networks and expounding on their ideas of strengthened civil societies and Asian cultural renewal in international forums. Inevitably, this trend began to call into question ASEAN's deliberately value-neutral and exclusively state-centric diplomatic culture.

In the wake of the embarrassing Cambodia episode, in which ASEAN had been maneuvered into a de facto violation of the noninterference rule, Anwar voiced an idea that seemed obvious to many, namely that ASEAN needed more robust principles for the conduct of intramural relations. He suggested that ASEAN adopt a policy of "constructive intervention," in which the participants " . . . should invite each others' services to boost each others' civil society, human development, education and national economy to avoid the kind of political crisis experienced by Cambodia." (Haacke 1999, 582).

Disaffection with noninterference further mounted in the fall of 1997, when fires from Indonesia blanketed Malaysia, Singapore, and parts of

Thailand with a dangerous haze for weeks at a time over a nine-month period. The haze issue laid bare the extent to which domestic policies had transborder effects. Indonesia's fires were set by plantation companies, many of whom were immune from regulation by virtue of their connections to President Suharto and his family. Despite repeated appeals from its neighbors, the Indonesian government appeared unwilling to take the firm measures required to limit the damage and prevent its recurrence. The problem had arisen before, in 1994–1995, after which ASEAN had drafted an action plan to prevent its recurrence. However, for ASEAN to address the problem at its root, that is, the lack of enforcement, it would have to apply pressure on Jakarta to reform its forestry policies and in so doing highlight the endemic corruption at the heart of the regime. Naturally, this prospect was excluded by the noninterference principle. But at the same time, the haze undermined the domestic legitimacy of the governments in affected countries and thus amounted to a form of "interference" of the sort the ASEAN protocols aimed to prevent. The haze crisis activated the most vocal components of civil society in most Southeast Asian countries, the environmental NGOs, who criticized their governments for not protecting the public interest by dealing more firmly with Indonesia (Cotton 1999).

The economic crisis of 1997–1998 cast an even harsher spotlight on the inter-relatedness of ASEAN members' domestic politics. Some governments' effort to conceal damaging economic data frustrated efforts to calm panicked financial markets. More seriously, Suharto's dangerous brinkmanship with the IMF and Mahathir's inflammatory broadsides against Western neocolonial domination undercut Thai and Philippine efforts to pursue an accommodationist strategy toward the IMF and other Western governments.

In response to these accumulated frustrations and the perception that ASEAN was failing to make any impact, the foreign minister of the new reformist Thai government advanced a proposal for a modification of the noninterference principle at ASEAN's 1998 ministerial meetings in Manila. Surin Pitsuwan declared that, if they were to confront the realities of globalization and interdependence that the crisis had revealed so starkly, "ASEAN members perhaps no longer can afford to adopt a noncommittal stance and avoid passing judgment on events in a member country, simply on the grounds of non-interference."[23] He proposed that ASEAN adopt a new principle of "flexible engagement" that would allow proactive diplomacy to resolve domestic issues when these had important spillover effects or weakened the grouping's collective.

With the exception of the Philippines, the rest of ASEAN's members bluntly rejected the Thai proposal. The new ASEAN members strenuously argued that noninterference was the explicit contract on which they had entered the association. They feared that a sudden change in the rules would be inevitably used to put pressure on them to change their totalitarian political systems. Malaysia was obviously averse to a policy that would sanction criticism of heterodox economic strategies or authoritarian political practices. Singapore, too, feared that constructive engagement could jeopardize its security. The city-state had already seen a rapid deterioration of relations with both Malaysia and Indonesia over its role in the economic crisis, and it had no wish to enable such disputes to be elevated to the level of multilateral regional diplomacy. In sum, most ASEAN members were concerned that any change in the noninterference principle might open a Pandora's box of intramural conflict. This fear outweighed concerns that that ASEAN's consensus-bound diplomacy would condemn the association to a creeping obsolescence by preventing action on crucial intramural.

ASEAN REGIONALISM: OBSOLESCENCE OR CONTINUITY?

ASEAN began the 1990s with burgeoning confidence and ambitious goals. By the decade's end, it was fending off suggestions that it was a moribund organization in a declining region. Critical observers noted that ASEAN's post–Cold War initiatives were built on a questionable premise, namely that a group of marginal powers could extend ASEAN's traditional model of intramural relations based on consultation, consensus, and conflict-avoidance, to achieve expanded goals in a rapidly changing regional environment (Buszynski 1997). Some went further, arguing that the grouping's regional model was increasingly obsolete (Narine 1999; Haacke 1998).

These analyses are overstated. Given the magnitude of Southeast Asia's recent challenges and the limited resources of its member states, ASEAN's failure to achieve definitive resolutions is unsurprising. A better measure of regional cohesion is the grouping's ability to preserve existing levels of cooperation and advance them through incremental reforms. Indeed, in the midst of recent turmoil one may expect key continuities in the premises of regional cooperation as well as tentative steps to strengthen the mechanisms for cooperation. Instead of spelling the breakdown of ASEAN regionalism, Southeast Asia's recent trials might instead prompt the organization to refocus on its more limited historic missions of stabilizing intramural relations and providing its members a multilateral instrument with which to partly mitigate their disadvantaged relations with outside powers. Other recent responses suggest that

ASEAN is capable of advancing regional cooperation by adopting more institutionalized and formal multilateral bargaining (Acharya 1999c). Finally, as the economic crisis fades and Southeast Asian states grapple with internal political challenges, the positive virtues of ASEAN's regional model have become visible again.

ASEAN In Asia's Geopolitical and Geoeconomic Systems

The conceit of ASEAN's regional outreach in the 1990s was that a group of relatively weak states could, by banding together, shape multilateral processes to enhance their own influence and moderate the economic and security behavior of Asia's dominant powers. Several years later, these ambitions appeared naïve. APEC and AFTA were ineffectual in the economic crisis, and the ASEAN Regional Forum had yet to address the region's core security challenges. There were indications that Southeast Asian states had begun to turn away from coordinated regional diplomacy to a new emphasis on bilateral external relations in order to secure their strategic and economic interests. For example, in 1999 the Philippines renewed its military access agreements with the United States and resumed joint military exercises. The next year Singapore, frustrated at delays in AFTA, began to negotiate bilateral free trade agreements with Australia, New Zealand, Japan, and other countries. Despite the severe blows to ASEAN's prestige and collective influence, however, the organization is likely to remain the indispensable forum for its members' extramural diplomacy and a key building block of Asia's international political economy.

There are several reasons for drawing this conclusion. Above all, Southeast Asian states' shared syndromes of dependency and marginality persist as powerful motives to maintain ASEAN as a counterweight to their bilateral relations with outside powers. It is often suggested that ASEAN members' differing strategic outlooks (e.g., their varying perceptions of Chinese and U.S. intentions) frustrate their ability to coordinate efforts in security affairs without a powerful unifying external threat. The collapse of the Communist threat, represented by Vietnamese expansionism, robbed the Southeast Asian states of their single overriding common purpose. But this reading of ASEAN's history is crucially incomplete. During the Cold War ASEAN organized not only to counter the specific Vietnamese threat but also to cope with the broader *uncertainties* emerging in its strategic environment. The group intensified its diplomatic role in the 1970s in response to the potential vacuum created by the U.S. withdrawal from Vietnam. Today, the geostrategic environment in East Asia is similarly in flux, and, as always, ASEAN remains peripheral to the calculations of the major players in the region. Although the United States has repeatedly pledged to maintain its forward presence and balancing role in East Asia, the long-term reliability of the U.S. security guarantee remains questionable, particularly for the Southeast Asian countries. U.S. efforts to encourage ASEAN to take stronger steps toward multilateral security cooperation are seen by many in the region as a signal that America wishes to reduce its commitments and transfer greater responsibility for deterring China to the Southeast Asian states themselves (Crispin 2000). Even if the United States maintains its role as Asia's strategic "balancer," mediating between China, Japan, and smaller powers, this would not address the full range of external security concerns and scenarios facing Southeast Asia's weak states. In this sense, it is the prospect of U.S. *neglect* that compels continued interest in regional security arrangements.[24]

Conversely, ASEAN has also pursued the goal of strategic *autonomy* during the Cold War, in order to minimize the risk that their dependence on the United States would impose greater obligations to the anti-Communist crusade than they would be able to meet. Most Southeast Asian countries (Thailand and Philippines being the obvious exceptions) had little desire to become directly embroiled in America's war in Indochina, despite their need to shelter under the U.S. security umbrella. A parallel situation prevails today, in that Southeast Asian states wish to preserve the U.S. role as a strategic balancer of China and Japan but do not want the countries to serve as pawns in a U.S. containment strategy or to increase American interest in and leverage over their domestic political economies.[25] The potential risks of overdependence were graphically illustrated in the eyes of many Southeast Asians by the U.S-backed Australian intervention in East Timor. ASEAN's members likewise share a common vulnerability to the destabilizing side-effects of any major rupture in relations between the United States, Japan, and China. The question, therefore, is not ASEAN's ability to resolve Asia's conflicts or alter the regional distribution of power, since its scope for positive diplomatic initiatives remains circumscribed by the interests and decisions of Asia's major powers. Rather, ASEAN and the ARF allow Southeast Asian states to buffer and counterbalance their security relations with external powers. It is in this context that ASEAN proper, and its ARF offshoot, allow the Southeast Asian states to manage extramural relations in ways that prevent great-power rivalries from exacerbating the grouping's internal tensions.

Third, each of Asia's major powers is favorably disposed to have ASEAN continue playing an important role in regional geostrategic affairs.

As the Timor affair suggests, a fragmented and conflict-ridden Southeast Asia would likely compel outside intervention that, in turn, could exacerbate tensions among the great powers. More positively, each of the region's major powers sees relations with ASEAN and the ARF as an important context in which to enhance its own diplomatic status. The United States has sought to encourage ASEAN and the ARF to take a more active role in deterring China from extending its military presence. Japan sees ASEAN as providing a multilateral structure within which it can safely expand its regional leadership role. For its part, China views ASEAN's quest for strategic autonomy with favor and wishes to encourage that tendency in the hopes of slowly balancing or even undermining America's strategic dominance in Asia (Cheng 1999; Dolven 1999).

The same strategic logic suggests that ASEAN will continue to pursue a coordinated geoeconomic diplomacy. The economic crisis confirmed Southeast Asian economies' profound dependence on the U.S. economy as well as the predominance in regional economic governance of the international financial institutions under U.S. control. At the same time, however, the crisis graphically illustrated how global market players have come to view Southeast Asia as a single economic unit. ASEAN's members recognize that they must pursue a coordinated approach to broad aspects of economic governance, such as financial sector regulation and investment promotion, if they are to restore their reputation with global investors and achieve a modicum of credibility in negotiating with the United States and the major global financial institutions. The association's Action Plan moved up the timetables for implementing tariff concessions under AFTA, but Malaysia soon backtracked by announcing it would delay by two years the liberalization of its sensitive auto sector, while Singapore began negotiating bilateral trade agreements outside the AFTA framework. Critics noted that Malaysia's backsliding undermined confidence in the region's commitment to economic integration, yet the episode paradoxically strengthened the AFTA program by prompting the creation of an explicit dispute resolution mechanism under the AFTA Council. Based on GATT article 28, the protocol would require members who postpone their liberalization commitments to compensate others whose exports were affected.[26] The end result moved ASEAN's economic integration project toward a more institutionalized process with supranational monitoring and regulation mechanisms.

Similar incremental progress occurred in the field of financial cooperation. After the United States quashed Japan's proposal for an Asian Monetary Fund (AMF) in 1997, ASEAN pledged to intensify consultation among its financial and central banking officials and began planning for a formal foreign-exchange-sharing mechanism to assist in balance-of-payments crises. In its 2000 Chiang Mai Initiative, ASEAN broadened its currency swap mechanism and forged bilateral complements to China, Japan, and South Korea. At ASEAN's December 2000 informal summit in Singapore, China publicly embraced the concept of an ASEAN-China free trade agreement.

The credibility of these initiatives is easily questioned, and few would suggest they herald the emergence of a cohesive East Asian economic bloc. They do, however, signal the continuity of ASEAN members' strategic interests in coordinated geoeconomic diplomacy. Two aspects of ASEAN's nascent monetary cooperation with Northeast Asia are particularly important in this regard. First, the Chiang Mai Initiative was undertaken in the face of U.S. public opposition.[27] Second, the growing economic alignment with the three Northeast Asian powers—Japan, South Korea, and China—contrasts with the general regional pattern of security relations. This points both to the growing parity of geoeconomic issues with traditional security concerns and to the relevant countries' desire to mitigate or counterbalance some of the vulnerability caused by their strategic dependency on the United States.

ASEAN's Intramural Cohesion in a Liberalizing and Fragmenting Region

ASEAN's role as a guarantor of intra-regional harmony has met with equally severe tests and dismaying results during the past three years. Some of these challenges derive from the devastating, but temporary, effects of the economic crisis. But even ASEAN's staunchest proponents recognize that the organization faces a qualitatively new political environment. Its members have experienced major political upheavals as social change and economic crises generated new challenges to authoritarian and patrimonial regimes. Trade and investment flows, migration and refugees, drug smuggling, piracy, and environmental destruction have expanded the scope of urgent cross-border challenges facing Southeast Asian states. ASEAN's enlargement and the uneven pace of reform among its members have vastly complicated the task of identifying common political values and benchmarks. The tension between growing interdependence and diverging identities and interests threatens to undermine ASEAN's historical raison d'être as the guarantor of a peaceful and prosperous region. As Vatikiotis (1999a, 83) puts it, " . . . centrifugal forces have already begun to exert themselves. There is a danger that Southeast Asia as a larger political entity will be divided by competing regional and extra-regional interests, especially in the wake of the economic crisis. These are the hard realities."

Such pessimism, while understandable in light of ASEAN's recent trials, is unwarranted. Two slightly paradoxical arguments suggest that ASEAN is likely to adjust to the region's internal convulsions, if only through ad hoc incrementalism. In the first case, the need for a fundamental transformation of ASEAN's regional model is often overstated. Its principles of sovereignty and noninterventionism do not, in any strict sense, preclude either the public airing of mutual disagreements or substantive negotiation over domestically sensitive issues. In the past, ASEAN governments often invoked the noninterference principle to persuade their counterparts to stifle criticisms voiced by NGOs or the public media, as when the Philippine and Malaysian governments obstructed local conferences on East Timor in order to placate the Suharto regime. Such an expansive interpretation of noninterference may be discarded without changing ASEAN's formal protocols. Likewise, despite the taboo on mutual criticism at the multilateral level, ASEAN has historically witnessed numerous public bilateral disputes touching on domestic matters in neighboring countries.[28] Changing political values and growing interdependence may work to give formerly sensitive issues a greater airing within ASEAN's deliberations, even if the organization continues to shun a formal dispute resolution role. For example, the 1998 Ministerial Meeting established an NGO working group on ASEAN Human Rights Mechanisms, and the individual members have reported to ASEAN on their establishment of national human rights commissions. ASEAN's Haze Action Plan has streamlined technical and financial cooperation in fighting fires in Indonesia, even if it has not addressed the problem's underlying causes.

In the security realm, an important precedent has been set that ASEAN may seek to mediate in cases of severe domestic turmoil in its member states. Embarrassed by the organization's paralysis in the East Timor crisis, leaders at the 1999 ASEAN summit endorsed the concept of having a "troika" of ASEAN states serve as an executive committee to engage in preventative diplomacy in domestic emergencies, including, if necessary, rapid deployment of peacekeepers. Such efforts to strengthen mechanisms for collective management of sensitive intra-regional issues may be dismissed as largely cosmetic. Yet they are symbolically important adjustments to ASEAN's diplomatic culture and hold out the prospect that the grouping is becoming less averse to discussing sensitive issues when they impact regional stability.

A second argument, however, points instead to the continuing relevance of the basic elements of ASEAN's approach to regionalism. Even as deepening interdependence creates counter-pressures for greater mutual engagement, Southeast Asian states retain their fundamental need for mutual forbearance from their neighbors. Notwithstanding the growth of democratic norms and civil society pressures, regime consolidation and sociopolitical stability remain core national interests throughout ASEAN's membership.[29] Cautious diplomacy that avoids exacerbating its members' dilemmas of domestic governance thus retains its priority in ASEAN diplomacy, over and above any effort to reach consensus on substantive political values or build capacities for multilateral dispute resolution (Ramcharan 2000). A broader view indicates that ASEAN's expansion has not led, as some feared, to the rise of cohesive factional blocs within the organization. In fact, the primary disputes have continued to occur between several of the original members. Notable examples include Malaysia and Singapore's ongoing rows over Singaporean access to Malaysian water, economic rivalry, and the Malaysian-owned railway station in Singapore. Malaysia and the Philippines fell into a bitter exchange when President Joseph Estrada criticized Malaysia for jailing Anwar Ibrahim. Meanwhile, Burma has found a reliable economic partner and diplomatic advocate in Singapore, and Vietnam made common cause with Malaysia and Indonesia in the wrangle over Cambodia's entry into the grouping. The reformist elements challenging ASEAN regimes are by no means all committed to liberal politics and economics, and even those that are may not demand that their governments seek to export democratic reform values to neighboring states. Opposition forces and NGOs include many who object to what they perceive as U.S. arrogance in imposing harsh economic medicine on the region; many such groups are generally disposed to favor enhanced ASEAN cooperation.[30] These examples suggest that ASEAN's more complex agenda is producing a cross-cutting and flexible pattern of issue-specific alignments among its members, rather than any self-reinforcing division into permanent sub-blocs.

CONCLUSION

Southeast Asia's diplomatic prestige endured a dizzying turnaround in the last decade of the twentieth century, as ASEAN's post–Cold War agenda first expanded and then foundered. The grouping's reversal of fortunes owed much to a devastating economic crisis that no one expected, but it also revealed the unrealistic expectations underpinning some aspects of the association's diplomatic projects. Southeast Asian leaders came to believe that their "soft-power," in the form of the ASEAN Way's familial consultations and consensus-based diplomacy, was sufficient to achieve solidarity and collective influence. As neorealist and liberal-institutionalist critics maintained, this notion contained more than a little overconfidence. Buszynski (1997, 576) acutely observed before the recent upheaval:

> The problems faced by ASEAN today are, in the main, a result of an attempt to adjust what was in the 1980s a small subregional association with limited functions to a major Asia-Pacific actor embracing an array of open-ended functions. The structure and the mechanisms that evolved within ASEAN to cope with the problems of the seventies and eighties are plainly inadequate today when the organization has taken upon itself a high-profile role.

ASEAN's dreams of projecting corporate strength in Asia's international relations were brought rudely to earth during the past few years. But the association's role in mediating relations between Southeast Asia and the wider world remains indispensable. Southeast Asian states require a regional counterweight to their asymmetric bilateral relations with outside powers, and the Asian economic crisis has exposed the dubious utility of the alternative regional multilateral institutions, notably APEC, or even the ARF, that once threatened to marginalize the association.

In the past year, moreover, ASEAN has recovered some of its momentum toward greater diplomatic cooperation. The grouping's internal structures and practices have come under pressure, but their resilience is manifest in the gradual progress toward more open and institutionalized approaches to regional order, even as core elements of the association's diplomatic model remain in place (Acharya 1999c). Efforts to identify common values and build a common regional identity will continue, but will remain adjunct to hard, but hopefully enlightened, bargaining to achieve shared interests and mitigate conflicting ones. In this respect, ASEAN's approach to regionalism remains vitally relevant to a changing world order that increasingly embeds interstate rivalries in more complex forms of interdependence and mutual vulnerability.

NOTES

1. "ASEAN's mode of activity, which has been expressed primarily in an informal process of confidence-building and trust creation, has never been directed to solving specific intra-mural problems . . . the very notion of a peace process misrepresents the remit of ASEAN as a multilateral security dialogue" (Leifer 1999, 25–26). The Bali Treaty provided for a formal dispute resolution mechanism under the aegis of an ASEAN High Council, but the process has never been invoked to resolve bilateral or wider disputes dividing its members. New provisions for the council's operation were adopted at an ASEAN summit in December 1998, but

most saw this as a token gesture of solidarity rather than a genuine departure in the direction of greater institutionalization. The few Southeast Asian boundary disputes that have been successfully negotiated were referred to outside arbitration bodies like the International Court of Justice. These include the Thai-Malaysian maritime boundary in the Gulf of Thailand and the Pedra Branca island in the Johor Straits between Malaysia and Singapore.

2. Members' bilateral security arrangements with outside powers were unconvincingly reconciled with ASEAN's pseudoneutralist ZOPFAN ideology by the fiction that all foreign bases and alliances were "temporary."

3. Leifer (1989) observes that even the most vaunted achievement of ASEAN's outward diplomacy, the reversal of Vietnam's Cambodia adventure, involved only a subsidiary role in a broader international coalition organized by two of Asia's great powers, China and the United States.

4. Examples included Malaysia's ties to Muslim separatist rebels in southern Thailand; Thailand's tolerance of Malaysian communist guerillas in the same territory; mutual hostility between Malaysia and Singapore over race riots prior to Singapore's ejection from the Malaysian Federation in 1965; lingering resentment in Indonesia over Sarawak and Sabah's incorporation into Malaysia; the Philippines' irredentist claim to Sabah; and Malaysian links to a brewing Muslim rebellion in Mindanao.

5. In the early 1990s, sub-ASEAN cooperation also emerged in the form of "growth triangles" linking Singapore with its neighboring Malaysian and Indonesian provinces and Malaysia's northern states with their Thai and Indonesian counterparts. Such efforts likewise focused largely on creating integrated logistical environments to attract external investment; only the initial triangle made significant progress.

6. The chief exception was APEC's Information Technology Agreement (ITA), endorsed at the 1996 Manila Summit, which committed APEC's members to eliminate tariffs on computing and information technology equipment. Even this agreement, however, was referred to the WTO for ratification.

7. One such proposal was for an Asian equivalent of the Council on Security and Cooperation in Europe. To the United States, the ARF held out the prospect of greater sharing of the regional security burden, particularly by facilitating an expanded role for Japan, without threatening U.S. bilateral alliance structure and overall strategic preeminence. China, long wary of security multilateralism as a cover for an American containment strategy, was attracted by the prospect that ASEAN's bid for greater strategic autonomy signaled an opportunity to woo the region to adopt a more independent diplomatic line and thus weaken U.S. strategic dominance over the long term (Cheng 1999).

8. Reinforcing such constructivist arguments was the notion that ASEAN's consensus-based diplomatic norms drew on cultural values and ideas about cooperation that were generalized throughout Asia.

9. The Paracel Islands are the subject of a separate dispute between Vietnam and China.

10. Indeed, the desire for insurance against Chinese assertiveness was presumed to be a major explanation for Vietnam's haste in reconciling with its erstwhile enemies in ASEAN in the 1990s.

11. In fact, none of the ASEAN countries had the necessary military transport and logistics capabilities to mount a successful intervention (Bostock 1999).

12. See *The Straits Times,* 25 September 1999, for criticisms of Howard by ASEAN members.

13. An embarrassing row emerged when Malaysia preemptively claimed that it had been asked to take the deputy command of the force, but later retreated when Timorese leaders objected and the position was given to Thailand.

14. Suchit Bunbongkarn, director of the Institute of Security and International Studies at Chulalongkorn University in Bangkok, quoted in Wain (1999).

15. During the Cold War era, several Asian countries, notably including Indonesia in the mid-1980s, had experienced severe financial crises, but found that Japan and the United States were unwilling to countenance a financial meltdown in their key regional allies. This time, however, the United States insisted on wrenching structural and policy reforms that would strike at the heart of the so-called Asian model of political economy that ASEAN countries practiced to varying degrees: high-debt industrial systems based on regulated banking oligopolies; government influence over the allocation of investment resources; and close government-business political ties. Many forecast the emergence of a pan-Asian resistance to the coercive imposition of Anglo-American capitalist rules on the region's political economies (Higgott 1998), yet the outcome suggested that ASEAN and its more powerful East Asian neighbors lacked sufficient cohesion to mobilize collective resistance.

16. When asked later why ASEAN hadn't used even its limited resources outside of the IMF frameworks, Singaporean leader Lee Kuan Yew frankly admitted, "We don't want to be telling [Thailand] what to do to reform its economy. It might take our relationship a long time to recover from that."

17. Referring to a competition for a major investment project between his country and Thailand, a Philippino Congressman commented that, "It's nice to talk about regional unity, but there's only going to be one General Motors plant. . . . We have to be prosperous before thinking across our borders." (Vatikiotis 1999b).

18. Brunei joined the founding five ASEAN members upon achieving independence in 1984.

19. The Philippines made a futile proposal for a multilateral dialogue between ASEAN and SLORC in 1995 after Myanmar applied to join ASEAN in 2000. When Malaysia assumed the ASEAN chair in 1996,

however, it unilaterally moved up the date for Myanmar's entry to 1997 (Moller 1998, 1090).

20. Carl Thayer, quoted in Hay 1999.

21. Noninterference took an ironic turn when, in an infamous 1992 speech to Philippine lawmakers, Singapore's Lee Kuan Yew declared that his host's economic malaise was the result of "too much democracy" and not enough discipline.

22. Even stable Singapore began to experiment with cultural liberalization and new mechanisms to encourage citizen "feedback."

23. Quoted in Haacke (1999, 585).

24. With regard to the Spratly islands dispute, Simon (1999, 11–12) observes that " . . . none of these [renewed U.S. bilateral agreements with Southeast Asian states] alters the basic U.S. policy of neutrality towards the dispute. . . . By taking advantage of . . . Washington's general passivity, Beijing indirectly calls into question the utility of the U.S. presence in the region. This situation also supports China's argument that U.S. alliances are relics of the past."

25. The Philippines, which has the most acute vulnerability in the region vis á vis China, felt compelled to upgrade its bilateral defense ties to the United States in 1999. Significantly, however, it rejected an American proposal to expand joint military exercises to include Thailand, Singapore, Canada, and Australia. A senior defense official explained that military ties to the United States would not be allowed to upset its regional ties, saying "[multilateralizing the exercises] might affect our bilateral relationship with countries (which are) not necessarily U.S. allies." *New Straits Times,* 13 November 2000.

26. In this case, the aggrieved party was Thailand, which had received major investments by U.S. automakers in anticipation of a liberalized regional auto market.

27. *The Nation* (Bangkok), 8 May 2000. Congruent with its close strategic alignment with the United States, Singapore also voiced reservations about efforts to escape the disciplines imposed by the IMF.

28. A notable recent example was the Philippines' and Indonesia's criticism of the Malaysian government's treatment of its former Deputy Prime Minister, Anwar Ibrahim, in late 1998. See also Ramcharan 2000, 82–83.

29. Stability dilemmas are particularly acute in ASEAN's anchor member, Indonesia, and will likely remain so for several years to come. As the struggling giant struggles to consolidate its new political order while preserving its territorial integrity, it will maintain its support for the idea that ASEAN diplomacy should give priority to bolstering the stability of its member governments. Thus, for example, ASEAN issued a forceful statement in November 1999 supporting President Abdurahman Wahid and urging that Aceh remain part of Indonesia.

30. In ASEAN's 2000 summit meeting, the grouping agreed to insist on Myanmar's full participation in meetings of the ASEAN-Europe forum, ASEM.

REFERENCES

Abad, M. C. Jr. 1996. Re-engineering ASEAN. *Contemporary Southeast Asia* 18, no.3:237–253.

Acharya, Amitav. 1995. ASEAN and Asia-Pacific multilateralism: Managing regional security. In *New Challenges for ASEAN,* edited by A. Acharya and R. Stubbs. Vancouver: UBC Press.

———. 1997. Ideas, identity, and institution-building: From the "ASEAN way" to the "Asia-Pacific way"? *The Pacific Review* 10, no.13:319–346.

———. 1998. *Democratising Southeast Asia: Economic Crisis and Political Change.* Perth: Asia Research Centre, Murdoch University.

———. 1999a. A concert of Asia? *Survival* (London: IISS), 41, no.3:84–101.

———. 1999b. Imagined proximities: The making and unmaking of Southeast Asia as a region. *Southeast Asian Journal of Social Science.* 27, no.1:55–76.

———. 1999c. Realism, institutionalism, and the Asian economic crisis. *Contemporary Southeast Asia* 21, no.1:1–29.

——— and R. Stubbs, eds. 1995. *New Challenges for ASEAN.* Vancouver: University of British Columbia Press.

Aggarwal, V. K. and C. Morrison, eds. 1998. *Asia-Pacific Crossroads: Regime Creation and the Future of APEC.* New York: St. Martin's Press.

Alagappa, Muthiah. 1995. Regionalism and security: A conceptual investigation. In *Pacific Cooperation: Building Economic and Security Regimes in the Asia Pacific,* edited by A. Mack and J. Ravenhill. Boulder, CO: Westview Press.

———. 1997. Systemic change, security, and governance in the Asia Pacific. In *The New Asia-Pacific Order,* edited by C. H. Chee. Singapore: Institute of Southeast Asian Studies.

———. 1998. Asian practice of security: Key features and explanations. In *Asian Security Practice: Material and Ideational Influences,* edited by A. Muthiah. Stanford, CA: Stanford University Press.

Amer, Ramses. 1999. Conflict management and constructive engagement in ASEAN's expansion. *Third World Quarterly* 20, no.5:1031–1048.

ASEAN. 1998. *Statement on Bold Measures.* Paper given at the Third ASEAN Informal Summit, 16 December 1998, Hanoi, Vietnam.

Baker, Richard W. 1998. The United States and APEC regime building. In Aggarwal and Morrison, eds. 1998.

Beeson, Mark. 1999. Reshaping regional institutions: APEC and the IMF in East Asia. *Pacific Review* 12, no.1:1–24.

Bergsten, C. F., ed. 1997. *Whither APEC? The Progress to Date and Agenda for the Future.* Washington, D.C.: Institute for International Economics.

Bobrow, Davis B., Steve Chan, and Simon Reich. 1996. Southeast Asian prospects and realities: American hopes and fears. *The Pacific Review* 9, no.1: 1–30.

Bora, Bijit, and E. M. Graham. 1997. Can APEC deliver on investment? In *Whither APEC? The Progress to Date and Agenda for the Future,* edited by C. F. Bergsten. Washington, D.C.: Institute for International Economics.

Borrus, M., D. Ernst, S. Haggard, eds. 2000. *International Production Networks in Asia: Rivalry or Riches?* Routledge Advances in Asia-Pacific Business. London, Routledge.

Bostock, Ian. 1999. ASEAN wanting on rapid deployment. *Jane's Defense Weekly,* November 17.

Bowie, Alisdair, and Danny Unger. 1997. *The Politics of Open Economies.* New York: Cambridge University Press.

Busse, Nikolas. 1999. Constructivism and Southeast Asian security. *The Pacific Review* 12, no.1:39–60.

Buszynski, Leszek. 1997. ASEAN's new challenges. *Pacific Affairs* 70, no.4:555–79.

Buzan, Barry. 1998. The Asia-Pacific: What sort of region in what sort of world? In McGrew and Brook. 1998.

Chanda, Nayan, and Shada Islam. 1998. In the bunker. *Far Eastern Economic Review,* 6 August 1998, 24–18.

Chang, Li Lin, and Ramkishen S. Rajan. 1999. Regional responses to the Southeast Asian financial crisis: A case of self-help or no help? *Australian Journal of International Affairs* 53, no.3:261–281.

Chen, Edward K. Y., and Peter Drysdale, eds. 1995. *Corporate Links and Foreign Direct investment in Asia and the Pacific.* Pymble, NSW: Harper Educational, in association with the Pacific Trade & Development Conference.

Cheng, Joseph Y. S. 1999. China's ASEAN policy in the 1990s: Pushing for regional multipolarity. *Contemporary Southeast Asia* 21, no.2:176–204.

Chin, Kin Wah. 1995. ASEAN: Consolidation and institutional change. *The Pacific Review* 8, no.3:424–439.

———. 1999. ASEAN's engagement with EU and the US in the 21st century: The political and strategic dimensions. Paper given at the Malaysia Association of American Studies (MAS) International Conference, 14–15 September 1999, Kuala Lumpur.

Ching, Frank. 1999. An engaging East Asia. *Far Eastern Economic Review,* December 16, 1999.

Cotton, James. 1999. The "haze" over Southeast Asia: Challenging the ASEAN mode of regional engagement. *Pacific Affairs,* 72, no.3:331–351.

Crispin, Shawn. 2000. The American role. *Far Eastern Economic Review,* October 5, 2000.

Crone, Donald. 1993. Does hegemony matter?: The reorganization of the Pacific political economy. *World Politics* 45, no.4:501–525.

Dolven, Ben. 1999. Sharper image: ASEAN strives for credibility by tackling sensitive issues. *Far Eastern Economic Review,* 5 August 1999: 17–18.

———, and Lorien Holland. 1999. Softly, softly. *Far Eastern Economic Review* (10 June 1999): 28–30.

Funston, John. 1998. ASEAN: Out of its depth? *Contemporary Southeast Asia* 20, no.1.

———. 1999. Challenges facing ASEAN in a more complex age. *Contemporary Southeast Asia* 21, no.2:205–219.

Ganesan, N. 2000. ASEAN's relations with major external powers. *Contemporary Southeast Asia,* 22, no.2:258–278.

Garnaut, R, and P. Drysdale. 1995. *Asia Pacific Regionalism: Readings in International Economic Relations*. Pymble, New South Wales: Harper Educational Publishers.

Gilpin, Robert. 1997. APEC in a new international order. In Hellmann and Pyle 1997.

Grieco, Joseph. 1998. Political-military dynamics and the nesting of regimes: An analysis of APEC, the WTO, and prospects for cooperation in Asia-Pacific. In Aggarwal and Morrison 1998.

Haacke, Jurgen. 1998. The Asianization of regional order in East Asia: A failed endeavour? *Asian Perspective* 22, no.3:7—47.

———. 1999. The concept of flexible engagement and the practice of enhanced interaction: Intramural challenges to the "ASEAN way." *The Pacific Review* 12, no.2:581—611.

Hay, Lao Mong. 1999. An Indochinese caucus: After a conclave in Vientiane, fears of a split. *Asiaweek,* 5 November.

Hay, Simon J. 1996. The 1995 ASEAN summit: Scaling a higher peak. *Contemporary Southeast Asia* 18, no.3:254—274.

Head, W.P., and E. G. Clausen. 1999. *Weaving a New Tapestry: Asia in the Post—Cold War World: Case Studies and General Trends*. Westport, CT: Praeger.

Hellmann, Donald C. 1997. America, APEC, and the road not taken: International leadership in the post—Cold War interregnum in the Asia-Pacific. In Hellmann and Pyle 1997.

———, and Kenneth B. Pyle. 1997. Introduction. In *From APEC to Xanadu: Creating a Viable Community in the Post—Cold War Pacific,* edited by D. C. Hellmann and Kenneth B. Pyle. Armonk, NY: M.E. Sharpe.

Higgott, Richard. 1995. APEC—A sceptical view. In *Pacific Cooperation: Building Economic and Security Regimes in the Asia-Pacific Region,* edited by A. Mack and J. Ravenhill. Boulder: Westview Press.

———. March 1998. The politics of economic crisis in East Asia: Some longer term implications. *CSGR Working Paper Series* (February).

———, R. Leaver, and J. Ravenhill. 1993. *Pacific Economic Relations in the 1990s: Cooperation or Conflict?* Boulder, CO: Lynne Rienner.

Huxlley, Tim. 1996. Southeast Asia in the study of international relations: The rise and decline of a region. *The Pacific Review* 9, no.2:199—228.

Kawasaki, Tsuyoshi. 1997. Between realism and idealism in Japanese security policy: The case of the ASEAN regional forum. *The Pacific Review* 10, no.4:480—503.

Khong, Yuen Fong. 1997a. ASEAN and the Southeast Asian security complex. In Lake and Morgan 1997.

———. 1997b. Making bricks without straw in the Asia Pacific? *The Pacific Review* 10, no.2:289—300.

Korhonen, Pekka. 1998. *Japan and Asia Pacific Integration*. London: Routledge.

Lake, D, and P. Morgan, eds. 1997. *Regional Orders: Building Security in a New World*. University Park, PA: Penn State University Press.

Lasater, Martin L. 1996. The New Pacific Community: U.S. Strategic Options in Asia. Boulder, CO: Westview.

Leifer, Michael. 1989. *ASEAN and the Security of Southeast Asia.* London and New York: Routledge.

———. 1995. ASEAN as a model of a security community? In Soesastro 1995.

Leifer, Michael. 1996. The ASEAN regional forum. *Adelphi Paper* no. 302. Oxford: Oxford University Press.

———. 1999. The ASEAN peace process: A category mistake. *Pacific Review* 12, no.1:25–38.

Lim, Robyn. 1998. The ASEAN regional forum: Building on sand. *Contemporary Southeast Asia* 20, no.2:115–136.

Lintner, Bertil. 1998. Lightning rod: As Burma draws fire, all of ASEAN gets burned. *Far Eastern Economic Review* (12 November 1998).

McGrew, Anthony and Christopher Brook, eds. 1998. *Asia-Pacific in the New World Order.* New York and London: Routledge

Mack, A., and J. Ravenhill, eds. 1995. *Pacific Cooperation: Building Economic and Security Regimes in Asia-Pacific.* Boulder, CO: Westveiw Press.

Mak, J. N. 1998. The Asia-Pacific security order. In McGrew and Brook 1998.

Markillie, Paul. 2000. South East Asia: Living together. *The Economist,* 12 February.

Marlay, Ross, and Samuel S. Stanton. 1999. An unequal contest: China versus the Philippines in the South China Sea. In *Weaving a New Tapestry: Asia in the Post–Cold War World: Case Studies and General Trends,* edited by William P. Head and Edwin G. Clausen. Westport, CT: Praeger.

Means, Gordon. 1995. ASEAN policy responses to North American and European trading agreements. In Acharya and Stubbs.

Moller, Kay. 1998. Cambodia and Burma: The ASEAN way ends here. *Asian Survey* 38, no.12:1087–1104.

Mutalib, Hussein. 1997. At thirty, ASEAN looks to challenges in the new millennium. *Contemporary Southeast Asia* 19, no.1:74–85.

Muthiah, Alagappa. 1998. Asian practice of security: Key features and explanations. In *Asian Security Practice: Material and Ideational Influences,* edited by A. Muthiah. Stanford University Press, Stanford, California.

Narine, Shaun. 1997. ASEAN and the ARF: The limits of the "ASEAN Way." *Asian Survey* 37, no.10.

———.1999. ASEAN into the twenty-first century: Problems and prospects. *The Pacific Review* 12, no.3:357–380.

Nathan, K. S. 1996. Linkages between Asia-Pacific regional economic and security relations: Emerging trends in the post–Cold War era. In Shirk and Twomey.

Nesadurai, Helen. 1996. APEC: A tool for U.S. regional domination? *The Pacific Review* 9, no.1:31–57.

Nischalke, Tobias Ingo. 2000. Insights from ASEAN's foreign policy cooperation: The ASEAN way, a real spirit or a phantom? *Contemporary Southeast Asia* 22, no. 1:89–112.

Nye, Joseph. 1995. The case for deep engagement. *Foreign Affairs* 74, no.4:90–102.

Pangestu, Mari. 1997. Assessing APEC trade liberalization. In Bergsten 1997.

Petri, Peter. 1993. Is the United States bowing out of Asia? *Journal of Asian Economics* 4, no.2:283–300.

Pitsuwan, Surin. 2000. Heeding ASEAN's legacy. *Far Eastern Economic Review* (17 February 2000).

Pyle, Kenneth B. 1997. The context of APEC: U.S.-Japan relations. In Hellmann and Pyle.

Ramcharan, Robin. 2000. ASEAN and non-interference: A principle maintained. *Contemporary Southeast Asia* 22, no.1:60–88.

Rapkin, David P. 1995. Leadership and cooperative institutions in the Asia-Pacific. In Mack and Ravenhill.

Ravenhill, John. 1998. The growth of intergovernmental collaboration in the Asia-Pacific region. In McGrew and Brook.

Rix, Alan. 1993. Japan and the region: Leading from behind. In Higgott, Leaver, and Ravenhill.

Rodell, Paul A. 1999. Historical legacies and contemporary ASEAN-PRC relations. In Head and Clausen.

Severino, Rodolfo. 1999. The ASEAN way in Manila. *Far Eastern Economic Review,* 23 December.

Shirk, S., and C. P. Twomey, eds. 1996. *Power and Prosperity: Economics and Security Linkages in Asia-Pacific.* New Brunswick, NJ: Transaction Publishers.

Simon, Sheldon. 1995. Realism and neoliberalism: International relations theory and Southeast Asian security. *The Pacific Review* 8, no.1:5–24.

———. 1999. United States Strategy in the Asia Pacific for the 21st century: Regional and global implications. Paper read at MAAS International Conference on the EU, U.S., and ASEAN: Exploring New Strategies for Cooperative Engagement in the 21st Century, September 14–15, 1999, at Kuala Lumpur.

Soesastro, H, ed. 1995. *ASEAN Economic Cooperation in a Changed Regional and International Political Economy.* Jakarta: Centre for Strategic and International Studies.

Solingen, Etel. 1999. ASEAN, *Quo Vadis?* Domestic coalitions and regional cooperation. *Contemporary Southeast Asia* 21, no.1:30–53

Sukma, Rizal. 1999. ASEAN-US Relations: The case for cooperative engagement. Paper given at the Malaysian Association for American Studies International Conference on European Union, the United States, and ASEAN: Exploring New Strategies for Cooperative Engagement in the 21st Century, September 14–15, 1999, at Kuala Lumpur.

Tay, Simon S. C., and Obood Talib. 1997. The ASEAN regional forum: Preparing for preventive diplomacy. *Contemporary Southeast Asia* 19, no.3:252–268.

Vatikiotis, Michael. 1998. Divided they fall. *Far Eastern Economic Review* (December 17): 26–27.

———. 1999a. ASEAN 10: The political and cultural dimensions of Southeast Asian unity. *Southeast Asian Journal of Social Science* 27, no.1:77–88.

———. 1999b. Bloc mentality. *Far Eastern Economic Review* (December 9): 22–24.

Wah, Chin Kin. 1995. ASEAN: Consolidation and institutional change. *The Pacific Review* 8, no.3:424–439.

Wain, Barry. 1999. Another chance for ASEAN. *Asian Wall Street Journal,* 29–30 October.

Wesley, Michael. 1999. The Asian crisis and the adequacy of regional institutions. *Contemporary Southeast Asia* 21, no.1:54–73.

Whiting, Allen E. 1997. ASEAN eyes China. *Asian Survey* 37, no.4:299–322.

Yamazawa, Ippei. 1995. On Pacific economic integration. In Garnaut and Drysdale.

———. 1997. APEC and WTO in trade liberalization. In Bergsten, ed. 1997.

Zakaria, Haji Ahmad, and Baladas Ghoshal. 1999. The political future of ASEAN after the Asian crisis. *International Affairs* (London), 75, no.4:759–778.

PART IV

COMPREHENSIVE SECURITY

CHAPTER 8

AMERICAN VIEWS OF ASIA-PACIFIC SECURITY: COMPREHENSIVE OR MILITARY

DAVIS B. BOBROW

INTRODUCTION

It is unwarranted to claim extended foresight well into the twenty-first century about the particulars of the United States role in Asia-Pacific security. It is feasible to understand many of the factors that will shape it and their current implications for that evolving role. These factors and prospects not only shape near-term American behavior, but they affect the expectations others in the Asia-Pacific do and will have of the region. As others act in light of those expectations, American officials, experts, interest groups, and the general public can be expected to use those actions as evidence to justify, specify, and even possibly revise American policy.

My premises are that what a democracy does in foreign affairs, and the challenges it recognizes and concentrates on, follow from the joint effects of four sets of factors. The first consists of salient ideas among policy elites and policy intellectuals about security threats and opportunities, and about appropriate national security objectives as performance standards. The second features observable military and economic developments indexing absolute and relative national capabilities and interdependence stakes and vulnerabilities. The third involves widely held self-conceptions and related policy goals. The fourth comprises prevailing interpretations of others and their paths into the future. Together they shape the domestic context for national choices.

Political leaders find it enticing to talk and act in ways compatible with those sets of factors, and difficult to run counter to them. Political leaders have incentives to call attention to military and economic developments that fit with prevailing national self-conceptions and images of others, and slight those that do not. The policy instruments available at any point in time and sought for the future reflect the joint implications of those sets of factors.

SETTING THE STATE

The four sets of factors operate within a framework provided by American views of what actors are included in the Asia-Pacific and the domains of policy activity held to be of security relevance.

The core in the American conception of the Asia-Pacific is clear—Northeast and Southeast Asian and Oceanic polities including Taiwan. The inclusion of others is less consistent. Those others that may or may not be included are Russia (the Department of Defense 1998 *East Asia Strategy Report* and APEC do), India (a major 1995 RAND study by Wolf et. al, and the 2000 report of the blue-ribbon United States Commission on National Security/21st Century do), and the countries of the Latin American Pacific (as APEC does). Asia-Pacific policy will then be inconsistent sometimes building in these others and sometimes not doing so. One or more of these others may, of course, be part of the core defined by non-U.S. policy circles in the Asia-Pacific. When that is the case, there may well be differences about the implications for Asia-Pacific security of relations with and developments in Russia, India, and Pacific Latin America.

The second framing element is the extent to which security is held to be primarily military. As a template, the now several-decades-old Japanese conception of comprehensive security (*sogo anzen hosho*) surely includes military matters but goes far beyond them to encompass other policy areas externally and internally oriented, bearing on national safety, autonomy, and prosperity. Security becomes a "big tent" in terms of policies and participating institutions, governmental and nongovernmental, unilateral and multilateral. The policies and capabilities include: national defense and arms control; intelligence and crisis management; foreign economic matters of resource supply, trade, investment, and finance; development cooperation and within it foreign aid; science and technology; disaster preparedness; and by implication environmental and public health domains (Bobrow 1999, 1984).

The conception leaves open issues of relative priority and resource allocation between competing areas of policy and national capacity. It also refuses to specifically identify nations and movements that pose particular threats. More positively, these unsettled matters can be viewed as a reasonable way of treating two realities. First, different elements of comprehensive security have more or less pressing needs with changing circumstances. Flexibility should be retained to adapt to those variations. Second, the threat stemming from particular foreign sources varies from issue to issue and time to time. Firmly and publicly casting a given party as an enemy or security challenger would then be counterproductive.

In the intervening decades, American security analysis and policy communities have also come to think in more extended ways about security; that is, more policy areas and national capabilities have seen efforts at "securitization" (see Buzan, Waever, and de Wilde 1998, and the many writings cited in their notes and references). In the late 1980s and early 1990s, matters of national economic vigor and international competitiveness became security matters—"geoeconomics" (Luttwak 1993). More recently, under the mantle of "homeland defense" and "transnational threats," calls have been made for treating as central security matters terrorism, proliferation of weapons of mass destruction, information infrastructure vulnerabilities, drug trafficking, infectious diseases, and environmental degradation. For each of these, the importance of nonstate as well as state actors has been noted.[1] Attempts have been made to add marketization and democratization to the aims and means of national security strategy (The White House 1996).

While comprehensive security has been partially embraced, there is ample evidence that the prevailing conception does not match the initial Japanese version. The American conception differs in its emphasis on the military dimension and explicitly identified current or potential "evildoers," as well as in its emphasis on the export of particular economic and political institutions and retained unilateralism. Spending on nonmilitary aspects of foreign affairs as a share of the total federal budget has fallen to a 30 year low of less than 1 percent. The decline in the nominal and constant dollar value of the defense budget has been reversed in the context of robust economic performance. The United States. has persistently opposed the development priority emphasis for APEC suggested by Asian members in favor of a globalization and "opening" emphasis (Bobrow 1999; Bobrow and Kudrle 1999).

Comprehensive security, American style, in the Asia-Pacific seems to be driven by crises (e.g., the Asian financial events of 1997) and by suggestions of imminent or potential military threats (e.g., North Korean missile launches, accelerated Chinese nuclear modernization as in the Cox espionage report,[2] and Chinese declaratory and deployment threats to Taiwan). Seduction and transformation through commercial benefits and the export of institutions are pursued, but political-military considerations seem to provide the most potent rationale for them in domestic American politics.

SALIENT IDEAS

How America positions itself with regard to security in the twenty-first century in general and the Asia-Pacific in particular has been receiving a great deal of attention from political leaders, bureaucrats, and the analysts who work for and seek to influence them. That in part reflects the military and economic factors discussed in the next section. Yet prevailing ideas about threats, opportunities, and security performance objectives take on a life of their own as they provide interpretations of more objective and tangible developments. Those ideas prominent in official and expert discussion are widely known to counterparts in the other nations of the Asia-Pacific, and affect their judgments about the American agenda, their expectations of likely American motivations and conduct, and their estimates of American reactions to what others do or refrain from doing.

Perhaps the most important overarching conceptualization is that of power transition theory (PTR) (DiCicco and Levy 1999). It holds single power supremacy to be a desirable world condition and states that overtaking such a hegemonic power makes for assertion and aggression by a rising power and even major war. The crude indices for that prospect feature a challenger, or "peer competitor," characterized by large geographic and population size and rapid absolute and relative rates of growth in economic and military terms. As it rises, such a state will increasingly assert itself in international and regional affairs and seek to change the "rules of the game" of international affairs from those favored by the challenged hegemon (Gilpin 1981). Even if an overtaking is unlikely at a global level, it can occur with similarly negative consequences for peace and cooperation at a regional level.

China is held to be the likely peer competitor to the United States. While it will not attain that global standing before 2050, it can attain that standing in the Asia-Pacific much sooner, say 2015 (Tammen et al. 2000; Khalilzad et al. 1999). As such, it will be able to and, according to "state-centered realism" (Zakaria 1998), probably will challenge the U.S. "security manager" role in the Asia-Pacific. A "rising China will seek to enhance its status on a global scale . . . and to play a larger role in the settlement of major issues on a worldwide basis. This would involve inherent conflict with the U.S." (Khalilzad et al. 1999, 19).Others in the region will then have to reexamine their followership of the United States accordingly. That prospect is accelerated and made more likely by modern technologies lending themselves to "asymmetric warfare" against the dominant country in a for now "unipolar" system.

There are three ways to avoid this unattractive prospect. First, the current American superpower can simply grow its military and economic resources faster, thus avoiding being overtaken. Second, even if that is not done, the United States can form a concert with others in the region and as a whole stay well ahead of the Chinese challenger. Third, through a combination of unilateral and multilateral steps, China can be given sufficient incentives and disincentives to transform itself into a "like-minded" status quo nation accepting American preferred international practices and domestic political and economic systems (Kugler 1998).

Each of these proposals has visible backers and obvious flaws. Supremacy through unmatched growth is at best expensive, and at worst impossible (Kupchan 1998). In the long run it raises the specter of being prone to "imperial overreach." Nor is it clear what it would take to convince others to accept inferiority. The concert option assumes that possible followers in the Asia-Pacific will see sufficient congruence of interests with the United States, and will rely on U.S. commitments enough to place most of their eggs in that basket. The transformation possibility depends ultimately on the consent of the target.

Given the contingencies inherent in each approach, it is not surprising that there is no consensus on adopting or rejecting any one of them. The result seems to be to try to pursue them all under such labels as "congagement" (Khalilzad et al. 1999), with a dubious claim to their being compatible and indeed reinforcing. Placing the Chinese overtaking relatively far into the future also facilitates postponing sharp choices.

Advocates of supremacy emphasize that it is endangered (The United States Commission on National Security/21st Century 2000) and the correct course is to pursue "full spectrum dominance." That amounts to ensuring "the ability of U.S. forces operating unilaterally or in combination with multinational and interagency partners to defeat any adversary and control any situation . . . worldwide" (Chairman of the Joint Chiefs of Staff 2000).

At the same time, a concert should be pursued through a set of de facto and de jure operational alliances with at least potential, and ideally pre-established, commitments to burden-sharing. In the Asia-Pacific, that track is evidenced in continuing attempts to: get Japan to commit to regional involvements; foster military relationships with India; deploy an integrated regional theater missile defense involving the United States, Japan, South Korea, and Taiwan; and expand efforts at joint military activities between the United States and more than one ostensibly allied Asian state (see, for example, Center for Naval Analysis 1997, 1998, and 1999). In the framework of PTR, such measures amount to efforts to contain the Chinese challenger whatever the rhetorical claims to the contrary.

The transformation strategy adds to the deterrence and containment emphases of the first two options: pro-active economic, diplomatic, cultural, and military engagement. Yet from a PTR point of view, it seeks to keep the target inferior and subordinate. If unsuccessful at transformation, forms of engagement that contribute to the techno-economic advance of the challenger are self-defeating. They will then only accelerate the challenger's rise. Acceptance of such aspects of engagement by the challenger may then be less a sign of genuine transformation and more a stratagem to build toward a power transition.

With all their differences, the three PTR management options share a foundation. They differ on means to avoid a regional power transition but have in common the assumption that doing so is not only in the American interest but also in that of most governments and populations in the Asia-Pacific. Thus the United States has a license to export security arrangements, economic structures, and political institutions. Since such exports are "good medicine" others have no valid reason for objecting to them. And in any event, the United States is "the indispensable power" for peace and prosperity in the Asia-Pacific. The options also share the assumption that the United States will exert the necessary degree of policy effort without undercutting the bases of its current supremacy. That in turn implies that refusing to share the costs of carrying out American strategies amounts to undermining the chances of forestalling a power transition favoring China.

These ideas have American engagement and potential intervention as necessary conditions for the security of others in the Asia-Pacific, with little recognition that such stances might bring with it insecurity for others in the Asia-Pacific.

Regional and National Paths

American policy surely gives first place to military and economic factors, though not limited to those two sectors. Accordingly, policy-makers must sooner or later come to terms with the absolute and relative magnitudes and trends in each. How they do so will be significantly determined by the salient ideas just discussed, and by the latitude and preferences provided by the opinions summarized in later pages.

Military Features

A variety of measures shown in table 8.1 suggest increases in military capacity predominating in the Asia-Pacific but with notable national exceptions. The general pattern of increases in defense expenditures over

Table 8.1 Military Resources

	Index Changes Def. Exp. 1985–98 (1985 = 100) (constant $U.S.)	Changes Def. Exp. as % of CGE 1985–1995/1992–1997	Index Changes in Armed Forces Personnel 1985–1998 (1985 = 100)	Changes Def. Exp. as % of CGE 1985–1998/1990–1998	Index Changes Arms Received-constant $ 1987–1998/1992–1998 (87=100)(92=100)
Australia	111	-.6 / -.6	82	-1.5 / -.3	NA
China	130	-5.3 / -2.2	72	-2.6 / -.8	53 / 32
Taiwan	151	NA	85	-2.4 / NA	444 / 677
India	154	-3.0 / 1.9	93	0 / -.8	NA
Indonesia	147	-1.4 / 5.9	108	-.2 / -.6	104 / 652
Japan	121	-1.4 / .3	100	0 / 0	138 / 92
DPRK	34	NA	126	-8.7 / -6.2	16 / 273
Republic of Korea	144	-13.0 / -5.2	112	-2.0 / -.6	135 / 102
Malaysia	128	1.7 / -.4	100	-1.9 / -.9	352 / 229
Myanmar	164	18.7 / 1.2	188	-1.7 / -.4	1119 / 180
New Zealand	94	-1.2 / -.1	77	-1.4 / -.5	NA
Pakistan	133	-2.8 / 3.7	122	-.4 / -1.5	NA
Philippines	217	-1.0 / -2.3	103	.9 / 0	121 / 73
Singapore	280	7.0 / -7.8	132	-1.7 / .3	212 / 359
Thailand	76	-4.5 / -4.5	130	-3.5 / -.1	54 / 75
Vietnam	27	-91.2 / -3.4	47	-16 / NA	7 / 843
Russian Federation	NA	NA / 2.9	NA	NA / -9.1	NA
United States	72	-8.3 / -4.8	65	-3.3 / -2.1	NA

Sources: International Institute of Strategic Studies 1999; United Nations Development Program 2000; The World Bank 2000

the 1985–1998 period was accompanied by marked decreases in constant dollar terms, especially for North Korea, Thailand, Vietnam, and, importantly, the United States (and, most observers would add, the former Soviet Union). Buildup by this measure exceeded 50 percent for Taiwan, India, Myanmar, the Philippines, and Singapore.

The increases were for the most part accomplished and made sustainable because they could be achieved while reducing the military burden on national economic resources (GDP), especially in the late 1980s. More money was left for use on other aspects of security and for other purposes, although this "dividend" has been shrinking. For most of the national economies, the opportunity cost of military spending has been declining. The pattern for share (priority) in government activity (Central Government Expenditures, or CGE) is more complex. With few exceptions (Myanmar, Singapore), the defense share was reduced in the 1985–1995 period (most strikingly for South Korea and Vietnam). More recent years (1992–1997) have for the most part seen either a lessening in the reduction of the defense share (China, South Korea, New Zealand, Vietnam and the United States) or an actual increase (India, Indonesia, Japan, Pakistan, the Russian Federation). For most governments in the Asia-Pacific, priorities have been not only tending toward increased defense spending in absolute terms but also moving away from reduced priority in the allocation of government resources.

Such aggregate measures, of course, do not convey the dynamics of military force modernization, let alone the qualitative changes associated with nuclearization or even missile acquisition. A crude sense of modernization momentum can be gained from the combination of changes in defense spending and the personnel size of armed forces. Modernization is particularly intense when expenditures increase substantially while numbers of personnel decline substantially. China, Taiwan, and India stand out in these terms. So do some laggards where the opposite is the case—North Korea and Thailand. Military readiness and capability, especially for conventional warfare, tend to increase the most when both spending and personnel increase, so long as the growth of the former exceeds that of the latter. The data suggest just such a development from 1985 through 1998 for Indonesia, South Korea, Pakistan, the Philippines, and Singapore—and in more modest terms for Japan and Malaysia. The opposite is suggested for North Korea, Myanmar, and Thailand.

Military capacity growth countries are militarily more prominent than others in the region, be it as sources of threat, attractive allies and burden-sharers, or as autonomous actors. The United States then has reason to pay increased attention in military respects to China, Taiwan, India,

Table 8.2 Defense Spending Ratios: 1985 and 1998

	US	AUS	PRC	TAI	J	INDI	SEA5	NO.K	ROK
US	X	36.0	7.2	19.1	7.2	19.3	16.2	132.6	20.5
AUS	47.4	X	.2	.5	.2	.5	.5	3.7	.6
PRC	13	.27	X	2.6	1.0	2.7	2.2	18.3	2.8
TAI	40.1	.8	3.1	X	.4	1.0	.9	6.9	1.1
J	12	.3	.9	.3	X	2.7	2.3	18.4	2.9
INDI	41.2	.9	3.2	1.0	3.4	X	.8	6.9	1.1
SEA5	33.8	.7	2.6	.8	2.8	.8	X	8.2	1.3
NOK	62.1	1.3	4.8	1.5	5.2	1.5	1.8	X	.4
ROK	41	.9	3.2	1	3.4	1	1.2	.7	X

Notes: For 1998 read above the diagonal by rows; for 1985, read below the diagonal by columns. The SEA-5 consists of Indonesia, Malaysia, the Philippines, Singapore, and Thailand.

Source: Calculated from International Institute of Strategic Studies 1999.

266 Davis B. Bobrow

Japan, Indonesia, Pakistan, the Philippines, South Korea, Malaysia, and Singapore. Barring some special incentive, it has reason to pay less attention to North Korea, Thailand, and Vietnam.

Another facet of military modernization involves domestic versus international arms supply. Little in the way of international supply implies greater autonomy, but for those who begin with technological inferiority it also suggests more difficulty in matching advanced countries and a greater relative burden on domestic techno-industrial resources. These implications have applied increasingly from 1987 through 1998 to China, North Korea, Thailand, and Vietnam. Growth in international supply has the opposite implications. It also suggests greater external supplier linkages with the recipient because of supplier firm self-interest and enhanced de facto capacity for joint military operations. In regional perspective, Taiwan, Indonesia, Malaysia, Japan, the Philippines, South Korea, and Singapore stand out for the period as a whole—and most of them have predominantly American suppliers. The more recent 1992–1998 period show a massive increase for Taiwan, Indonesia, Singapore, and Vietnam and—less attractively from an American point of view—North Korea.

One crude and very imperfect way of getting at shifts in relative strength and military balances is by examining military spending ratios based on constant dollars. Table 8.2 provides pertinent data for 1998 and 1985 with the former as row entries above the diagonal and the latter as column entries below it.

Together, the observations show changes in relative military strength if we take spending as a crude surrogate for it. With due caution, these ratios have several suggestive implications. First, the U.S. margin over others has both declined and remained substantial. The implications are that U.S. military primacy persists and that it may be in long-run danger. Second, the same ratios imply that other states are increasingly important in regional balances relative to the United States, be it as sources of threats or as security partners. Third, with all its efforts, the persisting Chinese edge may have lessened relative to Taiwan, India, the ASEAN-5, and South Korea, though its near equality with Japan has gone substantially unchanged. Fourth, a Chinese military threat to a U.S. joined by one or another set of associated countries in the region lies more in the future than the present and may be deterred altogether if the patterns found are sustained. That provides a window of opportunity for efforts to persuade China that becoming even a regional peer-competitor is unrealistic. Finally, the gap between North Korea and South Korea and its security backers has increased, posing incentives to Pyongyang both for accommodation and dramatic measures to avoid others exploiting its decline.

ECONOMIC FEATURES

The growth prior to the Asian financial crisis, which facilitated the military developments sketched above, and the post-crisis imperatives for its resumption involve increased regional interdependence across the Asia-Pacific and within Asia-Oceania (Bobrow, Chan, and Reich 1996). Economic security based on growth thus becomes increasingly a function of normal relations between the pertinent countries and regional order and stability. As military capacity derives from export-led economic growth, it has the same requisites. As of 1998, almost 70 percent of member exports were intra-APEC (The World Bank 2000).

The absolute and growing importance of the stability and order beneficial to trade is suggested by table 8.3. Exports topped the 20 percent of GDP level in 1998 for all listed countries except India, Japan, Myanmar, Pakistan, and the United States. From a 1985 base, the role of exports increased, often very substantially, for all the countries for which data were available, except for Myanmar and Singapore. The role of imports in 1998 reached or exceeded the 20 percent level, except for China, India, Japan, Myanmar, and the United States. Growth in importance was the rule except for Japan, Myanmar, Pakistan, and Singapore. North Korea at the end of the century lagged behind only Myanmar with total external trade (including the ROK) in 1999 at only 12 percent of GDP (Noland, 2000). And both have failed to reap the growth benefits achieved by most others in the Asia-Pacific.

At the beginning of the twenty-first century, most nations of the Asia-Pacific have enormous domestic interests in a regional context conducive to trade. That suggests that they find external security provision by the United States tolerable if viewed as essential to those domestic interests. At the same time, vulnerability to trade disruption in the Asia-Pacific is less severe for India, Japan, North Korea, Myanmar, and the United States than for others. That may limit the price they are willing to pay for such U.S. provision.

The degree of economic interdependence also includes flows of capital as measured in table 8.4 by gross capital flows and gross foreign direct investment shares of purchasing power parity (PPP) GDP,[3] and of net foreign direct investment relative to gross domestic investment. With growing integration into world financial markets, governments and populations acquire stakes in investor confidence and in the order and stability conducive to it. Comparison of 1998 with earlier data for the countries for which such data were available shows increases on all three measures with the partial exceptions of Australia, Indonesia, and Japan. The 1998 degree of interdependence was particularly great for Australia,

Table 8.3 The Role of Trade (Goods and Services)

	Exports as Percentage of GDP		Imports as Percentage of GDP	
	1998	Index 1990–1998 (1990=100)	1998	Index 1990–1998 (1990=100)
Australia	21	120	21	125
China	22	123	17	121
Taiwan	NA	NA	NA	NA
India	11	155	14	141
Indonesia	54	207	44	185
Japan	10	104	10	94
DPRK	NA	NA	NA	NA
Republic of Korea	49	167	36	118
Malaysia	114	150	93	125
Myanmar	1	31	1	27
New Zealand	29	105	28	105
Pakistan	16	102	20	86
Philippines	56	203	60	180
Singapore	153	75	135	69
Thailand	59	173	42	102
Vietnam	44	165	52	155
Russian Federation	32	174	27	150
United States	12	122	13	119

Source: United Nations Development Program 2000; The World Bank 2000.

Malaysia, New Zealand, Singapore, and Thailand. It was particularly low for India, Pakistan, and the Russian Federation. The price acceptable for U.S. security provision may vary accordingly.

Other indications of growth and stability needs, of vulnerability and stakes, involve external debt and debt service burdens. The implied needs for the sort of security that enhances confidence in stability and growth apply to borrowers and lenders alike. A high level of external debt relative to GNP and of debt service relative to export earnings motivates borrowers to seek the continued support of lenders and access to foreign markets. It also gives lenders strong interests in the continuation or improvement of borrower economic performance and export success, and in the borrower's acceptance of associated economic policy conditionalities and repayment norms. Relevant data appear in table 8.5.

As of 1998, the countries listed had debt levels in excess of 50 percent of GNP, except for China, India, and South Korea. Other than South Korea, Malaysia, and the Philippines, all countries for which data were available had increased their debt burden relative to GNP from 1985.

Table 8.4 Capital Integration (%)

	Gross Private Capital Flows as % PPP GDP		Gross FDI as % PPP GDP		Net FDI as % Gross Domestic Investment	
	1988	1998	1988	1998	1980	1998
Australia	14.8	12.0	6.5	3.3	4.6	8.5
China	.6	2.3	.3	1.3	0	11.9
Taiwan	NA	NA	NA	NA	NA	NA
India	.2	.9	0	0.1	.2	2.6
Indonesia	.6	4.4	.2	.9	1.0	−2.7
Japan	7.4	20.7	1.7	1.0	.1	.3
DPRK	NA	NA	NA	NA	NA	NA
Republic of Korea	3.3	13.2	.5	1.6	0	8.1
Malaysia	4.2	7.6	.9	2.6	12.5	25.8
New Zealand	8.6	9.4	4.6	5.2	3.9	19.7
Pakistan	.7	1.6	.2	.3	1.4	4.6
Philippines	1.3	3.6	.5	.7	−1.1	12.8
Singapore	32.6	57.6	12.2	13.5	22.8	25.5
Thailand	2.8	5.9	.7	2.1	2.0	24.7
Vietnam	NA	NA	NA	NA	NA	15.4
Russian Federation	NA	1.9	NA	.4	NA	6.1
United States	6.9	10.3	2.0	4.6	3.1	7.5

Source: The World Bank 2000.

Most countries, if anything, reduced their debt service burden (in part because of adaptations by lenders), with the exception of Indonesia. Yet as of 1998 the debt service burden was near or above the 20 percent level for India, Pakistan, and Thailand in addition to Indonesia.

In sum, for much of the Asia-Pacific a good reputation in financial markets is desirable and manageable if the stability and liberalization conducive to exports and incoming capital are maintained. It is also clear that external security disruptions affecting trade and creditor confidence will limit national capacity to pursue most of any prevailing comprehensive security agenda. In these terms, China, India, and Japan (as well as the outcasts of North Korea and Myanmar) are less immediately vulnerable than many others. In general then, the United States enhances the comprehensive security of others in the Asia-Pacific as it facilitates exports, foreign investment, and credit, and damps disturbances which would hinder these economic performance aids. Yet some key regional powers are in a relatively strong, although possibly weakening, position to deny any quid pro quo the United States may seek to extract for such provision.

Table 8.5 Burden of External Debt

	External Debt (% of GNP)		Debt Service (% of Exports)	
	1985	1998	1985	1998
China	5.5	16.4	8.3	8.6
India	17.7	23.0	22.7	20.6
Indonesia	44.4	176.5	28.8	33.0
Republic of Korea	51.6	44.0	27.8	12.9
Malaysia	69.9	65.3	30.4	8.7
Myanmar	NA	NA	52.5	5.3
Pakistan	43.9	52.8	24.9	23.6
Philippines	89.1	70.1	31.6	11.8
Thailand	45.9	76.4	31.9	19.2
Vietnam	NA	82.3	NA	8.9
Russian Federation	NA	69.4	NA	12.1

Source: United Nations Development Program 2000.

AMERICA IN THE WORLD: GENERAL VIEWS

Patterns and trajectories of military and economic tangibles affect policy as interpreted in light of general world-role views. Even if these views are not limited to the Asia-Pacific, they have implications for what it is relatively easy and tempting in domestic political terms for American leaders to do with regard to that region. Policies that run counter to widely held attitudes pose the risk of substantial opposition at home, opposition that can be overcome, if at all, only with substantial effort. When public and elite attitudes are substantially different (Page and Barabas 2000), the political challenge involves how to either avoid public attention (as elites are relatively attentive no matter what measures are taken), or convert the public with the help of supportive elites.

As table 8.6 shows, majorities of the public have supported international activism by the United States for more than 50 years, seeing it as being in the American national interest. Elite polls over the 1978–1998 period show near unanimity for activism (Reilly 1999). That preference is accompanied over the same 20-year period by increases in those believing that the United States is a more important and powerful world leader than it was a decade earlier. America not only should be active but it also is increasingly important and feasible for it to shape the world. As of 1998, more than 70 percent of publics and elites expected the U.S. world role to increase in the coming decade (Reilly1999).

The extent to which the American world role rests primarily on economic or military pillars poses more of a puzzle, perhaps indicating that

Table 8.6 America's World Role (%)

	International Activism		Growing World Role	Share Foreign Policy Problems of Important Problems	
	Pro	Con		Public	Elites
1998	61	28	50	73	19.5
1994	65	29	47	11.5	11.4
1990	62	28	37	16.8	19.5
1986	64	27	41	25.9	41.6
1982	54	35	27	15.2	29.4
1978	59	29	29	11.1	23.3

Note: The question in columns 1 and 2 asks if U.S. international activism is in the interest of America. The question for column 3 asks whether the American world role will grow in the coming decade. The question for columns 4 and 5 asks what the most important problems facing the country are.
Source: Gallup Organization Poll Release April 1, 1999; Reilly 1999.

it is a question of which pillar seems more in danger of erosion at a particular point in time. By 1990, substantial public and elite majorities (66 percent and 71 percent) saw U.S. economic difficulties as undermining American world power (Reilly 1991). Public and, even more so, elite majorities had by 1998 concluded that economic strength was more important for international power and influence than military strength (Reilly, 1999).

Polls in 1999 and 1993 (Gallup Organization Poll Release May 19, 1999) suggest, however, that being number one militarily was more important than being number one in economic terms. Polls taken in 1993, 1995, 1997, and 1999 show high and increasing convictions in the importance of the U.S. remaining a military superpower and in the importance of American nuclear weapons for that status (Herron, Jenkins-Smith, and Hughes, 2000). Beliefs that defense strength and spending were inadequate had by 1999 reached levels not seen since the Reagan administration (Gallup Organization Poll Release May 19, 1999). In 1999, only 50 percent thought the U.S. more secure than at the end of the Cold War, and only 45 percent thought that international security had improved (Herron, Jenkins-Smith, and Hughes 2000).

While these attitudes support American international engagement and military supremacy, the perceived importance of foreign policy problems for the American public and elites has declined from Cold War levels. The implication is that rather than having a general mandate to act internationally, political leaders now have to make the case for specific actions, be they in the Asia-Pacific or elsewhere. While the general claim

Table 8.7 Conditions for Direct U.S. Involvement in External Situations (%)

	Participation			Motivating Purpose			
	Multilateral	Unilateral	Stand Aside	Humanitarian Relief	End Atrocities	Counter Aggression	Restore Democracy
1999	72				77		
1998	72	21			36		
1997		12	11				
1996	74	13	12				
1995					66		
8/1994				79	67		37
2/1994				65	41	41	
1993				67	57		47
1992				71	56	33	
1990	48	15	31				
1986	45	24	30				

Sources: Reilly 1999; Richman 1994b; Princeton Survey Research/Pew Center September 1997; Program in International Policy Attitudes, University of Maryland June 1996.

for a right to intervene is clear, the support for and thus probability of actually intervening in any particular situation is not.

Other data (table 8.7) suggest that there are three, not necessarily exclusive, bases for a domestically persuasive intervention case. One is that of burden-sharing, which involves contributions by other parties. There is a strong preference for multilateral rather than unilateral action in pursuit of all but the most direct security interests (the concert option). The presence of a credible show of sharing by others in the burdens of action will influence what U.S. leaders will believe they can readily do, especially if the intervention is a matter of public attention. In 1998, 72 percent of the public and 48 percent of elites opposed acting alone in crises. The chances of a U.S. intervention to assist, deter, or repel others (rather than just protect Americans) will depend on the commitments of others in the Asia-Pacific to joint action. That gives them influence on American policy and stimulates American internationalists to develop alliances and coalitions in the Asia-Pacific.

A second basis is one that involves a violation of fundamental humanitarian norms, supplying a moral obligation to act. Justification for the use of U.S. military forces is greater when faced with extreme mass suffering (starvation, persecution reaching the level of large-scale atrocities) than when faced with aggression or the challenge of restoring democratic political forms. In the latter set of circumstances, the use of U.S. forces is not readily embraced by the public. In the former, it tends to be accepted, but only after terrible events have already been acted out and then only to stop them with minimum American involvement (e.g., East Timor).

The third basis is a scenario in which a foreign development and its initiators can be persuasively portrayed as a direct threat to American world-role assumptions, especially as a current or emerging threat to domestic well-being. That case is most readily made when the situation seems to exemplify an already widely-recognized threat. As of mid-1998, substantial shares of the American public saw attacks against the United States in the next decade as likely, both by foreign terrorists (50 percent) and by foreign national nuclear weapons (35 percent) (Gallup/CNN/USA Today June, 1998). A broader picture of the profile of critical threats to U.S. vital interests found through direct questions in 1998 appears in table 8.8 (Part A).

Three points stand out. First, many of the critical threats reflect a comprehensive security "big tent" going well beyond military or even economic matters, especially for the public. As Asians are associated with those nonmilitary generic threats, they may well motivate regional U.S. action even if the Asian states involved are themselves not seen as hostile. Second, elites and large segments of the public view future Chinese

Table 8.8 Critical Threats and Very Important Goals (%)

A. *Critical Threats to the United States*

	1998 Public	1998 Elites	1994 Public	1994 Elites
International terrorism	84	61	69	33
Chemical and biological weapons	76	64		
Nuclear weapons in hostiles hands	75	67	72	61
AIDS, viral threats to public health	72	34		
China as a world power	57	56	57	46
Immigration into U.S.	55	18	72	61
Economic competition from Japan	456	14	62	21
Global warming	42	27		
Economic competition from low-wage countries	40	16		
Islamic fundamentalism	38	31	33	39
Russian military power	34	19	32	16
Regional ethnic conflicts	34	26		
Economic competition from Europe	24	16	27	11

Sources: Reilly 1999, 1995.

power as dangerous, but only among the public is such a view widely held about Japanese economic competition. Third, the intensity of support for action will mount as a given situation seems to pose several of the salient threats rather than just one, for example, China as a world power linked to proliferation of weapons of mass destruction, immigrants, global warming, and low-wage economic competition.

The threats recognized have a turning-point status because they pose interference with goals, that is, with outcomes desired for tangible self-interest and less tangible normative grounds for evaluating the American world role. Whatever their base, "very important" foreign policy goals provide a rationale for American action. Goal support (table 8.8, Part B) puts America first—minimizing direct threats of violence and economic setbacks—with less support for achieving broader improvements in a global or regional human condition.

Public and elite majorities appear for proliferation control, blocking drugs, combating terrorism, and maintaining military superiority. Combating world hunger is the only less self-interested goal with such strong support. The elite, but not the public, provide a majority for defending

Table 8.8 Critical Threats and Very Important Goals (%)

B. *Very Important Foreign Policy Goals for the United States*

	1998 Public	1998 Elites	1994 Public	1994 Elites	1990 Public	1990 Elites
Prevent spread of nuclear weapons	82	85	82	90	59	94
Protect jobs of U.S. workers	80	45	83	50	65	39
Combat IR terrorism	79	74				
Secure energy supplies	64	45	62	67	61	60
Combat world hunger	62	56	56	41		
Maintain world-wide military superiority	59	58	50	54		
Control illegal immigration	55	21	72	28		
Improve global environment	53	46	58	49	58	72
Reduce U.S. trade deficit	50	34	59	49	56	62
Strengthen United Nations	45	32	51	33	44	39
Defend security of allies	44	58	41	60	61	56
Promote human rights in other countries	39	41	34	26	58	45
Promote market economies abroad	34	36				
Protect weaker nations against aggression	32	29	24	21	57	28
Help bring democracy to other nations	29	29	25	21	28	26
Help improve standard of living of LDCs	29	36	22	28	41	42
Protect interests of U.S. business abroad			52	38	63	27

Sources: Reilly 1999, 1995, 1991.

American allies. The public is more strongly supportive of protection in economic matters (keeping jobs of American workers, limiting immigration, securing energy supplies, reducing the trade deficit) than are elites. Other data suggest that the public has more reservations about the benefits of economic openness and immersion in the world economy (globalization) than the elite (54 percent positive to 82 percent), and that fewer recognize the merits of active contributions required to sustain that openness (support for greater IMF contributions 25 percent to 82 percent) (Reilly 1999). That, however, does not mean either support for economic isolationism by the public or the elite, but rather a strong constituency for retaining unilateral options for economic protection as through tariffs (in 1998, 49 percent of the public and, a 20-year high 34 percent of elites) (Reilly, 1999).

When viewed through non-American eyes, the composite of general views suggests an America claiming international centrality and committed to maintaining a military edge. Yet that same America cannot confidently be predicted to intervene in concert situations only loosely linked to direct threats of domestic harm. The security umbrella may not open, at least in time for preventive action. While America is not hostile to a broad comprehensive security agenda, such an agenda does not have priority compared to more "realist" and parochial military and economic matters. And there are grounds for concern about the extent to which the United States will abide by the open economy practices on which Asian economic security has come to rely.

Views of Asia

Within the context of the general views summarized, the domestic, politically attractive space for American policy is affected by more specific views of the Asia-Pacific. The foreign policy importance of Asia has risen dramatically among the American public and elites from the single-digit percentages polls found in 1978, 1982, and 1986 (Reilly 1987). Nevertheless, Europe was still held to be more important than Asia in 1998 by the public (42 percent to 28 percent) and elites (51 percent to 37 percent). On often asked "thermometer" questions, which gauge warmth or favorableness of feelings, no Asian country rated as favorably as did any of the "white, English-speaking Commonwealth" nations or another NATO ally.

Yet China and Japan have come to be viewed, in that order, as the potential sources for threat to American foreign and security policy, replacing Russia (Reilly 1999; Princeton Survey Research/Newsweek 1999). When in 1998 Americans were asked to list countries in terms of their relevance to U.S. "vital interests," China and Japan were the top two countries named. Japan (table 8.9, Part B) has maintained its high ranking in a relatively stable fashion since 1998. China has from 1994 on regained the high position it held in 1978, after a noticeable decline about a decade ago.

Those two Asian states are held to differ strikingly in the nature and trend of their importance and threat (table 8.8, table 8.9, Part A). China is seen by elites (almost unanimously) and the general public as being of increasing world importance in the coming decade, and Japan as relatively less so (especially in the eyes of the elites). Chinese power as a critical threat to U.S. power has become a majority view among both American elites and the public to an increasing extent since 1990. Japan has declined as such in general and, particularly with respect to economic competition. By 1999 China became the most frequently named military threat, the most important nuclear threat at that; and it rivaled Japan as the greatest economic threat (Fox News/Opinion Dynamics 1999; Herron, Jenkins-Smith, and Hughes 2000). China after 1983 was predominantly thought of as an enemy, or unfriendly (as contrasted with an ally, or friendly), an image that soared in the second half of 1999, until China was thought of by Americans as an enemy (33 percent) more consistently than a long list of other nations in various parts of the world. For the most part, public majorities have viewed China unfavorably for the last two decades, reaching the historical high of 69 percent in mid-1999 (Gallup Organization Poll Release June 3, 1999).

Containment and isolation of China would then seem to be the most popular course, especially since 1999 public majorities thought China had little promise of becoming either a democracy or a free market economy (Princeton Survey Research/Pew, March 1999). Yet considerations of military and economic potential have modified that implication, in line with some of the general world views introduced earlier. Chinese security cooperation in the nuclear realm was held in 1994 by very substantial majorities to be a more important consideration than human rights and market access (Richman 1994b). As for the human rights-trade priority, public opinion provides no clear mandate for making either one more important, according to polls in 1998 and 1999 (Gallup Organization Poll Releases June 3, 1999 and November 1999). American politicians have substantial domestic political reasons to try to make security implications the central theme in justifying policies toward China while pursuing dual, and even contradictory, tracks about economic engagement and human rights.

Since 1994, majorities have had a far different view of Japan. In the economic realm public and especially elite majorities for the last decade

Table 8.9 Who Counts in Asia? (%)

A. *Rising Powers and Sources of Danger*

	Rising China		Rising Japan		Country Most Dangerous to U.S.	
	Public	*Elites*	*Public*	*Elites*	*China*	*Japan*
1998	69	97	59	46	16	9
1994	66	91	66	47	11	11
1992					8	32
1990						

Sources: Reilly 1999, 1995; Richman 1994a.

Table 8.9 Who Counts in Asia? (%)

B. U.S. Vital Interests and Relationship

	In China		In Japan		China as Enemy or Unfriendly	View China Unfavorably
	Public	Elites	Public	Elites		
1999					63	56
1998	74	95	87	94	33	51
1997					36	50
1994	68	95	85	96	37	51
1993					36	39
1990	47	73	79	95		
8/1989						54
2/1989						13
1986	60	89	77	98		
1983					21	52
1982	64	87	82	97		
1978	70	93	78	99		64*

*indicates a 1979 poll.

Sources: Reilly 1999, 1995, 1991, 1987, 1983; Gallup Organization Poll Release March 31, 1999 and June 3, 1999; Harris Poll August 1999; Richman 1994a. Harris Poll Website: www.publicagendaonline.org.

have held Japan to practice unfair trade. Elites, however, almost unanimously view internal developments in Japan as key for dealing with the Asian financial crisis (Reilly 1999). On balance, Japan is then held to be a security partner (by 62 percent of the public in a 1999 Harris poll), and key to both security and economic policy goals in the Asia-Pacific—but a country prone to inappropriate economic behavior, which implies a continuing need for corrective and vigilant American steps. The difference in suspicion levels for China and Japan is suggested by the presence in 1994 polling of only very thin public and elite majorities for U.S. spying on Japan, but strong majorities for such activities targeting China (Reilly 1995).

General and elite public demand for and expectations of American Asia-Pacific policy are primarily for policy toward China and Japan, but not exclusively so. While less important, they also involve policy with regard to Taiwan, both Koreas, and India (table 8.10). In terms of vital interests, South Korea has in the past decade had substantial support among publics, with very strong majorities among elites. That has been less the case for Taiwan, but majority or near-majority support for that position has been maintained for the past two decades, and sporadic questions in the last decade have yielded public pluralities holding each to be allies, or friendly (Harris Poll of 1999; Richman 1994a). Thermometer questions show a slight improvement in feelings about South Korea and Taiwan, but only to a neutral point. As for India, substantial public minorities hold it to be a country in which the United States has a vital interest, and for the elite it has become (73 percent in 1998) a rising power. Yet thermometer readings remain mildly negative.

With regard to U.S. use of force in two major possible invasion cases in East Asia, opinions differ, with neither providing a strong presumption that such an American response would or would not occur. Data appear in table 8.11.

For a North Korean invasion of South Korea, public majorities (column 1) have opposed such a response since 1974, while elite majorities (column 2) have supported it. The public position here stands in contrast to the public's strongly negative view of North Korea (Richman 1994a; Reilly 1999). Yet even in the context of a North Korean nuclear weapons buildup, a military response is seen as less attractive than a diplomatic or economic sanctions one (Richman 1994b). As for a Chinese invasion of Taiwan, the public has moved to near majority support from predominant opposition to a military response, as has the elite, but with a decline from 1986. The domestically attractive course for U.S. leaders is then to hold out security guarantees to South Korea and Taiwan but also to exert effort to be sure that such measures are not called on.

Table 8.10 Vital Interests and Regard: Taiwan, South Korea, and India (%)

| | U.S. Vital Interests | | | | | | Warmth of Feelings | | |
| | Taiwan | | South Korea | | India | | Taiwan | South Korea | India |
	Public	Elites	Public	Elites	Public	Elites	Taiwan	South Korea	India
1998	52		54	82	36		51	50	46
1994	49		65	90	31				
1990	46	47	49	80			48	47	48
1986	53	48	58	80	36	55			
1982	51	44	43	66	30	57			

Sources: Reilly 1999, 1995, 1991, 1987, 1983; Gallup Organization Poll Release June 3, 1999.

Table 8.11 U.S. Military Response to Aggression (%)

	DPRK of the ROK		PRC of Taiwan	
	Public	*Elites*	*Public*	*Elites*
1999			47	
1998	30	74	27	51
1994	39	82		
1990	44	57		
1986	24	64	19	64
1974	14	19	17	11

Sources: Reilly 1999, 1995, 1991, 1987, 1975; ICR/ABC poll August 1999.

WHAT TO EXPECT OF THE UNITED STATES?

In combination, the considerations discussed suggest what the U.S. role will be in the Asia-Pacific in the coming years.

The country scope of the policy will add India to East and Southeast Asia, Australia, and New Zealand. Economic and military policy domains will continue to be most central, with continuing claims to primacy in both. Priority for one or the other will fluctuate depending on which is perceived to be on a path of decline. Other aspects of comprehensive security, particularly those involving hunger, the environment, and public health will receive American policy attention, but far less so than economic and military matters.

In the two primary domains, active efforts will be most likely in the face of presumptive threats to the domestic well-being of the United States. Such threats in the military arena most obviously involve long-reach weapons of mass destruction in the hands of others in the Asia-Pacific. In the economic domain, special emphasis will go to threats, to ensure the smooth functioning of international capital markets, and to the international or domestic competitiveness of major American goods and services industries. Those economic threats include the loss of anticipated economic opportunities in the region as well as in the domestic U.S. market.

Bilateral relations in the world and their salience as domestic political issues will give first place to China and Japan. Relations with both countries will continue to have an element of tension or suspicion, but especially so with China, with an emphasis on carrot-and-stick measures couched in terms of threat management. The always looming negatives about China will, for Japan, take the form of frustration with apparent foot-dragging and parochialism about buying into American grand recipes for the region and world. There is little prospect of U.S. withdrawal or isolation. There is a very high probability that the United States, barring major domestic economic reversals, will claim a "number one role" and expect it to be acknowledged by others; the United States will most likely take offense to initiatives by others that seem to run counter to that role, be it with regard to weapons of mass destruction, financial architectures, or independent attempts to change the political status quo.

In military matters, conviction about the feasibility and desirability of primacy will result in the pursuit of superiority, an adverse reaction to those who seem to be on a path of rivalry or denial, and a strong desire to have others bear more of a military regional balancing and deterring role. These mixed preferences suggest less an enhanced U.S. military presence or commitments than a greater emphasis on arms sales, defense industrial cooperation, and the political and technical infrastructure for coalitions and regional security joint action. Key countries in such a potential coalition will be Japan, India, South Korea, Taiwan, and Singapore.

The actual use, as contrasted with the display, of military capacity will be reactive and fleeting with regard to human suffering, and highly uncertain with regard to countering aggression against third parties. Neither aggressors or attacked third parties will be able to predict with confidence what the United States will do should such situations arise.

A vigorous if inconclusive debate will continue without clear resolution as to whether or not those emphases will suffice. That debate will go on while attempts are made to enhance the case for the transformation option through preventive diplomacy, including economic diplomacy measures to divert China and North Korea from a threatening path. Success with regard to the former will be measured by a host of yardsticks reaching well beyond military matters, including a search for evidence of a profound Chinese political and economic transformation. In contrast, with North Korea it will more be a matter of buying time for erosion processes well underway to work further.

The prospects in the economic arena for an equivalent to the support of a military buildup by nonchallengers and nonpariahs are less certain. Policies that would enhance the economies of others in the region by the United States bearing some costs or risks are likely, even if economic good times prevail in America, to require some combination of public inattention and elite mobilization (especially of major firms in the private sector) to support them. Both are less likely in times of perceived economic stress. At all times, those policies are more likely to succeed if wrapped in a military, security-enhancing, rationale. In bad times, a persuasive rationale of that sort will be necessary and not just facilitative. And the "good economic times" of America in the second half of the 1990s are unlikely to continue uninterrupted long into the twenty-first century.

The place of China in American policy toward the Asia-Pacific is clearly of the most fundamental importance, and also the most conflicted. Dramatic forecasts that U.S. China policy will make clear choices, be it for unilateral deterrence, multilateral containment, comprehensive economic engagement, or human rights conditionality, are appealing but unrealistic. Given substantial domestic constituencies for each, it is far more likely that U.S. administrations will try to have their cake and eat it too, by trying to pursue all three of the previously mentioned motivations, as they have and are doing. Emphases will shift from time to time, but no one will emerge as a clear victor. The triggers and onset of shifts in emphases will largely be a function of events and developments in and by China. There will be little support for, and indeed some resentment of, initiatives by third parties in the Asia-Pacific, which will lessen U.S. latitude to pursue any of the three policy lines.

One may with good reason observe that the preceding forecasts are ones of continuity more than change. That, I think, is the American preference. The feasibility of that preference will, of course, depend on de facto cooperation with it by others in the Asia-Pacific, as they believe it is their best available choice.

NOTES

1. See, for example, the National Defense Panel Report of 1998, Presidential Decision Directives 62 and 63 of the same year, the Environmental Protection Agency's *Environmental Security,* publication of 1999, and the National Intelligence Council's *The Global Infections Disease Threat and Its Implications for the United States* of 2000.

2. The charges were levied in the Final Report of the Select Committee on U.S. National Security and Military/Commercial Concerns with the People's Republic of China, U.S. House of Representatives, 1999. For a summary and cogent, well-informed rebuttal, see May 1999.

3. Gross private capital flows sum "values of direct, portfolio and other investment inflows and outflows . . . excluding changes in the assets and liabilities of monetary authorities and general government. Gross foreign direct investment . . . includes equity capital, reinvestment of earnings, other long-term capital and short-term capital." The use of a PPP base is conservative, working to decrease the percentages (The World Bank 1999, 327).

REFERENCES

Bobrow, D. B. 1999. Hegemony management: The United States in the Asia-Pacific. *The Pacific Review*, 12, no.2:172–96.

———. 1984. Playing for safety: Japan's security practices. *Japan Quarterly*, 31, no.1: 33–43.

———and S. R. Hill. 1991. Non-military determinants of military budgets: The Japanese case. *International Studies Quarterly*, 35, no.1: 39–61.

———, S. Chan, and S. Reich. 1996. Southeast Asian prospects and realities: American hopes and fears. *The Pacific Review*, 9, no.1: 1–30.

———and R. T. Kudrle. 1999. Foreign direct investment in the context of regionalism. Pp. 57–86 in *Racing to Regionalize: Democracy, Capitalism, and Regional Political Economy*, edited by K. P. Thomas and M. A. Tetreault. Boulder: Lynne Rienner.

Buzan, B., O. Waever and J. de Wilde. 1998. *Security: A New Framework for Analysis.* Boulder: Lynne Rienner.

Center for Naval Analysis. 1999, 1998, 1997. *Trilateral Naval Cooperation: Japan, U.S., Korea.* Washington, D.C.: Workshops I, II, and III.

Chairman of the Joint Chiefs of Staff. 2000. *Joint Vision 2020.* Washington, D.C.: U.S. Government Printing Office.

The Department of Defense. 1998. *The United States Security Strategy for the East Asia-Pacific Region.* Washington, D.C.

DiCicco, J. M. and J. S. Levy. 1999. Power shifts and problem shifts: The evolution of the power transition research program. *Journal of Conflict Resolution*, 43, no.6: 675–704.

The Gallup Organization Poll Releases. (Various years). Available at: www.gallup.com/poll/releases.

Gilpin, Robert. 1981. *War and Change in World Politics.* New York: Cambridge University Press.

Herron, K. G., H. C. Jenkins-Smith, and S. D. Hughes. 2000. *Mass and Elite Views on Nuclear Security: U.S. National Security Surveys 1993–1999.* Vol. I. Albuquerque, NM: University of New Mexico Institute for Public Policy.

International Institute for Strategic Studies. 1999. *The Military Balance 1999–2000.* Oxford: Oxford University Press.

Khalilzad, Z. et al. 1999. *The United States and a Rising China.* Santa Monica, CA: RAND.

Kugler, J. 1998. The policy implications of power parity. *Conflict Management and Peace Science* 16, no.2: 99–124.

Kupchan, C. A. 1998. After Pax Americana: Benign power, regional integration, and the sources of a stable multipolarity. *International Security* 23, no. 2: 40–79.

Luttwak, E. N. 1993. *The Endangered American Dream: How to Stop the United States from Becoming a Third World Country and How to Win the Geo-Economic Struggle for Industrial Supremacy.* New York: Simon and Schuster.

May, M. M., ed. 1999. *The Cox Committee Report: An Assessment.* Stanford: Center for International Security and Cooperation.

National Intelligence Council. 2000. *The Global Infectious Disease Threat and Its Implications for the United States.* NIE99–17D, January. Available at: www.odci.gov/cia.publications.nie/report/nie99–17d.

Noland, M. 2000. Economic integration between North and South Korea. *Korea's Economy 2000,* no.16: 67–70, Washington: Korea Economic Institute of America.

Page, B. I. and J. Barabas. 2000. Foreign policy gaps between citizens and leaders. *International Studies Quarterly.* 44, no.3: 339–64.

Reilly, J. E., ed. 1999. *American Public Opinion and Foreign Policy 1999.* Chicago: Chicago Council on Foreign Relations.

———1995. *American Public Opinion and Foreign Policy 1995.* Chicago: Chicago Council on Foreign Relations.

———.1991. *American Public Opinion and Foreign Policy 1991.* Chicago: Chicago Council on Foreign Relations.

———. 1987. *American Public Opinion and Foreign Policy 1987.* Chicago: Chicago Council on Foreign Relations.

Richman, A. 1994a. The American public's "rules of military engagement" in the Post–Cold War Era. Paper presented at the annual meeting of the American Political Science Association, 2 September, New York.

v.1994b. American public's attitudes toward U.S. international involvement in the post–Cold War era. Paper presented at the annual meeting of the International Studies Association, 29 March, Washington.

Tammen, R. et al. 2000. *Power Transitions.* Chatham, NJ: Chatham House.

United States Commission on National Security/21st Century 2000. *Seeking a National Strategy: A Concert for Preserving Security and Promoting Freedom,* Phase II Report. Washington, D.C.: Government Printing Office.

United States Environmental Protection Agency (1999). *Environmental Security: Strengthening National Security through Environmental Protection.* Washington, D.C. 160-F-99–001.

The White House. 1996. *A National Security Strategy of Engagement and Enlargement.* Washington, D.C.: Government Printing Office.

Wolf, C., Jr. et al. 1995. *Long-Term Economic and Military Trends 1994–2015: The United States and Asia.* Santa Monica, CA: RAND, MR-627-OSD.

The World Bank. 2000. *2000 World Development Indicators.* Washington, D.C.: World Bank.

———. 1999. *1999 World Development Indicators.* Washington, D.C.: The World Bank.

United Nations Development Program. 2000. *Human Development Report 2000.* New York: Oxford University Press.

Zakaria, F. 1998. *From Wealth to Power: The Unusual Origins of America's World Role.* Princeton: Princeton University Press.

CHAPTER 9

A Reinvigorated
Version of Japan's
Comprehensive Security:
Key to Stability
in the Asia Pacific*

SUEO SUDO

INTRODUCTION

Since the end of the Cold War, the world has seen some dramatic events unfold, such as the "revolution" in Eastern Europe, the demise of the Soviet Union, heightened regional conflicts, and widening economic globalization. In the Asia Pacific, while the dissolution of the Cold War structure progressed slowly and incrementally in its own ways, economic growth among the region's members reached unprecedented heights until a financial crisis broke out in July 1997, first hitting Thailand but immediately engulfing all Northeast and Southeast Asian countries. Just as the collapse of the Suharto regime in Indonesia amply illustrates, the financial crisis confirms that "business of Asia cannot exist—or be analyzed—in a political, social, or strategic vacuum."[1]

Under these critical circumstances, a necessary task for the Asian region is to review its past developments and see what remedies need to be administered to its real or potential underlying structural weaknesses, wherever they can be located. Equally needed is a hard look at the strategic implications of the multifarious effects of globalization in the post–Cold War era. The crisis has shown that a nation's security today, in what editor Hsiung calls the "geoeconomic age," is vulnerable to unforeseen threats stemming from the volatility of globalized capital in the world market.[2] In this light, the term "security," for nations in Asia Pacific as elsewhere, should be construed more broadly than mere military defense to include political, social, and economic dimensions. Given the fact that the economically hard-hit Asian countries were all victims of ravaging external forces, in certain cases (such as Japan) exacerbated by domestic institutional inadequacies, it is incumbent upon the region's countries to plot a new framework for regional security, as befitting the post–Cold War era.[3]

The purpose of this chapter is two-fold: (1) to analyze the development and limitations of the only regional security forum in the Asia Pacific, the ASEAN, after the attack of the recent financial crisis; and (2) to argue that a reinvigorated schema of comprehensive security—beyond the traditional military security—which can be taken from the Japanese example, could serve as an alternative framework for Asia Pacific's regional security, to meet the security needs in the new era.

JAPAN'S QUEST FOR A
NEW CONCEPT OF SECURITY

Japan's security policy has been shaped by Article 9 of its Constitution, which prohibits the use of force in settling international conflicts and the possession of "offensive" weapons.[4] While clinging to an alliance with the United States, Japan has had to depend on all possible nonmilitary means, especially diplomatic and economic, to safeguard the country's security. Having achieved the status as an economic power during the early 1970s, Japan, however, had to endure three major trying events at the same time. They were: the oil crisis of 1973–1974, the breakdown of international economic order (the so-called Nixon Shock), and the rise of burden-sharing in Japan's common defense program with the United States. As a result, it was almost inevitable that the Japanese developed a deep sense of vulnerability in respect of their economic, social, and military security. Thus came Japan's concept of "comprehensive security."

JAPAN'S ADOPTION OF THE COMPREHENSIVE SECURITY CONCEPT

In July 1980, the Study Group on Comprehensive National Security, appointed by Prime Minister Masayoshi Ohira, submitted its report to the government. Reflecting on the altered international order, the report characterized current international relations in terms of the transition from the era of Pax Americana to that of "peace through responsibility sharing." In order to enhance its security in the new era, it stressed that

Japan must actively seek to contribute to the maintenance and strengthening of the international system as well as keep up its self-reliant efforts. The report pointed out:

> In considering the question of Japan's security, the most fundamental change in the international situation that took place in the 1970s is the termination of clear American supremacy in both military and economic spheres. Militarily, it has become necessary for the allies and friends to strengthen their self-reliant efforts, especially in the area of conventional forces. Economically, U.S. economic strength has declined both in absolute terms and in relative terms against the economic development achieved by Europe and Japan.[5]

There were two major characteristics of the proposed policies. First, while recommending six specific policies—increasing military cooperation with the United States; strengthening Japan's defense capability; persuading the Soviet Union that Japan was neither weak nor threatening; providing greater energy security; ensuring greater food security; and improving crisis management of large-scale national disasters such as earthquakes—the report urged the establishment of an effective Comprehensive National Security Council within the Japanese government to replace the limited National Defense Council. Second, referring to Southeast Asia, the report declared: "Should a war break out in the Korean Peninsula or should the Indochina conflict greatly intensify the tension over the entire Southeast Asian region, Japan cannot remain unaffected. Accordingly, it must be Japan's responsibility to perform a political role for the stabilization of these areas."[6] The proposal of this concept was thus a high point in the evolution of Japan's new comprehensive security policy.

Prime Minister Zenko Suzuki, soon after taking over from the Ohira Administration, promised to undertake greater commitment to improving Japan's defense capabilities within its territories and in the surrounding sea and air space, extending the Japanese defense perimeter to 1,000 nautical miles southward from Tokyo and Osaka. Ministries concerned soon took the necessary steps in its wake. The Foreign Ministry, for instance, came up with a new concept of foreign assistance, which defined Japan's aid as "the cost of building an international order so as to achieve the comprehensive security of Japan." The Ministry of International Trade and Industry more specifically called for promoting economic security as part of the country's comprehensive security, and for the use of a blend of economic, political, and military tools to achieve the goal.[7] Thus, by propounding the concept of comprehensive security, the Japanese government intended to find a new and wider basis for Japan's international role as well as to promote its own defense goals.

In the mid-1980s, at the height of the Cold War, Prime Minister Yasuhiro Nakasone formulated his defense policy in accordance with the same concept. Nakasone's advisory group, called the "Peace Problem Study Group" and headed by Masataka Kosaka of Kyoto University, submitted a report to the government in December 1984, known as the "Comprehensive Security Policy for the International State of Japan." In contrast to the earlier report by Ohira's study group, the 1984 report contained three different elements. First, it characterized the world as having entered the stage of "multilateral management," in which Japan would be expected to perform a larger role. Second, it reappraised the 1976 Defense Outline and found it obsolete. Third, it advocated the removal of the one percent of GNP ceiling on the defense budget, in order that Japan could "play a greater defense role."[8]

Since the inception of the concept of "comprehensive national security" under three succeeding Japanese administrations foreign aid policy emerged as a catchword of Japanese diplomacy. In the early 1980s, therefore, Tokyo employed an active policy of awarding economic aid to nations deemed important for the sake of Japanese as well as international security, as exemplified by its dramatic increase of aid to Turkey, Pakistan, and Thailand, and denial of aid to Vietnam in 1980. Moreover, major effects of Japan's comprehensive security policy can be seen in four main areas. First, Japan broadened its defense perimeter. Second, it significantly reinforced security cooperation with the United States. Third, it loosened the constitutional as well as existing defense constraints to allow a more active security role. Fourth, Japan expanded its political role in the international arena.

POLICY FRAMEWORK OF COMPREHENSIVE SECURITY

Many international relations scholars define security as the ability of a state to defend itself against external military threats. Realists, in particular, emphasize the anarchical nature of the international system, which compels states to maximize their own power in the pursuit of national interests. They also believe that war is a necessary form of self-help in preserving one's national interests, including survival, against an unfavorable power distribution in the system, since states cannot rely on international institutions to achieve the same purpose.[9] This conventional concept of national security is thus exclusively focused on the protection of a nation's territorial integrity and political sovereignty from external inroads.

Table 9.1 Policy Framework of Comprehensive Security

Levels	Military Security	Economic Security
Multilateral	1 Creation of a more peaceful international order 2 International cooperation through arms control and confidence-building measures	1 Maintenance of free trade system 2 Resolution of the North-South problem
Intermediary	1 An alliance, or cooperation, with countries sharing political ideas and interests	1 Promotion of friendly relations with a number of nations that are important to a nation's economy
Domestic	1 Consolidation of denial capability at its base 2 Fostering of denial capability of the state and society as a whole	1 A certain degree of self-sufficiency 2 Maintenance of the nation's economic strength

Source: Sogo anzen hosho senryaku [Comprehensive National Security] (Tokyo: Okurasho insatsukyoku, 1980), pp. 23–24.

The notion of comprehensive security shared by Japan and the ASEAN countries, on the other hand, has a much broader spectrum of security in mind and a correspondingly bigger "bag of tools" for its protection. The concept, as shown above, is broader than that which was embraced in the traditional state-to-state relations; it is wider than military defense. A good example is the Indonesian concept of "national resilience." As President Suharto explained: "National resilience is an inward-looking concept, based on the proposition that national security lies not in military alliances or under the military umbrella of a great power but in self-reliance deriving from domestic factors such as economic and social development, political stability and a sense of nationalism."[10] Not only Indonesia, but other ASEAN states, likewise pursue similar security policies. Malaysia, for one, adopts a similar concept of comprehensive security, while Singapore stresses total security in order to maintain its political survival. In other words, comprehensive security is meant to draw attention to other aspects that have often been omitted in the traditional definition of security.

Another implication is that comprehensive security is not just a statement of goals and objectives but also a policy framework. The Japanese government contended that in responding to military and nonmilitary threats states need, first, to prevent or eliminate threats through influencing the surrounding environment; second, to promote friendly relations with other like-minded nations; and, third, to cope with actual threats by self-reliance, including military defense. With its emphasis on economic security, the concept posits that peace and prosperity are better served by all-around strength than by military power alone.[11] In other words, it is a comprehensive strategy to be pursued at three different levels in two fields, as shown below:

Given the fact that Japan and ASEAN share a quite identical approach to national security, it is not surprising that they sought a forum to deal with regional security issues in the post–Cold War era. The question here is whether Japan's and ASEAN's comprehensive security policy is adequate in taking care of the region's security in the new era. Before answering the question, let us examine the ASEAN Regional Forum, a by-product of Japan-ASEAN joint effort based on the broadened concept of comprehensive security.

THE ASEAN REGIONAL FORUM (ARF)
AS A COMPREHENSIVE SECURITY MECHANISM

In an attempt to create a regional security forum for the first time in the region's history, Japan and ASEAN made joint efforts over the last decade. In Japan, it was the Ministry of Foreign Affairs rather than the Defense Agency that formulated Japan's ARF policy. In Southeast Asia, it was the ASEAN-ISIS, or the ASEAN Institute of Strategic and International Studies, established in 1990 as part of a private think-tank of the region. As a continuation of Japan-ASEAN dialogue, taking advantage of the institutionalization of Japan-ASEAN relations such as the Post-Ministerial Conference (PMC), Japanese foreign ministry officials were invited in their "private" capacities in June 1991 to attend the ASEAN-ISIS meeting aimed at preparing an ASEAN-ISIS report to the 1991 ASEAN-PMC. It became clear, according to a participant, that both ASEAN and Japan had developed, in tandem, a number of similar security conceptions, including the idea that the ASEAN-PMC might be an appropriate forum for security discussions.[12]

At the 1991 ASEAN-PMC, therefore, Japan's Foreign Minister Taro Nakayama stated that the annual PMC meetings should become a forum for political dialogues in the field of security as well as economic cooperation and diplomacy, and proposed that senior officials of ASEAN and its dialogue partners prepare a report on security matters. Ever since Nakayama's proposal for a multilateral security forum, Japan has been playing an active role in promoting a security dialogue in Asia and the Pacific. Together with the first dispatch of a Japanese SDF mission to participate in the United Nations peacekeeping efforts in September 1992 (Cambodia) and a positive statement by Prime Minister Miyazawa in

Bangkok in January 1993, the establishment of the ASEAN Regional Forum (ARF) has, for the Japanese, been a diplomatic success.

CONVERGENCE OF
REGIONAL SECURITY CONCEPTS

To put the joint efforts by Japan and ASEAN into perspective, we need to distinguish three different types of multilateral security arrangements: common security, cooperative security, and comprehensive security.[13]

The concept of common security, originating in the 1982 report of the Palme Commission, focuses on the external military threats by assuring the need and common interest to ensure mutual survival under conditions of strategic interdependence. The central purpose of common security is to achieve international security through disarmament and arms control as a means to avoid ultimate nuclear warfare. It is well known that Western Europe adopted this strategy at the Conference on the Security and Cooperation in Europe (CSCE) in 1975, after which it evolved steadily and gained further legitimacy. Its success through the 1980s led to the call for similar approaches in Asia, as Soviet, Canadian, and Australian proposals were vindicated.

In September 1990, Canadian Secretary of State for External Affairs Joe Clark proposed a "North Pacific Cooperative Security Dialogue," which was based on a new concept of "cooperative security." The goal of cooperative security is to stabilize relations among states that are neither adversaries nor friends. It emphasizes the importance of political and diplomatic rather than military, means to achieve security. Thus, the central purpose is to prevent the emergence of manifest security threats in a region covered by the participants. It also places great stress on preventive diplomacy—a proactive nonmilitary approach to security that seeks to prevent conflict from reaching the stage where resort to military force will appear necessary. The CSCE has transformed itself from a common security system to a cooperative security system with the end of Cold War confrontation.

However, ASEAN and Japan rejected the scheme of a North Pacific Cooperative Security Dialogue because Asian countries, given their diversity, are not ready to accept any CSCE-type security arrangement. Instead, they came up with a new security approach, utilizing the existing framework of ASEAN-PMC. The new approach is called "comprehensive security" and gained strong backing from other countries in the region, as explained by some observers: "In sharp contrast to the strong military orientation of the Western-derived concept of 'common security,' 'comprehensive security,' which is perhaps the most widely endorsed security concept in the region, stresses non-military means of achieving and maintaining security."[14] In other words, cooperative security can work well only if there is a supportive security organization, like the North Atlantic Treaty Organization to complement the CSCE's preventive diplomacy. Well versed in the Asian security environment, Japanese leaders proposed a security forum, which was to utilize the existing security networks of PMC.

Therefore, this Japanese initiative was very significant. It was the first time Japan had endorsed a multilateral security dialogue and it was done while the United States was still officially opposed to the idea. In fact, the Foreign Ministry persuaded reluctant Americans to endorse the Nakayama proposal. Moreover, setting up a multilateral venue for security dialogue had another policy implication. According to Yukio Sato, "it is important for Japan to place herself in multilateral venues, wherein the countries which are worried about the future direction of Japanese defense policy can express their concern."[15] These attempts reveal that Japan wanted to utilize a multilateral security forum to complement the existing security networks, not to replace them. Accordingly, Japan envisages its own role as a "political broker" rather than a regional "policeman." As such, Japan's approach to the ARF was closely linked to the concept of comprehensive security, mainly developed by the Foreign Ministry. It also meant that Japan has come to endorse the extension of the "ASEAN's model" of regional security, which is based on consultation and consensus. The question here is whether the ARF based on multilateralism can make a significant difference in the evolution of the region's security.

DEVELOPMENT OF THE ARF PROCESS

The first ARF was held in July 1994 in Bangkok with six member states of ASEAN, seven dialogue partners (the United States, Japan, Australia, New Zealand, Canada, South Korea, the European Union), and five observers (Russia, China, Vietnam, Laos, Papua New Guinea) in attendance. During the two-hour session, Japanese Foreign Minister Yohei Kono stated that Japan would continue its basic security policies, which embraced an exclusively defense-oriented stance, the Three Non-Nuclear Principles, and the strengthening of a nonproliferation regime. Regarding regional security, Kono confirmed that the presence and engagement of the United States in the region is a prerequisite for regional peace and stability, yet efforts should be made to promote increased mutual confidence through the ARF process and to establish and improve the security environment from a long-term perspective. For this purpose, Kono proposed holding concrete discussions on "Mutual Reassurance Measures" in three areas: information sharing, personnel exchanges, and cooperation toward the promotion of global activities.[16]

In February 1995, a Philippine-China row began when Manila disclosed that the Chinese had built military-style structures on Mischief Reef, just 170 kilometers off the Philippine island of Palawan. In subsequent developments, the Philippine Navy removed Chinese markers on Pennsylvania Reef, Jackson Atoll, Second Thomas Reef, First Thomas Shoal, and Half Moon Shoal, and detained four Chinese fishing vessels near the contested reef. Although China explained its construction was to "provide shelters for Chinese fishermen," the incident triggered a chain reaction. First, it led to a decision by the Philippines to modernize its armed forces, with special emphasis on a conventional army. Second, Vietnam began to strengthen its relations with the Philippines as well as the United States. Third, Indonesia also changed its previous policy of neutrality toward China. This occurred after China's unexpected move to include Indonesian-owned Natuna Island into its territorial claims in the South China Sea.[17]

In dealing with China's alleged encroachment into the disputed territories, ASEAN tried to find resolution within the framework of the ARF, but to no avail. At the second ARF, held in August 1995, China successfully opposed a proposal that working groups be set up within the ARF to prepare policies on specific issues in between ministerial meetings. Although Foreign Minister Kono insisted that the territorial and jurisdictional dispute in the South China Sea should be taken up in ARF, it is understood that such a critical issue is beyond its scope. For the ARF was formed as a loose, informal, and ad hoc multilateral forum. In other words, the ARF may eventually have the power to resolve concrete security issues, but that is not likely to happen any time soon. Nevertheless, the final report stressed that "the ARF recognizes that the concept of comprehensive security includes not only military aspects but also political, economic, social and other issues."[18]

The third ARF, in July 1996, saw some progress in the field of confidence- building, such as dialogue on security perceptions, defense policy publications, enhancing high-level defense contacts and exchanges among defense staff colleges and training, and UN register of conventional arms. At the same time, the ARF formulated conditions for the admission of new members: (1) all new participants, who will be sovereign states, must subscribe to and work cooperatively to help achieve the ARF's key goals, (2) a new participant is admitted only if it can be demonstrated that it has an impact on the peace and security of the "geographical footprint" of key ARF activities, (3) efforts must be made to control the number of participants to a manageable level to ensure the effectiveness of the ARF, and (4) all applications for participation are to be submitted to the Chairman of the ARF, who will consult all the other ARF participants at the SOM (senior official meeting) and ascertain whether a consensus exists for the admission of the new participant. Furthermore, China's positive postures for ARF were all the more welcomed. However, the fact that the ARF had to take up the issue of human rights suggests a growing prominence of the influence of Western powers.[19]

The fourth ARF, held in July 1997 in Malaysia with 21 foreign ministers from Asian and Western nations, had very limited results. There were four main issues, such as the latest conflict in Cambodia, human rights in Myanmar, the Japan-U.S. guidelines, and new developments in the Korean peninsula. Most important was the issue of human rights in Myanmar, which has proven the most divisive one between ASEAN and Western states. U.S. Secretary of State Madeleine Albright strongly urged that: "It really is ASEAN's responsibility to convince the SLORC to open up a political dialogue with Aung San Suu Kyi's political party." Despite growing pressures against Myanmar, the ARF was confident with its policy of "constructive engagement," because the purpose of admitting Myanmar was to keep it out of China's sphere of influence. Subang Jayva of Malaysia, who chaired the fourth ARF, noted diplomatically in his Chairman's statement that the ARF "has played a positive role in enhancing mutual understanding and trust, promoting greater transparency as well as strengthening peace and stability in the region.[20]

In the midst of the Asian financial crisis, the fifth ARF was held in July 1998 in Manila. Main issues discussed were nuclear proliferation, elections in Cambodia, human rights in Myanmar, and the security implications of the ongoing financial crisis. Most important was the issue of nuclear tests in India and Pakistan, but the Chairman's statement did not refer to either country by name despite strong requests from the United States. This indicates that ASEAN was mindful of its long observed principle of "noninterference." In fact, ASEAN members for the first time addressed the issue during the foreign ministers meeting, where the Philippines and Thailand advocated the adoption of "flexible engagement." Although ASEAN did not agree to change its basic principle, the fact that the issue was raised at the meeting is likely to prove to be a taboo-breaking event in the long run. At the same time, many participants addressed, for the first time, nonmilitary issues, which would have a significant impact on regional security. For instance, U.S. Secretary of State Madeleine Albright devoted more than half of her opening statement to such nonmilitary concerns as peace between people and their leaders, AIDS, human rights, corruption, environmental protection and humanitarian needs.[21]

The last two meetings, held in July 1999 in Singapore and July 2000 in Thailand, had mixed results. Since the possibility of a North Korean missile launch was one of the focal points at the 1999 forum, it is significant that the ARF was unanimous in naming North Korea's missile development a destabilizing element in the region. However, ASEAN had to admit that it was the United States and China, not ASEAN, that led the discussion of regional security. Although ASEAN came up with a surprising proposal to draft a new code of conduct for the South China Sea, this ARF meeting showed the diminishing role of ASEAN in the ARF process. In a similar vein, at the 2000 forum, although North Korea for the first time attended, the forum ended as a talk shop without achieving any progress in respect of designing a mechanism for preventive diplomacy and a code of conduct for the South China Sea.[22] Without doubt, given the various proposals for reforming the ARF, it is clear that a deep sense of insecurity in Asia invariably persists.

SECURITY IMPLICATIONS OF THE ASIAN FINANCIAL CRISIS: THREE ISSUES

The end of the Cold War and the financial crisis in Asia have renewed interest in regional approaches to peace and security. As the region's soul searching continues, it is becoming a common belief that, compared to Western Europe, Asia-Pacific peace appears more fragile because the region has fewer liberal democracies, plus a more modest level of economic interdependence among its members; and it lacks Europe's multilateral institutions.[23] The financial crisis began when the Bank of Thailand announced a managed float of the Thai national currency on July 2, 1997. The value of the baht declined immediately by around 18 percent, forcing the Thai government to seek IMF assistance. By the end of July, the Philippines, Malaysia, and Indonesia had also floated their currencies, which prompted further depreciations and stock markets turbulence in the region.[24] The crisis was said, in some quarters, to have hit Asian countries because of inherent structural weaknesses. Others pointed to external predatory forces. Regardless of its real origins, the crisis pointed up a question of concern to the region's economic security. It required a fresh new look because security conditions of the 1990s were quite different from those of the previous decade. The significant lesson from a temporal comparison is that while the concept of Comprehensive Security did broaden the traditional concept of national security, it did not "deepen" it. In any renewed quest for a regional security commensurate with the post–Cold War conditions, we need to examine the following three issues if the concept is to have a "deepening" effect, namely: (1) redefining state-society relations with emphasis on human security, (2) making economic interdependence stable through policy coordination, and (3) strengthening multilateral institutions for preventive diplomacy. Hence, a new version of comprehensive security.

REDEFINING STATE-SOCIETY RELATIONS: DEMOCRATIZATION AND HUMAN SECURITY

In light of the financial crisis, Asia-Pacific countries, many are agreed, need to recorder their state-society relations. As one observer put it: "What the region needs is to put in place a political system that places value on accountability and transparency, that controls corruption and sets up an administrative and regulatory system that is suited to the age of globalization."[25] In fact, globalization is causing deep cleavages between those who have capital, skills, and resources and those who do not.

Without any doubt, economic performance of Asian countries during the 1970s and 1980s was remarkable and even exceptional, as compared with that of other developing countries. Once known as the locale of "Oriental despotism," Asia has by and large changed its negative image into a positive one, following its economic "miracle." For pragmatic reasons, most Asian countries have sought economic development to the neglect of democracy, if the latter means accountability, the rule of law, pluralism, and respect for human rights. Some, in fact, have done so at the expense of democratization, much to the chagrin of Western countries.

Nevertheless, rapid economic growth in the region has created a broad middle-class base, and with it a greater concern for civil society and democracy. It is claimed that the lack of democratization is likely to hinder greater participation of the populace, including the middle class, in the policy process, whereby hampering the further broadening of a nation's economic base. As the fate of the Marcos and Suharto regimes suggests, brutal violations of human rights and the continuing neglect of adequate working conditions of labor can have highly destabilizing effects on a political system. And, with the spread of discontent, more especially if exacerbated by the rise of political dissidents; increasing flows of refugees and foreign workers; and in some cases the activism of NGOs echoing the discontent; a country's external relations may also deteriorate and become destabilized.[26]

Addressing the democratization issue, many Asian countries need to redefine their state-society relations with emphasis on institutional pluralism. The demand for civil society is strongest in Thailand and the

Philippines, but the collapse of the Suharto regime in Indonesia has encouraged the forces of democracy in other countries, including Malaysia, because the recent financial crisis has indicated that democratic regimes may be more efficient in dealing with economic turmoil than authoritarian ones. As one observer cogently put it: "The crisis has helped East Asians discover the importance of civil society in economic development. Thus far, it has been the 'missing link' in the social, political, and economic 'space' that has been occupied predominantly by the state and market."[27]

In fact, the economic crisis has a healthy effect on the prospects for democracy and better governance, as exemplified by the "effective mobilization of the angry middle class in Thailand in support of a new constitution, the partial reigning in of President Suharto's children in Indonesia, and the election of long-time democracy advocate Kim Dae Jung in South Korea."[28] Without doubt, globalization of the economy is likely to open up societies and polities to the outside world whereas ideas, values, culture, and other elements of human life move freely across national boundaries.

The post–Cold War developments in the Asia Pacific have also generated new problems and challenges, which necessitate the "deepening" of the concept of security. It is now considered necessary to expand the concerns of security to encompass environment degradation, deadly diseases, and overpopulation, resulting in a new dimension of human security based on sustainable development.[29] This seems critical, as the haze problem caused by forest fires in Kalimantan and Sumatra since 1997 amply demonstrates. In this context, what Prime Minister Obuchi proposed during his visit to Vietnam in December 1998 may testify to Japan's commitment to human security: "The second area where our efforts are needed is placing emphasis on human security. Human security is a concept that takes a comprehensive view of all threats to human survival, life and dignity and stresses the need to respond to such threats. Japan will continue to address this area, utilizing its official development assistance and multilateral frameworks such as APEC. Japan has decided this time to contribute U.S.$4.2 million for the establishment of the Human Security Fund under the United Nations so that international organizations concerned can provide support in a flexible and timely manner to projects that are to be implemented in this region."[30]

MAKING ECONOMIC INTERDEPENDENCE
STABLE THROUGH POLICY COORDINATION

The second issue concerns the ways and means to manage emerging economic interdependence in the Asia-Pacific region. Ever since the Plaza

Accord of 1985, the rapid appreciation of the Japanese yen expedited the massive inflow of Japanese capital into Asian economies, hastening closer economic interdependence, especially in the field of production. Increased economic interdependence in turn created multilateral networks, some of which are embodied in formal intergovernmental institutions and others that are overlapping second track networks. As one observer summed up: "Increased economic interaction established the notion of an Asia-Pacific region encompassing North America, East and Southeast Asia, and the Southwest Pacific. Moreover, interdependence created new issues, particularly in the economic realm, that could not be addressed in one country. This put a premium on multinational research and policy discussion networks, both to formulate realistic approaches taking into account the circumstances of all the major actors involved, and to disseminate the results to policy-makers."[31]

However, we have come to realize that neither states' policies nor institutional responses were adequate to deal with the financial crisis. The price to pay was heavy, as described by Indonesian Foreign Minister Ali Alatas: "We have now come to realize, because of the crisis, how interdependent we are, how interconnected our problems are. Now we see that it cannot remain as a problem exclusive to Thailand, it inevitably could infect us. So our problems are interconnected, our interdependence towards one another has grown, and we realize in times of crisis we must be able to show the world that we are able to cooperate even more closely with each other."[32]

What is found lacking is obviously the much-needed policy coordination among the Asia-Pacific countries. Suffice it to say that the annual meetings of ASEAN-ARF or APEC have been confined largely to the exchange of opinions without necessarily effecting policy coordination. There may be many reasons for this, but the doctrine of noninterference within either forum could be the most direct culprit and, hence, most serious problem. According to Thai Foreign Minister Surin Pitsuwan: "It is time that ASEAN's cherished principle of non-intervention is modified to allow it to play a constructive role in preventing or resolving domestic issues with regional implications. When a matter of domestic concern poses a threat to regional stability, a dose of peer pressure or friendly advice at the right time can be helpful."[33]

In a way, since the financial crisis, we have witnessed the gradual erosion of the noninterference doctrine in Southeast Asia in the form of countries' mutual watching over each other's economic policies. This economic monitoring agreement may develop toward institutionalizing closer coordination of national economic policies and performance and fostering rule-based transparency in governance. Politically, it is interesting to note that many ASEAN members openly criticized the Mahathir government of Malaysia for its treatment of former Deputy Prime Minister Anwar Ibrahim. Indeed, Philippine President Estrada's explicit comment that "Anwar was not being given due process and that is a human right violation" was a taboo-breaking action.[34]

STRENGTHENING MULTILATERAL INSTITUTIONS FOR PREVENTIVE DIPLOMACY

The financial crisis has also shown that regional institutions could not respond adequately. In strengthening multilateral institutions in the Asia-Pacific region, ASEAN and its extended forum, ARF, need to be restructured. Timing seems to be ripe, for instance, as one scholar argues that "the political, economic, and strategic considerations that have made ASEAN a success within Southeast Asia do not necessarily apply to the more powerful states of the Asia-Pacific region. Therefore, ASEAN is an inappropriate model for the ARF."[35] In view of the ARF's main goal of "engaging China," moreover, the ARF has encountered a serious problem because "China's constant strategic pressure in the South China Sea has ASEAN in disarray. The ARF is doing little more than giving China opportunities to divide and rule."[36]

On the question of strengthening the ARF, we need come to grips with three main defects of the ARF: a structural anomaly, the inapplicability of ASEAN's procedures, and the misguided notion of basing it on a cooperative security. The first problem could be dealt with when the ARF relinquishes some of its present burdens and concentrates on the security of Southeast Asia. For instance, the issues of Taiwan and the Korean Peninsula exemplify the weakest link for the ARF. In this respect, the concerned Northeast Asian countries should approach the establishment of a Northeast Asian security forum. The second problem could be resolved if ASEAN agrees to modify the noninterference principle so as to deal promptly and effectively with regional security issues. The third defect could be handled if the ARF embraces critical elements of regional balance of power. That is to say, the Japan-U.S. alliance, anchored on the concept of regional partnership, may well be the best vehicle to balance competing political, economic, and security interests in the region. In so doing, ASEAN would have to bring in the United States more deeply and find functional linkages with the Japan-U.S. alliance.[37]

In this respect, it is significant that in September 1997, Prime Minister Hashimoto and President Clinton issued new security guidelines for the post–Cold War era to deal with the volatile situation on the Korean Peninsula, the unresolved crisis across the Taiwan Strait, and other potential problems in the Asia-Pacific region. However, the new document explains that the concept of "situation in areas surrounding Japan," covered under the joint agreement, is "not geographical but situational." Officials from several Asian nations have expressed concern about the expanded security role of Japan. To ease this anxiety, Japan proposed "a trilateral security dialogue" that may evolve into a formal mechanism through which Japan and the United States consult with China, as well as its neighbors, on security matters. Without doubt, this move would bode well for the formation of a multilateral security network in Asia.[38]

ASEAN countries have expressed their support for the redefinition of Japan-U.S. security relations. As one observer explained, "a strong U.S. presence in the region is always a prerequisite for a healthy and positive balance of power in the region. And since that is to be maintained primarily through the U.S.-Japan alliance, it has become a real anchor for peace and stability in the region, although burden-sharing with others in the region, including ASEAN, is also becoming more important for keeping the support for the alliance in the U.S. and Japan."[39]

With these modifications of the major security parameters, more attention can be paid to preventive diplomacy in the Asia Pacific region. So far, China has vehemently opposed any move that infringes on China's territorial rights, be it confidence-building measures or preventive diplomacy. Despite China's persistent objection, however, the time seems to be ripe for introducing a mechanism of preventive diplomacy. To practice preventive diplomacy in the region, however, further institutionalization is needed. In particular, the ARF will have to (1) agree on a set of norms and principles for executing preventive diplomacy; (2) establish a nexus of working mechanisms and institutions to link with other international, regional, and subregional institutions; and (3) move toward greater institutionalization of its own processes, balancing greater initiative and autonomy with accountability to and access by member states.[40] As a first step, the ARF could start with minimal institutions such as a Regional Risk Reduction Center and Special Representatives to undertake fact-finding missions and offer good offices. In this respect, ASEAN's decision to set up a "Troika" mechanism to address regional issues in November 1999 bodes well for the initiation of preventive diplomacy in the region.[41]

CONCLUSIONS

The above analysis suggests that Tokyo's formulation of a "comprehensive security" policy in the early 1980s corresponded closely to ASEAN's pursuit of "national and regional resilience," which eventually resulted in the joint sponsorship for the ARF in the early 1990s. As a result, we can argue that "comprehensive security is emerging as a norm in Asia."[42] However, the far-reaching financial crisis has proved that the old premises of comprehensive security are not tenable, thus necessitating the reinvigoration and deepening of the very concept of comprehensive security per se.

The intent here is to reinvigorate the old concept by replacing the Cold War security structure with a multilateral process and framework endowed with the following two attributes: First, it must be geared toward reassurance, rather than deterrence; second, it must promote both military and nonmilitary security. More specifically, the new notion of comprehensive security should stress the following three tasks:

1. Each state is to strengthen its legitimacy by adjusting to changing societal needs and demands, so as to promote a civil society that supports the rationales and cooperative policies of the state;
2. In tandem with the progress in industrialization and economic interdependence beyond national borders, each state is expected to come to terms with the region's common interests, so as to deal with the management risks emanating from increasing interdependence; and
3. while geared toward securing stability in interstate relations through balance of power and the maintenance of a mechanism for multilateral dialogue, this "diplomatic culture" is expected to exercise increasing influence over the behavior of area states in the long run.[43]

As ASEAN has been recovering from the brutal financial crisis, a greater security role for it within the Asia Pacific region is inevitable. The challenge of the 1990s was how the association could retain its momentum while reinforcing its politicosecurity relations with extraregional powers, including Japan. For Japan, on the other hand, the question was how it could broaden its diplomatic horizon. Through the 1990s, Japan's political role expanded substantially, as exemplified by the Tokyo meeting on Cambodia, the first Japanese participation in UN peace-keeping (PKO in Cambodia), Japan's active participation in the ARF, and its proactive role in the Asian financial crisis. These cases of Japan's political and economic initiatives differ significantly from its political role during the Cold War. In a renewed quest for a regional security concept relevant to the post–Cold War era, therefore, a "deepened" version of regional security is called for. Given the increasing interdependence among

Asia Pacific countries, what is needed is a new strategy, incorporating accountability, interdependence, and multilateralism, based on the reinvigorated concept of comprehensive security.

NOTES

* This research was partly supported by the Pache Research Subsidy of Nanzan University, which is duly acknowledged here.

1. Paul Dibb et al. "The Strategic Implications of Asia's Economic Crisis," *Survival* 40, no.2 (Summer 1998): 5. See also Graeme Cheeseman, "Asia-Pacific security discourse in the wake of the Asian economic crisis," *The Pacific Review* 12, no.3 (1999): 333–356.

2. For globalization and security, see especially S. Lynn-Jones, et al., eds., *Global Dangers: Changing Dimensions of International Security* (Cambridge: The MIT Press, 1995) and Paul Stares, ed., *The New Security Agenda: A Global Survey* (Tokyo: Japan Center for International Exchange, 1998).

3. Tony Tan, "Steps for Asia-Pacific Security," *International Herald Tribune,* January 20, 2000, p. 8. The study of international and national security has come under a close scrutiny in recent years, as one scholar contends: "the field of security studies seems poorly equipped to deal with the post–Cold War world, having emerged from the cold war with a narrow military conception of national security and a tendency to assert its primacy over other public policy goals. Its preoccupation with military statecraft limits its ability to address the many foreign and domestic problems that are amenable to military solutions." David Baldwin, "Security Studies and the End of the Cold War," *World Politics* 48, no.1 (October 1995): 132.

4. See Tetsuo Umemoto, "Comprehensive Security and the Evolution of the Japanese Security Posture," in Robert Scalapino, et al., eds., *Asian Security Issues* (Berkeley: Institute of East Asian Studies, University of California, 1988), pp. 28–49; and Sueo Sudo, *Southeast Asia in Japanese Security Policy* (Singapore: Institute of Southeast Asian Studies, 1991) for the evolution of Japan's security policy.

5. Sogo anzen hosho gurupu, *Sogo anzen hosho senryaku* [Comprehensive security strategy] (Tokyo: Okurasho insatsukyoku, 1980). See also Robert Barnett, *Beyond War: Japan's Concept of Comprehensive National Security* (Washington, D.C.: Pergamon, 1984); Shinkichi Eto and Yoshinobu Yamamoto, *Sogoampo to mirai no sentaku* [Comprehensive security and the future choice] (Tokyo: Kodansha, 1991); and Akihiko Tanaka, *Anzen hosho* [National Security] (Tokyo: Yomiuri shimbunsha, 1997), chapter 9, for further analyses on Japan's comprehensive security.

6. Yuichiro Nagatomi, ed., *Masayoshi Ohira's Proposal* (Tokyo: Foundation for Advanced Information and Research, 1988), p. 236.

7. See Gaimusho, *Keizai kyoryoku no rinen* [Rationales of Economic Cooperation] (Tokyo: Kokusai kyoryoku suishin kyokai, 1981); Tsusansho, *Keizai anzen hosho* [Economic security] (Tokyo: Tsusho sangyo chosakai, 1982).

8. Heiwamondai kenkyukai, *Kokusai kokka Nihon no sogo anzen hosho seisaku* [Comprehensive security policy of International State of Japan] (Tokyo: Okurasho insatsukyoku, 1985).

9. See especially Kenneth Waltz, *Theory of International Politics* (Reading, MA: Addison-Wesley, 1979), John Mearsheimer, "Back to the Future: Instability in Europe After the Cold War," *International Security* 15, no.1 (summer 1990): 5–56, and Aaron Friedberg, "Ripe for Rivalry: Prospects for Peace in a Multipolar Asia," *International Security* 18, no.3 (winter 1993–1994): 5–33.

10. Roger Irvine, "Making Haste Less Slowly: ASEAN from 1975," in Alison Broinowski, ed., *Understanding ASEAN* (London: Macmillan, 1983), p. 40. See also M. Alagappa, "Comprehensive security: Interpretations in ASEAN countries," in *Asian Security Issues,* edited by Robert Scalapino, et al. (Berkeley: Institute of East Asian Studies, University of California, 1988), pp. 50–78; and J. N. Mak, *ASEAN Defence Reorientation 1975–1992* (Canberra: Strategic and Defence Studies Centre, Australian National University, 1993), pp. 11–13.

11. See especially Anny Wong, *Japan's Comprehensive National Security and Its Economic Cooperation with the ASEAN Countries* (Hong Kong: The Chinese University of Hong Kong, 1991).

12. Yukio Sato, "1995 nen no fushime ni mukatte," [Toward a turning point in 1995] *Gaiko Forum* (January 1994): 12–23.

13. This section is based mainly on the following works: David Dewitt, "Common, Comprehensive, and Cooperative Security," *The Pacific Review* 7, no.1 (1994): 1–15; Akiko Fukushima, *Japanese Foreign Policy: The Emerging Logic of Multilateralism* (London: Macmillan, 1999), pp. 107–125.

14. Paulin Kerr, et al., "The Evolving Security Discourse in the Asia Pacific," in *Pacific Cooperation: Building Economic and Security Regimes in the Asia-Pacific Region,* edited by Andrew Mack and John Ravenhill (St. Leonards: Allen & Unwin, 1994), p. 252.

15. Yukio Sato, "Emerging Trends in Asia-Pacific Security," *The Pacific Review* 8, no. 2 (1995): 273–274.

16. Gaimusho, *Gaiko seisho 1995* [Diplomatic Bluebook 1995] (Tokyo: Okurasho insatsukyoku, 1995), p. 35.

17. *Far Eastern Economic Review* (August 3, 1995): 22; (June 8, 1995): 15; and (27 April 1995): 28.

18. Chairman's Statement of the Second ARF, 1 August 1995, Bandar Seri Begawan, Brunei.

19. *Asahi Shimbun,* 24 July, p. 9.

20. *The Economist,* 2 August 1997, p. 20; Chairman's Statement of the Fourth ARF, July 27, 1997, Subang Jaya, Malaysia.

21. Graeme Cheeseman, "Asia-Pacific Discourse," p. 345; *Mainichi Shimbun,* 28 July 1998, p. 3.

22. *Far Eastern Economic Review* (August 5, 1999): 17–18; *Asahi Shimbun,* 28 July 2000, p. 6.

23. See Bruce Russett, "A Neo-Kantian Perspective on Democracy, Interdependence and International Organizations in Building Security Communities," in *Security Communities,* edited by Emmanuel Adler and Michael Barnett. (Cambridge: Cambridge University Press, 1998), pp. 368–94; Joseph Grieco, "Systemic Sources of Variation in Regional Institutionalization in Western Europe, East Asia, and the Americas," in *The Political Economy of Regionalism,* edited by E. Mansfield and H. Milner. (New York: Columbia University Press, 1997), pp. 164–187; and Terumasa Nakanishi," Ajia niokeru sogo anzen hosho no kadai," [Tasks of Comprehensive Security in Asia] in *Ajia wa dokawaruka,* edited by T. Nakanishi. (Tokyo: Nihon keizai shimbunsha, 1993), pp. 323–344.

24. Major works on the financial crisis are Morris Goldstein, *The Asian Financial Crisis: Causes, Cures, and Systemic Implications* (Washington, D.C.: Institute for International Economics, 1998), T. J. Pemple, ed., *The Politics of the Asian Economic Crisis* (Ithaca: Cornell University Press, 1999); and H. Arndt and Hal Hill, eds., *Southeast Asian Economic Crisis* (Singapore: Institute of Southeast Asian Studies, 1999).

25. *Far Eastern Economic Review* (February 12, 1998): 49.

26. See especially Anek Laothamatas, ed., *Democratization in Southeast and East Asia* (Singapore: Institute of Southeast Asian Studies, 1997).

27. Hadi Soesastro, "Civil Society and Development: The Missing Link," *The Indonesian Quarterly* (Third Quarter 1999), p. 257.

28. Richard Cronin, "Asian Financial Crisis: An Analysis of U.S. Foreign Policy Interests and Options," Washington, D.C.: CRS Report for Congress, Congressional Research Service, Library of Congress, April 23, 1998, p. 17. See also Prasert Chittiwatanapong, "Challenges of and Responses to Globalization: The Case of South-east Asia," in *Globalism, Regionalism and Nationalism,* edited by Yoshinobu Yamamoto (Oxford: Blackwell Publishers, 1999), pp. 70–92.

29. For human security, see Michael Renner, *Fighting for Survival* (New York: W.W. Norton, 1996); and Keith Krause and Michael Williams, eds., *Critical Security Studies* (Minneapolis: University of Minnesota Press, 1997).

30. Keizo Obuchi, "Toward the Creation of a Bright Future for Asia," Ministry of Foreign Affairs, Japan, December 16, 1998.

31. Charles Morrison, "Interdependence, Policy Networks, and Security in Asia-Pacific," in *Asia-Pacific Security: The Economics-Politics Nexus,* edited by S. Harris and A. Mack (St. Leonards: Allen & Unwin, 1997), p. 131.

32. *Far Eastern Economic Review* (February 29, 1999): 37.

33. *Bangkok Post,* 13 June 1998, p. 5; *Far Eastern Economic Review* (August 6, 1998): 24–28.

34. *Straits Times,* 7 October 1998, p. 22. See also Carolina Hernandez, "To-wards Re-Examining the Non-Intervention Principle in ASEAN Politi-cal Co-Operation," *The Indonesian Quarterly* (Third Quarter 1998): 164–170; and Michael Richardson, "ASEAN Struggles to Change Its Reputation as Weak, Helpless and Divided," *International Herald Tribune,* 22 April 1999, p. 4.

35. Shaun Narine, "ASEAN and the ARF: The Limits of the ASEAN Way," *Asian Survey* 37, no.10 (October 1997): 962. See also Michael Wesley, "The Asian Crisis and the Adequacy of Regional Institutions," *Contemporary Southeast Asia* 21, no.1 (April 1999): 54–73, for a precise analysis on the role of ASEAN, APEC and ADB during the crisis.

36. Robyn Lim, "The ASEAN Regional Forum: Building on Sand," *Contem-porary Southeast Asia* 20, no.2 (August 1998): 115.

37. For a further discussion, see Sueo Sudo, "Toward a Japan-U.S.-ASEAN Nexus," in *The Japan-U.S. Alliance,* edited by Masashi Nishihara. (Tokyo: Japan Center for International Exchange, forthcoming). See also Rizal Sukma, "ASEAN and the ASEAN Regional Forum: Should 'the driver' be replaced?" *The Indonesian Quarterly* (Third Quarter 1999): 236–255.

38. Michael Green and Patric Cronin, eds., *The U.S.-Japan Alliance: Past, Present, and Future* (New York: Council on Foreign Relations, 1999).

39. Jose T. Almonte, "Ensuring Security the 'ASEAN Way,'" *Survival* 39, no.4 (winter 1997–1998): 80–82. Masashi Nishihara suggests that "the Guidelines are intended to give an indirect support for the ARF." See his "Chiikianzenhosho no atarashii chitsujo wo mezashite [In Search of a New Regional Security Order]," *Gaiko Forum* (November 1997): 40.

40. Simon Tay and Obood Talib, "The ASEAN Regional Forum: Preparing for Preventive Diplomacy," *Contemporary Southeast Asia* 19, no.3 (December 1997): 265–266. For a possibility of preventive diplomacy in the Asia Pa-cific, see *Yobogaiko nyumon,* edited by Mitsuro Donowaki. [Introduction to Preventive Diplomacy] (Tokyo: Foresuto shuppan, 1999), pp. 175–185.

41. *Asahi Shimbun,* 29 November 1999, p. 1.

42. M. Alagappa, ed., *Asian Security Practice* (Stanford: Stanford University Press, 1998), p. 625. See also Kurt Radtke and Raymond Fedema, eds., *Comprehensive Security in Asia* (Leiden: Bril, 2000) for a recent assessment of the concept.

43. Hitoshi Nakanishi, "Sogo anzen hosho seisaku no saikosei," [The Re-structuring of Comprehensive Security Policy] in *Nihon, Amerika, Chugoku,* edited by Ryosei Kokubun (Tokyo: TBS Buritanika, 1997), p. 130.

CHAPTER 10

CHINA IN SEARCH OF COMPREHENSIVE SECURITY

RICHARD WEIXING HU

China is considered more secure from any possible foreign invasion today than at any time in the last 50 years. As two American scholars put it, "[i]n all four regions around its periphery—Inner Asia, Northeast Asia, Southeast Asia, and South Asia—China is more secure today than at any other time since the establishment of the PRC," in 1949.[1] There is no doubt that China's regional security environment has been greatly improved over the last two decades. No foreign power or military alliance poses an immediate threat to China's territorial security. Thanks to its rapid economic growth over the last two decades, China now has much better "comprehensive national power" (*zhonghe guoli*)[2] to defend itself. However, despite the much stronger military and economic capabilities China has today, the Chinese leaders still demonstrate a deep sense of insecurity in their policy statements.[3] The sense of insecurity, as one analyst notes, could come from the political uneasiness of the Chinese Communist Party (CCP) in power.[4] It could also be due to the traditional "preparing for the worst" mentality (*ju an si wei*) held by the Chinese rulers in history. But, if we put aside "regime security," the question of how secure China is today seems to have more to do with the changing nature of security than China's power status.

Many people in China have come to accept that growing comprehensive national power does not mean comprehensive national security. National security, according to some Chinese scholars, depends on three factors: global and regional security situation (*anquan xingshi*), comprehensive national power, and national security strategy (*anquan zhanlue*). A peaceful international situation and a state's strong comprehensive national power do not necessarily give the state a favorable security environment. On the contrary, a state with relatively weak comprehensive national power may enjoy a stable security environment even during international turmoil situation.[5] Thus, to understand China's security environment and security strategy, we must appreciate how Chinese policy makers view international situation and, particularly, where they see threats to China's security.

The Chinese leaders' threat perception has gradually evolved since the end of the Cold War. Although the policy research that is closely linked to and reflective of official thinking still emphasize traditional security concerns, such as national sovereignty, territorial integrity, military defense, and military balance of power, Chinese scholars and security experts now increasingly recognize an array of new security threats. As the trend of globalization, accompanied by regionalization and democratization, was rigorously transforming the post–Cold War international relations, they began to discuss nontraditional security threats, ranging from environmental degradation to drug trafficking, to China's national security. Although none of these problems is a strictly novel concern, they are all considered "new" in the sense of being increasingly perceived as security threats. The increase of comprehensive national power, in some sense, can neither prevent these new security threats nor address them adequately. That's why there is growing consciousness and perception in China calling for "comprehensive security" (*zonghe znquan*).

This chapter attempts to examine the Chinese perspective of comprehensive security through a review of the recent Chinese literature in national security studies. The term "comprehensive security" has become popular in Chinese policy speeches and international relations analysis in recent years. In the debate over the "new security concept" (*xin anquan guan*), many scholars and security experts challenge the military-centered conception of security. To them, although military security is still essential, the notion of "security" has become more polysemantic. China must view security from a more comprehensive and nontraditional perspective. Related to that, they argue that Beijing must have a comprehensive security strategy, something similar to what the Japanese government adopted in the 1970s.[6]

TRADITIONAL VS. NONTRADITIONAL SECURITY THREATS

The term "security" (*anquan*) in China, for a long time, has been a synonym of national defense (*guofang*). China's national security strategy, for a long time, has largely concentrated on military defense against external invasion. Chinese leaders, from Mao Zedong to Deng Xiaoping, all had long revolutionary war experiences and understood well the importance of military power. For Mao, "political power grows out of the barrel of a gun" (*qiangganzi limian chu zhengquan*) and a political regime must also be sustained by military power. For Deng, while he understood the importance of military power for the regime's survivability, his first priorities were to modernize the economy and put the Chinese military power on a sound basis. From Mao and Deng to the current CCP leaders, they have all shared basic tenets of political realism in international relations. Chinese leaders believe nation-states are the most important actors in international politics, and the supremacy of national sovereignty shapes concerns and behavior of nation-states in today's international system, which is still a Westphalian one. They tend to view international relations more in terms of power and national interest and look on international institutions and norms with a great deal of suspicion.[7]

Derived from their realist approach to international relations, Chinese policy-makers tend to view the search for national security primarily a matter using military power to defend against foreign invasion and coercion. According to realism, a state can take unilateral action (such as increasing military capability) or balancing maneuvers (forming alliance with other states) to defend itself. But no matter what course of action it takes, the chief responsibility of managing security lies squarely on the state. It is the state's responsibility to take care of security for the nation, and military strength is the most important tool to do the job. Looking at Chinese leaders' speeches and policy analyses, the "traditional security" type of thinking is still prominent and strong. As a matter of fact, the defense against "traditional security" threats to China is considered the most important task in national security strategy.

China's assessment of the international security environment is largely skewed toward traditional security concerns. Chinese analysts view today's international security situation as a mixture of an overall détente and regional turmoil (*zongti huanhe, jubu dongdang*). As the recent *National Defense White Paper 2000* states, "The security situation in the Asia-Pacific region has been on the whole stable. . . . However, in today's world, factors that may cause instability and uncertainty have markedly increased. The world is far from peaceful. There is serious disequilibrium in the relative strength of countries."[8] New negative developments in the security of the Asia-Pacific region, such as the proposed U.S. Theater Missile Defense (TMD) system in Asia, Taiwan's separatist tendency, the expansion of the U.S.-Japanese security cooperation, and the East Asian financial crisis all make Beijing feel the heat in its security environment.

The bombing of the Chinese Embassy in Belgrade in 1999 and the tension in the Taiwan Strait have reinforced the Chinese perception of the salience of traditional security challenge China is facing. After the Cold War, China criticized the West as still sticking to the "Cold War mentality" in dealing with China. It opposed absolute security based on military supremacy, coercion, and military alliance. But before the U.S. cruise missiles hit the Chinese Embassy in Belgrade on May 7, 1999, killing three Chinese journalists and injuring more than 20 diplomats there, very few people in China considered a war involving China and the United States likely. The bombing suddenly brought a war in distance to a war close to home. It not only led to a nation-wide public outburst of anti-U.S. sentiments but also generated strong national support for defense modernization and preparation for future high-technological war vis-à-vis the West. The likelihood of war involving China and the United States, likely in the Taiwan Strait, is no longer something remote. The Chinese leaders and the public were reminded, again, of the urgency of defense modernization programs. Some security experts even argue that, as the "new" gunboat diplomacy appears in world politics, China can not underestimate the danger of the Western neo-interventionism to its security. China must seriously consider and prepare for a U.S. military intervention in the Taiwan Strait as it did in Kosovo.[9]

Although traditional security concerns are still predominant in Chinese security policy, nontraditional security issues began to gain attention in recent security debates. It is understandable why Chinese leaders and scholars still put nation's traditional security in the highest priority. But as the debate on the new security concept (*xin an quan guan*) indicates, the Chinese notion of security is changing. No matter how important traditional security issues may be, leaders cannot afford to ignore the increasing salience of nontraditional issues. With the end of the Cold War, the importance of military power is declining in world politics. More and more Chinese scholars began to question the prevailing orthodoxy of military defense in security thinking. Security concerns, they argue, are not one-dimensioned. Instead, states must consider a much wider set of security challenges, such as drug trafficking, terrorism, organized transnational crimes, environment degradation, civil and ethnic conflict, and resources scarcity. As one Chinese scholar writes, the connotation of security has become much more broadened and inclusive. There is a horizontal extension of the parameters of security policy to include a larger set of security problems as well as a vertical extension of the traditional referent object of security policy.[10] That is to say, China must reconsider the questions of "security of what" and "security for whom." The new parameters of security include nonmilitary issues, such as economic and environmental problems, as well as societal problems, such as poverty, natural disasters, crimes, social discrimination, and unemployment. The broadening of security concerns makes the referent object of security include not just states, governments, and regimes, but also social groups and individual citizens.

This conceptual shift or broadening can be best described by a concept popularized by the UNDP since 1994—"human security."[11] Instead of focusing on military defense of the state, human security emphasizes on the individual's welfare and freedom from hunger, attack, and discrimination. Security of an individual is considered to be just as important as that of the state. For some Chinese policy analysts, the possibility of interstate war still exists, but international competition occurs more in market than in territory today. Some of them argue that national security threat not only arises from abroad but also may originate internally from such problems as domestic terrorism, deterioration of the ecological system, and natural calamities.[12] They believe that, with further opening up to the outside world and China's integration into the global economy, the scope of national security has to be enlarged accordingly, especially in economic aspects. Economic security is vital for China's steady economic growth. To be secure in economic development, China must make sure its "economic interests are free from interruptions or threats posed by any internal or external elements."[13] Military power is necessary to defend China's economic interests and development, but economic security can not depend on military protection alone. Security problems used to be something that in the past had been reserved almost exclusively for military or defense-related concerns. Now, the rising concerns on these issues gradually changed the public's perception and attitudes toward security. Security problems can not be dealt with by military means alone; they require a broader and more comprehensive approach in national security strategy.

A new way of thinking or paradigm is quietly appearing in the policy community that agrees China must have a comprehensive security strategy. As one senior scholar observes, "without military means, modernized national security does not work, nor does it work with military means alone. Military security must be considered only one component in a comprehensive national security strategy."[14] Although there are few systematic studies on nontraditional security issues, there are more and more journal articles and books discussing the emerging nontraditional security concerns in China. Most Chinese scholars agree that the spectrum on security should be widened. China's national security strategy cannot be downgraded as national defense strategy. National security strategy can be divided into different categories, such as political security, economic security, military security, scientific and technological security, social security, informational security, ecological security, food security, resources security, and even cultural security. As a whole, they make the national comprehensive security strategy.[15] In dealing with comprehensive security issues, Chinese leaders are advised by scholars to establish a U.S.-type of national security council within the government structure, which can coordinate foreign and security policy-making. The Chinese leadership is reported to be carefully studying the feasibility of establishing a Chinese-style national security system that can handle security-related matters in a comprehensive way.[16]

The Chinese Notion of Comprehensive Security

The concept of comprehensive security has been widely used in the Asia Pacific region. The term was first created and became popular in Japan after the 1973 Oil Crisis, which exposed Japan's vulnerability in the world economic system and its dependence on imported oil from the Middle East. Following the oil crisis, the Japanese government sponsored a series of studies on the economic and nonmilitary aspects of its security, and the concept of "comprehensive security" was later created and adopted by the Ohira Administration (1978–1980) as a principle of its security policy. In 1980 a *Report on Comprehensive National Security* was submitted and accepted by the Suzuki Administration as official security strategy. Recognizing its vulnerability on resources dependence and the decline of U.S military and economic superiority, the Japanese government began to define security in a holistic way, emphasizing the multidimensional sources of a threat, both military and nonmilitary, to its security and national well being. In addition to dealing with traditional military threats, the comprehensive security strategy identified nonmilitary sources of challenge, such as disruption of international trade, natural disasters, and food and energy shortages, as security threats. While stressing the need to maintain conventional military capability and alliances, the Japanese approach to comprehensive security broadened the scope of security notions and helped elevate security policy to the highest level of policy agenda. In sum, the Japanese comprehensive national security is largely derived from external threat; it stresses economic security because of the country's dependency on external resources.

The ASEAN countries also enthusiastically took up the concept of comprehensive security in their policy deliberation. As David Dewitt notes, at least three ASEAN members—Indonesia, Malaysia, and Singapore—have developed distinctive notions of security that go beyond military objectives and instruments, while the Philippines also recently developed a similar doctrine to guide its approach to security.[17] Similar to the Japanese approach, the ASEAN states stress the nonmilitary threats and the nonmilitary instruments to deal with the threat. But different from the Japanese, they tend to focus more on internal concerns, such as war by proxy, subversion, ethnic and racial conflict, and drug trafficking.

Different from the Japanese and ASEAN approaches, the Chinese notion of comprehensive security concerns both internal and external threats. As some Chinese scholars put it, "China's security notion is a comprehensive one. On one hand, it stresses the importance of nation's sovereignty, territorial integrity, and non-violability. On the other hand, it accepts and pays attention to the political and social stability of the nation, economic security, and other emerging security issues, such as energy and environment."[18] To Chinese scholars, the end of the Cold War has fundamentally changed the international system and relations among nations. The new international environment has redefined China's security agenda.[19] As the threat from foreign invasion dramatically disappeared, the importance of internal stability has been elevated in the policy agenda. A state will have legitimacy problems if it fails to provide basic welfare for the bulk of the population or exhibits any of the following characteristics: repression, corruption, nonexistent political infrastructures, or competing centers of authority. Although the political stability in China is not as fragile as expected from the outside and Beijing does not see a severe, immediate threat to the regime, the Chinese leadership is sensitive to nontraditional security problems from inside. These security concerns include: (1) ethnic minority problems, such as possibilities of separatist movement, with or without external involvement, and terrorism; (2) problems of political dissidents and any forces that openly challenge the CCP (e.g., *Fa Lun Gong*); (3) social problems of overpopulation, poverty, massive unemployment, and income disparity between individuals and regions; (4) crimes, drug abuse and trafficking, and AIDS; (5) social menaces, such as corruption, that undermine the regime; and (6) high-tech crimes and Internet safety. Most of these are emerging challenges in the post–Cold War era. To the Chinese leaders, internal instabilities invite foreign intervention. Internal and external threats are often connected (*neiyou waihuan*). If you cannot put your house in order, external enemies will take advantages of the vulnerability.

Most Chinese scholars agree that China is facing security threats, both internal and external, and traditional and nontraditional security threats often overlap with each other. As a whole, comprehensive security should be a state in which national political, economic, and military interests are free from threat and disruption, internal and external, traditional and nontraditional. To achieve comprehensive security, a state must have a holistic way to cope with security problems. Comprehensive security is thus an integrated system of political, economic, military, environmental, information, psychological, and even cultural security.[20]

Debating national comprehensive security, Chinese scholars emphasize the importance of the indispensability between security and development (*shengcun yu fazhan*). As some scholars argue, national survival and economic development are complementary to each other. Economic development has become both the end and means for national security strategy.[21] In the post–Cold War international relations, economic development has become the primary determinant of the rise and fall of major powers in world politics. The main domain of international rivalry has shifted to the economic realm, and the essence of competition is the contest for comprehensive national capabilities. The collapse of the Soviet Union has testified the significance of winning the race in comprehensive national power. The 1991 Gulf War and 1999 Kosovo War demonstrated, again, the importance of comprehensive national power, especially in science and technology, as the primary determinant in future international struggle.[22] International competition, particularly in the long run, is a competition of comprehensive national capabilities, not just military power. Military power is a dependent variable, instead of independent variable, of national economic power.

The emerging concept of comprehensive security not only means the enlargement of security spectrum for Chinese policy makers, but also calls for more comprehensive means to deal with security problems. In addressing the "new" security problems, many Chinese scholars believe the means to achieve national security objectives have become "soft" (*ruan hua*).[23] As the military means is no long the sole means to achieve security goals, other nonmilitary means such as economic means, political, and diplomatic, and even cultural means are more and more used in international relations. In recent years, Beijing began to use more diplomatic and nonmilitary means to its regional security problems. Beijing has sought partnerships with almost all its neighbors as well as major Western powers. China has also sought to reduce tension and stabilize its territorial disputes with Asian neighbors through negotiation and treaties on border disputes. For disputes that cannot be solved, Beijing seeks to shelve them and maintains status quo. In regional reorganizations, Beijing has become more active in participating regional arrangements, such as APEC and ARF, to promote consensus and stability.

Over the last two years, Beijing has also staged a PR campaign about its "new security concept" in the international community. The Chinese leaders have actively promoted it as a new international norm by arguing that the world cannot have a new order without a new security concept, and that the new security concept is essential for enduring international peace and stability.[24] According to China's White Paper on National Defense 1998, international security "should be based on mutual trust and common interests. We should enhance trust through dialogue, seek security through cooperation, respect each other's sovereignty, solve disputes through peaceful means and strive for common development.[25] On March 26, 1999, President Jiang Zemin delivered a policy speech at the UN Committee on Disarmament in Geneva. He used the opportunity to argue that "[we] must establish a new Security Concept applicable to the need of new times."[26] In the UN Millennium Summit, President Jiang Zeming again appealed to world leaders that "The Cold War mentality must be abandoned once and for all, and a new security concept based on mutual trust, mutual benefit, equality and cooperation should established."[27]

GLOBALIZATION AND SOURCES OF CHINA'S INSECURITY

The changing nature of security challenges is largely shaped by globalization and its impact on security. While nobody disagrees that globalization has had a positive effect on economic development, few have fully appreciated what are the adverse effects of globalization on national security and governance. Globalization does not change the territorial division of nation-states but creates strong transnational forces that penetrate into societies. Economic liberalization, free trade, economic interdependence, "real time" communication and information flow, and technology transfer create threats as well as opportunities for a relatively "closed" state like China. Globalization has contributed to energy and environment problems, migration, organized crime, and terrorism. As a result, it undermines national sovereignty and makes states "defenseless," or less defendable to external threats.

The Chinese leaders have missed no opportunities to criticize the unequal benefits created by globalization between the rich and poor countries.[28] The intrusion of geoeconomics into international relations has greatly increased nontraditional security challenges to countries like China. Globalization, on one hand, is the prime and beneficent source of China's economic growth and prosperity. But on the other hand, it also makes China more dependent upon others for support and cooperation. Economic security is a very popular term in China. As China's economy increasingly integrates into the regional and global economic system, the degree of economic interdependence with other countries has become a hot issue in debate. As China opens up its market to foreign competition, required by its WTO commitment, the Chinese economy has exposed itself to the international fluctuation and market forces. It means a substantial reduction of government's capacity to control the economy, and leaves fewer administrative leverages to defend the national industry, market, Renminbi's value, and monetary stability. An unstable macroeconomic environment makes it difficult to sustain high economic growth, which is vital for the regime's survival. During the Asian financial crisis in 1997 and 1998, Beijing was particularly keen to learn lessons from the experiences of Southeast Asian countries, where adverse effects of economic liberalization left them defenseless against international speculative forces in the financial market. For Beijing's leaders, domestic financial order, resulting in economic prosperity, is one of the most important security issues. They eventually decided to move slowly and cautiously in opening up the capital market, full Renminbi convertibility, and market access in the service sector.

As foreign investment continuously pours in, China's national industry (especially many state-owned enterprises, SEOs) is facing a life-or-death situation. In contrast to government rhetoric, more and more scholars argue the government should strike a balance between protecting national industries and opening markets to foreign investment. Growing foreign economic presence in China following the WTO accession will further reduce barriers for foreign companies to enter the China market. The degree of foreign control, especially in the vital sectors of the economy, is considered by some as a threat to China's economic sovereignty. One scholar argues, "if our national industry shrinks as a result of absorbing foreign direct investment . . . if the dominant role of socialist public ownership and the leadership role of state-owned enterprises are weakened or discarded, then our country will have been utilized by foreign capital. Our open policy will have failed."[29]

Globalization is also the transmission belt for liberal democratic ideas to the Chinese society. Beijing is sensitive to the Western "peaceful evolution" through transnational cultural and economic activities. Globalization and economic integration make it easier for foreign companies and political forces to penetrate into the Chinese economic system and society. In addition to economic control, the Chinese leaders are increasingly concerned with political and cultural messages transmitted through commercial activities and social exchanges, which makes the defense against the Western "peaceful evolution" of China almost impossible. The Chinese young generation have already become more adaptive to the Western popular culture than the older generation. As *New York Times* columnist Ronald Steel writes, "Unlike traditional conquerors, [the West] is not content merely to subdue others: We insist that they be like us."[30] To Chinese writers, dealing with the Western ideological and cultural engagement is a more challenging job for the Chinese leaders. It requires great political wisdom to strike a balance between the nation's long-term strategy of opening up to the outside world and preserving social stability and regime security.

China's rapid economic development has also produced many severe social challenges. Economic wealth increase raises the expectation of political reform. The disparity between different regions and social groups could intensify potential social instabilities. Food and energy problems could get worse as the economy grows. If China can still produce sufficient food for its people in the next twenty years, there will be no easy solution for the energy shortage China will face in the future. China will become more dependent on foreign oil supply as domestic production declines. With a rapid pace of economic development and urbanization, China also faces growing environment protection concerns, resulting from industrialization and atmosphere and water pollution. The government has come to realize the seriousness of environmental degradation and its long-term impact on economic development. All these problems have bearing on national security strategy.

The Internet or cyberspace security is another new source of insecurity. China's Internet users have grown rapidly over last ten years. The latest survey by the official China Network Information Center (CNNIC) estimated there were 16.9 million users in China by June 2000.[31] Over the last two years, the number of users has been doubling every 6 months. A very conservative estimate would put the number of users in China at least 30 million by 2002. As the government, business, and society get increasingly dependent on the network, cyberspace has become the new frontier for national defense and government control. In recent years the Chinese government has tried different ways to control cyberspace but was not very successful. The security concern it has is two-fold: First, it worries about "illegal border crossing" from the outside world and has yet to find ways to keep sophisticated net users inside the screened area on the Internet. There are strong political implications for Internet control and regulation. But government regulations and censorship are always falling behind technology development, and it is getting harder and harder to control cyberspace and information flow across national borders. Second, Beijing has growing concerns on its future dependence on the Western information technology (IT). As U.S. IT products prevail in the Chinese market, the government fears it will be difficult to defend China's virtual borders against foreign intrusion. As the Chinese leaders learned from the Kosovo war and the latest IT development, information warfare will be vital for national defense. As an editorial in the *PLA Daily* argues, China will not be able to effectively defend its sovereignty and territorial integrity unless it can defend its virtual borders and maintain information security. The West attempts to use IT technology controlling other countries, and China must be vigilant about IT colonialism from the West.[32]

SOFT POWER AND COMPREHENSIVE SECURITY

In the new security concept debate, Chinese scholars and security experts also began to reflect on more profound issues on security and national power. They asked questions about why "comprehensive national power" does not bring comprehensive security. Twenty years ago, Deng Xiaoping convinced the nation that China must concentrate on economic development and modernization and that it will be more secure when its comprehensive national power increases. For Deng, China can only achieve national greatness and security through economic development and stronger power status. There has been a national consensus in favor of Deng's idea, and China's economic reforms and development have proven to be successful. However, with growing comprehensive national power, China's security has not improved accordingly. In foreign affairs, Beijing began to pursue an independent and peaceful foreign policy, hoping to maintain a favorable international environment for its domestic economic development. In Sino-U.S relations, Beijing has tried to avoid confrontation, increase mutual trust, and reduce troubles. But Beijing often finds itself with very limited leverage over Washington. It sometimes becomes wishful thinking to have a stable, long-term "strategic partnership" with the United States. China's lack of influence in its relations with other major powers directly contributes to its source of insecurity.

In reflection, many scholars find that the nation's understanding of comprehensive national power is too narrowly focused on hard power, while it neglects the salience of soft power in international relations. Hard power is useful but no longer adequate enough to deal with new security threats. National security also depends on how much influence a country has over others, and soft power, sometimes, is more relevant and salient in power relations. As China's economy grows, it has more and more interests to defend all over the world, but there is a growing capability gap between interest and capability. When it comes to defending its national interests and security, the means and power available must be relevant to the issues they address. Hard power cannot solve human rights disputes or prevent moral aspiration of Western values penetrating into the Chinese society. Moreover, China's rapid economic growth has increased its comprehensive national power, but it also fueled "China threat" concerns in the West. Good image could help to reduce the concerns. But it requires more than image to win others' trust.

Soft power is such an ideational source of power in international relations. According to Joseph Nye, soft power is the ability to influence other's preferences with intangible power resources such as culture, ideology, and institutions. It is in contrast to hard power, which is usually associated with tangible resources like military and economic strength.[33] Soft power encompasses at least the following elements: diplomatic skill; mobilization of international organization resources; domestic administrative competence; intellectual leadership; political and ideological appeal; cultural and moral attractiveness; and domestic cohesion. World history has proved that no country can become a world power without adequate soft power, and soft power has come to be more relevant a means to address some emerging security concerns.

China has far to go before it has acquires such soft power. After the collapse of communism in the Soviet Union and Eastern Europe, the socialist system seems to have run out of its course. While China's economic development has become more vigorous, its political system has remained rigid. The communist leadership continues to postpone political reforms, which leaves the domestic political system fragile. The political fragility severely undermines China's prospect to be a world power. When Beijing continues to be on the defense on human rights issues, its system is unlikely to generate moral and cultural appeal to other states. The Chinese government has tried to turn around the human rights struggle with the West, but the road to legitimacy has proven to be an uphill battle thus far.

The rise of China has caused suspicion and fear in the Western countries, rather than earning respect from them. Ideological concerns and power politics make the West view China more as a strategic competitor than a strategic partner. As the "democratic peace thesis" suggests, liberal democracies do not go to war against other liberal democracies. In this sense, as Michael Doyle terms it, they have created a "separate peace" in the world.[34] China not only has an image problem with the West, but also lacks the means and skills to mobilize political resources in the international society. The political resources include influences in international media, international governmental organizations (IGO) and nongovernmental organizations (NGO), and key bilateral relations. The Chinese leaders are happy with the hard power increase but neglect the importance of translating hard power into soft power, especially into international institutional power. In the end, it becomes more a rule-taker than a rule-maker in international affairs. Beijing has yet to learn effectively to use international organizations, both IGOs and

NGOs, to pursue its interests internationally. Some Chinese scholars have realized this problem and have argued that China must learn how to protect its national interests by employing both "soft" and "hard" means (*ran ying liang shou*).[35]

CONCLUSION

The new security concept is gaining momentum in China. More and more Chinese scholars have come to accept that China faces a new security environment today. The nature of security threats has changed from traditional sources of threat (military) to nontraditional sources of threat. China's focus on security must move from a single dimension to multiple dimensions, from external threats to internal sources as well. There is an increasing awareness on nontraditional security concerns, such as economic-related security, environmental degradation, transnational crime, and cyberspace security. But in answering the question of *security for whom,* most scholars, as can be ascertained from the research literature, still use the state as the reference point. Only limited consideration is given to human security at the individual level. Related to that, the proposed solutions of new security issues are still focused on state strategy in dealing with security challenges. Most scholars still view the state as the solution, instead of the cause, of security problems.

In answering the question of *by what means* and *at what cost,* there is growing consensus that increasing comprehensive national power does not mean comprehensive national security. As globalization has created an array of nontraditional security threats, ranging from environmental degradation and energy security to China's national security. Deng Xiaoping's prescription of increasing comprehensive national power can neither prevent new security threats nor address them adequately. The Chinese leaders have a too-narrow fixation with comprehensive national power. China may have acquired more hard power to defend its national interests, but it still lacks adequate soft power to manage favorable security relations with other major powers. To have comprehensive security, it must have power, both hard and soft, to cope with the new security challenges.

NOTES

1. Andrew Nathan and Robert Ross, *The Great Wall and the Empty Fortress: China's Search for Security,* (New York: W. W. Norton, 1997), p. 156.
2. The term has been widely used by Chinese leaders and scholars since the early 1990s in discussing China's national strategy and long-term eco-

nomic development. Deng Xiaoping used this term to emphasize that China's long-term goal should be catching up with world major powers by the middle of the twenty-first century in terms of overall national power. According to some Chinese scholars, China's comprehensive national power status now can roughly be ranked at the same level as that of Japan, not a global power, but, rather, a regional power. See Yan Xuetong, *Zhongguo Guojia Liyi Fengxi* [Analysis of China's National Interest] (Tianjin: Tianjin Remin Chubanshe, 1996), pp. 88–95.

3. See, for example, *China's National Defence in 2000* (White Paper), issued by the State Council Information Office, 17 October 2000.

4. Fei-ling Wang, "Self-Image and Strategic Intentions: National Confidence and Political Insecurity," in Yong Deng and Fei-ling Wang, eds., *In the Eyes of the Dragon: China Views the World* (Rowman & Littlefield, 1999), pp. 21–46.

5. Guo Zhenyuan, "Zengyang kuandai dangxian he weilai de zhongguo guoji anquan huanjing" [How Should We Assess China's Current and Future International Security Environment], *Zhongguo pinglun* (China Review) (November 2000): 20.

6. Barry Buzan argued that the concept of security must be broadened to incorporate military, political, economic, societal, and environment security in the twenty-first century. See Barry Buzan, "New Patterns of Global Security in the Twenty-first Century," *International Affairs* 67 (July 1991): 433.

7. For a good discussion on China's realist approach to international relations, see Thomas Christensen, "Chinese Realpolitik," *Foreign Affairs,* 75, no.5 (September/October 1996): 37–52.

8. The Information Office of the PRC State Council, *China's National Defence in 2000.* See *Renmin ribao,* 17 October 2000. For the English version of the White Paper, see *China Daily,* 17 October 2000.

9. See, for example, Yan Xuetong, "Guoji huanjing ji waijiao sikao" [The International Environment and Reflections on Our Foreign Affairs], *Xiandai guoji guanxi* [Contemporary International Relations], no.8 (1999): 7–11; and Chu Shulong and Wang Zaibang, "Guayu guoji xingshi he wo duiwai zhanlue ruogan zhongda wenti de sikao" [Reflections on International Situation and Some Important Issues of Our Foreign Strategy], *Xiandai guoji guanxi,* no.8 (1999): 1–6.

10. Pang Zhongying, "Broad Security, Economic Security, and Security Cooperation," *Ouzhou* (Europe), no.1 (1997): 35–38.

11. For further discussion on the subject, see UNESCO Division of Human Rights, Democracy, and Peace, *Non-Military Aspects of International Security* (Paris: UNESCO Publishing, 1995), p. 258.

12. Ibid.

13. Liu Jianping, "Guojia jingji anquan wenti yanjiu shuyao" [A Survey of Studies on National Economic Security], Renmin Ribao [People's Daily], 30 January 1999, p.6.

14. Shen Qurong, "Danyuan heping jianghui biande genjia chengshou—dui yashou weilai de zhengzhi sikao" [May Peace Become More Mature—Political Reflections on the Future of Asia], *Xiandai guoji guanxi,* no.7 (1996).

15. See, for example, Zhao Ying, *Xingde guojia anquanguan* [New National Security Concept] (Kunming: Yunnan Remin Chubanshe, 1992); and Li Yunlong, "Yatai diqu quanmian anquan hezuo" [Comprehensive Security Cooperation in the Asia Pacific], *Xiandai guoji guanxi,* no.5 (1996): 23–25.

16. For more discussion, see Duan Silin, "Zhonggong dui tai xinsilu" [New Thinking in CCP's Taiwan Strategy], *Guang jiaojing* [Wide Angle], no.337 [16 October 2000]: 18–21.

17. David Dewitt, "Common, Comprehensive and Cooperative Security," *Pacific Review* 7, no.1 (1994): 3–4.

18. Chu Sulong and Peng Chunyan, "Postwar New Developments in the International Security Theories," *Xiandai guoji guanxi,* no.4 (1999): 32.

19. See Weixing Hu, "China's Security Agenda after the Cold War," *Pacific Review* 8, no.1 (1995): 117–135.

20. Tang Yongsheng and Cheng Hainan, "On Comprehensive Security," *Ou Zhou* [Europe], no.3 (1997): 43.

21. Ibid., p.44–45.

22. For more discussion, see Tong Jiemin, "Seize Opportunities to Develop Economic and Trade Relations with the European Union," *Guoji maoyi* [International Trade] (February 1995): 13–17.

23. See Fu Mengzi, "Chong jingji anquan jiaodu tan dui feichuantong anquan de kanfa" [My Views on Nontraditional Security from the Perspective of Economic Security], *Xiandai guoji guanxi,* no.3 (1999):1–2; Pang Zhongying, "Broad Security"; Tong and Cheng "On Comprehensive Security," p.45.

24. Cheng Ruisheng, "Lun zhongguo di yatai anquan de xin fangzhen," [China's New Guidelines To Asian Pacific Security], *Guoji wenti yanjiu* [International Studies], no.3 (1999): 1–6.

25. Information Office of the State Council, China's National Defense 1998, July 1998. For English version, see *Beijing Review,* August 10–16, 1998.

26. Jiang Zeming's speech can be viewed at http://www.peopledaily.com.cn/ item . . . /jiangzm/1999.

27. President Jiang Zemin's speech at the UN Millennium Summit, New York, 6 September 2000.

28. President Jiang Zeming's speech at the APEC summit in Brunei, 15 November 2000.

29. Zhou Guangchun, "Duiwai kafang zhong de mingzu gongye yu guonei shichang wenti," [The Issues of National Industry and Domestic Market during the Open Door Policy Period], *Qiushi* [Seeking the Truth], no.6 (1996):14–18.

30. Quoted from James L. Watson, "China's Big Mac Attack," *Foreign Affairs,* (May/June 2000): 121.

31. Quoted from Kathleen Hartford, "Cyberspace with Chinese Character-istics," *Current History* (September 2000): 255.

32. *Jiefangjun bao* [PLA Daily], 10 February 2000, cited in *Xin Pao* [Hong Kong], 11 February 2000, p.14.

33. Joseph S. Nye, Jr., *Bound to Lead: The Changing Nature of American Power* (New York: Basic Books, 1990), pp.188–201.

34. Michael W. Doyle, "On the Democratic Peace," *International Security* 19, no.4 (1995).

35. See, for example, Pei Minxing, "Chengli guojia anquan weiyuanhui he ran shili" [Establishing National Security Council and Soft Power], *Xin Pao* (Hong Kong), 24 January 2000, p.7.

PART V

ASIA PACIFIC
AFTER THE CRISIS

CHAPTER 11

REALISTIC EXCHANGE RATES: A POST-ASIAN FINANCIAL CRISIS PERSPECTIVE

LOK SANG HO

INTRODUCTION

In the wake of the Asian financial crisis, jitters remain over the chance that another crisis is brewing. But before we know a workable way of preventing a repeat of what happened in 1997–1998, we need to address what constitutes a real currency crisis. And, we need to know that there are different currency crises and that there is a link between exchange rate and a currency crisis.

Just about everyone is concerned about currency crises. Currency crises can ruin enterprises, destroy jobs, cause inflation, send interest rates sky-high, and arbitrarily and unfairly redistribute wealth. Innocent people get hurt. Life savings can be lost. Even governments may fall. The Asian financial crisis has forcefully put the message across: currency crises can shatter lives and topple governments. There does not seem to be anything worse than a full-blown currency crisis.

Some economists have tried to come up with "early warning systems" that can raise an alarm before crises strike (Chote 1998, xv, 62; Kaminsky et al.1997). Perhaps the size of the current account deficit relative to the GDP, perhaps the size of the government budget deficit, and perhaps some other indicators such as the country's degree of dependency on short-term foreign debt, could serve the purpose. Apart from such early warning systems, some economists have provided their own definitions of what constitutes a currency crisis. Some say that if the exchange rate should fluctuate beyond a certain range, one could say a crisis has occurred. But it appears that such systems are not of much use. On any of these counts Hong Kong, for example, has neither been vulnerable to a currency crisis nor has faced any crisis at all. But Hong Kong is widely believed to have suffered greatly from the currency attack that it endured in 1997 and 1998. Officially at least, Hong Kong's unprecedented recession of 5.3 percent in 1998 was due to the Asian financial crisis. Hong Kong's overnight interbank lending rate briefly breached 280 percent on October 23, 1997, on the back of a massive attack on the Hong Kong dollar that sent the stock market plunging. The crux of the crisis was that people did not believe that the prevailing exchange rate could hold.

I would define a *true currency crisis* as a situation in which the prevailing exchange rate has lost credibility and tension has developed in the financial market and in the economy. To avoid exchange rate crises, the exchange rate has to be at a level that is credible. A credible exchange rate is such that it is consistent with full employment and balance of payments equilibrium over the long term. Clearly an excessively high exchange rate erodes the country's competitiveness, and unemployment may ensue. Clearly the exchange rate cannot hold if the country keeps losing its foreign exchange reserves. In the short run, however, because of speculative pressures, perhaps triggered by the contagion (or spread of the effects of the currency instability to other economies), market players may sell the currency in huge volumes, thus creating pressure for it to depreciate. Such short-term selling need not, however, undermine the current exchange rate's long-term credibility if the country's foreign exchange earnings match its foreign exchange payments. As long as the latter is the case and the exchange rate is consistent with full employment, I would say the current exchange rate is inherently defendable. Even though there may be an appearance of a currency crisis, there is no true crisis. I will call such situations "*apparent crises.*" Whereas the currency should devalue when there is a true crisis, devaluation is not warranted under apparent crises. Not only should the central bank not devalue the currency, but it also must not raise interest rates to fend off the short-term selling. Since the currency is defendable, it should be defended. There is a third kind of currency crisis, which I call "*disguised currency crisis.*" There need not be market pressures for the currency to devalue. Indeed, quite the reverse may be true. A currency may become increasingly overvalued due to market pressures, to the extent that the exchange rate becomes incompatible with full employment. Thus, overvaluations may occur under a regime of linking with a host country as well as under a regime of floating exchange rate.

The next section will examine two cases of true currency crisis. I argue that currency crises need not be a result of excessive short-term borrowing, lack of fiscal discipline, excessive money supply growth, or crony capitalism. While any one of these factors, acting on its own or in conjunction with others, will erode investors' confidence and prompt a currency crisis, perfectly "straight economies" could also run into trouble. Hong Kong is a case in point. Hong Kong's currency crisis in 1997 belongs to the true crisis category even though it was well-behaved fiscally and its financial institutions followed all the basic rules of prudence. The Thai baht debacle, on the other hand, provides a case of true currency crisis arising from excessive short-term borrowing coupled with a link to the U.S. dollar.

The third section will examine two cases of apparent currency crises. The Malaysian and the Singapore economies were hit by currency devaluation pressures in 1997, not withstanding strong economic fundamentals and a dearth of evidence that their currencies were grossly overvalued.

The fourth section will present the Japanese yen as a case of disguised currency crisis. The yen has been floating all along, and pressures were mounting for it to appreciate rather than depreciate. Yet it had, over the years, appreciated to such levels that its economy stagnated.

What all this means is that neither a floating exchange rate regime—with or without bands—nor a fixed exchange rate regime will free us from the threat of currency crises. The conclusion argues that it is in the interest of the international financial community to maintain exchange rates at sustainable or defendable rates. A concerted effort, through a mechanism fully supported by all the world's major economies, should be made to protect such exchange rates.

THE HONG KONG CASE
VS. THE THAI CASE

It is obvious that Hong Kong was under great stress during the Asian financial crisis. The Forward Exchange Rate for the U.S. dollar in terms of the Hong Kong dollar showed a huge premium—over 6,000 points for the 12-month contract in January 1998. That is, whereas HK$7.75 converted to one U.S. dollar in the spot market, the market expected that in a year's time more than HK$8.3 would be needed to buy one U.S. dollar. Along with such expectations for the HK dollar to depreciate, interest rates in Hong Kong went up dramatically. As interest rates went up, the stock market went down. During the week ending on October 23, 1997, the stock market lost 23.34 percent of its value. As table 11.1 shows, pressures on the Hong Kong dollar lingered on through 1998, but by March 1998 they had eased considerably.

Table II.I Forward Exchange Rate as Compared with the Spot Exchange Rate
(HKD against USD)

Honk Kong Daily-Middle Rate	Spot	1 month	3 month	6 month	9 month	1 year
15 Oct 1997	7.7385	90	280	535	800	1000
17 Oct 1997	7.7400	90	295	565	850	1125
20 Oct 1997	7.7420	145	445	825	1150	1400
21 Oct 1997	7.7475	265	750	1500	1850	2250
22 Oct 1997	7.7475	550	1350	1650	2950	3750
23 Oct 1997	7.6900	1550	2950	4050	4900	6000
24 Oct 1997	7.6900	1050	1850	2750	3500	4300
27 Oct 1997	7.7305	750	1550	2550	3100	3800
29 Oct 1997	7.7335	400	1000	1950	2700	3200
31 Oct 1997	7.7305	350	1100	2050	2800	3600
3 Nov 1997	7.7325	225	650	1500	2050	2750
10 Nov 1997	7.7325	650	1800	3050	3950	5000
12 Nov 1997	7.7295	575	1600	2700	3550	4500
19 Nov 1997	7.7295	305	1200	2550	3550	4750
21 Nov 1997	7.7305	205	850	2000	3250	4250
28 Nov 1997	7.7303	155	730	1600	2450	3450
3 Dec 1997	7.738	125	750	1850	2650	3650
5 Dec 1997	7.737	80	630	1700	2650	3550
8 Dec 1997	7.7385	48	525	1500	2300	3450
12 Dec 1997	7.7493	260	1000	2400	3800	5000
19 Dec 1997	7.75	65	625	1780	3050	4050
24 Dec 1997	7.75	65	625	1900	3350	4450
31 Dec 1997	7.75	95	655	1850	3100	4150
5 Jan 1998	7.75	195	900	2250	3650	4950
7 Jan 1998	7.7345	255	1000	2500	3850	5250
9 Jan 1998	7.747	580	1650	3250	5050	6800
14 Jan 1998	7.744	500	1400	2750	4050	5800
19 Jan 1998	7.74075	495	1400	2950	4450	5950
23 Jan 1998	7.738	245	1175	2750	4250	6050
26 Jan 1998	7.7422	325	1300	2950	4550	6150
2 Feb 1998	7.738	165	780	2050	3550	4850
6 Feb 1998	7.7375	100	655	1650	2750	4150
11 Feb 1998	7.739	45	425	1350	2300	3400
16 Feb 1998	7.7395	110	650	1750	2950	4150
20 Feb 1998	7.746	65	465	1100	2550	3300
25 Feb 1998	7.7465	30	345	1020	1800	2850
2 Mar 1998	7.7438	25	295	920	1650	2450
6 Mar 1998	7.744	70	445	1200	2050	2950
9 Mar 1998	7.74355	65	410	1150	2000	2950
13 Mar 1998	7.7455	43	335	1050	1850	2850
19 Mar 1998	7.748	2.5	175	750	1400	2300
23 Mar 1998	7.74875	15	87.5	540	1050	1700
25 Mar 1998	7.748	14.5	120	625	1250	2000
30 Mar 1998	7.7463	2.5	130	625	1200	1900

Source: Hong Kong Monetary Authority

Why was the Hong Kong dollar subjected to so much selling pressure? The world certainly knows well that Hong Kong has about the world's biggest foreign exchange and fiscal reserves in per capita terms. Hong Kong has no official foreign debt and only a tiny official internal debt. Hong Kong's bank regulators imposed on its banks standards that far exceed the Basle capital asset ratio requirements, and none of its financial institutions was under any imminent risk of insolvency. The reason, according to my analysis, is that the market did not believe that the exchange value of the Hong Kong dollar could hold—given that the U.S. dollar had appreciated so much against most other currencies, the HK-U.S. dollar link, and Hong Kong's recent inflation history. The market lost confidence in the Hong Kong dollar because it believed that without a large devaluation of the currency Hong Kong's economy would not be able to compete with others. Because of the strength of the U.S. dollar and given the history of high inflation, the market had good reasons to suspect that the Hong Kong dollar had to depreciate. In the end, the HK dollar did not depreciate, but Hong Kong went through a painful period of deflation and adjustment.

Like the Hong Kong dollar, the Thai baht had been informally linked to the U.S. dollar for quite some time. Over the years, Thailand had lost competitiveness because of new competition from the emerging economies. It had been falling into debt steadily, and short-term borrowing from overseas had fueled an unsustainable real estate boom. Meanwhile, its current account deficit had grown bigger and bigger, while its foreign exchange reserves were becoming smaller and smaller. The immediate urge to sell the baht, however, was prompted by the fall of Finance One, the biggest finance company in the country. The decision to devalue the baht on July 2, 1997 was first welcomed by the financial markets. The stock market actually rose almost 8 percent that day, showing that the devaluation was seen as a positive move to deal with a long-standing problem realistically. However, with Thailand's foreign exchange reserves dwindling to dangerous levels, investors continued to be worried, particularly as the central bank suspended the operations of 16 finance companies. On August 5, Bangkok unveiled an austerity plan in line with IMF recommendations and suspended another 48 finance companies.

The Hong Kong dollar and the Thai baht were attacked for different reasons. In the former case it was because the U.S. dollar link had taken the HK dollar exchange rate to increasingly incredible levels, particularly given the devaluations of other Asian currencies. In the latter case it was because of gross weakness in economic fundamentals. In the end, however, the central banks of both economies panicked and raised interest rates to unprecedented levels, bringing ruinous effects across the entire economy. Ultimately, Hong Kong had to face a period of painful deflation[1] while Thailand had to struggle with cleaning up its financial mess.

MALAYSIA AND SINGAPORE

Malaysia and Singapore were innocent victims of the contagion. Although Malaysia in 1996 had a current account deficit at 4.6 percent of its GNP, this represented a big improvement over 1995, when the current account deficit was as high as 10.2 percent of the GNP. The gross savings rate was maintained at a high level of about 40 percent, while inflation was mild. Singapore had an ongoing and growing current account surplus since 1988 and had an even higher savings rate. Singapore also boasts one of the world's highest per capita foreign exchange reserves.

Based on the economic fundamentals, neither country had a need to depreciate its currency. However, to maintain their competitiveness when other currencies in the region had depreciated, it would make sense for them to depreciate relative to the U.S. dollar. A larger depreciation than this would be unnecessary. This tactic was followed by Singapore, which allowed its exchange rate to depreciate from S$1.4305 to the dollar, on July 1, 1997, to S$1.6755 to the dollar by year-end—a decline of 15.48 percent. The prime lending rate was not raised until November 1997, and it peaked at 7.79 percent through August 1998, and then was reduced decisively to 5.9 percent by the end of 1998. Malaysia had much more humble reserves and depreciated much more and raised interest rates much more to defend the ringit. The base lending rate offered by the commercial banks went up to 12.27 percent by mid 1998 from about 10 percent in 1997. The average lending rate offered by merchant banks was 18.71 percent by the end of January 1998. It was only in September 1998, after capital controls had been imposed, that interest rates started to decline noticeably. The high interest rates and the capital controls cost the Malaysian economy much growth. Real GDP declined 7.5 percent in 1998. In contrast, Singapore's GDP growth, at 0.4 percent, though down significantly from 8.4 percent the previous year, remained positive in 1998.

The judgement that the currency crises suffered by Singapore and Malaysia were not warranted is vindicated by the big current account surpluses of the two countries after the devaluations. Singapore's current account surplus jumped 40 percent in 1998, to 25.4 percent of the GDP. Malaysia's current account showed a surplus equal to 13.7 percent of the GDP in 1998, which rose further to 16.9 percent of the GDP in 1999. As it happened, Malaysia never accepted any aid from the IMF. The economy bounced back 5.4 percent in 1999 and is expected to register a 5.8 percent growth in 2000.

JAPAN:
A CASE OF DISGUISED CURRENCY CRISIS

On appearance, Japan had no currency crisis. People do not speak of a currency crisis if the currency is subject to appreciation pressures prompted by strong current account surpluses. However, Japan's economy has been battered by the strength of the yen. The formation of the property price bubble is a direct result of the accumulation of huge amounts of savings. The subsequent burst of the bubble and the insolvency of many Japanese banks that followed were direct results of the strength of the yen, which is itself predicated on the strong current account balance.

As I (Ho, 2000, chapter 11) explained, Japan's high savings rate is actually very much the source of its economic woes. "If the Japanese had consumed more, it would not have so much money to pump into real estate. The current account surplus would not have been so big. The yen would not have been so strong. And the asset price bubble would not have formed, let alone burst."

On the eve of the global stock market crash in 1987, the Nikkei index, fueled by strong savings, had already breached the historical high of 26,000. Yet portfolio diversification considerations suggest that it would make sense to put some of the new savings in the stock market, some money in real estate, and some money on overseas assets. The continued accumulation of savings pushed the Nikkei Index and property values higher and higher (table 11.2). By the end of 1989 the Nikkei was close to 39,000. When the yen hit a new high in 1991, however, it became apparent that it made less and less sense to put more money into the domestic stock market and the domestic property market. Interest in acquiring Japanese assets reversed. Yet, thanks to an efficient manufacturing sector and a highly successful export effort, notwithstanding large capital outflows, the yen broke through historical highs. Between 1990 and 1995, the yen-dollar exchange rate moved from a low of 160 yen to the dollar to a high of around 80 yen to the dollar. As the yen appreciated, home assets, which are denominated in yen, became even more expensive. The incentive to sell increased while the incentive to buy disappeared. No wonder property prices and stock prices nose-dived. A couple of months after the yen's U.S. dollar exchange rate peaked at around 80 yen to the dollar in April 1995, the Nikkei had fallen below 15000. The land price index had also been shaved by half. Commercial land was particularly hard hit. About 60 percent of the peak value was lost.

Table 11.2 Asset Prices and Exchange Rates in Japan, 1984–1997

Year	Stock Price Index	Property Price Index	Exchange Rate (Yen/$)	Economic Growth
1997	15258.7	44.9	129.9	1.4
1996	19361.3	48.6	116.0	5.1
1995[a]	19868.1	54.7	102.9	1.5
1994	19723.1	63.2	99.8	0.6
1993	17417.2	71.4	111.9	0.3
1992	16924.9	87.0	124.6	1.0
1991[b]	22983.8	103.0	125.2	3.8
1990[c]	23848.7	100.0	135.4	5.1
1989[d]	38915.9	76.9	143.4	4.8
1988	30159.0	61.8	125.9	6.2
1987	21564.0	48.3	138.5	4.2
1986	18701.3	38.4	160.1	2.9
1985	13113.3	33.6	200.6	4.4
1984	11542.6	31.3	251.6	3.9

Source: Bank of Japan. Data for the Land Price Index is for comprehensive use in 6 major cities and is cited from *Statistics of Japan 1998*, published by the Statistical Bureau of Japan.

Notes: Stock price indices are for end of the month at end of the year, the land price indices are average values for the year.

[a]April 1995 saw the yen touching 80 yen to the dollar, then weakening rapidly. The weakening of the yen triggered a dramatic rise in stock prices that lasted about a year.

[b]1991 saw the yen rising to a nearly all-time high, having reversed a brief depreciation against the dollar in 1989. Property prices peaked.

[c]1990 saw the property market jumping, following the sharp surge in the stock market the previous year.

[d]1989 saw the stock market hit a peak and the yen hit a trough.

While domestic asset prices plummeted, the value of overseas assets also declined in yen terms as the yen continued to appreciate against foreign currencies. Because Japan is a net creditor nation, by definition Japan has more foreign-currency denominated assets and foreign currency-denominated liabilities. Appreciation of the yen hurt directly the balance sheets of Japan's business sector and indirectly those of Japan's banks, even if the latter were prudent enough to ensure that their own foreign liabilities matched their foreign assets.

Why the stock market bubble burst in 1990 and the property price bubble burst in 1991 is not an easy question to answer. Ito and Iwaisako (1995, see especially p. 32ff.) could not find a valid explanation for the stock price increase in the second half of 1989 and the land price increase in 1990 using any asset-pricing model based on fundamentals or rational bubbles. The evidence does show, however, that exchange movements certainly played some role. We know that stock prices are much more sensitive to emerging economic trends and that they tend to lead property prices and turns in the macroeconomy. The yen's depreciation in 1989 increased the attractiveness of Japanese assets and triggered a boom in asset prices. It also slowed the outflow of Japanese capital. The excessive stock price increase, coupled with the realization that the yen's depreciation in 1989 was only a temporary blip, triggered a sell-off in 1990. The sharp declines in the stock market in turn aggravated the property sell-off in 1991.

One would ask why in the long years of secular appreciation of the yen, from 360 to the dollar in early 1971, through around 125 yen to the dollar in 1988, nothing serious happened. The evidence is quite clear that during these years Japan had invested aggressively in enhancing its productivity and overseas. Through such investments, it managed to preserve its competitiveness so that the manufacturing sector was still going strong in 1988, notwithstanding an already strong yen. *Over the years, however, the accumulation of savings and the absence of alternative instruments of investment inevitably took domestic asset prices to higher and higher levels.* On the back of such price gains, yen appreciation really made it attractive to sell Japanese assets. The result is a trail of bad debts, bank failures, and a stagnant economy.

Historically, "super strength" of currencies has always spelled disaster for economies. Hong Kong in 1985 was on the verge of a recession because the U.S. dollar to which it was linked was so strong. The UK economy on the eve of the sterling crisis of 1992 also suffered serious unemployment and fiscal deficits for the same reason. The paradox is that a freely floating exchange rate does not guarantee that the exchange rate would be at a level compatible with both internal balance (full employment and fiscal balance) and external balance (balance of payments equilibrium). While a linked exchange rate may become overvalued relative to what is needed for internal balance and external balance by virtue of the strength of the host currency, a floating exchange rate may become overvalued for internal balance by virtue of massive capital inflows or massive current account surplus.

CONCLUSIONS

All the above suggests that neither floating exchange rates nor fixed exchange rates will protect us from currency crises. Various innovations, including the crawling peg or the idea of an optimal band for exchange rate movement, are really beside the point unless the exchange rate is consistent with the requirements for full employment and macroeconomic stability and is able to hold its place. Paradoxically, in the short term our globalized capital markets may not allow such a stability-compatible exchange rate to hold its place. Because of nervousness, herd behavior, or some temporary shocks, the market could bring about an exchange rate way below what is warranted. Hong Kong in 1983, just prior to the introduction of the linked exchange rate system, had seen such a scenario, with the Hong Kong dollar falling to about HK$10 to the U.S. dollar. The Indonesian rupiah fell below 15,000 rupiah to the dollar in June 1998, before rising back to about 8,000 rupiah to the dollar by year-end. Mirroring the decline in the exchange value of the rupiah, Indonesian inflation shot up, to over 80 percent in August, September, and October 1998. Similarly, recent declines in the value of the Euro were causing the specter of high inflation. Such exchange rates are inconsistent with economic stability, contribute to run-away inflation, and engender social instability.

People normally do not refer to a strong currency as being "under crisis." But if the strength of the currency is sapping the health of the economy, it really is the source of an economic crisis. The strength of the yen has cost the country a decade's growth. Fiscal measures to stimulate the economy and save the banks only led to fiscal deficits, as much as 10 percent of the GDP. Such ratios are widely regarded as unsustainable and unacceptable, and it is more than three times the threshold limit allowed under the Maastricht Treaty for European currencies to join the monetary union.

To conclude, there are exchange rates that are needed for economic stability and the world has to act together to bring them about because the market will not automatically do so. Fixed exchange rates, floating exchange rates, crawling pegs, and floating bands—none will suffice. What is needed is analysis and understanding of what exchange rates are compatible with stability of the financial markets and the economy. What is needed is a global effort to bring these exchange rates about. We need a strong IMF, or some other international body, to do the job. Knowing what is needed is the first step toward dealing with a problem. Countries in Asia, having suffered a big blow from the financial crisis, should work together to achieve this knowledge.

NOTES

1. As chapter 18 of Ho (2000) shows, the problems that the Hong Kong Special Administrative Region faced after the hand-over were exacerbated by the misguided housing policies adopted by the new administration.

REFERENCES

Chote, Robert, ed. 1998. *Financial Crises and Asia*. CEPR Conference Report, No. 6. London: Centre for Economic Policy Research; distribution by Brookings Institution, Washington, D.C.

Ho, Lok Sang. 2000. *Principles of Public Policy Practice.* Boston: Kluwer Academic Publishers.

Ito, Takatoshi and Iwaisako, Tokuo. 1995. Explaining asset bubbles in Japan. National Bureau of Economic Research Working Paper #5358 (November).

Ito, Takatoshi, Eiji Ogawa and Yuri Nagataki Sasaki. 1998. How did the dollar peg fail in Asia? *NBER Working Paper* # 6729 (September).

Kaminsky, Graciela, Saul Lizondo, and Carmen Reinhart. 1997. Leading indicators of currency crises. *IMF Working Paper:* WP/97/70. Washington, D.C.: International Monetary Fund, July.

PART VI

CONCLUSIONS

CHAPTER 12

THE EMERGENT GLOBAL AND ASIAN REGIONAL ORDER: COMPLEMENTARITY AND DIVERGENCE

JAMES C. HSIUNG

Contrary to a general assumption that international relations (IR) scholars are concerned solely with explanation but not prediction, there is no lack of scholarly attempts to divine world order in the coming millennium. For example, in a special issue of the *International Studies Review*, Davis B. Bobrow (who is also a contributor to the present book) lined up an international group of IR scholars to offer their "conjectures" about the next millennium (Bobrow-ISR 1999). They did so from a wide range of perspectives including: realpolitik, economic systems, new social technology, identity change, and the like.[1] But our book is of a different sort, in at least two distinct ways.

First, most other discussions of the future world order follow in the tradition of the three waves of debates/dialogues in the short history of the IR field, as cogently extrapolated by Yosef Lapid (1989) and Davis Bobrow (in Bobrow-ISR 1999, 3–5). Ours, as has been shown, takes into consideration not only the "mainstream" views in the IR field—plus the empirical developments in the traditional (post-1500 A.D.) experience of the world system that they reflect—but also the very different views and experience of the nations in the Asia Pacific region. Second, unlike other studies offering visions about the next millennium, our book does not purport to offer a "prediction" of the new century's world order per se. Rather its aim is to suggest a way to reach a contour of such a world order; and it does so by speculating on the possible "trajectory" through which the new order is most likely to emerge.

In sum, using a framework that reveals an interrelated linkage, this book searches for a prevision of the emergent global order in tandem with the Asian regional order. The region in effect serves both as an illustration of the new world order and as a test of its universality (or lack of it). In this quest, we are mindful that the dawn of the new millennium follows the end of a tumultuous century that was full of paradoxes, as manifested in its many great triumphs and setbacks, plus many unprecedented innovations and breakthroughs (see the Foreword above). It only follows that the shape of the emergent world order, and the regional order as well, is anticipated by the bequests and unfinished agendas of the departing century. In addition, certain landmark trends that surfaced after the Cold War, some buoyed or swayed by preexisting conditions, may also cast a decisive influence on the emergent world order as well. Globalization is a ready example; a contrary trend of regionalism is another.

BEQUESTS OF THE PAST CENTURY
ON THE TWENTY-FIRST CENTURY

Of the various bequests, three stand out as the most noteworthy for their far-reaching effects. They are inherent in three genres of sea change. The first is the spread of wealth beyond the traditional (post-1800 A.D.) "core" of the world economy to the East, which, according to the world-system literature, had enjoyed dominance in the preexisting global economy long before the rise of the West. After 1492, Europeans used the silver extracted from the American colonies (later backed by gunboat diplomacy) to gain entry into an expanding Asian market. Ever since, and especially after 1800, East Asia declined and has remained in the "periphery."[2] With its newly achieved economic "miracles" over the last three decades, despite the financial crisis of the late 1990s, the Asia Pacific region demonstrates formidable credentials prompting many to claim that it will once again be the "center of the world"[3] in the twenty-first century.

Second, the spread of the Western-type democracy as a functioning political system from Europe and North America to expanding parts of Asia Pacific is an unprecedented development in world history. This trend is most likely to continue into the new century, although it is not so certain that it necessarily augurs well for the peace and stability of the region, as in the tortuous path of Indonesia's journey to democracy since the late 1990s. As has been shown (chapter 3), the removal of the strong hand of the Suharto regime has only exacerbated ethnic and religious diversities in Indonesia, resulting in massive racial conflicts and riots, further abetted by the violence of a military let loose from its traditional moorings. The chaos only gave fillips to secessionist forces in Aceh beyond East Timor, creating further threats to the country's political and economic stability.[4]

Along with the tides of democratization, the concomitant spread of free-trade values to nearly all members of the Asia Pacific group, regardless of their political ideologies at home, is nevertheless a reasonably decisive factor in the region's favor, looking into the new century, when geoeconomics will eclipse the geopolitical dictate that has dominated the Westphalian system since its very inception.

The third bequest from the twentieth century derives from the fall of communism in Eastern Europe and in the Soviet Union, the very progenitor of Leninist Marxism.[5] While this genre of change may give pause to many in the Third World to reflect on whether the West is justified in calling it proof of the "victory of capitalism," the fact is that only in Asia Pacific can one find the last clustering of robust Communist regimes. This cluster includes China, North Korea, and Vietnam among the Indochinese states. Yet, all are shifting gears in their economies to allow the market to play a more decisive role in lieu of the erstwhile state planner. But taking to heart Gorbachev's failures leading to the Soviet Union's collapse, they have apparently learned not to try precipitous political reforms before economic ones take firm root.

After enumerating the above three bequests, most analysts would probably be contented and then proceed to ascertain the possible effects of this total legacy on the new era. I would, however, add that these sea changes must be viewed against the backdrop of a development of dire consequence, namely, that of hegemonic decline. I use the term in more than just its political sense, but in the broader connotation of the theory of hegemonic stability. The theory holds that stability of the international economic system is a collective good, the production of which depends on the role of a hegemon. The function of this hegemonial leader is to bear the necessary cost of stability[6] while exacting compliance (by other members) with the rules of the liberal international economic order that it (the hegemon) has helped create. Although the theory, with all its robust explanatory power, is disputed by radicals and Gramscians alike,[7] the fact remains that with the decline of the United States as the hegemonic leader in the global economic system,[8] a role it has played since the end of World War II. The world has seen the weakening of the Bretton Woods system (built on its twin institutional pillars: the IMF and the World Bank) after 1971, the demise of the GATT and its replacement by the World Trade Organization (WTO) since 1995, and the rise of regional blocs such as the EU and the NAFTA. This drift of regionalism, needless to say, is a derogation from the ideal scenario of a *global* economic order in the true sense of the term. Likewise in the Asian region, the regionalism trend resulted in the rise of the Asia Pacific Economic Cooperation forum (APEC), since 1989 (as Richard Feinberg discusses it in chapter 6, in comparison with FTAA). Equally, the same regionalism trend accounts for the recent expansions in the function of the Association of South East Asian Nations (or ASEAN, as outlined in chapter 7 by Greg Felker).

Again, most commentators, including scholars specializing in international political economy (IPE), would probably be content with having thus identified a linkage between hegemonic decline and the rise of regional super trading blocs. But I would go one step further, to suggest another development of major consequence affecting international relations, as is germane to our concern with the emergent world order. I am referring to the arrival of a peculiar competition between geoeconomics and geopolitics, over which the sole surviving superpower has at best only partial control. Relatively speaking, geoeconomics (guided by concerns of economic security) is a uniting force, as it calls for collective action among nations. On the other hand, geopolitics, with its emphasis on ideology and geography (i.e., concerns of national defense in the traditional [military] sense) creates contention and power clashes (see chapter 1).[9] But as a caveat and update, it should be noted that geoeconomic interests (or search for economic security) may also revive the traditional conflicts in the scramble for scarce vital resources such as oil and other strategic minerals, in what one author (Klare 2000, 403) calls the "return of resource wars."

The peculiar tug of war between the geopolitical and geoeconomic pulls, in fact, may complicate the existing ethnic, religious, and cultural diversities that are responsible for the ambivalence and hesitancy of the region's states and that have been dogging its institution-building efforts, such as the ASEAN. Although created in 1967 in anticipation of the U.S. phase-out from the Vietnam War and the region, ASEAN is in a perpetual state of confusion as to the mission it is mandated to serve. It is today torn between (1) the reality of its members' continuing dependence on external powers for their national security (a geopolitical dictate), on the one hand, and (2) what it is expected to do for its members in promoting intra-ASEAN economic cooperation[10] and, following the recent financial crisis, fending off turbulence in the global financial market as well as attacks by external predators (a geoeconomic concern), on the other. To a certain extent, this is also the dilemma facing the Asian members of the APEC, which may explain their hesitancy and halting endorsement of moves for fuller institutionalization and liberalization.

While it is safe to say that geoeconomic considerations may anticipate cooperation over conflict between major powers across the Pacific region, including China, Japan, the United States, and even Russia,[11] the continuance of a geopolitical side-show falling within the bailiwick of traditional national security may indeed call into question whether the conflictual reflex will not disrupt the general geoeconomic disposition toward collaboration. In this broad context, the state of relations between China and the United States (in league with Japan) will almost certainly determine the prospect of peace, stability, and prosperity at both the regional and global levels (we will come back to this specific point later). What will happen to China as a major power and, more important, where it will be vis-à-vis the United States on the totem pole of world politics, will obviously determine the world's balance of power and, for our purpose, the shape of world order and Asian regional order.

Concededly, what is going to happen in China's internal politics will in part hold the key to these questions. This book, by definition, falls within the international relations field. Space does not allow it to look into the likely domestic developments within China,[12] or any other country, for their own sake. Nevertheless, we did have occasion to address China's performance under pressure during the Asian financial crisis (chapter 3). We have noted China's envied record of emerging from the crisis largely unscathed—as contrasted with the sad consequence from unsafeguarded liberalization befalling Thailand and South Korea, among others. China offers a lesson for the others in the region that maintaining some measure of "macroeconomic control," as the Chinese do, is the best guarantee against the ravaging forces of globalized capital while the economy is opening up to the global markets. As we have seen, those Asian countries that promptly introduced or reinstituted effective control of their currency market (as did Malaysia and South Korea in midstream) were able to get out of the crisis and the consequential economic slump sooner than others (see chapters 3 and 4 above). The pattern confirms Alvin So's thesis of "Asianization" (chapter 4), in that falling back on "Asian values" or, to be more exact, on the "Asian developmental state" model, has proven to be the best defense of Asian nations against the destabilizing force of globalization. This is a trend surely to continue into the new century, as the region copes with deepening globalization.

AN EVALUATION

The above three sea changes, all bequests of the past century, may be interrelated, but, in light of the Asian experience, they need not be. A Western ideologue may typically argue, for example, that democracy has brought wealth to the East Asian countries in a process that proves the victory of capitalism. But as I have argued elsewhere (Hsiung 1993, 236), the Asian "tigers" achieved their phenomenal economic success nearly two decades before anyone of them even began the first step in the long trek toward democracy (Hong Kong was a colony until mid-1997). Only in Japan did the two paths converge, and then only because of U.S. tutelage after the end of World War II. Even in Japan, the long one-party rule by the powerful Liberal-Democratic Party, 1955 through 1993, coincided with the best years of Japan's economy. To a large extent, whether the East Asian economic "miracle" is proof of the victory of capitalism depends largely on how much credit one assigns, or denies, to the region's Confucian cultural mix (along with other possible causes).

Although so many Western commentators were in such a hurry to jump to the conclusion that Asian values were dead as soon as the largely externally-fueled financial crisis broke out in 1997, the reality paradoxically proves just the opposite. In retrospect, the Confucian cultural mix probably deserves more credit than it has received for the economic success of all Asian countries that share "Asian values" in common, although the mix of its content may vary from case to case.

The unexpected short duration of the economic slump triggered by the financial crisis, and the region's prompt recovery, which was achieved without a tight-belt austerity program or the dire structural reforms initially called for by the IMF, can only confirm that the root cause of the crisis was not domestic frailties or inherent flaws of the Asian mode of development (see chapters 2, 3, and 4; and, more especially, chapter 11 for a theoretical explication of this conclusion). In this light, the financial crisis will prove to be a temporary roadblock rather than evidence of fatal inherent shortcomings destined to prevent the region's high performance economies from fulfilling the widely held pre-1997 expectations that the twenty-first century would be the Pacific Century.[13]

The Unfinished Agenda from the Past Century

Equally, the emergent world order of the new era is anticipated by the unfinished agenda of the past century. Under "unfinished" agenda, I am subsuming both (1) the *unfulfilled* agenda carried over from the past century, and (2) *additional new* agenda items emanating from totally new sources after the Cold War. One example in the latter category is the arrival of truly globalized capital markets, accelerating the pace and momentum of globalization like never before. The ravaging forces released in the wake of globalization, such as the casino syndrome created by the hot-money flows, which largely accounted for the attack on the Asian economies, have in turn engendered a new impetus for greater regionalism in Asia Pacific, surmounting the region's traditional diversity and division (as Richard Feinberg and Greg Felker have argued in chapters 6 and 7, respectively). In fact, in reaction to the external attack on their economic security, Asian nations have found the pull toward the European Union more irresistible than ever (see chapter 5, by Brian Bridges above), going beyond their earlier aversion to the United States due to harrying contentions over the definition of human rights (chapter 3).

In my 1993 study (Hsiung 1993, 254f), extrapolating from an earlier study of triadic games, I calculated that there was a 67 percent chance that Asia Pacific and North America would align on the same side, against Europe, the largest of the three super trading blocs in terms of total combined GDP and a number of other measures (251). This finding, based on realist power-ratio calculations, corroborates both the alliance-making experience of nations and Waltzian neorealist theory. Consistent with his theory that in anarchy, power calculations determine states' alliance behavior, Kenneth Waltz (1979, 127) counsels: "Secondary states, if they are to choose, flock to the weaker side; for it is the stronger side that threatens them." The fact that the Asian group chose instead to ally with the stronger of the two larger blocs testifies either that geoeconomic alliance-making calls for different strategies or that some extraneous factor(s) tipped the balance, making pure geopolitical power calculations an inadequate guide for policy. While the United States was shunned by the Asian countries because its human-rights foreign policy was a great turn-off (*New York Times*, 3 March 1996, 3), Bridges' study (chapter 5) finds a geoeconomic pull between EU and the Asian Pacific and suggests that both share an uneasiness, though for different reasons, about their American connection.

As has been shown earlier in this book (chapter 1), a likely candidate for the new century's systemic value is the call for "social justice" (including but not limited to distributive justice), which means, among other things, the debunking of international social Darwinism ("survival for the fittest") that underpinned the myth of the "Whiteman's Burden" of yore and that in effect rationalized the deprivation and exploitation of the poor and less-powerful nations.

Traditional conceptions of world order, sustained by the implicit international social Darwinism, assume that stability is best maintained through hierarchy or entrenched inequality among states. Globalization since the late 1990s, however, forces the world to rethink inequality (Hurrell and Woods 1999, 8–35). Global institutions such as the IMF and the Bank for International Settlements were beginning to address more directly issues like poverty, inequality, and equity (2). Quests for solutions to these became, for these and other institutions, a more immediate goal of sustainable development, which used to be only a concern for the United Nations General Assembly, a political organ in which the poor nations have a numerical majority.

True, the characteristic systemic value of the twentieth century, "self-determination" (i.e., decolonization), precipitated the instant destruction of the long-held vast colonial empires of the West. Yet, in its wake, the gulfs separating the haves and the have-nots have been widening. An estimated three billion people, or half of the world's population, live on under U.S.$2 per day.[14] According to the UNDP, the highly indebted, poverty-stricken nations also face high rates of malnutrition, as well as infant mortality, disease, and illiteracy (UNA-USA 2000a, 144). Sustainable development, therefore, remains a high-priority item on the unfulfilled agenda from the last century, carried forward into the new.

In a move indicative of what is forthcoming on the threshold of the new century, the world's richest nations, including the United States, Japan, and European and other industrial powers, joined in an agreement, at the end of 2000, to forgive loans to twenty-two of the world's poorest countries for the year. They acted in fulfillment of a promise to accelerate debt relief and to give a token of the West's unprecedented prosperity to the world's poor nations (*New York Times,* 23 December 2000, p. 6). Although the debt-relief program, announced jointly by the World Bank and the IMF, was more immediately a victory of an eclectic coalition of religious organizations, the fact that the creditor nations were willing to oblige, it should be stressed, portrays an awareness that the wealthy must act in the world's onerous task of poverty reduction. While the amount forgiven was small—$20 billion out of a total stock estimated to be $125 billion, if the debt was to be paid off before year's end—it is the thought that counts. It offers encouraging signs of a shared conviction that, to paraphrase Abraham Lincoln loosely, "we cannot have half of the world prosperous and the other half hopelessly impoverished." For our purpose here, the significance of this implied acceptance of a "one-worldness" is matched only by a presumptive readiness, on the part of the debt-forgiving nations, to curb the reflex of international Social Darwinism that has guided international relations since 1648.

The ultimate solution to the world's poverty reduction, of course, lies in generating development so that the poor can lift themselves out of the quagmire of poverty. The buzz word for the next century, therefore, is development. At the United Nations Millennium Summit in September 2000, when virtually all the world's leaders gathered in

New York to discuss the collective future of humankind, one of the two issues stressed in all the speeches was *development,* the other one peace (UNA-USA 2000b).

In view of the rising importance of human security in the age of "comprehensive security," a large part of the task of development concerns human development. In addition to personal security of people against violence or deprivation by their own governments, such as witnessed in "ethnic cleansing" or other genocidal acts, human development entails also the removal of such other sources of human insecurity as income inequity, illiteracy, infectious diseases, and shortages of clean water, food, and housing (as discussed in chapters 1 and 3).

Under the clarion call of social justice, I might add, the notion of sustainable development also extends to the protection of an individual's right to life and of a nation's right to a way of life against the threat of environmental degradation (Kiss 1992, 235). An agenda item facing both rich and poor nations in the new century, therefore, is the deterioration of our environment, such as is found in diminished water resources, continuing land degradation, and global climate change, among other things.

In this book, we have lumped economic security and environmental security, as well as human security, under the generic rubric of "comprehensive security,"[15] as contrasted to the traditional concerns of security as merely national defense. In three chapters (chapters 8, 9, and 10), we have seen the positions of as many countries (United States, Japan, and China) presented by Davis Bobrow, Sueo Sudo, and Richard Hu, respectively. Although the scope and emphasis of the concept may vary, one compelling conclusion is that all three countries embrace "comprehensive security" as a strategic guidance for national policy. There is a comparable awareness that the traditional notion of security conceived only in military terms is defunct and must be stretched to accommodate economic, environmental, and human dimensions, responding to the dire challenges of the new age driven by high technology, resource depletion, population explosion, and climate change.

The finding as such confirms that at least on the question of "comprehensive security," there is universal consensus.[16] This serves to substantiate an assertion we made earlier, that the Asia Pacific region may offer a confirmation of the universality of parts of the emergent world order in the new century. Conversely, the full-hearted embrace of currency-control policies by Asian nations, and their turning inward to an "Asianization" solution, in the wake of the recent trauma (see chapters 3, 4, and 7), offers evidence of national behavior contrary to the general trends associated with globalization elsewhere. To its Western advocates, globalization requires unreserved liberalization. This process may, in and of itself, set in motion a force that diminishes the ability of national governments to set their own agenda and control their own fate (see Steve Chan's discussion in chapter 2 above). What is happening in the Asia Pacific since 1997, thus, offers a refutation of any claim to universality that Western advocates may assert for their assumed globalization culture.

In addition, mitigation of the hierarchy in our Westphalian system, where power still nearly determines all things, remains ultimately as an unavoidable item on the new century's global agenda. Under conditions of resource scarcity, where optimal global resource management holds the key to the survival of the human species and our ecosystem, power would make no sense if it cannot be channeled to productive purposes through collective action in collaboration with the disfranchised and the powerless. Some of this mitigating trend, however, was already in evidence toward the latter part of the post-1945 world order, as can be seen in the conclusion of the Law of the Sea Convention (CLOS-III) in 1982. One unprecedented provision in the Convention (Article 125) is that landlocked states are now entitled to the "freedom of transit through the territory of [neighboring] transit states by all means of transport" to and from the sea. This is the first time ever in history that landlocked states, otherwise deprived of an outlet of their own to the sea, are endowed with such a right (not privilege), and, as such, they are no longer at the mercy of their neighbors.[17] The development demonstrates an underlining growing sense of world community in which the usual hierarchy of nations built on the power configuration, in this case on the haphazard distribution of natural endowment, is gradually coming loose, if not sufficiently leveled down as yet. And, with it, the social Darwinism that rationalized such a hierarchy among nations has received its first significant dent. Its further chipping away remains an agenda item for the new century.

TELESCOPING THE FUTURE
OF TWENTY-FIRST CENTURY WORLD ORDER
AND THE ASIA PACIFIC: A SUMMING UP

To recapitulate, we have identified *social justice* as the new systemic value that will highlight the "mission" for nations in world affairs and provide a "grammar" for their behavior in our Westphalian system. Under the new guiding star of social justice, the goals to be pursued by nations in the new century, both in their individual and collective endeavors, will not only be peace, but also equity. A natural confirmation of this speculation will be if states are found to accept certain ends of the world community on par with, or even higher than, the egoistic goals of their own.

A clear trend in this direction was already in evidence toward the end of the second half of the twentieth century, as can be seen in the two examples given above, viz.: the wide acceptance of obligations by states in the control of the environment, including the global commons, and their willingness to grant transit rights to landlocked states.

At the next tier, we have also identified a few items high on the collective agenda of the "global village" in the new century, such as globalization, comprehensive security, and human development. All are tasks that entail collective action. Hence, multilateralism and "other help" will increasingly replace unilateral self-help by states in the interest of international governance. This is so because the name of the game for all nations is global survival—that is, survival from the rampaging threats of environmental degradation and the ravaging forces of globalization.

We have also seen that other trends, such as regionalism (or localization), may spin off from the deepening process of globalization. "Asianization" represents such a contrary development, arising from the Asian region's reaction to the recent financial crisis. Likewise, the trend of democratization, while irresistible in general, may in peculiar instances (such as in Indonesia thus far) veer off to the treacherous shoals of instability. Other items such as tackling the hierarchy of nations, which is thus far determined by the power configuration across the system, will continue to mark the pursuit of nations in the realm of world politics.

This takes us to the next question, the polarity of our Westphalian system in the new century. We have seen that no matter whether Binnendijk's (1999) prognostication or the Organskiite group's (Tammen 2000) scenario comes true, China is destined to come out on top. The difference will be between a China that will be one of the two poles in a new U.S.-China bipolarity (as Binnendijk suggests) and, alternatively, a China that will "overtake" the United States to become the next sole superpower (as the Organskiite Power Transition theory adherents conclude). In either event, from our standpoint, the projected systemic value of social justice will not be in jeopardy. If anything, judging by the oft-professed Chinese support for a "fair, just, and reasonable" new international order,[18] it will only receive an assist from China's ascent.

FUTURE OF THE GLOBAL ORDER: A CHANCE FOR PEACE AND EQUITY TO WORK?

If the emergent global order sketched in the book, as outlined in this concluding chapter, is a true approximation of what will come to pass, then what is that which statesmen must do, or watch against, in order for peace and equity to have a chance to work? While the new systemic value (social justice) may become a universal culture, offering a guide for all nations, it does not automatically guarantee that peace and equity will come true by themselves, even if major powers are willing to lend their support. Certain conditions must be present; and major decision-makers must abide by certain rules or eschew certain intuitive reflexes.

In the first place, true statesmanship must allow for the fact that different nations may see the same issue(s) from totally different time horizons (Stein 1990, 106–108). For instance, we have seen certain "rogue states," prompted by a motivation to play Microsoft to America's IBM in order to compete, or just to assure their own security, develop their own limited ballistic missile systems(chapter 3).[19] It takes true statesmanship, on the part of our decision-makers, to know how to face this challenge squarely, lest overreaction leads to counterproductive escalating spirals. As Paul Bracken (1999, 153) cogently points out, it is America's overseas forward bases that have become hostages to missile attack. To protect these bases ("Achilles' heels"), and to protect America's homeland, the United States came under increasing pressures to build its own Theater Missile Defense (TMD) and National Missile Defense (NMD) systems in response. But in the final analysis, at stake is not who is ahead in technology (undoubtedly, the United States is). Rather, the question the "rogue states" (and others) may be asking is why it is necessary for Washington to maintain these overseas bases, if not for the pursuit of "global supremacy"—which Bracken calls an "irresistible temptation when it comes on the cheap" (155). It is one thing if the current ballistic missile race is about national defense. Let us not forget that national defense is as much as a concern for the "rogue states" (and others) as for us. But it is quite another if our decision-makers should think it is a race in technology, or, worse, about ideology. That was how the United States got trapped into the Vietnam War.

In a perceptive analysis of the U.S.-China divergence, Ellis and Koca (2000) offer an interesting list of contrasting concerns of how Washington and Beijing misperceive each other from their disparate horizons. For instance, many in Washington are transferring what they can extrapolate from successful U.S. deterrence of the former Soviet Union to their strategic thinking about China. Others view China, alternatively, through the prism of the Gulf War (and Saddam Hussein) and Kosovo (and Milosovic). Again from the U.S. standpoint, Beijing's avowed determination to stop Taiwan's separatist drift is a threat of aggression and a challenge to the United States, because of U.S. commitment to defend the island's security. But as the mainland Chinese view it, Taiwan's separatism is a "regime survival" issue for Beijing (Ellis and Koca 2000, 3). This is so precisely because China is still unflinchingly guided by what

Takashi Inoguchi (Bobrow-ISR 1999, 174) calls the "Westphalian paradigm of world politics" (based on territorial states), to a much greater extent than is the United States. On the other hand, add Ellis and Koca, China has its problems, too, when it tries to view the U.S. willingness to respond to external aggression from the perspective of the Somalia analogy,[20] rather than the Pearl Harbor analogy. In short, misreading each other's intentions through one's own horizon is the best recipe for disaster, in the new century as well as in the last.

Second, it is not enough for nations to have a mere synchronic view of events; they need to have an intertemporal view, when, for instance, it comes to the matter of environmental security. In all previous centuries, the fixation on war and its effects focused mainly on the present generation (hence, synchronic view). But on matters of environmental degradation, the next generations are likely to feel the effects more acutely, if the present generation takes no precautions. Hence, only from an intergenerational view will nations fully appreciate the depth and extent of the damage that environmental degradation is to inflict on humankind. Only then will this generation fully realize its onerous responsibility toward posterity. Peace and equity, thus, will have intertemporal qualities to them in the age of comprehensive security (Weiss 1992, 385–412; and Weiss 1989).

Thomas Friedman of the *New York Times* reported in his column that some Chinese students who were demonstrating for democracy at Tiananmen Square in 1989 found themselves outside the U.S. Embassy throwing stones in 1999 after the "Americans bombed the Chinese Embassy in Belgrade" ("The Five Myths," *New York Times*, 27 October 2000).[21] This example, I hope, will wake up our decision-makers in Washington to the fact that their policy (or nonpolicy) directed at the present leadership in Beijing may negatively impact on the younger generations among the Chinese, whose minds we are trying to win in the first place. It requires an intertemporal perspective to appreciate this point, but it is important for peace and equity in the new century, more so than in the last.

Third, unilateralism versus multilateralism is another quandary confronting peace and equity in the new era. Typical of old-fashioned unilateral self-help, the usual United States policy reflex has been to go it alone, as in instances from aiding the Contras fighting the Sandinista government in Nicaragua (in the early 1980s), to invading Panama and abducting its chief of state Manuel Antonio Noriega (December 1989), to developing a National Missile Defense (NMD) since the 1990s. But in the age of comprehensive security, especially in combating deterioration of the environment, such as ozone depletion, global warming, loss of biological diversity, and the spread of infectious diseases, collective action (i.e., multilateralism) must prevail. Decision-makers will have to learn to reorder their mental paradigms (Pirages 1978, 7) accordingly.

And, fourth, a closely related issue is that certain selective bilateral policies may not necessarily be up to the challenge in the new age of multilateral interdependence. As Yoichi Funabashi (2000, 76) points out, the U.S.-Japan "privileged" relationship, which is an example of selective bilateralism par excellence, does not work any longer, because all its three premises are anachronistic. First, the long-standing separation of economic and security issues is no longer possible in the age of comprehensive security. Second, Japan's "privileged" status vis-à-vis the United States (and its "preponderance over China") is no longer so secure. Tokyo suspects that U.S. pursuit of its relationship with China, in a geoeconomic game, may come at Japan's expense. And, third, Japan is starting to question its own order of priorities, as the U.S.-Japan alliance often trumps Japan's national interests. For example, Japan's intent to engage Iran and Myanmar comprehensively, in trade and investment relations, has been frustrated by its own ties with Washington because of the latter's preoccupation with human rights issues. The bottom line is that in the age of multilateral interdependence, it will be increasingly more difficult to neatly sort out, for example, national defense, economics, and human rights interests than in the past.

FUTURE OF PEACE AND EQUITY IN ASIA PACIFIC? THE REQUISITES FOR REGIONAL ORDER

Similarly, certain prerequisites must be present before peace and equity will have a chance to work out in the Asian region. Certain adjustments on the part of key decision-makers in assessing the intentions of their counterpart players will be necessary, at the regional level as at the global level, lest their misreadings of each other's minds jeopardize the chances of peace and equity. In addition, in the age of multilateral interdependence, decision-makers will learn that bilateral relationships cannot be detached from the tangle of multilateral relations

First and foremost, in the Asian region, there must be prior stability in the delicate U.S.-China-Japan triadic relationship, which has replaced the strategic U.S.-China-USSR triangle of the 1980s in importance. Other than China and Japan, the Asian region is comprised of weak states whose geopolitical security has thus far been dependent on external guarantors. Furthermore, the intra-regional regimes (such as the ASEAN) they rely on for the furtherance of their geoeconomic interests are not completely insulated from external interference (as has been shown in chapters 4 and 7). Without stability in the U.S.-China-Japan triad, no external power could credibly guarantee the geopolitical security of the weak states in the region, as will become clear below.

Thomas Christensen (1999) has unraveled the complexity of the causes for the triadic instability in the U.S.-China-Japan tangle. The first is a "security dilemma" in that the recent upgrading of the U.S.-Japan alliance to include Japan in a joint research of theater missile defenses (TMD), is bound to provoke China (and, I would add, Russia) to respond in kind, including the development of a counter-TMD system of its own (hence, a spiral).[22] Christensen notes two other exacerbating factors that may provoke further spirals: First, Chinese historical memories of Japanese aggression (1931–1945) make China especially allergic to increases in Japanese military activism. Second, because of Bejing's apprehensions that Taiwan is steadily moving toward an irreversible separatist course, any acquisition of even defensive weapons by Taiwan or Japan (a potential Taiwan ally) threatens mainland China and may provoke spirals. (How much more so if Taiwan, as has been rumored, should be included in the U.S.-Japan TMD scheme!) Under the title "U.S. Triggers Arms Race in Asia," the *Far Eastern Economic Review* (3 August 2000, 16) concludes that this is exactly what the U.S. scheme is doing in the region.

In an unusually strident dissent, however, Jennifer Lind (2000) challenges Christensen's thesis, raising the specter of "fifty years of dogs that don't bark." For 50 years, she claims, "Japan and Taiwan have made the kind of military moves that Christensen argues will create spirals." After asserting that the anticipated spirals did not occur (hence, the dogs did not bark), she concludes that Christensen's hypothesis is falsified. I would, however, raise a question about whether there were intervening variables that made it unnecessary for the dogs to bark. There were indeed two, which, I think, would resolve the dispute.

The first intervening variable was Japan's erstwhile low military profile after 1945, as expressed in its cap on annual defense spending at 1 percent of GNP during much of the Cold War era. A number of developments changed all this since the late 1980s, especially after 1990. First, under President Ronald Reagan, the United States exerted pressures on Japan to increase its share of the mutual security burden in the Asian region, thus relieving part of the U.S. responsibility correspondingly. As a result, the Japanese agreed, under the Reagan-Suzuki communiqué of 1981, to protect their territory, air, and sea lanes of communication to a range of 1,000 miles. In 1987, the Japanese cabinet under Prime Minister Nakasone reversed the long-standing cap of annual defense spending. Five years later, Japan overcame another taboo when it adopted an unprecedented measure known as PKO, under which contingents of Japanese "self-defense forces" would be allowed to join United Nations peace-keeping missions in the world's trouble spots (Auer 1992).

Then came the Persian Gulf War, precipitated by Iraq's invasion of Kuwait (1990), cutting off Japan's Persian Gulf oil supplies instantly, which made Japan feel particularly vulnerable. Even worse, the 1990 East Asia Strategic Initiative (EASI) of the Bush Administration, which called for phased reduction of U.S. military presence in the Asian region to the 100,000 troop level, further alarmed the Japanese that they might have to fend for themselves. Furthermore, Japan's economic recession since 1989 dramatically daunted the Japanese self-confidence. When polled by the Asahi Shimbun in August 1994 about which country would likely be the hegemon in Asia Pacific in the twenty-first century, 44 percent of the Japanese named China, followed by 33 percent favoring the United States. Only 16 percent picked Japan.[23] This has to be read in conjunction with World Bank projections (in 1992) that the combined total GDP of Greater China (mainland, Hong Kong, and Taiwan), estimated at $9.8 trillion by 2002, would beat the $9.7 billion GDP of the United States. And, Greater China's combined net import volume, totaling $639 billion, would surpass Japan's $521 billion import by 2002 (Kristoff 1993). If such perceived China threats fueled Japan's new China-bashing binge, they also accounted for precipitous increases in its annual defense budget, which went up from the world's third largest in 1991 to the second largest by 2000. The change in Japanese attitude also anticipated a revitalization of the Japan-U.S. alliance, which in turn alarmed China (Garrett and Glaser 1997). Hence, one can expect Lind's dogs to become restless, waiting for an occasion to bark.

The second intervening variable accounting for Lind's dogs not barking for 50 years, as I argued elsewhere (Hsiung 2000a, 120f), was the simple fact that until the death of President Chiang Chink-kuo (CCK) in 1988, Taiwan never wavered in its adherence to the "One China" principle. This pledge, which can be traced back to CCK's father, President Chiang Kai-shek, from 1950 on, convinced Beijing that Taiwan would not cut its umbilical cord from the mainland, in the legal as well as political sense. It thus disarmed Beijing politically, deprived it of a pretext for resorting to force in the Taiwan Strait, and, more important, turned it from a deadly rival into a potential partner by creating the expectation (through repeated assertions of Taiwan's "One China" commitment) that eventually mainland China and the island would emerge reunited from their current split. The "shadow of the future" was, thus, brought into play through an "iterated game" (Axelrod 1984), to the benefit of peace and tranquillity in the Taiwan Strait. Hence, no dogs were barking. To complete the parable, it was as though the dogs found the supposed offender a temporarily estranged member of the family. Keeping a vigilant watch, maybe whining? Yes. But barking? No, and no need to.

But after 1988, things were becoming increasingly unstuck. CCK's successor, Lee Teng-hui, began to waver on Taiwan's "One China" commitment. We have noted (in chapter 3) that Lee's "two states" theory, advanced in July 1999, began to unravel the cross-Strait relationship. Then came the March 2000 election, which ushered in a new administration headed by Chen Shui-bian, whose party (DPP) platform openly championed a separatist route for the island, and who himself refused to recognize there is "one China." Despite repeated proddings by Beijing, Chen even refused to acknowledge he is a fellow "China-person" (chung-kuo-ren). Hence, the erstwhile effective protective screen (Taiwan's "One China" commitment) that kept the dogs not barking for fifty years is no more. All indications are that Beijing is seriously preparing for the eventuality of an armed solution to the mainland-Taiwan division impasse outstanding since 1949.[24] Lind's dogs, it appears, are not only prepared to bark, but to bite if necessary.

All told, Lind is both analytically unconvincing (she concludes the area is "primed for peace") and empirically wrong, as she grossly omits the fierce barking of the dogs in 1995–1996. In a nine-month period, Beijing unleashed not one but three waves of nuclear "missile testing" across the Taiwan strait, the closet salvoes exploding less than 6 miles off Keelung, to warn Taiwan's President Lee about his perceived flirtation with a separatist adventure (Ross 2000). The U.S. dispatch of two carrier battle groups to cruise through the Taiwan Strait, in a "show of force" to calm down Taiwan's jitters, almost precipitated a direct nuclear confrontation with the PLA, which was conducting "military exercises" in the Strait.

Admittedly, it is harmless for an analyst like Lind to be so oblivious of lessons from the past and of the reasons behind both the dogs barking and not barking. But decision-makers cannot afford such luxury. Lee Kuan Yew, Singapore's Senior Minister (FEER 2000), issued a grave warning presumably directed at all government leaders, including the United States, that the Taiwan powder keg could ignite a conflagration that will engulf the entire region. It might even embroil the United States in a nuclear holocaust that nobody wants. Oftentimes, well-meaning analysts raise the question on whether China, with its present military capability and modest defense expenditures (about U.S.$15 billion annually), can or cannot take Taiwan by force (e.g., O'Hanlon 2000). But this is the wrong question to pose. As the late patriarch Deng Xiaoping put it, "We'd rather have it proven that we tried but failed [to stop it] even by force, than be accused [by our disgruntled compatriots and posterity] of not trying to stop Taiwan going independent."[25]

Earlier, I raised the issue of stability within the U.S.-China-Japan triad, precisely with the U.S.-Japan alliance in view. Apparently, many in Japan have apprehensions about the stability. Japanese Nobel laureate (for literature) Ohe Kenzaburo, for instance, once told a pen pal that he was fearful of the outcome of a conflict between the United States and China over the question of Taiwan. Because of its alliance relationship, Japan would be embroiled in a conflict that it did not choose and that might escalate into a nuclear holocaust. From the ashes of such a nuclear conflict, he figured, some form of life may still be found in the two combatant nuclear giants, China and the United States. But, Kenzaburo rued, there would be absolutely nothing left in Japan or Taiwan in the conflict's wake (Han Xiu 2000). By now, I hope it is clear why stability in the U.S.-China-Japan triadic relationship is a sine qua non for geopolitical peace in the Asian Pacific region.

Second, if equity in the regional context means generically the furtherance of the socioeconomic well-being of the Asian nations, then the role of the United States, with necessary adaptations, may remain crucial for at least the first two decades of the twenty-first century. I use this time frame because to my knowledge no analyst, not even among the most maverick, has predicted any contending power likely to replace the United States as the next hegemon in the Asian region before 2020. While the United States may or may not be able to bring a Pareto-optimal state to the region, it is still powerful enough, despite the hegemonic decline alluded to above, to affect negatively the outcome of institution-building by the area states. Without U.S. blessings, for instance, Japan was reluctant to join the "ASEAN+3" (Japan, China, and South Korea), a scenario first proposed by Malaysian Prime Minister Mahathir back in the 1980s. Without U.S. backing, the proposed Asian Monetary Fund, concocted as part of a regional package responding to the financial crisis of the late 1990s, did not even get off the ground, despite Japanese initial impetus.

The United States, though, does not hold a veto on the freedom of the region's several states to protect their economic security by unilateral (as opposed to region-wide multilateral) means. One example is the uncoordinated initiative to institute or reintroduce unilateral currency control in mid-stream by countries such as Korea, Malaysia, etc., in order to contain the damage done to their economies from the recent crisis.

As we have seen from the crisis, external threats to the region's economic security came from two sources: the casino effects of globalized capital and attacks by external manipulators out to make a kill.[26] While the first problem, involving turbulence created by hot money flows in the global capital markets, can be controlled by heightened internal control against overborrowing from abroad, the second requires international multilateral remedies. External speculators thus far can operate in the dark and get away with predatory "killings" precisely because there are no international rules and mechanisms restraining them. Many mainstream economists in the West have directed their attention to alleged domestic structural flaws in Asian nations, such as "crony capitalism," although it has been proven that the crisis was brought on more by exogenous factors, including manipulation by external speculators (e.g., mammoth hedge funds), than by domestic failings (chapters 3, 4, and 11). The reversal by Paul Krugman (1999) of his early support of the by-now discredited endogenous thesis should set an example for other, still recalcitrant economists to follow. It should also provide a plausible justification for international regimes to be instituted for the control and restraint of international monetary speculators for the future. While the Asian region, as has been noted (chapter 3, 4, and 7), has established its modest early warning system, its efficient functioning would conceivably depend on U.S. support to a larger extent than Washington has appeared willing to give thus far. For one thing, U.S. support would make the monitoring mechanism no longer limited to one region, and hence more effective against the amorphous monetary speculators who operate globally.

Loksang Ho (chapter 11) concludes his penetrating analysis of currency crises with the suggestion that no one country, nor the open market, can bring about exchange rates that are compatible with stability of the financial markets and the economy. It takes a global effort by the world community to do it. Moreover, let me add, this is an area in which the United States can reclaim some of its credentials as the hegemonic leader of the global economic system.

Besides, in the age of geoeconomics, China's real threat to the weak states in Southeast Asia may in fact be in the economic domain. For instance, China's competitiveness in manufacturing (exports up in 2000 to an annual 30 percent) was reported by the *Economist* (2 December 2000, 42) as one factor driving down Southeast Asian currencies. In addition, manufacturers in the area are feeling the heat as China-based firms are said to get the "largest bite" of foreign investment in Asia outside Japan. If all this is true, then the U.S. role as a possible external "guarantor" of the security of the small Southeast Asian states would lose its meaning, unless it could be redirected and geared toward the economic security of these states. Otherwise, under the circumstances, a natural tendency for these states would be to beef up their collective defenses, in the new geoeconomic game, by optimizing the protective mechanisms within ASEAN.

Third, if past lessons can be a guide, a prerequisite for peace and equity in Asia Pacific in the new century would depend on something that may sound ethereal, namely, the perceptions and assumptions of major decision-makers. I raise this point because decision-makers do not always react to the true reality as it objectively exists, so much as to the reality (or stimuli) that they perceive or assume to be true; This is testified to by the misreading of minds among key European leaders that triggered World War I (Snyder 1989).

It is indisputable that peace and stability in the Asia Pacific hang, to a large extent, on the role of China. However, while much depends on China's future performance (even shaping up domestically), much also depends on the perceptions and assumptions of the other major actors, in particular the United States. A couple of examples may help illustrate this point.

First, U.S. analysts and politicians, with some exceptions, share a deeply held consensus that China is the most formidable threat to U.S. interests in Asia in the Post–Cold War era (e.g., Betts 1996). Without getting into the merits of this debatable claim, let me note for illustration that Japan, by contrast, is usually perceived as peace-loving and democratic. Ironically, it takes a native Japanese professor, Saburo Ienaga (1996), of the Tokyo University of Education, to tell us that the postwar Japanese educational system "glorifies war" and, equally important, that the government in Tokyo systematically censors all textbooks used in the Japanese school system, notwithstanding the fact that the country is widely recognized as a democracy abroad. Again, ironically, it takes a naturalized Japanese citizen and former German Jesuit priest, Prof. Peter J. Herzog (1993) of Sophia University, to document with massive evidence that Japan has what he calls a "pseudo-democracy." China, on the other hand, is not known to similarly "glorify war" in teaching its schoolchildren. And, if China inspects textbooks used in its schools, that situation is reflected in the fact that it is not called a "democracy" abroad. But does all this matter? Yes, if key decision-makers order their foreign policy toward the target country accordingly.

Parenthetically, the purpose of this discussion is not to knock Japan. Rather, it is to dramatize the contrast in which China, relative to Japan, is perceived by the outside world, including major-decision makers, such as those on Capitol Hill and in the government of President George W. Bush.

My second example of a discrepancy in world perception is in regard to Goa and Tibet. Portugal possessed a historic right of transit to Goa and three other enclaves through the intervening territory of India from the eighteenth century, a right that survived British colonization and the 1947 independence of India that was guaranteed under international law (as affirmed by the International Court of Justice in 1960).[27] But when Portugal failed to cede its Goa enclave to the new Republic of India, the latter in 1961 occupied the territory *by force*. As Wolfgang Friedmann (1964, 314) observes, "however morally defensible [under] the principle of decolonization . . . it was contrary to India's obligations [not to resort to the use of force] under the Charter" of the United Nations. Outside a small nucleus of international law professors such as Friedmann, nevertheless, the Indian move was not considered an invasion, much less an aggression. It was soon forgotten by the world and is not even mentioned in popular books on the history of international relations since 1945.[28]

In contrast, Tibet, as a part of China (albeit under the old concept of suzerainty), was not only firmly established in the annals of history but was confirmed by an international treaty concluded in 1907 between two foreign powers, Britain and Russia, who pledged to respect China's suzerain rights in Tibet.[29] What better proof does one need to show that Tibet was *not* an independent state unrelated to China!

This fact notwithstanding, much of the scholarly and official world oftentimes considers China's administration in Tibet as a "subjugation" (e.g., Calvocoressi 1991, 401). Worse, its takeover by the new Communist regime in Beijing in 1950, one year after the Chiang Kai-shek government lost the civil war on the mainland, was condemned in Western literature as a "military invasion" (e.g., van Walt van Praag 1987, 142) or even as a "military conquest" (Neterowicz 1989, 33), as if Tibet was another independent state. Why this difference, as compared with India in respect of Goa? Obviously, people's perceptions and assumptions have a lot to do with it: In one case, the invasion was done by an acknowledged Western-type democracy, and in the other, the takeover involved a Communist regime. But does it matter? Yes, to reiterate, as long as key decision-makers follow their perceived reality and assumptions, however unfounded, they will order their policy accordingly; and the real truth will not matter.

Hence, more than anything else, the Asian region's peace and equity in the new century will, as in the past, depend very much on the perceptions and assumptions of the major powers outside the region. Samuel Huntington (1996, 309) charges that U.S. foreign policy thinking suffers from an inability to expunge its Cold War mentality. The charge simply confirms that old images, derived from perception and implicit assumptions, die hard.

The fourth, and last, factor to ponder in regard to the future of peace and equity in the Asia Pacific is Asian nationalism. Comparative studies of nationalism[30] usually attempt to trace all nationalisms to some common identifiable origin(s). But between Europe and Asia, there is a distinct generalizable difference. If it can be maintained that nationalism in

Europe arose in opposition to imperial rule (or the *ancien regime*) and is hence "anti-imperial," Asian nationalism has a more complicated pedigree. As noted earlier in this book (chapter 3), much of the Asian region lived under colonial rule until after World War II. Hence, Asian nationalism in most cases is postcolonial. Only in China was modern nationalism in part "anti-imperial," if that means it was in opposition to the monarchical system embodied by the Manchu dynasty, the last in the country's long dynastic history. But the people's revolt against the Manchu system was prompted by more than dynastic decadence. The most decisive factor why the revolt received such widespread support was, in the final analysis, the crushing weight of foreign (European and Japanese) encroachments, against which the then-existing imperial system had proved totally inept, putting China's national survival on the block. Hence, to save China, the nation realized it had to shake off the foreign "imperialist" yoke as well as to overthrow the dynastic rule at home. Hence, modern Chinese nationalism is both "anti-imperial" and "anti-imperialist."

Nationalism in Japan is neither postcolonial (Japan was itself a colonial power) nor anti-imperial. It was first antishogunal (but pro-imperial) and, then, revanchist (as mentioned in chapter 3). It was antishogunal because the Japanese since 1192 lived under a de facto government headed by a hereditary military leader, the shogun, who ruled with an iron hand, though nominally on behalf of the Tenno (Emperor), who enjoyed a cloistered quasitheocratic existence. Toward the end of the last of the three shogunal houses (the Tokugawa), Commodore Matthew Perry of the United States, arriving with his "black ship," succeeded in opening up Japan to the outside world.

The Treaty of Kanagawa that Perry exacted from the Japanese in 1854 was to many among the samurai class a humiliation and a reminder of Japan's weakness. Determined to save Japan from the fate that had fallen on a China that refused to change its ways when confronted by Western gunboat diplomacy, a group of samurai leaders in 1868 staged a bloodless coup that ended the Tokugawa shogunal rule and ostentatiously brought the young emperor Meiji back on the political saddle. The modernizing samurai leaders then appropriated the emperor's name in justifying their well-coordinated reform program, named the Meiji Reform, and in rallying popular support for it.[31] The nationalism thus generated was not anti-imperial, but anti-shogunal and pro-imperial (hence, the Meiji *Restoration*).

Thus far, we have accounted for three variations of Asian nationalism: anticolonial, anti-imperialist, and pro-imperial. Only the first two are externally directed. Their implicit external targets are the former colonialists (the West for Southeast Asia, but Japan for Korea and Taiwan) and former invaders and exploiters (both European and Japanese for China). Understandably, nationalism of the postcolonial or anti-imperialist variation is latently resentful, although not in all cases. In Hong Kong and Taiwan, for example, the nationalism is postcolonial but not necessarily anticolonial. But in Singapore and almost all other former colonies, postcolonial nationalism is anticolonial (Hsiung 2000b, 312). The subliminal bitterness against real or imagined external "predators" that can be found in nationalism of both the postcolonial and anti-imperialist sort has surfaced periodically, as in the Philippine eviction of the United States from its Subic Bay naval base in 1992 and as in the disputes with Washington over the meaning of human rights that produced the Bangkok Declaration signed by 49 Asian states in 1993 (Hsiung 1997, 121f).

Japanese revanchist nationalism, as we have observed in chapter 3, is a force whose orientation remains uncertain, if only because revanchism is an understudied subject. But to the extent it is externally directed (toward Japan's nemesis in World War II), one can reasonably expect a similar element of latent resentfulness (such as surfaced in Okinawa's stubborn opposition since the mid-1990s to continued U.S. bases there) that deserves to be watched, if only because it may have policy implications for both the United States and the Asian region.

In any event, we know that the immediate overriding concerns of postcolonial and anti-imperialist nationalism are political independence, territorial integrity, and national unification. After the Vietnamese unification, the next in line seems to be the unification of the two Koreas, toward which an important first step has been taken since the meeting of their presidents in June 2000. The only remaining case in the region is the reunification of mainland China and Taiwan.[32] This is why, until and unless a breakthrough is found, the Taiwan Strait remains the most fluid, unstable, and dangerous spot in the entire region for the twenty-first century. It is part of the unfortunate, unsettling legacy of nationalism left by the last century for the next.

In the wake of the externally fueled financial crisis of the late 1990s, one can reasonably expect the vigilant attitude associated with postcolonial and anti-imperialist nationalism to become more heightened in the region. An indication is in the increased interest in Asian regionalism (as opposed to Pacific-wide regionalism) among the Asian members of Asia Pacific. A bad sign for the United States is that these nations seem more drawn to Europe, as ASEM−3, which met in Seoul, October 2000, clearly demonstrates. Equally bad news for the United States is, as Brian Bridges notes (chapter 5), is that the Europeans and Asians share a common ambivalence about their respective American connection. Furthermore, contrary to U.S. predilections, he finds, the Europeans are paying more attention to China, replacing Japan as the centerpiece of EU's Asia policy. This may or may not complicate the question of stability within the U.S.-China-Japan triad, the sine qua non for peace and equity in the Asian region, in ways beyond our ability to foresee.

Conclusion

In closing, I am reminded of a book tantalizingly titled: *Thunder From the East: Portrait of a Rising Asia,* coauthored by Nicholas D. Kristof and Sheryl WuDunn (2000), both of the *New York Times.* It was the first such book after the Asian crisis to revive the speculation, albeit based on much data and analysis, that the twenty-first century will witness Asia's return to global prominence. As a preliminary indicator, the coauthors noted that Asia's GDP amounted to 33 percent of world output in 1998, up from only 17 percent in 1952, despite the financial crisis that gripped the region after mid-1997. But immediately the book received a "So what?" put-down review in a highly respectable journal written by a senior scholar, obviously an Asia-phobe, who shall remain nameless. Challenging the book's title, the review was dramatically entitled "The End of Asia,"[33] and his conclusion said just as much. I have learned, therefore, not to end this book by hazarding a conclusion nearly as upbeat as the Kristoff-WuDunn volume.

On the other hand, I have to be faithful to my conscience and my conviction, informed and buoyed as it is by the data and analyses presented in the preceding chapters as well as those available from other sources known to me. Hence, I will end by briefly examining two challenging but intelligent, if quixotic and condescending, questions raised by this anonymous reviewer-critic of the Kristof-WuDunn book, to wit: (1) What is Asia? and (2) Will the twenty-first century be remembered more for the "end of Asia" than for its rise? My reactions will follow the order in which the two questions were raised, and I will try to be restrained and professional.

What Is Asia?

For our purpose here, we may qualify "Asia" to read Asia Pacific, leaving out India and others in South Asia. A straight answer to the question is that Asia is now more than a geographic term. From our discussions in this book, we can safely say that Asia (that is, Asia Pacific) is a region that is distinct for its three shared properties: Asian values, the developmental state model, and an Asian nationalism that, as just discussed, shows three variations (postcolonial, pro-imperial/revanchist, and post-imperialist). There is no need to elaborate further on the third theme (Asian nationalism). Let me note that the first two (i.e., Asian values and the developmental state model) are closely related, though separate, properties (see discussions in chapter 3). As we have seen throughout the book, these two properties have both stood the region in good stead and have seen their credibility reconfirmed by the recent crisis. For convenience sake, let us identify the bedrock of "Asian values" as Confucian ethic,[34] which may be blended in varying degrees with other cultural contents such as Islam (as in Malaysia, Indonesia, and other places), Buddhism (Taiwan, Thailand, etc.), Shinto (Japan), Marxism (China), and Christianity (South Korea, the Philippines, etc.). By "Confucian ethic," we mean not the official Confucianism that used to be emphasized in the traditional *keju* system for careers in Chinese officialdom. Rather, we refer to the Confucian ethos ingrained in people's way of life and thinking patterns, passed down from generation to generation through family rearing and social mores—so deeply ingrained that not even the most iconoclast of governments can easily eradicate it.

If we can design a scale of high to low rankings in terms of the extent to which a nation is imbued with Confucian cultural influence, then we can identify the Asian nations in three groups on a sliding scale of high, medium, and low, viz.: (1) China, Singapore, Taiwan, and Hong Kong, (2) Malaysia, South Korea, and Thailand, and (3) the Philippines, Indonesia, and Japan. While this scale is admittedly very intuitive and unscientific, it will nevertheless serve an analytical purpose if it can provide a criterion for comparison. With this scale in view, we can attempt to see if a correlation, however haphazard, can be established between how deeply a country was exposed to the Confucian ethic and how it fared in the recent crisis. It so happens that those countries that are "high" on our list of Confucian imbuement (or contamination?) were among the first to recover from the crisis (as discussed in chapters 3 and 4, among others). Then came the ones that rank as "medium." Those that rank "low" in the above list were the last to recover. Japan, whose cultural mix today shows the least Confucian content, as compared with the other Asian societies, has yet to see its way out of the woods.[35]

In his projections about the future, post-crisis, economic landscape in the Asian region, Wang Gangmao (1999) identified five groups in descending order of their economic vitality, as gauged by their comparative standing on five indicators. He placed Singapore, Taiwan, Hong Kong, and mainland China in the top pack, or Tier One. It is potentially coincidental that all four are in the "high" Confucian zone. The correlation may or may not necessarily suggest a causality. Nor does it mean that a re-Confucianized Japan would necessarily be better able to cure its lingering economic setbacks. Nevertheless, the comparison as such leads us to a crucial point: At a minimum this much can be said, that it was *not* Asian values that sent the Asian economies tumbling down in the financial crisis of 1997–1998, as many Western critics had initially alleged. Thus, those who wrote hasty obituaries about the death of "Asian values," and those who gloated over Asian Tigers having joined the ranks of stuffed animals could have saved themselves the enormous subsequent embarrassment if they had at least thought twice before asserting their favorite conclusions.

During the height of the Asian financial crisis, an enthusiast of Western capitalism told a U.N audience that a "tragedy" from the crisis was that "non-Anglo-American routes to prosperous economies have been *de-legitimated*" (emphasis added), leaving Eastern Europe, Africa, and other parts of Asia no alternative model to "counterpoise to . . . Anglo-American capitalism."[36] The real tragedy, in hindsight, is that if Western analysts keep talking about Asia Pacific in like manner, their credentials as serious scholars will be "de-legitimated."

Furthermore, if those with an aversion to "Asian values" should be prompted by the idea that such values are bad for free trade and incongruent with a liberal policy on labor, their fears are unwarranted. During negotiations with the United States, which were in earnest progress toward the final months of the Clinton Administration in 2000, Singapore was willing to accept a so-called "Jordanian pact," named after a recently concluded U.S.-Jordan treaty that authorizes sanctions to enforce commitments on labor and environmental standards. Some U.S. trade groups, including the pact's staunch supporters, were surprised that Singapore would accept such an obligation despite its history of joining other Asian countries at the failed 1999 WTO conference in Seattle to oppose the linkage of labor and environmental standards. Singaporean officials explained that while their government still considered such linkage highly disruptive in the multilateral trade area, Singapore was confident that its own labor practices and environmental protections were close to Western standards (*Asian Wall Street Journal Weekly,* 11–17 December 2000, p. 2). Thus, Asian values can coexist with global free trade.

THE "END OF ASIA" IN THE TWENTY-FIRST CENTURY?

According to our unnamed reviewer-critic of the Kristof-WuDunn book, the twenty-first century will see the "end of Asia" for two reasons: (1) that the spread of capitalism and "Abrahamic ideology" (i.e., Judaeo-

Christian-Islamic culture) will wipe out Asia's "pre-Abrahamic culture"; and (2) that the rise of individual Asian societies, especially China and India, will make it "finally impossible to talk about 'Asia' as a political or cultural unit." In rebuttal, let me say that the root cause of this reviewer-critic's problem was that he, inadvertently echoing Churchill, whom he momentarily ridiculed elsewhere in the article, assumed that Asia was only a geographic name. Hence, the rise of strong, organized, human societies like China and India would make the maintenance of "Asia" as a geographic name no longer tenable.

More crucial was the critic's pronouncement that the spread of capitalism and Abrahamic ideology would obliterate Asian culture, which he calls the "last traces of pre-Abrahamic culture." The implied premise that all cultures must head toward oblivion, to be replaced by the "Abrahamic culture," is alarming, indeed bordering on the preposterous.

This unilinear view recalls to mind a similar common assumption among some self-flattering Western theorists during the 1960s, when whole groups of postcolonial states began to appear, that modernization meant the irradiation of Western culture. More specifically, the same modernization theorists proclaimed that prior "political development" (a code phrase for democracy) held the key to economic development in the less developed world. Now, four decades later, we have yet to see the claim substantiated by more empirical evidence. As has been demonstrated, in East Asia the pattern has been just the reverse: It was prior economic development that paved the way to democracy, as in both South Korea and Taiwan, not the other way around. And, to complete the irony, a "strong state" (code words for a soft authoritarian regime) in either case had proved instrumental in engendering prior economic success, approaching "miraculous" proportions, in the first place.

On the other hand, in a lengthy study, Varshney (2000, 718f) courageously points out that "long-lasting *democracies* of the developing world [in three continents] failed to eliminate poverty" (emphasis added). That is, they have failed dismally in the area of economic development, despite their prior political development (democracy).[37] Thus, the claim of the earlier Western modernization theorists has been turned on its head. As if to confirm this nasty point, recent reports revealed that the post-crisis economic woes plaguing two of the Asian tigers (South Korea and Taiwan) in much of 2000, or one year after the region had recovered from the crisis, were products of those countries' own march to advanced stages of democracy: South Korea's economy was threatened because democracy fostered strong unionized labor and loss of public confidence in the bureaucracy, which could no longer lead as before (*FEER,* 7 December 2000, p. 16f). And, in Taiwan, where the stock market lost 50

percent of its value, the economy was derailed by an atypical political instability ever since its March 18 election, a test of true democracy in itself, which trounced out the Kuomintang after over 50 years in power
(*FEER,* 19 October 2000, p. 16; *New York Times,* 5 December 2000, C-1).

The unfulfilled claim of the Western modernization theorists, as such,
is only matched by an as-yet unfulfilled belief held by many TV enthusi-
asts, since television first emerged, that the new medium would wipe out
radio broadcasting and the movie industry in no time. But over half a
century later, this has not happened. The TV, radio, and movie media
have proved to be able to coexist.

Earlier we noted how the Asian region survived a financial crisis
brought on by globalization. We have seen that Asian values survived the
crisis and that while globalization continues, the region has turned to
"Asianizaiton" as an answer. As has been shown, Asian regionalism can go
hand in hand with globalization. By the same token, there is no reason why
Asian values cannot coexist with the reviewer-critic's Ahrahamic culture.

In fact, if one applies the critic's logic in return courtesy, one could
claim, in reverse, that with the free dissemination of the by nature more
inclusive Asian culture[38] globally—in as many ways as the modern information age makes possible—it could in turn lead to the fall of Western
culture in due course,[39] more especially if Asia Pacific should attain the
heights that Kristof and WuDunn's data and analysis point to! While
logically consistent with the critic's argument, this inference would be so
ludicrous that no reasonable person would accept it.

If in the past Confucianism was not as "outgoing" and intrusive into
other lands, it was because never did Confucius enjoin his disciples to "go
to the end of the earth and preach the word of *tian,*" much less to do so
with a sword or gunboat diplomacy. The modern-day mass media, which
makes old-fashioned evangelism obsolete, would conceivably give Asian
culture an equal opportunity to be heard globally. But any sensible person would agree that mutual accommodation and coexistence between
cultures, rather than displacement and obliteration, would be the outcome from the free cross-dissemination of diverse cultures carried by
modern global communication flows, on the radio, on the tube, in print,
and in cyberspace. Occasional clashes may occur, but mutual accommodation will result. I doubt if the critic's "Abrahamic culture" can be as re-
fractory and overpowering vis-à-vis other cultures as he may wish it to be.
In this connection, I think it appropriate to heed a counsel from James
N. Rosenau (1997, 7) that we should prospect the future more in
"both/and" than in "either/or" terms.

Future historians looking back to the twenty-first century will prove
whether our unnamed critic of the Kristof-WuDunn volume was correct

in predicting the "end of Asia" or, alternatively, whether our study here correctly concluded that the century would witness the very likely rise or re-rise of Asia, for the reasons laid out through these pages. To put it another way, the question for future historians looking back to the twenty-first century is to decide whether the prediction by the unnamed critic—no matter how confidently and self-righteously it was stated— came true, or, on the other hand, whether the conclusion from a solid body of research such as is presented in this book was borne out empirically by subsequent events.

If there is any one sentence that could succinctly recapture the essence of this book, I think it would be that the twenty-first century will be an era of peace and equity—and that the increasing global consciousness of this duality is, to put it mildly, related to the rising Asian participation in the life of the global village.

NOTES

1. For an excellent and succinct summary plus conclusions derived from the various visions in comparative light, see the last essay, by Stuart J. Kaufman, in Bobrow ISR 1999, 193–221.
2. I discussed this point in the Foreword, but for details, see Frank 1998.
3. Frank (1998) in fact is referring to China as being the coming "Middle Kingdom" (or center of the world) once again. He is in agreement with Huntington (1996), Khalilzad et al. (1999), and the Organski group (Tammen et al. 2000).
4. For a discussion of the idea that globalization may undermine conventional liberal democracy, see Scholte 2000, 261–282.
5. Despite the fall of Leninist Marxism along with the collapse of the Soviet Union, Karl Marx was voted, in a BBC poll (London) in 1999, as the "Thinker of the Millennium," followed by Albert Einstein. A Reuters poll named Einstein and Marx as the two most influential thinkers of the past millennium.
6. The hegemon has to maintain a stable international monetary system, to provide open markets for goods, and to ensure access to oil at stable prices, in the global liberal economic order, to the benefit of members. Cf. Keohane 1984, at 139.
7. Charles Kindleberger (1973) proves the indispensability of a hegemon in the global economic order by demonstrating what brought on the Great Depression of 1929–1939. He identifies its cause as rooted in the lack of a leader who could create and enforce the rules of a liberal international economic order and to play the role of "lender of last resort." Radicals reject the theory. Antonio Gramsci (1971), on the other hand, sees the role of the hegemon as dispensing ideological leadership.
8. On hegemonic decline, see Keohane and Nye 1977, 42–46; Oye et al. 1987, 12–14; and Gilpin 1987, 77–79.

9. See also Ross 1999.

10. The cooperation extends to non-ASEAN nations like China, Korea, and Japan under the "ASEAN+3" formula.

11. Although Russia is mainly a European power, it has been a member of APEC since 1997, and half of Russia is in Asia. India, conceivably destined to play a dominant role in the area washed by the Indian Ocean, is another actor in the major power game, though this book is concerned with Asia Pacific.

12. It bears noting that the Chinese Communist Party now stakes its legitimacy on a new set of claims. It purports to represent (1) the developmental direction of the most advanced mode of production, (2) the forward orientation of cultural advance in China, and (3) the general will and broadest interests of the people. This theory of "three represents," as it is shortened in Chinese, is said to have policy implications See *People's Daily*, 2 Nov. 2000, p. 3. It should be noted that for the CCP to stake out its legitimacy on this claim of "three represents" is an important modification of the Leninist (and Maoist) claim of prescience based on avant-gardism.

13. Of the plethora of commentaries about the oncoming Pacific Century, see for example Linder (1986), McCord (1991), and Borthwick (1992).

14. As reported by World Bank President James Wolfensohn to an UNCTAD meeting, *World Ecology Report*, spring 2000. Cited in UNA-USA 2000a, 143.

15. For a comprehensive presentation of the diverse views on the "comprehensive security" question in Asia, see Radtke and Feddema 2000.

16. For a list of these buffeting problems, see "The Global 2000 Report to the President" by the Council on Environmental Quality and the U.S. Department of State, reproduced in Hastedt and Knickrehm 1994, 423–430.

17. Pursuant to the 1982 Law of the Sea Convention, landlocked Mongolia has set up a permanent maritime terminal station in China's coast city of Tianjin to facilitate the Mongolian access to and from the ocean.

18. The latest such instance was at the APEC's annual meeting in Brunei, when Jiang Zemin, China's President, sounded the same theme after lashing out at the widening gaps between North and South. To bridge these gaps he once again called for the creation of a "fair, just, and reasonable" new international economic order. See the text of the speech reproduced in *Renmin ribao*, 22 November 2000, p. 1.

19. I owe this idea initially to Paul Bracken 1999, 151.

20. The "Somalia analogy" is a reference to the episode of the lackadaisical U.S. intervention in the Somalia civil war, as part of the United Nations peacekeeping mission, in December 1993. Public and Congressional outrage at the killings of the UN peacekeepers prompted President Clinton to hastily withdraw all the Rangers in March 1994. See *A Global Agenda: Issues Before the 49th General Assembly of the U.N.*, edited by John Tessitore and Susan Woofson. A publication of the UNA-USA. Lanham, MD: University Press of America, 1994, 30–32.

21. James Miles (2000) reports similar Chinese student nationalism against the United States and Britain in the wake of the NATO bombing of the Chinese Embassy in Belgrade. The ire aroused by the bombing "triggered China's first mass protests at foreign powers [i.e., embassies and consulates] since the Cultural Revolution a quarter of a century earlier."

22. On Asian reactions to the U.S. missile defense system, see Green and Dalton 2000. On Chinese and Russian opposition to the U.S. TMD plan, see "Russia and China Unite in Criticism of U.S. Anti-Missile Plan," *New York Times,* 19 July 2000, p. 6. An excellent analysis of the reasons why Russia and China oppose the U.S. missile plan, is in Greg May 2000. See further Godwin and Medeiros (2000) for a cogent appraisal of China's view that the U.S. missile defense program is not a shield but a sword.

23. As reported in a *Christian Science Monitor* dispatch from Tokyo, 10 January 1995.

24. The "2000 China National Defense" White Paper, issued on October 16, 2000, promises PLA armed invasion in the event that Taiwan declares separatist independence or indefinitely refuses to negotiate for a permanent solution to the longstanding division between Taiwan and mainland China. See *Renmin ribao,* 16 October 2000, p. 1. In anticipation of the worst, Beijing reorganized its highest policy-making team on the Taiwan question to include three top-brass generals, Zhang Wannian, no. 2 man on the powerful CCP Military Affairs Commission; Xiong Guangkai, PLA's vice chief of staff; and Wang Zaixi, a major general known for his expertise in military strategy. See "Beijing Reorganizes Its Team Directing Taiwan Policy in Preparing for the Worst," *The Mirror* (Hong Kong), no. 281 (December 2000): 80f.

25. Deng to me in a six-hour private audience at his Beidaihe resort, 29 July 1987, where he revealed his inner thoughts, which I think are typical of the leadership in Beijing as a whole. Considering the overwhelming reaction that would result from Beijing's inaction if Taiwan should go independent, which would put the CCP's legitimacy on the line, Deng's remark was not without reason.

26. During the financial crisis that hit the Asian region, George Soros' Quantum Fund openly declared "war" on Hong Kong's financial market (*South China Morning Post,* 28 August 1998, p. 1).

27. ICJ, *Case Concerning Right of Passage Over Indian Territory* (Portugal vs. India) (Merits), Judgment of 12 April 1960.

28. For example, Peter Calvocoressi, *World Politics Since 1945,* which by 1991 had gone into the 6th edition (New York: Longman, 1991); and William R. Keylor, *The Twentieth-Century World: An International History,* 3rd ed. (New York and Oxford: Oxford University Press, 1996).

29. The Anglo-Russian Convention of 1907, text in *Treaties and Agreements with and Concerning China, 1894–1919,* ed., John V. A. MacMurray (New York: Oxford University Press); and text of provisions concerning Tibet, in *Treaties, etc., Between Great Britain and China,* 3rd ed., edited by

Edwarf Hertslet (London: Harison & Sons, 1908). For a discussion of the background, see Tung 1970.

30. Cf. Anthony D. Smith, "Theories of Nationalism: Alternative Models of Nation," in Michael Leifer 2000, 1–20.

31. For this part of Japanese developments, see Meyer 1993; and Burks 1956.

32. The question is further complicated by the steady, though often concealed, growth of a nativist Taiwan nationalism, especially since 1988. See Ching Cheong, "Will Taiwan Break Away? The Rise of Taiwanese Nationalism." Available online at: http://www.pspc.com.sg/books/general/.4579,htm.

33. The review was carried in *Foreign Affairs* 79, no. 6 (November/December 2000): 156–162.

34. "Asian values" are defined to include essentially respect for authority, stress on education, group rights over the individual (or esprit de corps), and exhortation to high savings. All of these are of Confucian origin.

35. Japan's banking crisis remains bogged down with domestic political division, and Japan enjoys the dubious distinction as the "world's biggest debtor," amounting to 114 percent of GDP. See "Japanese Bank Reform, Vital to the Economy, Snags on Political Reef," and "Japan's Massive Debt Bomb Ticks Ever Louder," in *Wall Street Journal,* 11 December 2000, p. 1 and p. 27. Other reports that the younger Japanese are increasingly more "individualistic" and Westernized (see, for example, "Japan's New Attitude," *Asiaweek,* 20 October 2000, pp. 42–48), suggest that the traditional contents, including Confucian, in the Japanese cultural mix are being further diluted.

36. Remarks by Professor Jeffrey Henderson, Manchester Business School, UK, quoted in the *UN Chronicle,* 21, no.3, at p. 27.

37. In Varshney's Table 1, he lists the following as the democracies in the developing world that have not been able to shake off poverty: India, Sri Lanka, Philippines, Botswana, Jamaica, Trinidad and Tobago, Costa Rica, and Venezuela (2000, 719).

38. Charles A. Moore (1967, 6f), commenting on the syncretism of Chinese culture, for example, speaks of a "somewhat difficult-to-understand attitude of 'both-and'—as contrasted with the Western tendency to think in terms of 'either/or,'" such that the fine lines of distinction and exclusiveness so typical of Western life and thought and even religion are not common to the Chinese mind."

39. For an exposition of backlashes against Western culture, see Benjamin Barber 1995.

REFERENCES

Auer, James C. 1992. "The Global Influence of Japanese Defense Efforts." In *The Pacific in the 1990s: Economic and Strategic Change,* edited by Janos Radvanyi. Lanham, MD: University Press of America.

Axelrod, Robert 1984. *The Evolution of Cooperation.* New York: Basic Books.

Barber, Benjamin. 1995. *Jihad vs. McWorld: How the Planet is Both Falling Apart And Coming Together and What This Means for Democracy.* New York: Times Books.

Betts, Richard K. 1996. "Wealth, Power, and Instability: East Asia and the United States after the Cold War." In Brown, Lynn-Jones, and Miller 1996.

Binnendijk, Hans. 1999. "Back to Bipolarity?" In *Strategic Forum* (May). Published by the Institute for National Strategic Studies, National Defense University.

Bobrow, Davis B. 1999. "Prospecting the Future." In Bobrow-ISR 1999, 1–10.

Bobrow- ISR 1999. "Prospects for International Relations: Conjectures about the Next Millennium." *International Studies Review* 1, no. 2l (Summer); special issue, edited by Davis Bobrow.

Borthwick, Mark. 1992. *Pacific Century: The Emergence of Modern Pacific Asia.* Boulder, CO: Westview Press.

Bracken, Paul. 1999. "The Second Nuclear Age." *Foreign Affairs* 79, no. 1: 146–156. Also his *Fire in the East: Rise of East Asian Military Power and the Second Nuclear Age* (New York: HarperCollins, 1999), from which his *Foreign Affairs* article was adopted.

Brown, Michael E., Sean M. Lynn-Jones, and Steven E. Miller, eds. 1996. *East Asian Security.* Cambridge, MS: MIT Press.

Burks, Ardath. 1956. "Part Two: The Government and Politics of Japan," in *Far East Governments and Politics,* by Paul Linebarger, Djang Chu, and Ardath Burks. Princeton, NJ: Van Nostrand.

Calvocoressi, Peter. 1991. *World Politics Since 1945,* 6th ed. London: Longman.

Christensen, Thomas J. 1999. "China, the U.S.-Japan Alliance, and the Security Dilemma in East Asia." *International Security* 23, no. 4 (Spring): 49–80.

Ellis, Jason D., and Todd M. Koca. 2000. "China Rising: New Challenges to the U.S. Security Posture." *Strategic Forum,* no. 175 (October). Published by the Institute for National Strategic Studies, National Defense University, Washington, D.C.

FEER. 2000. "Lee: The Cruel Game." *Far Eastern Economic Review* (8 June): 16–17.

Frank, Andre Gunder. 1998. *ReOrient: Global Economy in the Asian Age.* Berkeley, CA: University of California Press.

Friedmann, Wolfgang. 1964. *The Changing Structure of International Law.* New York: Columbia University Press.

Funabashi, Yoichi. 2000. "Japan's Moment of Truth." *Survival* 42, no. 4: 73–84. Quarterly published by the International Institute of Strategic Studies (IISS), London.

Garrett, Banning, and Bonnie Glaser. 1997. "Chinese Apprehensions about Revitalization of the U.S.-Japanese Alliance." *Asian Survey,* 37, no. 4: 383–402.

Gilpin, Robert. 1987. *The Political Economy of International Relations.* Princeton, NJ: Princeton University Press.

Godwin, H. B., and Evan S. Medeiros. 2000. "China, America, and Missile Defense: Conflicting National Interests." *Current History* 99, no. 638: 285–290.

Gramsci, Antonio. 1971. *Selections from the Prison Notebooks of Antonio Grasci.* New York: International Publishers.

Green, Michael J., and Toby F. Dalton. 2000. "Asian Reactions to U.S. Missile Defense." *NBR Analysis* 11, no.3. Available online at: http://www.nbr.org/publications/analysis/vol 11no3/index.html.

Han, Xiu. 2000. "Correspondences with Ohe Kenzaburo." *The Open Magazine* (Hong Kong), no. 162 (June 2000):92–93.

Hastedt, Glann, and Kay Knickrehm, eds. 1994. *Toward the 21ˢᵗ Century.* Englewood Cliffs, NJ: Prentice-Hall.

Herzog, Peter J. 1993. *Japan's Pseudo-Democracy.* New York: New York University Press.

Hsiung, James C. 1993. *Asia Pacific in the New World Politics.* Boulder, CO: Lynne Rienner.

———. 1997. *Anarchy and Order: The Interplay of Politics and Law in International Relations.* Boulder, CO: Lynne Rienner.

———. 2000. "Diplomacy Against Adversity: Foreign Relations under Chiang Ching-kuo," *Asian Affairs* 27, no. 2: 111–124.

———. 2000b. *Hong Kong the Super Paradox: Life After Return to China.* New York: St. Martin's Press.

Huntington, Samuel P. 1996. *The Clash of Civilizations: Remaking of World Order.* New York: Simon Schuster.

Hurrell, Andrew, and Ngaire Woods, eds. 1999. *Inequality, Globalization, and World Politics.* New York and London: Oxford University Press.

Ienaga, Saburo. 1996. "The Glorification of War in Japanese Education." In Brown, Lynne-Jones, and Miller 1996.

Inoguchi, Takashi. 1999. "Peering into the Future by Looking Back: The Westphalian, the Philadelphian, and the Anti-Utopian Paradigms." In Bobrow-ISR 1999.

Jervis, Robert, Richard Ned Lebow, and Janice Gross Stein, eds. 1989. *Psychology & Deterrence.* Baltimore, MD: Johns Hopkins University Press.

Keohane, Robert O. 1984. *After Hegemony: Cooperation and Discord in the World Economy.* Princeton, NJ: Princeton University Press.

———and Joseph S. Nye. 1977. *Power and Interdependence.* Boston: Little, Brown.

Khalilzad, Z, et al. 1999. *The United States and a Rising China.* Santa Monica, CA: RAND Corp.

Kindleberger, Charles. 1973. *The World in Depression, 1929–1939.* Berkeley, CA: University of California Press. Reissued in a revised edition in 1986.

Kiss, Alexandre. 1992. "The Implications of Global Change for the International Legal System." In Edith Brown Weiss 1992.

Klare, Michael T. 2000. "A Return to Resource Wars?" *Current History* 99, no. 641 (December): 403–407.

Kristof, Nicholas D. 1993. "The Rise of China." *Foreign Affairs* 72, no. 5: 59–74.

———, and Shirley WuDunn. 2000. *Thunder From the East: Portrait of a Rising Asia.* New York: Alfred A. Knopf.

Krugman, Paul. 1999. *The Return of Depression Economics.* New York: W.W. Norton. Reissued in paperback in 2000.

Lapid, Yosef. 1989. "The Third Debate: On the Prospects of International Theory in a Post-Positivist Era." *International Studies Quarterly* 33, no. 3 (September): 235–254.

Leifer, Michael, ed. 2000. *Asian Nationalism*. London and New York: Routledge.

Lind, Jennifer M. 2000. "Correspondence: Spirals, Security, and Stability in East Asia." *International Security* 24, no. 4 (Spring): 190–195.

Linder, Staffan B. 1986. *The Pacific Century: Economic and Political Consequences of Asian-Pacific Dynamism*. Stanford, CA: Stanford University Press.

McCord, William. 1991. *The Dawn of the Pacific Century: Implications for Three Worlds of Development*. New Brunswick, NJ: Transaction Publishers.

May, Greg. 2000. "Reality Check: Beijing Must Factor into Missile Defense Equation." The Nixon Center, available online at: http://www.nixoncenter. org-publications/Reality%20Check/6_09- 00ChinaNMD.html.

Meyer, Milton W. 1993. *Japan: A Concise History*, 3rd ed. Lanham, MD: Littlefield Adams.

Miles, James. 2000. "Chinese Nationalism, U.S. Policy and Asian Security." *Survival*, 42 no. 4 (Winter): 51–72. London: International Institute of Strategic Studies.

Moore, Charles A., ed. 1967. *The Chinese Mind: Essentials of Chinese Philosophy and Culture*. Honolulu, HI: East-West Center Press, University of Hawaii Press.

Neterowicz, Eva M. 1989. *The Tragedy of Tibet*. Washington, D.C.: Council for Social and Economic Studies.

O'Hanlon, Michael. 2000. "Why China Cannot Conquer Taiwan?" *International Security* 25, no.2:51–86.

Oye, Kenneth A., Robert J. Lieber, and Donald Rothchild. 1987. *Eagle Resurgent? The Reagan Era in American Foreign Policy*. Boston: Little, Brown.

Pirages, Dennis. 1978. *Global Ecopolitics: The New Context of International Relations*. North Scituate, MS: Duxbury Press.

Radtke, Kurt, and Raymond Feddema, eds. 2000. *Comprehensive Security in Asia: Views from Asia and the West on a Changing Security Environment*. Leiden, Boston, and Koln: Brill.

Rosenau, James N. 1997. *Along the Domestic-Foreign Frontier: Exploring Governance in a Turbulent World*. Cambridge: Cambridge University Press.

Ross, Robert. 1999. "The Geography of Peace: East Asia in the Twenty-First Century." *International Security* 23, no. 4 (Spring): 81–118.

———. 2000. "The 1995–1996 Taiwan Strait Confrontation: Coercion, Credibility, and the Use of Force." *International Security* 25, no. 2: 87–123.

Scholte, Jan Aart. 2000. *Globalization: A Critical Introduction*. New York: St. Martin's Press.

Snyder, Jack L. 1989. "Preceptors of the Security Dilemma in 1914." In Jervis, Lebow, and Stein. 1985.

Stein, Arthur A. 1990. *Why Nations Cooperate*. Ithaca, NY: Cornell University Press.

Tammen, Ronald, et al. 2000. *Power Transitions: Strategies for the 21st Century*. New York: Seven Bridges Press (Chatham House Publishers).

Tung, William. 1970. *China and the Foreign Powers: The Impact of and Reaction to Unequal Treaties*. Dobbs Ferry, NY: Oceana Publications.

UNA-USA. 2000a. *Global Agenda 2000–2001: Issues Before the 55th General Assembly of the United Nations,* edited by John Tessitore and Susan Woolfson. An annual publication of the United Nations Association of the United States of America. Lanham and New York: Rowman & Littlefield.

UNA-USA 2000b. "United Nations Hosts Millennium Summit." *The Interdependent* 26, no.3:5–7. New York: United Nations Association of the United States of America.

Van Walt van Praag, Michael C. 1987. *The Status of Tibet.* Boulder, CO: Westview.

Varshney, Ashutosh. 2000. "Why Have Poor Democracies Not Eliminated Poverty?" *Asian Survey* 60, no. 5: 718–736. Berkeley, CA: University of California Press.

Waltz, Kenneth N. 1979. *Theory of International Politics.* Reading, MA: Addison-Wesley.

Wang, Gangmao. 1999. Post-Crisis Economic Landscape: Re-Takeoff and Integration of East Asian Economies. Paper delivered at the International Conference on the Challenges of Globalization, 21–22 October 1999, Bangkok. Available online: fbawkm@nus.edu.sg.

Weiss, Edith Brown 1989. *In Fairness to Future Generations: International Law, Patrimony, and Intergenerational Equity.* Irving, NJ: Transaction Press.

———, ed. 1992. *Environmental Change and International Law: New Challenges and Dimensions.* Tokyo: United Nations University Press.

About the Editor
and Contributors:
A Biosketch

James C. Hsiung, Ph.D., Columbia University, New York, is Professor of Politics and International Law at New York University, where he teaches international relations theory, international law and governance, and East Asian politics and relations. He is author and editor of 17 books, not counting his numerous articles and book chapters. His most recent books are: *Asia Pacific in the New World Politics* (1993), *Anarchy and Order: The Interplay of Politics and Law in International Relations* (1997), and *Hong Kong the Super Paradox* (2000). A former executive editor of the Washington-based learned journal *Asian Affairs,* he holds the title of Honorary or Visiting Professor at several universities in China proper and Lingnan University in Hong Kong. He is also a former advisor or consultant to several Asian governments, including the Singaporean Ministry of Education.

Davis B. Bobrow is Professor of Public and International Affairs and Political Science, University of Pittsburgh. He has held visiting appointments at the Australian National University, Beijing University, the International University of Japan, and Saitama University. He is a past-president of the International Studies Association and a former member of the U.S. Defense Science Board. He has published widely on international security affairs and international political economy with special reference to the United States and East Asia. He recently edited *Prospects for International Relations: Conjectures about the Next Millennium* (Blackwell, 1999).

Brian Bridges is a Professor in the Department of Politics and Sociology at Lingnan University, Hong Kong, specializing in the politics and international relations of the Asia Pacific region. He studied in Wales (UK) and Japan, worked for the BBC and the Royal Institute of International Affairs (London) before joining Lingnan in 1993. He is interested particularly in North-east Asian affairs and in Europe's links with the Asia Pacific region. His most recent books are *Europe and the Challenge of the Asia Pacific* (1999) and a co-edited volume *Europe, China and the Two SARs* (2000). He has just finished writing a book on South Korea during and after the financial crisis.

STEVE CHAN is Professor of Political Science, Director of the Center for International Relations, and Interim Faculty Director for International Affairs at the University of Colorado, Boulder. He is also currently serving as Treasurer of the International Studies Association and the overall program coordinator for the 2001 Hong Kong convention being organized by the ISA and its partner associations. His research addresses issues of political economy, foreign policy, defense economics, and regionalism. His publications include a dozen books and over a hundred articles and chapters.

RICHARD FEINBERG, Ph.D. in international economics from Stanford, is Professor and Director of the APEC Study Center, Graduate School of International Relations and Pacific Studies, at the University of California, San Diego. He is Project Coordinator of the APEC International Assessment Network (APIAN); and he chairs the Board of Contributing Editors for the Institute of the America's e-publication, *America's Insights*. Moreover, he is Co-director of the Leadership Council for Inter-American Summitry and former Senior Director of Inter-American Affairs for the National Security Council, the White House, 1993–1996. His many publications include: *Summitry in the Americas; The Intemperate Zone: The Third World Challenge to U.S. Foreign Policy*; and *Subsidizing Success: The Expost-Import Bank in the U.S. Economy.*

GREG FELKER is Assistant Professor in the Division of Social Science of The Hong Kong University of Science and Technology. He received his Ph.D. from Princeton University in 1998. His specialization is the political economy of Southeast Asia, with a particular focus on patterns of industrialization, foreign investment, and technology transfer. He has also published articles on contemporary Malaysian politics. He is the co-editor (with Jomo K. S.) of *Technology, Competitiveness, and the State: Malaysia's Industrial Technology Policies* (1999).

LOK SANG HO, Ph.D. from the University of Toronto, began his career as an economist in the Ontario government in 1979 and continued on as Research Officer for the Ontario Economic Council. In 1983 he went back to Hong Kong to take up teaching at the Chinese University of

Hong Kong. At Lingnan University, which he joined in late 1995, he is currently Director of the Center for Public Policy Studies and Head of the Economics Department. He is also on the Advisory Council of the HK Institute for Monetary Research and a member of the Hong Kong Committee of PECC and the Trade Policy Forum. He was elected President of the Hong Kong Economic Association in 1999 and has been Managing Editor of the *Pacific Economic Review* since its launch in 1996. His latest book, *Principles of Public Policy Practice* (2000), adds to a list of some 70 journal articles and book chapters.

RICHARD WEIXING HU, Ph.D., University of Maryland, is Associate Professor of Political Science in the Department of Politics and Public Administration, University of Hong Kong. He teaches Chinese foreign policy, international political economy, and East Asian international relations. His research interests include political economy in the Greater China area, relations across the Taiwan Strait, Chinese defense policy, and Asian Pacific security. His latest publications include: *China's International Relations in the 21st Century* (with Gerald Chan and Daojiong Zha, forthcoming), and journal articles in *World Affairs, Pacific Review,* and *Brown Journal of World Affairs.*

ALVIN Y. SO is Professor and Head of the Division of Social Science at the Hong Kong University of Science and Technology. His research interests are in social classes, development, and democratization in Hong Kong, China, and East Asia. His recent publications include *Hong Kong's Embattled Democracy: A Societal Analysis* (1999), *The Environmental Movements in East Asia: Comparative Perspective* (co-editor, 1999), *Survey Research in Chinese Societies* (co-editor, forthcoming).

SUEO SUDO, Ph.D. from the University of Michigan, is Professor in the Faculty of Policy Studies at Nanzan University, Japan, where he also directs the Nanzan Asia Program (NAP). Prior to the current position, he was a fellow at the Chulalongkorn University in Thailand and at the Institute of Southeast Asian Studies in Singapore, and taught international relations at the University of Saga, Japan. His publications include *Southeast Asia in Japanese Security Policy* (1991); *The Fukuda Doctrine and ASEAN* (1992); and *The Structure of Southeast Asian International Relations* (1996).

INDEX